# — THE —
# QUOTABLE
# LAWYER
## REVISED EDITION

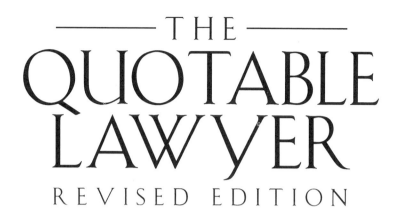

# THE
# QUOTABLE LAWYER

## REVISED EDITION

ELIZABETH FROST-KNAPPMAN
AND
DAVID S. SHRAGER

WITH THE ASSISTANCE OF SCARLET RILEY

A NEW ENGLAND PUBLISHING ASSOCIATES BOOK

Facts On File, Inc.

**The Quotable Lawyer, Revised Edition**

Checkmark Books
An imprint of Facts On File, Inc.
11 Penn Plaza
New York NY 10001

**Library of Congress Cataloging-in-Publication Data**

Frost-Knappman, Elizabeth.
    The quotable lawyer / Elizabeth Frost-Knappman and David S.
Shrager ; with the assistance of Scarlet Riley. — Rev. ed.
        p.    cm.
    Authors' names appear in reverse order on previous ed.
    "A New England Publishing Associates book."
    Includes bibliographical references and index.
    ISBN 0-8160-3753-1 (hc). — ISBN 0-8160-3778-7 (pbk).
    1. Law—Quotations   I. Shrager, David S.   II. Riley, Scarlet.
III. Title.
K58.F76  1998                          98-2522
340—dc21

Checkmark Books are available at special discounts when purchased in bulk quantities for businesses, associations, institutions or sales promotions. Please call our Special Sales Department in New York at 212/967-8800 or 800/322-8755.

You can find Facts On File on the World Wide Web at http://www.factsonfile.com

Text design by Grace M. Ferrara
Cover design by Cathy Rincon
Cover photograph by Arnold Katz Photography, Inc.

Printed in the United States of America

VB  FOF  10 9 8 7 6 5 4 3 2 1
    (pbk)  10 9 8 7 6 5 4 3 2 1

This book is printed on acid-free paper.

# CONTENTS

# CONTENTS

Dedicated to the memory of

*Lorena L. Frost*

# $\mathcal{I}$NTRODUCTION

From the time of the ancient Greeks, law has been the bedrock of civilized society. The Ten Commandments, the Code of Justinian, the Magna Carta and the United States Constitution represent a common thread of basic rules of conduct which govern the relationships among individuals and with their rulers or governments.

As society grew more complex and rule by dictatorial fiat or royal decree became intolerable, lawyers and jurists became necessary to interpret and apply the law, and to protect individual rights and liberties. As lawyers became advocates for a partisan viewpoint, whether before a court or jury, their success came to be determined by the skill and art of their persuasive communication. Lawyers and judges have become "word merchants" in the best sense. The successful advocate should be able to synthesize a complex legal precedent in a few pithy sentences and articulate a point of view within the sweep of a compelling sentence.

Lawyers and jurists have been among the most articulate professionals. Louis Brandeis, Felix Frankfurter, Ruth Bader Ginsburg, Learned Hand, Oliver Wendell Holmes, Jr., Barbara Jordan, William O. Douglas, Sandra Day O'Connor and Catharine MacKinnon are just a few of the many brilliant and quotable attorneys and jurists, whose names are now well etched in American jurisprudence. There is surely no subject for a book of quotations more deserving and appropriate than the law.

But the law has not been the object of discussion or quotation only by members of the judiciary and bar. Not surprisingly, the legal system has been the focus of comment by every sector of society. Lawyers as partisans and the sometime purveyors of ill tidings have been subjected to criticism over the ages. "First, let's kill all the lawyers" was simply the Shakespearean articulation of the practice of the ancient Greeks who first received the message from the bearer of ill tidings and then proceeded to kill the bearer. "The law's delay" may be seen as a pejorative reference to the predictable reaction of the citizen who perceives that his or her case is not being expeditiously handled by the legal system.

*The Quotable Lawyer* brings together approximately 3,000 of the best quotes concerning the law, made not only by jurists and lawyers, but also by priests, poets, playwrights, prophets, politicians, humorists, actors and activists. In this respect, the book gathers within one volume the best in the written and spoken word from a wide variety of sources, so long as the quotes serve the common theme of comments relating to the legal arena.

*The Quotable Lawyer* cites several hundred quotations by women. Other volumes, limiting themselves largely to comments by members of the legal profession, have omitted quotations by women. Although it is only in recent years that women have entered the law in large numbers, already including prestigious practitioners and jurists within their ranks, they have not been silent on the law, whether as writers, thinkers or activists. Their observations, from the 16th century on, will be found here.

The quotations have been organized in chapters in a topical fashion, and arranged chronologically within each chapter. Anonymous comments, biblical and Talmudic quotes, maxims, proverbs and folk sayings will all be found at the beginning of the chapters. Following each quotation, its author, source and approximate date are given. In the event the precise date of the quote could not reasonably be established, the biographical dates of the author are identified.

As a practical matter, the editors have not identified those men and women listed in the biographical section of *Webster's Tenth New Collegiate Dictionary*. Nor have they identified well-known contemporary figures, such as popular writers, entertainers and the like. Career descriptions have been supplied for obscure figures and those who are perhaps not widely known outside their field. In some instances, a career description is followed by a job description, which indicates the position held by the author at the time of the quotation, e.g., Donald Cressey, American educator; professor, University of California, Santa Barbara; Bernard Segal, American lawyer; president, American Bar Association; Frank Hague, American politician; mayor, Jersey City, New Jersey.

*The Quotable Lawyer* also contains an Index of Authors and an Index of Subjects, in which the quotations are topically arranged along with their entry numbers. This index also contains cross-references to other subjects under which related quotations can be located.

No edited work of this sort could have been completed without reference to the many collections that have come before. The volumes that have been particularly helpful are listed in the selective bibliography at the end of the book. Other sources are cited throughout the text.

The editors would like to express their appreciation to the following people for their generous help:

John Thornton, Joe Reilly, Eleanor Wedge and Adrian Saich for their invaluable editorial advice and assistance

Sarah Claudine Kurian and Scarlet Riley for their help in researching and compiling the quotations

Mark Carson, John Guinther and William Packard for contributing their favorite sayings

Laurie Likoff for her interest in revising this book

Elizabeth Frost-Knappman
David Shrager

# *1.* ACCOMPLICES

1.1 ❦ How near to guilt without actual guilt.

*Latin proverb*
*W. Gurney Benham,* Putnam's
Complete Book of Quotations,
Proverbs and Household Words, *1927*

1.2 ❦ He who helps the guilty shares the crime.

*Publilius Syrus, Latin writer*
Sententiae, *c.43* B.C.

1.3 ❦ He who profits by a crime commits it.

*Seneca,* 4 B.C. ?–A.D. 65
Medea, *1st century*

1.4 ❦ He who does not prevent a crime when he can encourages it.

*Seneca,* 4 B.C. ?–A.D. 65
Troades, *1st century*

1.5 ❦ No one shall be a thief with me as his helper.

*Juvenal*
Satires, *c.120*

1.6 ❦ Those who consent to the act and those who do it shall be equally punished.

*Sir Edward Coke,* 1552–1634
*W. Gurney Benham,* Putnam's
Complete Book of Quotations,
Proverbs and Household Words, *1927*

# *2.* ACCUSATIONS

2.1 ❦ Trust me, no tortures which the
    poets feign,
  Can match the fierce, the unutter-
    able pain,
  He feels, who night and day, devoid
    of rest,
  Carries his own accuser in his breast.

*Juvenal*
Satires, *c.120*

2.2 ❦ Let your accusations be few in number, even if they be just.

*Xystus I, pope*
The Ring, *c.120*

2.3 ❦ It warms the very sickness in my
    heart,
  That I shall live and tell him to his
    teeth,
  "Thus diddest thou."

*Shakespeare*
Hamlet, *IV, 7, 1600–1601*

2.4 ❦ Like a rough orator, that brings
more truth
Than rhetoric, to make good his
accusation.

*Philip Massinger*
Great Duke of Florence, *1627*

2.5 ❦ The best apology against false accusers is silence and sufferance, and
honest deeds set against dishonest
words.

*John Milton*
Apology for Smectymnuus, *1642*

2.6 ❦ Believe not each accusing tongue,
As most weak persons do;
But still believe that story wrong,
Which ought not to be true.

*Attributed to Richard Brinsley
Sheridan, 1751–1816*
*W. Gurney Benham,* Putnam's
Complete Book of Quotations,
Proverbs and Household Words, *1927*

2.7 ❦ In all criminal proceedings, the accused shall enjoy the right . . . to be
informed of the nature and cause of
the accusations, [and] to be confronted with the witnesses against
him.

*Constitution of the United States,
Sixth Amendment, 1791*

2.8 ❦ The breath
Of accusation kills an innocent
name,
And leaves for lame acquittal the
poor life,
Which is a mask without it.

*Percy Bysshe Shelley*
The Cenci, *1819*

2.9 ❦ The law does not expect a man to
be prepared to defend every act of
his life which may be suddenly and
without notice alleged against him.

*John Marshall, 1755–1835*
*Albert J. Beveridge, III,* Life of Marshall,
*1919*

2.10 ❦ It is not uncommon for ignorant
and corrupt men to falsely charge
others with doing what they imagine that they themselves, in their narrow minds and experience, would
have done under the circumstances. . . .

*John H. Clarke, American jurist*
Valdez v. United States, *244 U.S.
432, 450 (1917)*

2.11 ❦ The Constitution . . . speaks not
only of the freedom of speech but
also of trial by jury instead of trial
by accusation.

*Margaret Chase Smith*
Newsweek, *June 12, 1950*

2.12 ❦ When a man points a finger at someone else, he should remember that
four of his fingers are pointing at
himself.

*Louis Nizer*
My Life in Court, *1960*

2.13 ❦ Ours is an accusatorial and not an
inquisitorial system—a system in
which the state must establish guilt
by evidence independently and
freely secured and may not by coercion prove its charge against an accused out of his own mouth.

*Felix Frankfurter*
*In majority opinion that confessions
extracted by police coercion may not be
used in evidence, March 26, 1961*

# 3. ACTS

**3.1** ❦ Overlook our deeds, since you know that crime was absent from our inclination.

*Ovid*
Fasti, *c.8*

**3.2** ❦ Good laws are begot by bad actions.

*Macrobius*
Saturnalia, *c.400*

**3.3** ❦ Do as we say, and not as we do.

*Giovanni Boccaccio*
Decameron, 1348–1353

**3.4** ❦ The best way to keep good acts in memory is to refresh them with new.

*Francis Bacon*
Apophthagmes, *1625*

**3.5** ❦ A man wants no protection when his conduct is strictly right.

*William Murray, 1st earl of Mansfield,*
*English jurist; Chief Justice* Bird v.
Gunston *(1785), 3 Doug. 275*

**3.6** ❦ Never do today what you can do as well tomorrow; because something may occur to make you regret your premature action.

*Aaron Burr,* 1756–1836
*Marshall Brown,* Wit and Humor
of Bench and Bar, *1899*

**3.7** ❦ Our deeds determine us, as much as we determine our deeds.

*George Eliot*
Adam Bede, *1859*

**3.8** ❦ But the character of every act depends upon the circumstances in which it is done.

*Oliver Wendell Holmes*
Schenck v. United States, *249 U.S.*
*47, 52 (1919)*

**3.9** ❦ We cannot think first and act afterwards. From the moment of birth we are immersed in action, and can only fitfully guide it by taking thought.

*Alfred North Whitehead,* 1816–1947
*Franklin Pierce Adams,* F.P.A.
Book of Quotations, *1952*

**3.10** ❦ Inaction without more is not tantamount to choice.

*Benjamin N. Cardozo*
Richard v. Credit Suisse, *242 N.Y.*
*346, 351 (1926)*

**3.11** ❦ Action . . . stimulates hope.

*Louis Nizer*
My Life in Court, *1960*

# 4. ADVERSARY PROCESS

4.1 ❦ . . . my desire is . . . that mine adversary had written a book.

*Old Testament, Job 31:35*

4.2 ❦ And do as adversaries do in law—Strive mightily, but eat and drink as friends.

*Shakespeare*
*The Taming of the Shrew, I, 2,*
*1593–1594*

4.3 ❦ In case of defence 'tis best to weigh The enemy more mighty than he seems.

*Shakespeare*
*Henry V, II, 4, 1598–1599*

4.4 ❦ My prayer to God is a very short one: "O Lord, make my enemies very ridiculous!"

*Voltaire*
*Letter to M. Damilaville,*
*May 1767*

4.5 ❦ Treating your adversary with respect is giving him an advantage to which he is not entitled.

*Samuel Johnson*
*James Boswell,* The Life of Samuel Johnson, *1791*

4.6 ❦ When a man voluntarily engages in an important controversy, he is to do all he can to lessen his antagonist, because authority from personal respect has much weight with most people, and often more than reasoning. . . . Adams: You would not jostle a chimney-sweeper.
Johnson: Yes, Sir, if it were necessary to jostle him *down.*

*Samuel Johnson*
*James Boswell,* The Life of Samuel Johnson, *1791*

4.7 ❦ A man cannot be too careful in the choice of his enemies.

*Oscar Wilde*
*The Picture of*
*Dorian Gray, 1891*

4.8 ❦ It's not my enemies I worry about. It's my friends.

*Warren Harding, 1865–1923*
*New York Times, July 9, 1984*

4.9 ❦ [A farmer], before sunrise on a cold and misty morning, saw a huge beast on a distant hill. He seized his rifle and walked cautiously toward the ogre to head off an attack on his family. When he got nearer, he was relieved to find that the beast was only a small bear. He approached more confidently and when he was within a few hundred yards the distorting haze had lifted sufficiently so that he could recognize the figure as

only that of a man. Lowering his rifle, he walked toward the stranger and discovered he was his brother.

*Louis Nizer*
My Life in Court, *1960*

4.10 ❧ The business of the advocate, simply stated, is to win if possible without violating the law.

*Marvin E. Frankel, American jurist;*
*judge, U.S. District Court*
National Observer, *November 1, 1975*

4.11 ❧ . . . trials by the adversarial contest must in time go the way of the ancient trial by battle and blood.

*Warren Burger*
*Speech, American Bar Association,*
*Las Vegas, February 12, 1984*

# 5. ADVICE

5.1 ❧ If the old dog barks, he gives counsel.

*German proverb*
*W. Gurney Benham,*
Putnam's Complete
Book of Quotations, *1927*

5.2 ❧ Counsel is as welcome to him as a Shoulder of Mutton to a sick Horse.

*Proverb*
*Thomas Fuller,* Gnomologia, *1732*

5.3 ❧ Advice is judged by results, not by intentions.

*Cicero*
Ad Atticum, *c.66* B.C.

5.4 ❧ Who cannot give good counsel? 'Tis cheap, it costs them nothing.

*Robert Burton* Anatomy of
Melancholy, *1621*

5.5 ❧ If any whimsical notions are put into you by some enthusiastic counsel, the Court is not to take notice of their crotchets.

*George Jeffreys*
Hayes' Case *(1684), 13*
*How. St. Tr. 134*

5.6 ❧ Better counsel comes overnight.

*Gotthold Ephraim Lessing*
Emilia Galotti, *1772*

5.7 ❧ We ask advice, but we mean approbation.

*Charles Caleb Colton*
Lacon, *1820*

5.8 ❧ A lawyer's advice is his stock in trade.

*Attributed to Abraham Lincoln,*
1809–1865
*M. Francis McNamara,* Ragbag of
Legal Quotations, *1960*

*5.9* ❧ The fact that a lawyer advised such foolish conduct, does not relieve it of its foolishness. . . .

*Lucilius A. Emery, American jurist*
*Hanscom v. Marson, 82 Me. 288,*
*298 (1890)*

*5.10* ❧ It is always a silly thing to give advice, but to give good advice is absolutely fatal.

*Oscar Wilde*
*Portrait of Mr. W. H., 1890*

*5.11* ❧ He had only one vanity; he thought he could give advice better than any other person.

*Mark Twain*
*The Man That Corrupted*
*Halleyburg, 1900*

*5.12* ❧ [*Advice.*] The smallest current coin.

*Ambrose Bierce*
*The Devil's Dictionary, 1906*

*5.13* ❧ The advice of the elders to young men is very apt to be as unreal as a list of the hundred best books.

*Oliver Wendell Holmes*
*"The Path of the Law," Collected*
*Legal Papers, 1921*

*5.14* ❧ [When business people want] creative legal opinion, [lawyers] often give business advice, which is as good as my legal opinion. . . . They tell us "this is the law," when the truth and what they should be saying is, "this is our opinion of the law."

*Donald P. Kelly, American business*
*executive; president, Esmark Corporation*
*Address, American Bar Association,*
*Chicago, reported in the San Francisco*
*Examiner & Chronicle, August 14, 1977*

# 6. AFFIRMATIVE ACTION

*6.1* ❧ So-called formal equal opportunity has done a lot but misses the heart of the problem . . . The rules may be color-blind, but people are not.

*Patricia Williams*
*"The Obliging Shell: An Informal Essay*
*on Formal Equal Opportunity," 87*
*Michigan Law Review 1989*

*6.2* ❧ Racial classifications are suspect, and that means that simple legislative assurances of good intention cannot suffice.

*Sandra Day O'Connor, January, 1989*
*Peter Huber, Sandra Day O'Connor,*
*1990*

*6.3* ❧ Lots of white people think black people are stupid. They are stupid themselves for thinking so, but regulation will not make them smarter.

*Stephen Carter*
Reflections of an Affirmative Action
Baby, *1992*

6.4 ❦ The quiet but steady revolution in affirmative action puts individual rights over group rights.

*Susan Au Allen, to National Order of*
*Women Legislators*
*Speech, November 11, 1996, in* Vital
Speeches of the Day, *April 1, 1997*

# 7. AGING

7.1 ❦ The older I grow the more I distrust the familiar doctrine that age brings wisdom.

*H.L. Mencken*
Prejudices, *1922*

7.2 ❦ I used to think that the main-spring was broken by 80, although my father kept on writing. I hope I was wrong for I am keeping on in the same way. I like it and want to produce as long as I can.

*Oliver Wendell Holmes, Jr., circa 1925*
*Catherine Drinker Bowen,* Yankee
From Olympus, *1944*

7.3 ❦ In youth money is a convenience, an aid to pleasure. In age, it is a necessity, for when we are old we have to

buy even consideration and politeness from those about us.

*Dorothy Dix*
Dorothy Dix—Her Book, *1926*

7.4 ❦ At twenty a man is full of fight and hope. He wants to reform the world. When he's seventy he still wants to reform the world, but he knows he can't.

*Clarence Darrow*
Interview, *April 18, 1936*

7.5 ❦ I'm having a glorious old age. One of my greatest delights is that I have outlived most of my opposition.

*Maggie Kuhn*
Speech, Vermont state legislature, *1991*

# 8. AGREEMENTS

8.1 ❦ Agreement makes law.

*Latin legal maxim*
*W. Gurney Benham,* Putnam's
Complete Book of Quotations,
Proverbs and Household Words, *1927*

8.2 ❦ A lean agreement is better than a fat judgment.

*Proverb*
*Rosalind Fergusson,* The Facts On
File Dictionary of Proverbs, *1983*

*8.3* ❦ They two agreed like two cats in a gutter.

*Proverb*
*John Heywood,* Proverbs, *1546*

*8.4* ❦ Men keep agreements when it is to the advantage of neither to break them.

*Ascribed to Solon, c.630–c.560* B.C.

*8.5* ❦ The main object of conciliation lies in reaching a solution to a case based upon morals and with a warm heart.

*Confucius*
Analects, *c.500* B.C.

*8.6* ❦ We seldom attribute common sense except to those who agree with us.

*La Rochefoucauld*
Maximes, *1665*

*8.7* ❦ It is evident that many great and useful objects can be attained in this world only by cooperation. It is equally evident that there cannot be efficient cooperation if men proceed on the principle that they must not cooperate for one object unless they agree about other objects.

*Thomas Babington Macaulay*
Gladstone on Church and State, *1839*

*8.8* ❦ Ah! don't say you agree with me. When people agree with me I always feel that I must be wrong.

*Oscar Wilde*
The Critic as Artist, *1891*

# *9.* ALIBIS

*9.1* ❦ Poor men's reasons are not heard.

*German proverb*
*W. Gurney Benham,* Putnam's Complete Book of Quotations, Proverbs and Household Words, *1927*

*9.2* ❦ [*Alibi:*] a lie by which criminals escape punishment.

*Dublin barrister Marshall Brown,*
Wit and Wisdom of Bench and Bar, *1899*

*9.3* ❦ Better a bad excuse than none.

*Nicholas Udall*
Ralph Roister Doister, *c.1553*

*9.4* ❦ And, oftentimes, excusing of a fault Doth make the fault worse by the excuse.

*Shakespeare*
King John, *I, 1, 1596–1597*

*9.5* ❦ I know'd what 'ud come o' this here mode o' doin bisness. Oh Sammy, Sammy, vy worn't there a alleybi!

*Charles Dickens*
Pickwick Papers, *1836–1837*

*9.6* ☙ If your governor don't prove a alleybi, he'll be what the Italians call
reg'larly flummoxed.

*Charles Dickens*
Pickwick Papers, *1836–1837*

*9.7* ☙ He always has an alibi, and one or
two to spare:
At whatever time the deed took
place—
Macavity wasn't there.

*T.S. Eliot,* 1888–1965
Macavity: The Mystery Cat

# *10.* APPEALS

*10.1* ☙ Once a lawyer was arguing a case before three lord justices in the court
of appeal, dealing with an elementary point of law at inordinate
length. Finally, the master of the
rolls, who was presiding, intervened:
"Really," he protested, "do give this
court credit for some intelligence."
Quick as a flash came the reply:
"That is the mistake I made in the
court below, my lord."

*Anonymous*
*Archibald Edgar Bowker,* A Lifetime
with the Law, *1961*

*10.2* ☙ The point appears here in its virgin
state, wearing all its maiden blushes,
and is therefore out of place.

*Logan E. Bleckley, American jurist*
Cleveland v. Chambliss, *64 Ga. 352,*
*359 (1879)*

*10.3* ☙ If no appeal were possible . . . this
would not be a desirable country to
live in. . . .

*Charles Bowen, English jurist;*
*Lord Justice*
The Queen v. Justices of County of
London *(1893), L.R. 2 Q.B. 492*

*10.4* ☙ [*Appeal:*] In law, to put the dice into
the box for another throw.

*Ambrose Bierce*
The Devil's Dictionary, *1906*

*10.5* ☙ An appeal, Hinnissy, is where ye ask
wan coort to show its contempt f'r
another coort.

*Finley Peter Dunne*
Mr. Dooley Says: The Big Fine, *1906*

*10.6* ☙ In this Court dissents have gradually
become majority opinions.

*Felix Frankfurter*
Graves v. New York ex rel. O'Keefe
*306 U.S. 466; 83 L.Ed. 927; 59 Sup.*
*Ct. 595 (1939)*

*10.7* ☙ Appeal must be to an informed, civi-
cally militant electorate.

*Felix Frankfurter*
Baker v. Carr, *369 U.S. 186, 82 S.*
*Ct. 691, 7 L. Ed.2d 663 (1962)*

10.8 ❧ "[Dissents are] appeals to the brooding spirit of the law, to the intelligence of another day."

*Charles Evans Hughes, 1930–1941*
*Irving Kaufman, "Keeping Politics out*
*of the Court," New York Times,*
*December 9, 1984*

# 11. ARGUMENTS

11.1 ❧ A lawyer's primer: If you don't have
the law, you argue the facts; if
you don't have the facts, you argue
the law; if you have neither the facts
nor the law, then you argue the
Constitution.

*Anonymous*

11.2 ❧ He opens the door with an ax.

*English proverb*
*John Ray, English Proverbs, 1678*

11.3 ❧ The sergeant pleads with face on fire,
And all the court may rue it;
His purple garments come from
Tyre;
His arguments go to it.

*Epigram*
*Marshall Brown, Wit and Humor of*
*Bench and Bar, 1899*

11.4 ❧ Prepare your proof before you argue.

*Jewish folk saying*
*Joseph L. Baron, A Treasury of Jewish*
*Quotations, 1956*

11.5 ❧ An argument derived from the abuse
of a thing does not hold good against
its use.

*Latin legal phrase W. Gurney Benham,*
*Putnam's Complete Book of*
*Quotations, Proverbs and*
*Household Words, 1927*

11.6 ❧ There is no arguing with one who
denies first principles.

*Latin legal phrase*
*W. Gurney Benham, Putnam's*
*Complete Book of Quotations,*
*Proverbs and Household Words, 1927*

11.7 ❧ A legal decision depends not on the
teacher's age, but on the force of his
argument.

*Talmud, Bava Batra*

11.8 ❧ Do not attempt to confute a lion
after he's dead.

*Talmud, Gittin*

**11.9** ❧ No honest man will argue on every side.

> *Sophocles, 496?–406* B.C.
> Oedipus at Colonus, *c.408* B.C.

**11.10** ❧ In a just cause it is right to be confident.

> *Sophocles, 496?–406* B.C.
> *W. Gurney Benham,* Putnam's
> Complete Book of Quotations,
> Proverbs and Household Words, *1927*

**11.11** ❧ Arguments derived from probabilities are idle.

> *Plato*
> Phaedo, *c. late 4th century* B.C.

**11.12** ❧ We must make a personal attack when there is no argumentative basis for our speech.

> *Cicero*
> Pro Flacco, *c.58* B.C.

**11.13** ❧ In a heated argument we lose sight of the truth.

> *Publilius Syrus, Latin writer*
> Sententiae, *c.43* B.C.

**11.14** ❧ Who over-refines his argument brings himself to grief.

> *Petrarch*
> Vita di Madonna Laura, *c.1350*

**11.15** ❧ He draweth out the thread of his verbosity finer than the staple of his argument.

> *Shakespeare*
> Love's Labour's Lost, *V, 1,*
> *1594–1595*

**11.16** ❧ Be calm in arguing; for fierceness makes
> Error a fault, and truth discourtesy.

> *George Herbert*
> *"The Church Porch,"* The Temple,
> *1633*

**11.17** ❧ Bluster, sputter, question, cavil; but be sure your argument be intricate enough to confound the court.

> *William Wycherley*
> The Plain Dealer, *1677*

**11.18** ❧ He'd undertake to prove, by force
> Of argument, a man's no horse.
> He'd prove a buzzard is no fowl,
> And that a Lord may be an owl,
> A calf an Alderman, a goose a Justice,
> And rooks, Committee-men or Trustees.

> *Samuel Butler*
> Hudibras, *1663–1678*

**11.19** ❧ First settle what the case is, before you argue it.

> *Lord Chief Justice Howe*
> Trial of the Seven Bishops *(1688),*
> *12 How. St. Tr. 342*

**11.20** ❧ I know you lawyers can, with ease, Twist words and meanings as you please.

> *John Gay*
> Fables, *1727*

**11.21** ❧ Heat is in proportion to the want of true knowledge.

> *Laurence Sterne*
> Tristram Shandy, *1760*

**11.22** ❦ It seems to me that the defendant's counsel blows hot and cold at the same time.

*Justice Buller*
I'Anson v. Stuart *(1787), 1 T.R. 753*

**11.23** ❦ [Johnson said] . . . striking his foot with mighty force against a large stone, till he rebounded from it, "I refute it thus."

*Samuel Johnson*
*James Boswell,* The Life of Samuel Johnson, *1791*

**11.24** ❦ He is an ingenious council who has made the most of his cause; he is not obliged to join it.

*Samuel Johnson*
*James Boswell,* The Life of Samuel Johnson, *1791*

**11.25** ❦ This is the last hair in the tail of procrastination.

*Sir Lloyd Kenyon, English jurist; Lord Chief Justice; sitting in the Rolls Court, indignant at one of the parties, late 18th century*
*Marshall Brown,* Wit and Humor of Bench and Bar, *1899*

**11.26** ❦ Be brief, be pointed, let your matter stand
Lucid in order, solid and at hand;
Spend not your words on trifles but condense;
Strike with the mass of thought, not drops of sense;
Press to the close with vigor, once begun,
And leave—how hard the task!—leave off when done.

*Joseph Story*
Advice to a Young Lawyer, *1835*

**11.27** ❦ I was with you, Mr. Scott [Lord Eldon]—until I heard your argument.

*Edward Thurlow, English jurist; Lord Chancellor, 1731–1806*
*Sir Travers Twiss,* Life of Lord Eldon, *1844*

**11.28** ❦ The gentleman puts me in mind of an old hen which persists in setting after her eggs are taken away.

*Fisher Ames, American lawyer, 1758–1808, referring to opposing counsel*
*Theophilus Parsons,* Memoirs of Theophilus Parsons, *1859*

**11.29** ❦ The last point is perfectly new, and it is so startling that I do not apprehend it will ever become old.

*Sir William Henry Maule, English jurist*
Whitaker v. Wisbey *(1852), 12 C.B. 44, 58*

**11.30** ❦ Once, when he [Lord Mackay] was counsel in a case the presiding judge asked him whether he estimated it would be possible to start the next case after lunch time the next day: "Oh yes, my Lord," replied Mackay. "I'll certainly have finished my argument by then." "Yes, Mr. Mackay," said the judge, "I know you'll have finished, but will you stop?"

*Lord Mackay, Scottish jurist*
*Francis Cowper, "London Letter,"*
New York Law Journal, *April 8, 1963*

**11.31** ❦ The weapon of the advocate is the sword of the soldier, not the dagger of the assassin.

*Ascribed to Sir Alexander Cockburn, British jurist; Lord Chief Justice, 1802–1880*
*H. L. Mencken,* A New Dictionary of Quotations, *1946*

*11.32* ❧ Narrow-gauge statesmen grew red as turkey gobblers mouthing their ignorance against the (women lawyers') bill, and staid old grangers who had never seen the inside of a courthouse seemed to have been given the gift of tongues and delivered themselves of maiden speeches pregnant with eloquent nonsense.

> *Clara Shortridge Foltz, c. 1876, on debate on California senate floor*
> *Dawn Bradley Berry,* The 50 Most Influential Women in American Law, *1996*

*11.33* ❧ When facts were weak, his native cheek
Brought him serenely through.

> *Charles H. Spurgeon, English devine 1834–1892, commenting on an eminent lawyer*
> *W. Gurney Benham,* Putnam's Complete Book of Legal Quotations, Proverbs and Household Words, *1927*

*11.34* ❧ No mistake is so commonly made by clever people as that of assuming a cause to be bad because the arguments of its supporters are, to a great extent, nonsensical.

> *Thomas H. Huxley* Science and Education—Essays, *1897*

*11.35* ❧ "You are old," said the youth, "and your jaws are too weak
For anything tougher than suet;
Yet you finished the goose, with the bones and the beak.
Pray, how did you manage to do it?"
"In my youth," said his father, "I took to the law,
And argued each case with my wife,

And the muscular strength which it gave to my jaw
Has lasted the rest of my life."

> *Lewis Carroll, 1832–1898* "You Are Old, Father William"

*11.36* ❧ If the court please, I am about to illustrate it by diagrams, and I hope to make it so plain that the audience and perhaps the court will understand it.

> *James T. Brown, American lawyer, addressing a circuit court judge in Indiana*
> *Marshall Brown,* Wit and Humor of Bench and Bar, *1899*

*11.37* ❧ If the court will listen, the court will learn.

> *John A. Campbell, American jurist*
> *Marshall Brown,* Wit and Humor of Bench and Bar, *1899*

*11.38* ❧ But to generalize is to omit. . . .

> *Oliver Wendell Holmes*
> Donnell v. Herring-Hall-Marvin Safe Co., *208 U.S. 267, 273 (1908)*

*11.39* ❧ We see what you are driving at, but you have not said it, and therefore we shall go on as before.

> *Oliver Wendell Holmes*
> Johnson v. United States, *163 Fed. 30, 31 (1908)*

*11.40* ❧ One has to try to strike the jugular and let the rest go.

> *Oliver Wendell Holmes* Speeches, *1913*

**11.41** ❧ Lawyers earn their bread in the sweat of their browbeating.

> *James Huneker*
> Painted Veils, *1920*

**11.42** ❧ To be brief is almost a condition of being inspired.

> *George Santayana*
> Little Essays, *1920*

**11.43** ❧ The obvious is better than obvious avoidance of it.

> *H. W. Fowler*
> A Dictionary of Modern English
> Usage, *1926*

**11.44** ❧ To get the sympathy of the Tribunal for himself ought always to be one of the first objects of the advocate.

> *Richard Burdon Haldane*
> An Autobiography, *1929*

**11.45** ❧ The elaborate argument . . . does not need an elaborate answer.

> *Oliver Wendell Holmes*
> United States v. Wurzbach, *280 U.S.*
> *396, 399 (1930)*

**11.46** ❧ Holmes, when you strike at a king, you must kill him."

> *Ralph Waldo Emerson to Oliver*
> *Wendell Holmes*
> Harlan Phillips, Felix Frankfurter
> Reminiscences, *1960*

**11.47** ❧ A judge of the Massachusetts Supreme Judicial Court found the long-winded speeches of lawyers especially trying and advised them to take a course of reading risque books that they might learn to say things by innuendo.

> *Attributed to a judge of the*
> *Massachusetts Supreme Judicial Court*
> *Ed Bander,* Justice Holmes ex
> Cathedra, *1966*

**11.48** ❧ The brilliant, ruthless F. E. Smith, afterwards Lord Chancellor Birkenhead, was a master of the unanswerable *riposte*. Once when he was starting his opening speech for a plaintiff an impatient judge interrupted him saying: "I've read the pleadings in this matter and I don't think much of your case." "Oh, I'm very sorry to hear that, my lord" replied Smith smoothly, "but you'll find that the more you hear of it the more it will grow on you." On another occasion a judge unwisely said to Smith who was opening a complicated case: "I've listened to you for an hour and I'm none the wiser." "None the wiser, perhaps, my lord," said Smith, "but certainly better informed."

> *Frederick Edwin Smith, English jurist;*
> *Lord Chancellor* 1872–1930
> *Francis Cowper "London Letter,"* New
> York Law Journal, *August 28, 1961*

**11.49** ❧ Expediency may tip the scales when arguments are nicely balanced.

> *Benjamin N. Cardozo*
> Woolford Realty Co. v. Rose, *286*
> *U.S. 319, 330, 76 L.Ed. 1128, 52 S.*
> *Ct. 568 (1932)*

**11.50** ❧ A doctrine capable of being stated only in obscure and involved terms is open to reasonable suspicion of being either crude or erroneous.

*Sir Frederick Pollock, 1845–1937*
*Mark De Wolfe Howe,*
Holmes-Pollock Letters, *1946*

**11.51** ❧ The picture cannot be painted if the significant and the insignificant are given equal prominence. One must know how to select.

*Benjamin N. Cardozo, 1870–1938*
"Law and Literature," Selected
Writings of Benjamin Nathan
Cardozo, *edited by Margaret E. Hall,*
*1947*

**11.52** ❧ Or, supposing fishes had the gift of speech, who would listen to a fisherman's weary discourse on flycasting, the shape and color of the fly, the size of the tackle, the length of the line, the merit of different rod makers and all the other tiresome stuff that fishermen talk about, if the fish himself could be induced to give his views on the most effective methods of approach? For it is the fish that the angler is after, and all his recondite learning is but the hopeful means to that end.

*John W. Davis*
*Association of the Bar of the City of*
*New York,* The Argument of an
Appeal, *October 1940*

**11.53** ❧ Judicious omission is preferable to correct superfluity.

*Walter Kidde*
*Foreword,* We Give You Walter Kidde,
*1940*

**11.54** ❧ A phrase begins life as a literary expression; its felicity leads to its lazy repetition; and repetition soon establishes it as a legal formula, undiscriminatingly used to express different and sometimes contradictory ideas.

*Felix Frankfurter*
Tiller, Executor v. Atlantic Coast
Line Railroad Co., *318 U.S. 54, 68*
*(1943)*

**11.55** ❧ Moderation is power.

*George W. Keeton, ed.*
Harris's Hints on Advocacy, *1943*

**11.56** ❧ It is pretty hard to make the tail wag the dog.

*Sidney Post Simpson, American*
*educator; professor, Harvard Law*
*School, 1934–1945*
*Eugene C. Gerhart,* Quote It! *1969*

**11.57** ❧ . . . answers are not obtained by putting the wrong question and thereby begging the real one.

*Felix Frankfurter*
Priebe and Sons v. United States,
*332 U.S. 407, 420 (1947)*

**11.58** ❧ I give up. Now I realize fully what Mark Twain meant when he said, "The more you explain it, the more I don't understand it."

*Robert H. Jackson*
Securities Commission v. Chenery
Corporation, *332 U.S. 194, 214*
*(1947)*

11.59  ❧  Counsel searching for authority for lack of argument.

> *N. R. Jessel*
> *Arthur Goodhart,*
> Five Jewish Lawyers, *1949*

11.60  ❧  The petitioner's problem is to avoid Scylla without being drawn into Charybdis.

> *Robert H. Jackson*
> Montana-Dakota Utility Co. v.
> Northwestern Public Service Co., *341*
> *U.S. 246, 250 (1951)*

11.61  ❧  It is one thing, though, to recognize and properly apply a sound principle. It is quite another to run that same sound principle into the ground. It is one thing for a dog to have a tail. It is quite another for the tail to wag the dog.

> *Joseph C. Hutcheson, Jr., American jurist*
> Deal v. Morrow, *197 F.2d 821 (1952)*

11.62  ❧  If you want to win a case, paint the Judge a *picture* and keep it simple.

> *John W. Davis*
> *Annual meeting of Scribes,*
> *August 21, 1955*

11.63  ❧  Proceed. You have my biased attention.

> *Learned Hand, 1872–1961, speaking*
> *to a counsel who demanded the right to*
> *reargue a motion already heard*
> *M. Frances McNamara,* 2000 Famous
> Legal Quotations, *1967*

11.64  ❧  The best way to win an argument is to begin by being right. . . .

> *Jill Ruckelshaus, American*
> *government official*
> *Frederic A. Birmingham, "Jill*
> *Ruckelshaus: Lady of Liberty,"*
> Saturday Evening Post,
> *March 3, 1973*

11.65  ❧  Things in law tend to be black and white. But we all know that some people are a little bit guilty, while other people are guilty as hell. . . . However, once you get into the courtroom, you are doomed to do battle; then it becomes yes or no, guilty or not guilty. You cannot bring in a verdict that the defendant is a little bit guilty.

> *Donald R. Cressey, American educator;*
> *Professor, University of California,*
> *Santa Barbara*
> Center Magazine, *May–June 1978*

11.66  ❧  Among attorneys in Tennessee the saying is: When you have the facts on your side, argue the facts. When you have the law on your side, argue the law. When you have neither, holler.

> *Albert Gore, Jr.*
> Washington Post, *July 23, 1982*

11.67  ❧  In determining the outcome of a given case, a lawyer's flamboyance plays a part. His or her performance in the courtroom is responsible for about 25% of the outcome; the remaining 75% depends on the facts. Those who criticize flamboyant lawyers are just envious.

> *Melvin Belli*
> U.S. News & World Report,
> *September 20, 1982*

11.68  ❧  In saying what is obvious, never choose cunning, yelling works better.

> *Cynthia Ozick, 1928–*

11.69 ❧ Two wrongs don't make a right but they often appear the next best thing in legal disputes or tangles with lawyers.

*Deborah L. Rhode*
Lawyers, *in press*

# *12.* ASSASSINATION

12.1 ❧ Believe me, a thousand friends suffice thee not;
In a single enemy thou hast more than enough.

*Ali Ibn-Abi-Tlib,* c. 600–661, *Arabian religious leader and victim of assassination*
*Franklin Pierce Adams,* F.P.A. Book of Quotations, *1952*

12.2 ❧ Despotism tempered by assassination, that is our Magna Charta.

*Russian noble*
*Message to Count Münster on the assassination of Paul I, emperor of Russia, 1800*

12.3 ❧ Assassination has never changed the history of the world.

*Benjamin Disraeli*
Speech, *May 1865*

12.4 ❧ Assassination is the extreme form of censorship.

*George Bernard Shaw*
The Rejected Statement, *1903*

12.5 ❧ America is the place where you cannot kill your government by killing the men who conduct it.

*Woodrow Wilson*
*Address, in Helena, Montana, September 11, 1919*

12.6 ❧ Is it too much to hope that the martyrdom of our beloved President might even soften the hearts of those who would themselves recoil from assassination, but who do not shrink from spreading the venom which kindles thoughts of it in others?

*Earl Warren*
*Eulogy, on the death of President John F. Kennedy, November 24, 1963*

# 13. AUTHORITY

13.1 ❦ Fear God, and offend not the Prince
nor his laws,
And keep thyself out of the
Magistrate's claws.

*Anonymous*
Hundred Points of Good Husbandry,
*1557*

13.2 ❦ Great men in judicial places will
never want authority.

*Proverb*
*Sir Edward Coke,* Institutes of the
Lawes of England, *vol. 2, 1628–1641*

13.3 ❦ There is no king where there is
no law.

*Proverb*
*E. Gordon Duff, ed.,* Salomon and
Marcolphus, *1892*

13.4 ❦ Laws should have authority over
men, not men over laws. [when
asked why it was not permitted to
change any of the ancient laws].

*Pausanius, king of Sparta, c.400* B.C.
*Burton Stevenson,* Home Book of
Proverbs, Maxims and Familiar
Phrases, *1948*

13.5 ❦ He who lies hid in remote places is a
law unto himself.

*Publilius Syrus, Latin writer*
Sententiae, *c.43* B.C.

13.6 ❦ She made what pleased her lawful.

*Dante*
The Divine Comedy: Inferno,
*c.1310–1312*

13.7 ❦ Who to himself is law, no law doth
need, offends no law, and is a king
indeed.

*George Chapman*
Bussy D'Ambois, *1607*

13.8 ❦ His [Cardinal Wolsey's] own opinion was his law.

*Shakespeare*
Henry VIII, *IV, 2, 1612–1613*

13.9 ❦ It is not wisdom but Authority that
makes a law.

*Thomas Hobbes*
Dialogue of the Common Laws,
*c.1670*

13.10 ❦ . . . there is nothing too absurd but
what authority can be found for it.

*Sir Henry Manistry, English jurist*
Henderson v. Preston *(1888). 4*
T.L.R. 632, 633

13.11 ❦ The passing of an unjust law is the
suicide of authority.

*Pastoral letter of the American Roman
Catholic hierarchy, February 1920*

13.12  ❦ The strongest bulwark of authority is uniformity; the least divergence from it is the greatest crime.

*Emma Goldman*
*"The Individual, Society and*
*the State," 1940, in*
*Alix Kates Shulman, ed,*
Red Emma Speaks, *1983*

13.13  ❦ The young are too apt to believe what a great man says, especially if he be an authority in the profession they follow.

*George W. Keeton, ed.* Harris's Hints
on Advocacy, *1943*

13.14  ❦ Decisions of this Court do not have intrinsic authority.

*Felix Frankfurter* Adamson v.
California, *332 U.S. 46, 59 (1947)*

13.15  ❦ "The Judiciary is still the one place in our system where authority can be abused with virtual impunity."

*Steve Martini, attorney and writer*
The Judge, *1966*

13.16  ❦ The decision finally rests not upon appeals to past authority, but upon *what people want.*

*S. I. Hayakawa*
*Laurence J. Peter,* Peter's Quotations,
*1977*

# 14. BAR

**14.1** ❦ O lady, lady, all interruption and no
sense between us, as
if we were lawyers at the bar! but I
had forgot, Apollo
and Littleton never lodge in a head
together.*

*Anonymous*
*William Andrews, ed.,* The Lawyer in
History, Literature, and Humour,
*1896*

**14.2** ❦ I will for ever, at all hazards, assert
the dignity, independence, and integrity of the English bar; without
which, impartial justice, the most
valuable part of the English constitution, can have no existence.

*Thomas Erskine*
Trial of Thomas Paine *(1792), 22*
How. St. Tr. 358, 412

**14.3** ❦ I think of times when far
Aloof cold envy stood,
And brethren of the Bar
Professed good brotherhood—
No soulless etiquette,
But friendship warm and true—
With heart and hand we met
When this old wig was new.
No greedy hand was then
Projected for a fee;
We held no servile pen
To any lordly he;
And none of us demurred
The poor man's cause to sue,

For honour was the word
When this old wig was new.

*George Outram, 1805–1856*
*"When This Old Wig Was New"*

**14.4** ❦ Shall I ask what a court would be,
unaided? The law is made by the
Bar, even more than by the Bench.

*Oliver Wendell Holmes*
*"The Law,"* Speeches, *1913*

**14.5** ❦ Membership in the bar is a privilege
burdened with conditions.

*Benjamin N. Cardozo*
In re Rouss, *221 N.Y. 81, 84 (1917)*

**14.6** ❦ The unique advantage of the Bar as
a profession is that it offers in later
years to those who have succeeded
in it the sanctuary of the Bench. . . .

*Harold Macmillan*
A Man of Law's Tale,
*1953*

**14.7** ❦ The Senate no longer need bother
about confirmation of Justices but
ought to confirm the appointment
of law clerks.

*Robert H. Jackson, 1892–1954*
*John P. Frank,* Serving Justice,
*1974*

---

*i.e., law and letters do not flourish together

# *15.* BILL OF RIGHTS

15.1 ❦ Congress shall make no law respecting an establishment of religion, or prohibiting the free exercise thereof; or abridging the freedom of speech, or of the press; or the right of the people peaceably to assemble, and to petition the Government for a redress of grievances.

*Constitution of the United States, First Amendment, 1791*

15.2 ❦ The right of the people to be secure in their persons, houses, papers, and effects, against unreasonable searches and seizures, shall not be violated. . . .

*Constitution of the United States, Fourth Amendment, 1791*

15.3 ❦ No person shall be held to answer for a capital, or otherwise infamous crime, unless on a presentment or indictment of a Grand Jury, . . . nor shall any person be subject for the same offence to be twice put in jeopardy of life or limb; nor shall be compelled in any Criminal Case to be a witness against himself, nor be deprived of life, liberty, or property, without due process of law; nor shall private property be taken for public use, without just compensation.

*Constitution of the United States, Fifth Amendment, 1791*

15.4 ❦ In all criminal prosecutions, the accused shall enjoy the right to a speedy and public trial. . . .

*Constitution of the United States, Sixth Amendment, 1791*

15.5 ❦ What seems fair enough against a squalid huckster of bad liquor may take on a different face, if used by a government determined to suppress political opposition under the guise of sedition.

*Learned Hand*
United States v. Kirschenblatt, *1926*

15.6 ❦ Bills of rights give assurance to the individual of the preservation of his liberty. They do not define the liberty they promise.

*Benjamin N. Cardozo*
*"Paradoxes of Legal Science," in*
Selected Writings of Benjamin
Nathan Cardozo, *edited by*
*Margaret E. Hall, 1928*

15.7 ❦ Thoughts, emotions, and sensations [demand] legal recognition.

*Louis D. Brandeis*
The Curse of Bigness: Miscellaneous
Papers of Louis D. Brandeis, *1935*

15.8 ❦ Civil liberties had their origin and must find their ultimate guaranty in the faith of the people.

*Robert H. Jackson*
Douglas v. Jeannette, *319 U.S. 157,*
*182 (1943)*

**15.9** ❦ If there is any fixed star in our constitutional constellation, it is that no official, high or petty, can prescribe what shall be orthodox in politics, nationalism, religion, or other matters of opinion or force citizens to confess by word or act their faith therein.

*Robert H. Jackson*
West Virginia State Board of
Education v. Barnette, *319 U.S. 624,*
*638 (1943)*

**15.10** ❦ The very purpose of a Bill of Rights was to withdraw certain subjects from the vicissitudes of political controversy, to place them beyond the reach of majorities and officials and to establish them as legal principles to be applied by the courts. One's right to life, liberty, and property, to free speech, a free press, freedom of worship and assembly, and other fundamental rights may not be submitted to vote; they depend on the outcome of no elections.

*Robert H. Jackson*
West Virginia State Board of
Education v. Barnette, *319 U.S. 624,*
*638 (1943)*

**15.11** ❦ We set up government by consent of the governed, and the Bill of Rights denies those in power any legal opportunity to coerce that consent. Authority here is to be controlled by public opinion, not public opinion by authority.

*Robert H. Jackson*
West Virginia State Board of
Education v. Barnette, *319 U.S. 624.*
*641 (1943)*

**15.12** ❦ It is not only under Nazi rule that police excesses are inimical to freedom. It is easy to make light of insistence on scrupulous regard for the safeguards of civil liberties when invoked on behalf of the unworthy. . . . History bears testimony that by such disregard are the rights of liberty extinguished, heedlessly, at first, then stealthily, and brazenly in the end.

*Felix Frankfurter*
Davis v. United States, *328 U.S.*
*582. 66 S. Ct. 1256, 90 L.Ed. 1453*
*(1946)*

**15.13** ❦ Of course I know how illusory would be the belief that my vote determined anything; but nevertheless when I go to the polls I have a satisfaction in the sense that we are all engaged in a common venture. If you retort that a sheep in the flock may feel something like it; I reply, following Saint Francis, "My brother, the Sheep."

*Learned Hand*
The Bill of Rights, *1958*

**15.14** ❦ It seems as if the Department [of Justice] sees the value of the Bill of Rights as no more than obstacles to be overcome.

*Sanford H. Kadish, American*
*educator; professor, University of*
*California, Berkeley*
Los Angeles Times, *July 25, 1969*

# 16. BRIBERY

*16.1* ❦ He that buyeth magistracy will seek justice.

*English proverb*
*John Ray,* English Proverbs,
*1678*

*16.2* ❦ Bribes throw Dust into cunning Men's eyes.

*Proverb*
*Thomas Fuller,* Gnomologia, *1732*

*16.3* ❦ Death's boatman takes no bribe. . . .

*Horace*
Odes, *23* B.C.

*16.4* ❦ And if thou freely wilt, in bribes thy coyne bestowe,
Both judge, and jurie will bee prest, all favour thee to showe:
Yea Gods from heaven will hither come, all honour thee to doe.

*Stefano Guazzo*
Civile Conversation, *1574*

*16.5* ❦ Honesty stands at the gate and knocks,
and bribery enters in.

*Barnabe Rich, English writer and*
*soldier, 1542–1617*
The Irish Hubbub, *c.1617*

*16.6* ❦ Though the bribe be small, yet the fault is great.

*Sir Edward Coke*
Institutes of the Lawes of England,
*vol. 3, 1628–1641*

*16.7* ❦ Where many a Client Verdict miss'd,
For want of Greazing in the fist.

*Thomas D'Urfey*
Collins's Walk Through London,
*1690*

*16.8* ❦ Every man has his price, I will bribe left and right.

*Edward Robert Bulwer-Lytton,*
*1st earl of Lytton*
Walpole, *1875*

*16.9* ❦ When their lordships asked Bacon
How many bribes he had taken
He had at least the grace
To get very red in the face.

*Edmund C. Bentley, English*
*journalist and poet*
Baseless Biography, *1939*

*16.10* ❦ [It is] very much better to bribe a person than kill him. . . .

*Sir Winston S. Churchill*
*F. B. Czarnomski, ed.,* The Wisdom
of Winston Churchill,
*1956*

# 17. BUSINESS

17.1 ❦ The man of law who never saw
The wayes to buy and sell,
Wenyng to rise by merchandize,
I pray God speed him well.

*Attributed to Sir John Fortescue,*
*English jurist; Chief Justice,*
*c.1385–1479*
*W. Gurney Benham,* Putnam's
Complete Book of Quotations,
Proverbs and Household Words, *1927*

17.2 ❦ Corporations cannot commit treason, nor be outlawed, nor excommu-
nicated, for they have no souls.

*Sir Edward Coke*
Case of Sutton's Hospital *(1612), 5*
*Rep. 303; 10 Rep. 326*

17.3 ❦ Trade is the mother of money.

*Thomas Draxe, ?–1618*
Bibliotheca

17.4 ❦ . . . everyone thirsteth after gaine . . .

*Sir Edward Coke*
Institutes of the Lawes of England,
*vol. 3, 1628–1641*

17.5 ❦ Did you expect a corporation to
have a conscience, when it has no
soul to be damned and no body to
be kicked?

*Edward Thurlow, English jurist; Lord*
*Chancellor, 1731–1806*
*Wilberforce,* Life of Thurlow, *1775*

17.6 ❦ A corporation cannot blush. It is a
body, it is true; has certainly a
head—a new one every year; arms it
has and very long ones, for it can
reach at anything; . . . a throat to
swallow the rights of the community, and a stomach to digest them!
But who ever yet discovered, in the
anatomy of any corporation, either
bowels or a heart?

*Howell Walsh*
*Speech, Tralee assizes, c.1825*

17.7 ❦ The selfish spirit of commerce
knows no country, and feels no passion of principle but that of gain.

*Thomas Jefferson, 1743–1826*
*Letter to Larkin Smith*

17.8 ❦ The rule of my life is to make business a pleasure, and pleasure my
business.

*Aaron Burr, 1756–1836*
*Letter to Pichon, secretary of the*
*French Legation at Washington, D.C.*

17.9 ❦ I think that there is nothing, not
even crime, more opposed to poetry,
to philosophy, ay, to life itself, than
this incessant business.

*Henry David Thoreau*
Life Without Principle, *1854*

17.10 ❦ The ways by which you may get
money almost without exception
lead downward.

*Henry David Thoreau*
Life Without Principle, *1854*

17.11 ❦ It must be remembered that all trade is and must be in a sense selfish. . . .

*John Duke Coleridge, English jurist;*
*Lord Chief Justice*
Mogul Steamship Co. v. McGregor,
Gow & Co. *(1888), L.R. 21 Q.B.D.*
*553*

17.12 ❦ The director is really a watch-dog, and the watch-dog has no right, without the knowledge of his master, to take a sop from a possible wolf.

*Timothy Bower, English jurist*
In re North Australian Territory Co.,
*1892*

17.13 ❦ Don't steal; thou'lt never thus compete successfully in business. Cheat.

*Ambrose Bierce*
The Devil's Dictionary, *1906*

17.14 ❦ The gambling known as business looks with austere disfavor upon the business known as gambling.

*Ambrose Bierce*
The Devil's Dictionary, *1906*

17.15 ❦ . . . the most enlightened judicial policy is to let people manage their own business in their own way.

*Oliver Wendell Holmes*
Dr. Miles Medical Co. v. Park & Sons
Co., *220 U.S. 373, 411 (1911)*

17.16 ❦ . . . mere money-making cannot be regarded as the legitimate end [of business] since with the conduct of business human happiness or misery is inextricably interwoven.

*Louis D. Brandeis*
*Address, Brown University, 1912*

17.17 ❦ . . . while I should be the last to say that the making of a profit was not in itself a pleasure, I hope I should also be one of those to agree that there were other pleasures than making a profit.

*Learned Hand*
Thacher et al. v. Lowe, *288 Fed. 994,*
*995 (1922)*

17.18 ❦ . . . the notion that a business is clothed with a public interest and has been devoted to the public use is little more than a fiction intended to beautify what is disagreeable to the sufferers.

*Oliver Wendell Holmes*
Tyson and Brother v. Banton, *273*
*U.S. 418, 446 (1927)*

17.19 ❦ To say that only those businesses affected with a public interest may be regulated is but another way of stating that all those businesses which may be regulated are affected with a public interest.

*Harlan Fiske Stone*
Tyson and Brother v. Banton, *273*
*U.S. 418, 451 (1927)*

17.20 ❦ The business of America is business.

*Calvin Coolidge, 1872–1933*
*Franklin Pierce Adams, F.P.A. Book*
of Quotations, *1952*

17.21 ❦ Strong responsible unions are essential to industrial fair play. Without them the labor bargain is wholly one-sided.

*Louis D. Brandeis*
The Curse of Bigness: Miscellaneous
Papers of Louis D. Brandeis, *1935*

**17.22** ❧ When . . . you increase your business to a very great extent . . . the man at the head has a diminishing knowledge of the facts, and . . . a diminishing opportunity of exercising a careful judgment upon them.

*Louis D. Brandeis*
*Alpheus Thomas Mason,* Brandeis: A Free Man's Life, *1946*

**17.23** ❧ What to an outsider will be no more than the vigorous presentation of a conviction, to an employee may be the manisfestation of a determination which it is not safe to thwart.

*Learned Hand*
National Labor Relations Board v. Federbush Co., Inc., *121 F.2d 954, 957 (1941)*

**17.24** ❧ When I hear artists and authors making fun of business men I think of a regiment in which the band makes fun of the cooks.

*H. L. Mencken*
A New Dictionary of Quotations, *1946*

**17.25** ❧ Of course there's a different law for the rich and the poor; otherwise who would go into business?

*E. Ralph Stewart*
*Laurence J. Peter,* Peter's Quotations, *1977*

**17.26** ❧ The legal system is in part responsible for the very size and growth [of big business and big government]. And too often when the individual finds himself in conflict with these forces, the legal system sides with the giant institution, not the small businessman or private citizen.

*Edward M. Kennedy*
*Address, American Bar Association, New York, reported in the* Washington Post, *August 8, 1978*

**17.27** ❧ It's not just our lunch, but our carcasses, that Microsoft is after.

*Gary Reback, lawyer*
*James Daly,* "The Robin Hood of the Rich," Wired, *August 1997*

# 18. CASES

18.1 ❧ The laws are adapted to those cases which most frequently occur.

*Legal maxim*

18.2 ❧ A rotten case abides no handling.

*Shakespeare*
2 Henry IV, *IV, 1, 1597–1598*

18.3 ❧ I have betrayed myself with my own tongue;
The case is altered.

*Ben Jonson*
The Case Is Altered, *1598*

18.4 ❧ Decided cases are the anchors of the law, as laws are of the state.

*Francis Bacon*
De Augmentis Scientiarum, *1623*

18.5 ❧ Every case stands upon its own bottom.

*Sir Francis Pemberton, English jurist;*
*Chief Justice*
Fitzharris' Case *(1681), 8 How.*
*St. Tr. 280*

18.6 ❧ I accede to the authority of that case, although I think it is a very strong decision. It does not convince me; it overcomes me.

*Sir Edward Hall Alderson, English*
*barrister*
Mearing v. Hellings *(1845), 14*
*M&W 711, 712*

18.7 ❧ Hard cases, it is said, make bad law.

*John Campbell, British jurist; Lord*
*Chief Justice*
Ex parte Long *(1854), 3 W.R. 19*

18.8 ❧ This case reminds me of one in which I likened the Plaintiff's case to a colander, because it was so full of holes.

*Sir George Jessel, English jurist*
Ex parte Hall *(1882), 19 Ch. D.*
*580, 584*

18.9 ❧ My wonder is really boundless,
That among the queer cases we try,
A land-case should often be groundless,
And a water-case always be dry.

*John G. Saxe, American lawyer and*
*poet, 1816–1887*
*Marshall Brown,* Wit and Humor of
Bench and Bar, *1899*

18.10 ❧ The mere advocate, however brilliant, will lose the most cases, though he may win the most verdicts.

*B. F. Butler, American general and*
*politician*
Autobiography and Personal
Reminiscences, *1892*

18.11 ❧ A case is only an authority for what it actually decides. I entirely deny it can be quoted for a proposition that may seem to follow logically from it.

Such a mode of reasoning assumes that the law is necessarily a logical code, whereas every lawyer must acknowledge that the law is not always logical at all.

*Hardinge Stanley Giffard,*
*1st Earl Halsbury, English jurist; Lord*
*Chancellor*
Quinn v. Leathem *(1901),*
*A.C. 495, 506*

18.12 ❦ Great cases like hard cases make bad law. For great cases are called great, not by reason of their real importance in shaping the law of the future, but because of some accident of immediate overwhelming interest which appeals to the feelings and distorts the judgment.

*Oliver Wendell Holmes*
Northern Securities Co. v.
United States,
*193 U.S. 197, 400–401 (1904)*

18.13 ❦ General propositions do not decide concrete cases.

*Oliver Wendell Holmes*
Lochner v. New York *198 U.S. 45,*
*76, 49 L. Ed. (1905)*

18.14 ❦ Cases were decided in the chambers of a six-shooter instead of a supreme court.

*O. Henry,* 1862–1910
Law and Order

18.15 ❦ No two cases are exactly alike. A young attorney found two opinions in the New York Reports where the facts seemed identical although the

law was in conflict, but an older and more experienced attorney pointed out to him that the names of the parties were different.

*Cuthbert W. Pound, American jurist*
*"American Law Institute Speech of*
*Judge Pound," 5* New York State
Bar Association Bulletin
*265, 267 (1933)*

18.16 ❦ I long have said there is no such thing as a hard case. I am frightened weekly but always when you walk up to the lion and lay hold the hide comes off and the same old donkey of a question of law is underneath.

*Oliver Wendell Holmes,* 1841–1935
*Mark De Wolfe Howe,*
Holmes-Pollock Letters, *1946*

18.17 ❦ There is an old and somewhat foolish saying that "Hard cases make bad law," and therefore the law must be left as it is. It would be equally true to say, "Bad law makes hard cases," and therefore the law must be amended. The real truth lies somewhere between. Mere freaks of fortune should not be made an excuse for weakening a law which is sound. But a law which is seen to multiply hard cases . . . is not worth preserving, for the law was made for man, not man for the law.

*A. P. Herbert,* 1890–1971
Uncommon Law, *1936*

18.18 ❧ The law itself is on trial in every case as well as the cause before it.

*Harlan F. Stone, 1872–1946*
*Laurence J. Peter, Peter's Quotations,*
*1977*

18.19 ❧ Law students are trained in the case method, and to the lawyer everything in life looks like a case. His first thought in the morning is how to handle the case of the ringing alarm clock.

*Edward B. Packard, Jr.*
Columbia Forum, *Spring 1967*

18.20 ❧ You don't approach a case with the philosophy of applying abstract justice—you go in to win.

*Percy Foreman*
Newsweek, *February 3, 1969*

18.21 ❧ I'm sick and tired of hearing about the number of cases disposed of when we discuss the judicial system. The chief justice should know that the job of the courts is not to dispose of cases but to decide them justly. Doesn't he know that the business of courts is justice?

*Jim R. Carrigan, American jurist;*
*justice, Supreme Court of Colorado,*
Los Angeles Herald-Examiner,
*August 3, 1977*

18.22 ❧ Of every hundred cases, ninety win themselves, three are won by advocacy, and seven are lost by advocacy.

*A. Fountain*
Wit of Wig, *1980*

18.23 ❧ We're approaching space-age technology with Model-T statutes and cases.

*Lori B. Andrews, American lawyer,*
*describing infertility cases and the law*
New York Times,
*June 27, 1984*

# *19.* CERTAINTY

19.1 ❧ Too much subtlety in law is condemned, and so much exactitude destroys exactness.

*Latin legal phrase*
*W. Gurney Benham,* Putnam's
Complete Book of Quotations,
Proverbs and Household Words, *1927*

19.2 ❧ That is sufficiently certain which can be made certain.

*Legal maxim*

19.3 ❧ Better an ounce from the ground than a pound from the roof.

*Talmud, Yevamot*

*19.4* ❦ Doubt cannot override a certainty.

*Talmud, Yevamot*

*19.5* ❦ It is better the law should be certain, than that every Judge should speculate upon improvements in it.

*John Scott, Lord Eldon*
Sheldon v. Goodrich *(1803),*
*8 Ves 481, 497*

*19.6* ❦ The power of the lawyer is in the uncertainty of the law.

*Jeremy Bentham*
*Letter to Sir James Macintosh, 1808*

*19.7* ❦ The glorious uncertainty of the law was a thing well known and complained of, by all ignorant people, but all learned gentlemen considered it as its greatest excellency.

*Richard Brinsley Sheridan*
Parliamentary History, *1820*

*19.8* ❦ Being a lawyer, I don't like to advise parties to go to law. I know the glorious uncertainty of it, as it is called.

*Horace Mayhew, English journalist*
The Image of His Father, *1848*

*19.9* ❦ . . . it is always probable that something improbable will happen.

*Logan E. Bleckley, American jurist*
Warren v. Purtell, *63 Ga. 428, 430*
*(1879)*

*19.10* ❦ Our life is wrought of dreams and waking, fused
Of truth and lies. There lives no certitude.

*Arthur Schnitzler*
Paracelsus, *1899*

*19.11* ❦ Delusive exactness is a source of fallacy throughout the law.

*Oliver Wendell Holmes*
Truax v. Corrigan, *257 U.S. 312, 342*
*(1921)*

*19.12* ❦ We must distinguish between the sound certainty and the sham . . . and then, when certainty is attained, we must remember that it is not the only good that we can buy at too high a price.

*Benjamin N. Cardozo*
Growth of the Law, *1924*

*19.13* ❦ They do things better with logarithms.

*Benjamin N. Cardozo*
Paradoxes of Legal Science, *1928*

*19.14* ❦ The law is not a series of calculating machines where definitions and answers come tumbling out when the right levers are pushed.

*William O. Douglas*
*"The Dissent, A Safeguard of*
*Democracy," 32* Journal of The
American Judicial Society, 105 (1948)

# *20.* CHANGE

*20.1* ❦ Every innovation occasions more harm and derangement of order by its novelty, than benefit by its abstract utility.

*Legal maxim*

*20.2* ❦ Can an Ethiopian change his skin, or a leopard his spots?

*Old Testament, Jeremiah 13:23*

*20.3* ❦ You can not step twice into the same river, for other waters are continually flowing on.
It is in changing that things find repose.

*Heraclitus,* fragments 21, 23

*20.4* ❦ The laws of a state change with the changing times.

*Aeschylus*
Seven Against Thebes,
*467* B.C.

*20.5* ❦ Ancient laws remain in force long after the people have the power to change them.

*Aristotle*
Politics, *c.322* B.C.

*20.6* ❦ That which is a law today is none tomorrow.

*Robert Burton, English clergyman and writer*
The Anatomy of Melancholy, *1621*

*20.7* ❦ The law is like apparel, which alters with the time.

*John Dodderidge, English jurist*
Jones v. Powell *(1628), Palm. 536, 538*

*20.8* ❦ The law is not the same morning and night.

*George Herbert*
Jacula Prudentum, *1651*

*20.9* ❦ When I hear any man talk of an unalterable law, the only effect it produces upon me is to convince me that he is an unalterable fool.

*Sydney Smith, English essayist*
Peter Plymley's Letters, *1807*

*20.10* ❦ Laws and institutions must go hand in hand with the progress of the human mind.

*Thomas Jefferson, 1743–1826*
*Laurence J. Peter,* Peter's Quotations, *1977*

*20.11* ❦ I do not allow myself to suppose that either the convention or the League have concluded to decide that I am either the greatest or the best man in America, but rather they have concluded it is not best to swap horses while crossing the river, and have further concluded that they might not make a botch of it in trying to swap.

*Abraham Lincoln*
*Address to a delegation from the National Union League,*
*June 9, 1864*

**20.12** ❧ If truth were not often suggested by error, if old implements could not be adjusted to new uses, human progress would be slow.

*Oliver Wendell Holmes*
*The Common Law,*
*1881*

**20.13** ❧ In law . . . the evil of lax definitions . . . has not been without compensation. Men are very ready to accept new ideas, provided they bear old names.

*John Chipman Gray, American jurist*
*"Some Definitions and Questions*
*in Jurisprudence," 6*
*Harvard Law Review 21 (1893)*

**20.14** ❧ . . . it is a step for further advance to see what has been won from chaos already.

*John Chipman Gray, American jurist*
*"Some Definitions and Questions in*
*Jurisprudence," 6*
*Harvard Law Review 21 (1893)*

**20.15** ❧ Law is merely the expression of the will of the strongest for the time being, and therefore laws have no fixity, but shift from generation to generation.

*Brooks Adams, American historian*
*The Law of Civilization and Decay,*
*1896*

**20.16** ❧ After all, that is what laws are for, to be made and unmade.

*Emma Goldman*
*"The Social Aspects of Birth Control,"*
*Mother Earth,*
*April 1916*

**20.17** ❧ Our course of advance, therefore, is neither a straight line nor a curve. It is a series of dots and dashes.

*Benjamin N. Cardozo*
*The Paradoxes of Legal Science, 1928*

**20.18** ❧ The law is a living growth, not a changeless code.

*Inscription carved over the entrance to*
*the Yale Law School, 1929–1931*

**20.19** ❧ A year ago, if I had $100 in gold in my pocket, I was a law-abiding citizen; if I perchance had a pint of whiskey I was a criminal. Today, if I have the whiskey, I am a law-abiding citizen; but if I have the gold, I am a criminal violating the law.

*Lester Jesse Dickinson, American politician*
*Speech, Cleveland, Ohio, January 5, 1934*

**20.20** ❧ We accept the verdict of the past until the need for change cries out loudly enough to force upon us a choice between the comforts of further inertia and the irksomeness of action.

*Learned Hand*
*Speech, Supreme Judicial Court of*
*Massachusetts, November 21, 1942*

**20.21** ❧ To ask for overt renunciation of a cherished doctrine is to expect too much of human nature. Men do not repudiate the doctrines and dogmas to which they have sworn their loyalty. Instead they rationalize, revise, and reinterpret them to meet new needs and new circumstances, all the while protesting that their heresy is the purest orthodoxy.

*William Fullbright*
*Old Myths and New Realities, 1964*

**20.22** ❧ Just because we cannot see clearly the end of the road, that is no reason for not setting out on the essential journey. On the contrary, great change dominates the world, and unless we move with change we will become its victims.

*Robert F. Kennedy*
*Farewell statement, Warsaw, Poland,*
*reported in the* New York Times,
*July 2, 1964*

**20.23** ❧ Law must be stable, and yet it cannot stand still.

*Roscoe Pound, 1870–1964*
*Kenneth Redden,* Modern Legal
Glossary, *1983*

**20.24** ❧ Change just for the sake of change is not necessarily good. But, change to adapt to the situation is *survival.*

*"Adapt—or Lose!"* Ohio State Bar
Association Report, *vol. XL, no. 21*
*(May 22, 1967)*

**20.25** ❧ Law must become the principal instrument of social change but it must move faster and in a more responsive way to social needs. In the question of racial integration, for example, if we were to move at the same rate as the first nine years since the Supreme Court decision, it would take us another nine centuries to do the job effectively.

*Ramsey Clark*
New York Times, *December 14, 1969*

**20.26** ❧ Don't agonize. Organize.

*Florynce R. Kennedy*
*Gloria Steinem, "The Verbal Karate of*
*Florynce Kennedy, Esq."*
Ms., *1973*

**20.27** ❧ Had Rip Van Winkle gone away and come back today . . . and if he went into the courts, the principal changes he would have observed would have been the wearing apparel, the increased number of judges and the air conditioning. Most of the rest would be the same as when he began his legendary exile in the Catskill Mountains.

*Warren E. Burger*
*Address to the Economic Club,*
*New York,*
*reported in the*
Wall Street Journal,
*March 15, 1974*

**20.28** ❧ That man is a creature who needs order yet yearns for change is the creative contradiction at the heart of the laws which structure his conformity and define his deviancy.

*Freda Adler, American educator*
Sisters in Crime, *1975*

**20.29** ❧ Women must organize and think strategically about creating ongoing pressure for change. Access is easy. Getting in law schools and getting a job is easy. To actually change the structure at law schools and law firms is really difficult.

*Mary Baker*
*"Back to the Future,"* Perspectives,
*Fall 1997*

# 21. CHARACTER

21.1 ❦ Man's advocates are repentance and good deeds.

*Talmud, Shabbat*

21.2 ❦ Our characters are the result of our conduct.

*Aristotle*
Nicomachean Ethics, *c.335* B.C.

21.3 ❦ Character is habit long continued.

*Plutarch*
Moralia: Education of Children, *c.95*

21.4 ❦ Confidence in others' honesty is no light testimony of one's own integrity.

*Michel de Montaigne*
Essais, *1588*

21.5 ❦ Good sense is, of all things among men, the most equally distributed; for every one thinks himself so abundantly provided with it, that those even who are the most difficult to satisfy in everything else, do not usually desire a larger measure of this quality than they already possess.

*Descartes*
Discourse of the Method of Rightly Conducting the Reason and Seeking Truth in the Sciences, *1637*

21.6 ❦ Humility is a Vertue all preach, none practise, and yet every body is content to hear.

*John Selden, 1584–1654*
Table-Talk, *1689*

21.7 ❦ Every single Act either *weakeneth* or *improveth* our Credit with other Men; and as an habit of being *just* to our Word will *confirm*, so an habit of too freely *dispensing* with it must necessarily *destroy* it.

*George Savile, 1st marquess of Halifax,*
*English politician, 1633–1695*
The Complete Works of George Savile, First Marquess of Halifax, *1912*

21.8 ❦ He that leaveth nothing to Chance will do few things ill, but he will do very few things.

*George Savile, 1st marquess of Halifax,*
*English politician, 1633–1695*
The Complete Works of George Savile, First Marquess of Halifax, *1912*

21.9 ❦ It is a general Mistake to think the Men we like are good for every thing, and those we do not, good for nothing.

*George Savile, 1st marquess of Halifax,*
*English politician, 1633–1695*
The Complete Works of George Savile, First Marquess of Halifax, *1912*

21.10 ❦ It is the nature of all greatness not to be exact. . . .

*Edmund Burke*
*"Speech on American Taxation,"*
*April 19, 1774*

21.11 ❧ Character is much easier kept than recovered.

*Thomas Paine*
The Crisis, *1776–1783*

21.12 ❧ You, my lord, are a judge; I am the supposed culprit. I am a man; you are a man also. By a revolution of power we might change places, though we could never change characters.

*Robert Emmet, 1778–1803*
*Speech to judge when on trial for treason*

21.13 ❧ Character is like a tree and reputation like its shadow. The shadow is what we think of, the tree is the real thing.

*Abraham Lincoln, 1809–1865*
*Franklin Pierce Adams,* F.P.A. Book of Quotations, *1952*

21.14 ❧ In my opinion the best character is generally that which is the least talked about.

*Sir William Erle, English jurist;*
*Chief Justice*
The Queen v. Rowton *(1865), 34*
*L.J.M.C. 63*

21.15 ❧ I think there should be no occasion on which it is absolutely, as a point or rule of law, impossible for a man to redeem his character.

*John Duke Coleridge, English jurist;*
*Lord Chief Justice*
In re Brandreth *(1891), L.J. 60*
*Q.B.D. 504*

21.16 ❧ If you will think about what you ought to do for other people, your character will take care of itself.

*Woodrow Wilson*
*Address at Pittsburgh 1914*

21.17 ❧ I don't say embrace trouble. That's as bad as treating it as an enemy. But I do say meet it as a friend, for you'll see a lot of it and had better be on speaking terms with it.

*Oliver Wendell Holmes, 1841–1935*
*Eugene C. Gerhart,* Quote It! *1969*

21.18 ❧ . . . it cannot be said that by common experience the character of most people indicted by a grand jury is good.

*Oliver Wendell Holmes*
Greer v. United States, *245 U.S.*
*559, 561 (1918)*

21.19 ❧ Risk! Risk anything! Care no more for the opinions of others, for those voices. Do the hardest thing on earth for you. Act for yourself. Face the truth.

*Katherine Mansfield, in 1922*
The Journal of Katherine Mansfield,
*1927*

21.20 ❧ . . . to be civilized is to be potentially master of all possible ideas, and that means that one has got beyond being shocked, although one preserves one's own moral and aesthetic preferences.

*Oliver Wendell Holmes, 1841–1935*
*Mark De Wolfe Howe,*
Holmes-Pollock Letters, *1946*

**21.21** ❦ We can forgive a man the defects of his qualities, if only he has the qualities of his defects.

*Oliver Wendell Holmes,* 1841–1935
*Irving Dilliard,* The Spirit of Liberty,
*1960*

**21.22** ❦ The heroic hours of life do not announce their presence by drum and trumpet, challenging us to be true to ourselves by appeals to the martial spirit that keeps the blood at heat. Some little, unassuming, unobtrusive choice presents itself before us slyly and craftily, glib and insinuating, in the modest garb of innocence. . . . Then it is that you will be summoned to show the courage of adventurous youth.

*Benjamin N. Cardozo,* 1870–1938
*"Law and Literature," in* Selected
Writings of Benjamin Nathan
Cardozo, *edited by Margaret E. Hall,*
*1947*

**21.23** ❦ . . . one of my best French quotations "On ne régne sur les âmes que par le calme." He was never in a hurry, never anxious to make an effect or sensation. He sat still and men came to him.

*Sir Winston S. Churchill*
A Roving Commission, *1941*

**21.24** ❦ Absolute discretion is a ruthless master. It is more destructive of freedom than any of man's other inventions.

*William O. Douglas*
United States v. Wunderlich, *342*
*U.S. 98, 101 (1951)*

**21.25** ❦ Of those qualities on which civilization depends, next after courage, it seems to me, comes an open mind, and, indeed, the highest courage is, as Holmes used to say, to stake your all upon a conclusion which you are aware tomorrow may prove false.

*Learned Hand*
*Irving Dilliard,*
The Spirit of Liberty, *1960*

**21.26** ❦ Still, I know of no higher fortitude than stubbornness in the face of overwhelming odds.

*Louis Nizer*
My Life in Court, *1960*

**21.27** ❦ . . . there is more respect to be won in the opinion of this world by a resolute and courageous liquidation of unsound positions than by the most stubborn pursuit of extravagant or unpromising objectives.

*George W. Kennan*
*"Kennan on Vietnam,"*
New Republic, *February 26, 1966*

**21.28** ❦ I have spent many years of my life in opposition, and I rather like the role.

*Eleanor Roosevelt*
*Joseph P. Lash,* Eleanor: The Years
Alone, *1972*

**21.29** ❦ Be nobody's darling;
Be an outcast.

*Alice Walker, "Be Nobody's Darling,"*
Revolutionary Petunias and
Other Poems,
*1973*

**21.30** ❦ Courage in the courtroom is more important than brains. If I were hiring a lawyer and had to choose between one that was all brains and one that was all guts, I would take the guts.

*Percy Foreman*
Los Angeles Times, *May 16, 1976*

**21.31** ❦ I have a brain and a uterus and I use them both.

*Patricia Schroeder*
*Esther Stineman,* American Political Women, *1980*

**21.32** ❦ Toughness doesn't have to come in a pinstripe suit.

*Dianne Feinstein*
Time, *June 4, 1984*

**21.33** ❦ I don't think unnecessary suffering builds character at all. It doesn't make you a better person, it makes you a bitter person . . .

*Geraldine A. Ferraro*
Ferraro: My Story, *with Linda Bird Francke, 1985*

**21.34** ❦ If I am going to be criticized for doing what I believe in, I might as well just keep doing what I believe in.

*Hillary Rodham Clinton, 1994*
*Dawn Bradley Berry,* The 50 Most Influential Women in American Law, *1996*

**21.35** ❦ The idea that I would check my brain at the White House door is something that just doesn't make any sense to me.

*Hillary Rodham Clinton*
*Claire G. Osborne,* The Unique Voice of Hillary Rodham Clinton, *1997*

# 22. CHEATING

**22.1** ❦ Feather by feather the goose is plucked.

*Scottish proverb*
*W. Gurney Bentham,* Putnam's Complete Book of Quotations, Proverbs and Household Words, *1927*

**22.2** ❦ A false balance is an abomination to the Lord.

*Old Testament, Proverbs 11:1*

**22.3** ❦ My revenue is the silly cheat.

*Shakespeare*
The Winter's Tale, *IV, 2, 1610–1611*

**22.4** ❦ He is not cheated who knows he is being cheated.

*Sir Edward Coke*
Institutes of the Lawes of England, *vol. 1, 1628–1641*

**22.5** ❦ Many men *swallow* the being
cheated, but no man can ever
endure to chew it.

*George Savile, 1st marquess of Halifax,*
*English politician*
Maxims, *1693*

**22.6** ❦ 'Tis no sin to cheat the devil.

*Daniel Defoe*
History of the Devil,
*1726*

**22.7** ❦ To cheat a man is nothing; but the
woman must have fine parts, indeed,
who cheats a woman.

*John Gay*
The Beggar's Opera, *1728*

**22.8** ❦ He'll cheat without scruple, who
can without fear.

*Benjamin Franklin*
Poor Richard's Almanack, *1743*

**22.9** ❦ Thou shalt not steal; an empty feat,
When it's so lucrative to cheat.

*Arthur Hugh Clough*
The Latest Decalogue, *c.1849*

**22.10** ❦ It's heads Law wins, tails they lose.

*William De Morgan*
It Can Never Happen Again, *1909*

# 23. CHILDREN

**23.1** ❦ The unwise man and the forweaned
[spoiled] child have but one law.

*English proverb*
*Richard Morris, ed.,* Trinity College
Homilies: Old English Homilies of
the Twelfth Century, *1873*

**23.2** ❦ Let children support their parents or
be imprisoned.

*Roman law*

**23.3** ❦ Let nothing which is disgraceful to
be spoken of, or to be seen,
approach this place where a child is.

*Juvenal*
Satires, *c.120*

**23.4** ❦ Infants have no privilege to
cheat men.

*Peter King, English jurist; Lord*
*Chancellor*
Evroy v. Nicholas *(1733), 2 Eq. Ca.*
*Ab. 489*

**23.5** ❦ The law of grab is the primal law of
infancy.

*Antoinette Brown Blackwell, American*
*feminist and writer,* The Sexes
Throughout Nature, *1875*

**23.6** ❦ There are no illegitimate children—
only illegitimate parents.

*Leon R. Yankwicho*
*Opinion,* Zipkin v. Mozon,
*June 1928*

*23.7* ❦ It is said that famous men are usually the product of unhappy childhood. The stern compression of circumstances, the twinges of adversity, the spur of slights and taunts in early years, are needed to evoke that ruthless fixity of purpose and tenacious mother-wit without which great actions are seldom accomplished.

*Sir Winston S. Churchill*
Marlborough, His Life and Times,
*1933–1938*

*23.8* ❦ All adults stand accused . . . the society responsible for the welfare of children has been put on trial. There is something apocalyptic about this startling accusation; it is mysterious and terrible like the voice of the Last Judgment: "What have you done to the children I entrusted to you?"

*Maria Montessori*
The Secret of Childhood, *1936*

*23.9* ❦ It's clear that most American children suffer too much mother and too little father.

*Gloria Steinem*
New York Times, *August 26, 1971*

*23.10* ❦ I've been struck by the upside-down priorities of the juvenile-justice system. We are willing to spend the least amount of money to keep a kid at home, more to put him in a foster home, and the most to institutionalize him.

*Marian Wright Edelman, American lawyer*
*Margie Casady,*
*"Society's Pushed-Out Children,"*
Psychology Today, *June 1975*

*23.11* ❦ [A] 12-year old-child photographed while masturbating surely suffers the same psychological harm whether the community labels the photograph "edifying" or "tasteless."

*Sandra Day O'Connor*
New York v. Ferber, *458 U.S. 747*
*(1982)*

*23.12* ❦ Apparently we just don't feel that all American children of all colors and social classes are our children, the way I think a Swede quite easily feels that a child up in Lapland is very precious to a worker in Stockholm.

*Mary Ann Glendon, lawyer,*
*Harvard professor*
Bill Moyers, *A World of Ideas, 1989*

*23.13* ❦ Where I come from, grandparents and family members are supposed to take care of neglected children. It's an obligation, not something you do for a government paycheck.

*Judy Sheindlin*
Don't Pee on My Leg and
Tell Me It's Raining, *with Josh Getlin*
*1996*

# 24. CITIZENSHIP

24.1 ❦ The crowd of changeable citizens.

*Horace*
*Odes, 23* B.C.

24.2 ❦ If a man be gracious and courteous to strangers, it shows he is a citizen of the world.

*Francis Bacon*
*Essays, 1612*

24.3 ❦ Citizens are not born, but made.

*Baruch Benedictus de Spinoza*
*Tractatus Politicus, 1676*

24.4 ❦ Before Man made us citizens, great Nature made us men.

*James Russell Lowell, 1819–1891*
*"On the Capture of Certain*
*Fugitive Slaves."*

24.5 ❦ Every citizen or subject of another country, while domiciled here, is within the allegiance and the protection, and consequently subject to the jurisdiction, of the United States. . . .

*Horace Gray, American jurist; judge,*
*U.S. Supreme Court*
*United States v. Wong Kim, Ark.,*
*169 U.S. 649, 42 L.Ed. 890, 18 Sup.*
*Ct. 456 (1898)*

24.6 ❦ If cats were born in an oven would they be biscuits?

*Finley Peter Dunne, 1867–1936, in*
*reference to United States v. Wong Kim,*
*Ark., 1898, which held that all Chinese born*
*in the United States were citizens*
*M. Frances McNamara, 2,000*
*Famous Legal Quotations, 1967*

24.7 ❦ The power of citizenship as a shield against oppression was widely known from the example of Paul's Roman citizenship, which sent the centurion scurrying to his higher-ups with the message: "Take heed what thou doest: for this man is a Roman."

*Robert H. Jackson*
*Edwards v. California, 314 U.S. 160,*
*182 (1941)*

24.8 ❦ It is not the function of our government to keep the citizen from falling into error; it is the function of the citizen to keep the Government from falling into error.

*Robert H. Jackson, U.S. judge*
*American Communications*
*Association v. Douds, May 1950*

24.9 ❦ As citizens of this democracy, you are the rulers and the ruled, the law-givers and the law-abiding, the beginning and the end.

*Adlai E. Stevenson*
*Speech, Chicago, September 29, 1952*

24.10 ❦ Men and women are biological facts. Ladies and gentlemen—citizens—are social artifacts, works of political art. They carry the culture that is sustained by wise laws, and traditions of civility.

*George Will*
*Introduction, The Pursuit of*
*Happiness, and Other Sobering*
*Thoughts, 1978*

# 25. CIVIL DISOBEDIENCE

25.1 ❦ Men of most renowned virtue have sometimes by transgressing most truly kept the law.

*John Milton*
Tetrachordon, *1644–1645*

25.2 ❦ If a law commands me to *sin I will break it*; if it calls me to *suffer*, I will let it take its course *unresistingly*. The doctrine of blind obedience and unqualified submission to any human power, whether civil or ecclesiastical, is the doctrine of despotism, and ought to have no place 'mong Republicans and Christians.

*Angelina Grimké, American abolitionist*
*"Appeal to the Christian Women of the South,"* Anti-Slavery Examiner, *September 1836*

25.3 ❦ Must the citizen ever for a moment, or in the least degree, resign his conscience to the legislator? I think that we should be men first, and subjects afterward.

*Henry David Thoreau*
Civil Disobedience, *1849*

25.4 ❦ The only obligation which I have a right to assume is to do at any time what I think right.

*Henry David Thoreau*
Civil Disobedience,
*1849*

25.5 ❦ Under a government which imprisons any unjustly, the true place for a just man is also a prison.

*Henry David Thoreau*
Civil Disobedience, *1849*

25.6 ❦ Unjust laws exist: shall we be content to obey them. . . .

*Henry David Thoreau*
Civil Disobedience, *1849*

25.7 ❦ I will have no laws. I will acknowledge none. I protest against every law which an authority calling itself necessary imposes upon my free will.

*Pierre Joseph Proudhon*
Idée générale de la révolution, *1851*

25.8 ❦ I submit that an individual who breaks a law that conscience tells him is unjust, and who willingly accepts the penalty of imprisonment in order to arouse the conscience of the community over its injustice, is in reality expressing the highest respect for the law.

*Martin Luther King, Jr.*
Why We Can't Wait, *1964*

25.9 ❦ The right to defy an unconstitutional statute is basic in our scheme. Even when an ordinance requires a permit to make a speech, to deliver a sermon, to picket, to parade, or to assemble, it need not be honored when it is invalid on its face.

*Potter Stewart*
Walker v. Birmingham, *388 U.S. 307,*
*87 S. Ct. 1824, 18 L.Ed.2d 1210 (1967)*

*25.10* ✾ One can say categorically that there is no constitutional right of civil disobedience to a valid law.

*Archibald Cox*
*Mark De Wolfe Howe*
*and J. R. Wiggins,* Civil Rights, The
Constitution and The Courts, *1967*

*25.11* ✾ Social protest and even civil disobedience serve the law's need for growth. . . .

*Archibald Cox*
*Mark De Wolfe Howe and*
*J. R. Wiggins,* Civil Rights,
The Constitution and The Courts, *1967*

*25.12* ✾ The core of the evil in true civil disobedience is that it weakens the bonds of law and compels the state to resort to power.

*Archibald Cox*
*Mark De Wolfe Howe and*
*J. R. Wiggins,* Civil Rights, The
Constitution and The Courts, *1967*

*25.13* ✾ . . . those whose conscience demands that they defy authority in some ways that involve great consequences must be willing to accept some penalty. . . .

*Joseph Wood Krutch*
*"If You Don't Mind My Saying*
*So . . . ,"* American Scholar, *Winter*
*1967–1968*

*25.14* ✾ While the State may respectfully require obedience on many matters, it cannot violate the moral nature of a man, convert him into a serviceable criminal, and expect his loyalty and devotion.

*Liane Norman, American educator*
*"Selective Conscientious Objection,"*
Center Magazine, *May/June 1972*

*25.15* ✾ The defiance of established authority, religious and secular, social and political, as a world-wide phenomenon may well one day be accounted the outstanding event of the last decade.

*Hannah Arendt*
*"Civil Disobedience,"* Crises of the
Republic, *1972*

*25.16* ✾ Disobedience is the worst of evils. This it is that ruins a nation.

*Jean Anouilh, 1910–1987*
*Laurence J. Peter,* Peter's Quotations,
*1977*

# *26.* CIVIL RIGHTS

*26.1* ✾ The law, in our case, seems to make the right; and the very reverse ought to be done—the right should make the law.

*Maria Edgeworth, Irish novelist*
The Grateful Negro, *1802*

*26.2* ✾ No man is good enough to govern another man without that other's consent.

*Abraham Lincoln*
*Speech, Peoria, October 16, 1854*

**26.3** ❦ . . . in view of the Constitution, in the eye of the law, there is in this country no superior, dominant, ruling class of citizens. There is no caste here. Our Constitution is color-blind, and neither knows nor tolerates classes among citizens . . .

*John Marshall Harlan*
Plessy v. Ferguson, *163 U.S. 537, 559–560 (1896)*

**26.4** ❦ In respect of civil rights, all citizens are equal before the law. The humblest is the peer of the most powerful.

*John Marshall Harlan*
Plessy v. Ferguson, *163 U.S. 537, 559 (1896)*

**26.5** ❦ . . . most people, no doubt, when they espouse human rights, make their own mental reservations about the proper application of the word "human."

*Suzanne LaFollette, American feminist and writer*
*"The Beginnings of Emancipation,"*
Concerning Women, *1926*

**26.6** ❦ The Fourteenth Amendment . . . nollifies sophisticated as well as simple-minded modes of discrimination.

*Felix Frankfurter*
Lane v. Wilson, *307 U.S. 268, 275 (1939)*

**26.7** ❦ Distinctions between citizens solely because of their ancestry are by their very nature odious to a free people

whose institutions are founded upon the doctrine of equality.

*Harlan Stone*
Hirabayashi v. United States, *320 U.S. 81 (1943)*

**26.8** ❦ A license cannot be revoked because a man is red-headed or because he was divorced, except for a calling, if such there be, for which red-headedness or an unbroken marriage may have some rational bearing.

*Felix Frankfurter*
Barsky v. Board of Regents, *347 U.S. 442, 470 (1954)*

**26.9** ❦ . . . in the field of public education the doctrine of "separate but equal" has no place. Separate educational facilities are inherently unequal.

*Earl Warren*
Brown v. Board of Education of Topeka, *347 U.S. 483, 74 S. Ct. 686, 98 L.Ed. 873 (1954)*

**26.10** ❦ We come then to the question presented: Does segregation of children in public schools solely on the basis of race, even though the physical facilities and other "tangible" factors may be equal, deprive the children of the minority group of equal educational opportunities? We believe that it does.

*Earl Warren*
Brown v. Board of Education of Topeka, *347 U.S. 483, 74 S. Ct. 686, 98 L.Ed. 873 (1954)*

**26.11** ❦ It may be true that the law cannot make a man love me. But it can keep him from lynching me, and I think that's pretty important.

*Martin Luther King, Jr.*
Wall Street Journal,
*November 13, 1962*

26.12 ❦ I don't want to be told that I must love a woman or a man because of their color, any more than I want to be told that I must hate them because of their color. I love and hate only a few, and their color may have as little or as much to do with it as their height or the color of their hair or the way they walk. It is for themselves in their totality that I am drawn to them or recoil from them—for their totality and their humanity.

*Max Lerner*
"Notable & Quotable," *Wall Street Journal, March 29, 1963*

26.13 ❦ . . . a century after the Emancipation Proclamation, no American should have to demonstrate in the streets in order to be admitted to a hotel or to eat at a lunch counter or to see a motion picture.

*Editorial, "The Civil Rights Message,"*
New York Times,
*June 20, 1963*

26.14 ❦ I have a dream that one day on the red hills of Georgia, the sons of former slaves and the sons of former slave-owners will be able to sit together at the table of brotherhood. . . . That one day even the state of Mississippi, a state sweltering with the heat of oppression, will be transformed into an oasis of freedom

and justice. . . . That my four little children will one day live in a nation where they will not be judged by the color of their skin but by the content of their character.

*Martin Luther King, Jr.*
*Address, Lincoln Memorial, during the*
*National March on Washington,*
*August 28, 1963*

26.15 ❦ . . . there is no constitutional right for any race to be preferred . . . If discrimination based on race is constitutionally permissible when those who hold the reins can come up with "compelling" reasons to justify it, then constitutional guarantees acquire an accordion-like quality . . .

*William O. Douglas*
De Funis v. Odegaarde, *416 U.S.*
*312 (1974)*

26.16 ❦ The law changes and flows like water, and . . . the stream of women's rights law has become a sudden rushing torrent.

*Shana Alexander*
State-by-State Guide to Women's
Legal Rights, *1975*

26.17 ❦ Preferring members of any one group for no reason other than race or ethnic origin is discrimination for its own sake. This the Constitution forbids. . . .

*Lewis F. Powell, Jr.*
University of California v. Bakke,
*438 U.S. 265, S. Ct. 2733, 57*
*L.Ed.2d 750 (1978)*

26.18 ❦ Civil rights groups hold no monopoly position among those discontent with legislative or executive action who seek the aid of the courts.

*Ruth Bader Ginsburg*
15 Georgia Law Review 539,
*1981*

26.19 ❦ . . . we should be especially sensitive to the rights of those whose choices upset the majority.

*Harry A. Blackmun*
Bowers v. Hardwick,
*June 30, 1986*

# *27.* CLIENTS

27.1 ❦ Who lied to me about his case,
And said we'd have an easy race,
And did it all with solemn face?
It was my client.

*Anonymous*
*Jacob M. Braude,* Lifetime Speaker's
Encyclopedia, *1962*

27.2 ❦ A client twixt his attorney and counsellor is like a goose twixt two foxes.

*Proverb*
*Rosalind Fergusson,* The Facts On File
Dictionary of Proverbs, *1983*

27.3 ❦ He that is his own lawyer has a fool for a client.

*Proverb*
*Rosalind Fergusson,* The Facts On File
Dictionary of Proverbs, *1983*

27.4 ❦ Lawyers' gowns are lined with the willfulness of their clients.

*Proverb*
*Rosalind Fergusson,* The Facts On File
Dictionary of Proverbs, *1983*

27.5 ❦ From your confessor, lawyer and physician,
Hide not your case on no condition.

*Sir John Harington, English writer*
Metamorphosis of Ajax, *1596*

27.6 ❦ Good counsellors lack no clients.

*Shakespeare*
Measure for Measure, *I, 2,*
*1604–1605*

27.7 ❦ Never fear the want of business. A man who qualifies himself well for his calling, never fails of employment in it.

*Thomas Jefferson*
*Letter to Peter Carr, June 22, 1792*

27.8 ❦ I would rather have clients than be somebody's lawyer.

*Louis D. Brandeis*
*Ernest Poole, Interview,* American
Magazine, *vol. 71, no. 492, 1911*

**27.9** ❧ . . . ideal client—"the very wealthy man in very great trouble."

*John C. Sterling, American publisher*
*John C. Payne, "Lawyers and the Laws*
*of Economics," 46 American Bar*
*Association Journal 365 (April 1960)*

**27.10** ❧ Most of the clients that I represent in a criminal case I detest. . . . As a matter of fact, . . . the more I become involved emotionally in my client's cause, the less I am able to [do] for him.

*Joseph A. Ball, American lawyer; president,*
*American College of Trial Lawyers*
*Speech, American Bar Association, reported*
*in the Los Angeles Herald-Examiner,*
*August 23, 1970*

**27.11** ❧ You can't earn a living defending innocent people.

*Maurice Nadjari*
*New York Post, May 8, 1975*

**27.12** ❧ If there is any truth to the old proverb that "one who is his own lawyer, has a fool for a client," the Court . . . now bestows a *constitutional* right on one to make a fool of himself.

*Harry Blackmun*
*Faretta v. California (1975)*

**27.13** ❧ There is never a deed so foul that something couldn't be said for the guy; that's why there are lawyers.

*Melvin Belli*
*Los Angeles Times,*
*December 18, 1981*

# 28. COMMON LAW

**28.1** ❧ The unwritten law—the "common law."

*Latin legal phrase*
*W. Gurney Benham, Putnam's*
*Complete Book of Quotations,*
*Proverbs and Household Words, 1927*

**28.2** ❧ Things which restrict the common law are to be interpreted rigidly.

*Latin legal phrase*
*W. Gurney Benham, Putnam's*
*Complete Book of Quotations,*
*Proverbs and Household Words, 1927*

**28.3** ❧ We ourselves of the present age, chose our common law, and consented to the most ancient Acts of Parliament, for we lived in our ancestors 1,000 years ago, and those ancestors are still living in us.

*Sir Robert Atkyns, English jurist*
*Trial of Sir Edward Hales (1686), 11*
*How. St. Tr. n. p. 1204*

**28.4** ❦ Its [The common law's] origin . . . is as undiscoverable as the Head of the Nile.

*Sir Matthew Hale*
*History of the Common Law, 1713*

**28.5** ❦ The common law is nothing else but statutes worn out by time. . . .

*Sir John Eardley Wilmot, English jurist;*
*Chief Justice*
*Collins v. Blantern (1767), 2 Wils,*
*K.B., 341, 348*

**28.6** ❦ The first requirement of a sound body of law is, that it should correspond with the actual feelings and demands of the community, whether right or wrong.

*Oliver Wendell Holmes*
*The Common Law, 1881*

**28.7** ❦ The common law is not a brooding omnipresence in the sky but the articulate voice of some sovereign or quasi-sovereign that can be identified. . . .

*Oliver Wendell Holmes*
*Southern Pacific Co. v. Jensen, 244*
*U.S. 205, 221 (1917)*

**28.8** ❦ [Common law] stands as a monument slowly raised, like a coral reef, from the minute accretions of past individuals, of whom each built upon the relics which his predecessors left, and in his turn left a foundation upon which his successors might work.

*Learned Hand*
*"Review of Judge Cardozo's* The
Nature of the Judicial Process," *35*
Harvard Law Review, *481 (1922)*

**28.9** ❦ We always exempt ourselves from the common laws. When I was a boy and the dentist pulled out a second tooth, I thought to myself that I would grow a third if I needed it. Experience discouraged this prophecy.

*Oliver Wendell Holmes, 1841–1936*
Think, *October 1959*

**28.10** ❦ . . . Churchill never minded contemplating the mystery of death. Once a friend inquired: "What makes you think you will reach the bar of Heaven?" He interjected with solemn assurance: "Surely the Almighty must observe the principles of English common law and consider a man innocent until proven guilty."

*Sir Winston S. Churchill, 1874–1965*
New York Times, *February 1, 1965*

# 29. COMPETITION

29.1   ✿   One bush, they say, can never hide two thieves.

*Aristophanes*
*The Wasps, 422* B.C.

29.2   ✿   Not hate, but glory, made these chiefs contend. . . .

*Alexander Pope*
*Verse translation of Homer's "Iliad"*
*1715–1720*

29.3   ✿   Free competition is worth more to society than it costs.

*Oliver Wendell Holmes*
*Vegelahn v. Guntner, 167 Mass. 92,*
*44 N.E 1077, 1080 (1896)*

29.4   ✿   [W]e have found nothing to take the place of competition excepting monopoly, which is but a modern form of slavery.

*Clarence Darrow, 1857–1938*
*Arthur and Lila Weinberg,*
*Verdicts Out of Court,*
*1963*

29.5   ✿   For excesses of competition lead to monopoly. . . .

*John Gardner*
*Excellence: Can We Be Equal and*
*Excellent Too?,*
*1961*

29.6   ✿   I'm a competitive person, but I have never understood people's competitiveness at the expense of their colleagues.

*Geraldine A. Ferraro*
*Ferraro: My Story, with Linda*
*Bird Franke, 1985*

# 30. CONFESSION

30.1   ✿   Silence [in court] may be equivalent to confession.

*Talmud, Yevamot*

30.2   ✿   Confession of our faults is the next thing to innocency.

*Publilius Syrus, Latin writer*
*Sententiae, c.43* B.C.

30.3   ✿   The confession of evil works is the first beginning of good works.

*St. Augustine, 354–430*
*Franklin Pierce Adams, F.P.A.*
*Book of Quotations, 1952*

30.4   ✿   Confess and be hanged.

*Christopher Marlowe*
*The Jew of Malta, 1589*

**30.5** ❧ Hamlet: Confess yourself to heaven: Repent what's past; avoid what is to come.

*Shakespeare*
*Hamlet, III, 4, 1600–1601*

**30.6** ❧ He's half absolv'd who has confessed.

*Matthew Prior*
*Alma, 1715–1717*

**30.7** ❧ There is no refuge from confession but suicide; and suicide is confession.

*Daniel Webster*
*Argument on the murder of Captain*
*White, April 6, 1830*

**30.8** ❧ A confession is wholly and incontestably voluntary only if a guilty person gives himself up to the law and becomes his own accuser.

*Robert H. Jackson*
*Ashcraft v. Tennessee, 322 U.S. 143,*
*161 (1944)*

# *31.* CONFORMITY

**31.1** ❧ Once conform, once do what other people do because they do it, and a lethargy steals over all the finer nerves and faculties of the soul.

*Virginia Woolf*
*"Montaigne,"*
*The Common Reader,*
*1ST series, 1925*

**31.2** ❧ Conformity is the jailer of freedom and the enemy of growth.

*John F. Kennedy*
*Speech,*
*September 25, 1961*

**31.3** ❧ Only dead fish swim with the stream.

*Linda Ellerbee*
*Move On, 1991*

# *32.* CONSCIENCE

**32.1** ❧ It is always Term-Time in the Court of Conscience.

*Proverb*
*Thomas Fuller, Gnomologia, 1732*

**32.2** ❧ No guilty man is ever acquitted at the bar of his own conscience.

*Juvenal*
*Satires, c.120*

*32.3* ❦ Conscience and reputation are two things. Conscience is due to yourself, reputation to your neighbor.

*St. Augustine, 354–430*

*32.4* ❦ My conscience hath a thousand several tongues,
And every tongue brings in a several tale,
And every tale condemns me for a villain.

*Shakespeare*
*Richard III, V, 3, 1592–1593*

*32.5* ❦ Why should not Conscience have vacation
As well as other Courts o' the nation?

*Samuel Butler*
*Hudibras, 1663–1678*

*32.6* ❦ Two things fill my mind with everincreasing wonder and awe . . . the starry heavens above me and the moral law within me.

*Immanuel Kant*
*Critique of Pure Reason, 1787*

*32.7* ❦ Labor to keep alive in your breast that little spark of celestial fire, called Conscience.

*George Washington, 1732–1799*
*Moral Maxims: Virtue and Vice,*
*Conscience*

*32.8* ❦ A man's vanity tells him what is honour,
a man's conscience what is justice.

*Walter Savage Landor, English writer*
*Imaginary Conversations, 1824*

*32.9* ❦ The sting of conscience, like the gnawing of a dog at a bone, is mere foolishness.

*Nietzsche, 1844–1900*
*Human All-too-Human*

*32.10* ❦ The roots of valid law . . . are, and can only be, within the individual conscience.

*Harold J. Laski*
*The State in Theory and Practice,*
*1935*

*32.11* ❦ Conscience is the inner voice which warns us somebody may be looking.

*H.L. Mencken*
*A Mencken Chrestomathy, 1949*

# *33.* CONSEQUENCES

*33.1* ❦ When anything is forbidden, everything which leads to the same result is also forbidden.

*Latin legal expression*
*W. Gurney Benham,* Putnam's
Complete Book of Quotations,
Proverbs and Household Words, *1927*

*33.2* ❦ It is the common fate of the indolent to see their rights become a prey to the active.

*John Philpot Curran, Irish jurist*
*Speech upon the Right of Election,*
*1790*

33.3 ❧ If a man will make a purchase of a chance he must abide by the consequences.

*Sir Richard Richards, English jurist*
*Hitchcock v. Giddings (1817), 4*
*Price, 135*

33.4 ❧ The degree of civilization which a people has reached, no doubt, is marked by their anxiety to do as they would be done by.

*Oliver Wendell Holmes*
*The Common Law, 1881*

33.5 ❧ Logical consequences are the scarecrows of fools and the beacons of wise men.

*Thomas H. Huxley*
*Animal Automatism, 1884*

33.6 ❧ You may not sell the cow and sup the milk.

*Proverb quoted by Edward*
*Macnaghten, 1st baron, English jurist*
*Nordenfelt v. Maxim Nordenfelt*
*Guns and Ammunition Co. (1894),*
*L.R. App. Cas. (1894), p. 572*

33.7 ❧ Consequences cannot alter statutes, but may help to fix their meaning.

*Benjamin N. Cardozo*
*In re Rouss, 116 N.E. 782, 785*
*(1917)*

# 34. CONSTITUTION

34.1 ❧ What are twenty acts of Parliament amongst friends?

*John Selden, 1584–1654*
*Table-Talk, c.1689*

34.2 ❧ It [the Constitution] is a good canvas, on which some strokes only want retouching.

*Thomas Jefferson*
*Letter to James Madison, July 31, 1788*

34.3 ❧ . . . no society can make a perpetual constitution, or even a perpetual law. The earth belongs always to the living generation. . . . Every constitu-

tion then, and every law, naturally expires at the end of 19 years.

*Thomas Jefferson*
*Letter to James Madison,*
*September 6, 1789*

34.4 ❧ Our Constitution is in actual operation; everything appears to promise that it will last; but in this world nothing is certain but death and taxes.

*Benjamin Franklin*
*Letter to Jean-Baptiste Le Roy,*
*November 13, 1789*

34.5 ❧ We, the people of the United States, in Order to form a more perfect Union, establish Justice, insure domestic Tranquility, provide for the common Defense, promote the general Welfare, and secure the Blessings of Liberty to ourselves and our Posterity, do ordain and establish this Constitution for the United States of America.

*Framers of the Constitution*
*Preamble to the Constitution of the*
*United States, 1789*

34.6 ❧ The American constitutions were to liberty, what a grammar is to language: they define its parts of speech, and practically construct them into syntax.

*Thomas Paine*
*The Rights of Man, 1791*

34.7 ❧ We must never forget that it is a constitution we are expounding.

*John Marshall*
*McCulloch v. Maryland, 17 U.S.*
*(4 Wheat.) 316, 415 (1819)*

34.8 ❧ A Constitution should be short and obscure.

*Napoleon Bonaparte, 1769–1821*
*Franklin Pierce Adams, F.P.A.*
*Book of Quotations, 1952*

34.9 ❧ Laws and institutions must go hand in hand with the progress of the human mind . . . We might as well require a man to wear the coat that fitted him as a boy, as civilized society to remain ever under the regime of their ancestors.

*Thomas Jefferson, 1743–1826,*
*referring to constitutions*
*Franklin Pierce Adams, F.P.A.*
*Book of Quotations,*
*1952*

34.10 ❧ But there is a higher law than the Constitution. . . .

*William H. Seward*
*Speech, U.S. Senate,*
*March 11, 1850*

34.11 ❧ The Constitution of the United States was made not merely for the generation that then existed, but for posterity—unlimited, undefined, endless, perpetual posterity.

*Henry Clay*
*Speech, U.S. Senate, 1850*

34.12 ❧ "We, the people of the United States." Which "We, the people"? The women were not included.

*Lucy Stone, American suffragist*
*Speech, reported in the*
*New York Tribune*
*April 1853*

34.13 ❧ A majority held in restraint by constitutional checks and limitations, and always changing easily with deliberate changes of popular opinions and sentiments, is the only true sovereign of a free people.

*Abraham Lincoln*
*First inaugural address,*
*March 4, 1861*

34.14 ❧ If by the mere force of numbers a majority should deprive a minority of any clearly written constitutional right, it might, in a moral point of view, justify revolution.

*Abraham Lincoln*
*First inaugural address,*
*March 4, 1861*

34.15 ❦ The Constitution of the United
States is a law for rulers and people,
equally in war and in peace, and covers with the shield of its protection
all classes of men, at all times, and
under all circumstances.

*David Davis, American jurist*
Ex parte Milligan, *71 U.S.*
*(4 Wall.) 2, 120–21 (1866)*

34.16 ❦ I am sworn to uphold the Constitution as Andy Johnson understands it
and interprets it.

*Andrew Johnson, c.1865–1869, in*
*vetoing the act of Congress that created*
*the National Bank*
*Thad Stem, Jr. and Alan Butler,* Sam
Ervin's Best Short Stories, *1973*

34.17 ❦ What's the Constitution between
friends?

*Timothy J. Campbell, American*
*politician; Tammany Hall (New York*
*City) congressman*
*Communication to President Grover*
*Cleveland, c.1885*

34.18 ❦ Our Constitution is color-blind.

*John M. Harlan*
Plessy v. Ferguson, *163 U.S. 537,*
*559, 41 L.Ed. 256, 263, 16 S. Ct.*
*1138 (1896)*

34.19 ❦ Constitutions are intended to preserve practical and substantial rights,
not to maintain theories.

*Oliver Wendell Holmes*
Davis v. Mills, *194 U.S. 451, 457*
*(1904)*

34.20 ❦ . . . the accident of our finding certain opinions natural and familiar,
or novel, and even shocking, ought
not to conclude our judgment upon
the question whether statutes embodying them conflict with the Constitution of the United States.

*Oliver Wendell Holmes*
Lochner v. New York, *198 U.S. 45,*
*76 (1905)*

34.21 ❦ We are under a Constitution, but
the Constitution is what judges
say it is.

*Charles Evans Hughes*
*Speech, Elmira, New York,*
*May 3, 1907*

34.22 ❦ Constitutional rights like others are
matters of degree.

*Oliver Wendell Holmes*
Martin v. District of Columbia, *205*
*U.S. 135, 139 (1907)*

34.23 ❦ . . . the Constitution of the United
States is not a mere lawyers' document: it is a vehicle of life, and its
spirit is always the spirit of the age.

*Woodrow Wilson*
Constitutional Government in the
United States, *1908*

34.24 ❦ Whenever the Constitution comes
between men and the virtue of the
white women of South Carolina, I
say—to Hell with the Constitution!

*Cole L. Blease, American politician;*
*governor, South Carolina*
*Public statement, 1911*

34.25 ❧ Constitutional law like other mortal contrivances has to take some chances.

*Oliver Wendell Holmes*
Blinn v. Nelson, *222 U.S. 1, 7 (1911)*

34.26 ❧ There is truth in the reply of a great lawyer when asked how the lawyers who formed the United States Constitution had such a mastery of legal principles: "Why, they had so few books."

*Charles Warren*
*"The Colonial Lawyer's Education,"*
A History of the American Bar, *1911*

34.27 ❧ But the provisions of the Constitution are not mathematical formulas having their essence in their form; they are organic living institutions transplanted from English soil. Their significance is vital, not formal. . . .

*Oliver Wendell Holmes*
Gompers v. United States, *233 U.S. 604, 610 (1914)*

34.28 ❧ The Fourteenth Amendment . . . was adopted with a view to the protection of the colored race, but has been found to be equally important in its application to the rights of all. . . .

*Oliver Wendell Holmes*
United States v. Mosley, *238 U.S. 383, 388 (1915)*

34.29 ❧ Our constitution . . . is an experiment as all life is an experiment.

*Oliver Wendell Holmes*
Abrams v. United States,
*250 U.S. 616, 630, 63 L.Ed. 1175, 1180, 40 S. Ct. 17 (1919)*

34.30 ❧ Without general elections, without freedom of the press, freedom of speech, freedom of assembly, without the free battle of opinions, life in every public institution withers away, becomes a caricature of itself, and bureaucracy rises as the only deciding factor.

*Rosa Luxemburg,* 1870–1919
*Paul Froelich,* Die Russische
Revolution, *1940*

34.31 ❧ Constitutional rights should not be frittered away by arguments so technical and unsubstantial. "The Constitution deals with substance, not shadows."

*Louis D. Brandeis*
Milwaukee Social Democratic
Publishing Co. v. Burleson, *255 U.S. 407, 431 (1921)*

34.32 ❧ The great generalities of the Constitution have a content and a significance that vary from age to age.

*Benjamin N. Cardozo*
The Nature of the Judicial Process,
*1921*

34.33 ❧ If the thing has been practiced for two hundred years by common consent, it will need a strong case for the Fourteenth Amendment to affect it. . . .

*Oliver Wendell Holmes*
Jackson v. Rosenbaum Co., *260 U.S. 22, 31 (1922)*

*34.34* ❧ The interpretation of constitutional principles must not be too literal. We must remember that the machinery of government would not work if it were not allowed a little play in its joints.

*Oliver Wendell Holmes*
Springer v. Philippine Islands, *277 U.S. 189, 209–210 (1928)*

*34.35* ❧ The United States Constitution has proven itself the most marvelously elastic compilation of rules of government ever written.

*Franklin D. Roosevelt*
*Radio speech, March 2, 1930*

*34.36* ❧ If the provisions of the Constitution be not upheld when they pinch as well as when they comfort, they may as well be abandoned.

*George Sutherland, American jurist*
Home Building & Loan Assn. v. Blaisdell, *290 U.S. 398, 483 (1934)*

*34.37* ❧ Do the people of this land . . . desire to preserve those [liberties] so carefully protected by the First Amendment. . . . If so, let them withstand all *beginnings* of encroachment. For the saddest epitaph which can be carved in memory of a vanished liberty is that it was lost because its possessors failed to stretch forth a saving hand while yet there was time.

*George Sutherland, American jurist*
Associated Press v. National Labor Relations Board, *301 U.S. 103, 141 (1937)*

*34.38* ❧ If the Constitution is to be construed to mean what the majority at any given period in history wish the Constitution to mean, why a written Constitution?

*Frank J. Hogan*
*Presidential address, American Bar Association, San Francisco, July 10, 1939*

*34.39* ❧ . . . the ultimate touchstone of constitutionality is the Constitution itself and not what we have said about it.

*Felix Frankfurter*
Graves v. New York ex rel. O'Keefe, *306 U.S. 466; 83 L.Ed. 927; 59 Sup. Ct. 595 (1939)*

*34.40* ❧ While the Declaration was directed against an excess of authority, the Constitution was directed against anarchy.

*Robert H. Jackson*
The Struggle for Judicial Supremacy, *1941*

*34.41* ❧ Is that which was deemed to be of so fundamental a nature as to be written into the Constitution to endure for all times to be the sport of shifting winds of doctrine?

*Felix Frankfurter*
West Virginia State Board of Education v. Barnette, *319 U.S. 624, 642 (1943)*

**34.42** ❧ The Constitution does not provide for first and second class citizens.

*Wendell L. Willkie*
An American Program, *1944*

**34.43** ❧ The Constitution was built for rough as well as smooth roads. In time of war the nation simply changes gears and takes the harder going under the same power.

*Harold H. Burton, American jurist*
Duncan v. Kahanamoku,
*327 U.S. 304, 342 (1946)*

**34.44** ❧ Our protection against all kinds of fanatics and extremists, none of whom can be trusted with unlimited power over others, lies not in their forbearance but in the limitations of our Constitution.

*Robert H. Jackson*
American Communications
Association v. Douds, *339 U.S. 382,*
*439 (1950)*

**34.45** ❧ . . . the validity of a doctrine does not depend on whose ox it gores.

*Robert H. Jackson*
Wells v. Simonds Abrasive Co., *345*
*U.S. 514, 525 (1953)*

**34.46** ❧ The Constitution favors no racial group, no political or social group.

*William O. Douglas*
Uphaus v. Wyman, *364 U.S. 388,*
*406 (1960)*

**34.47** ❧ We believe . . . that when the men who met in 1787 to make a Consti-

tution made the best political document ever made, they did it very largely because they were great compromisers.

*Learned Hand*
Irving Dilliard, The Spirit of Liberty,
*1960*

**34.48** ❧ Can any of you seriously say the Bill of Rights could get through Congress today? It wouldn't even get out of committee.

*F. Lee Bailey*
Newsweek, *April 17, 1967*

**34.49** ❧ The layman's Constitutional view is that what he likes is Constitutional and that which he doesn't like is unconstitutional. That about measures up the Constitutional acumen of the average person.

*Hugo L. Black*
New York Times, *February 26, 1971*

**34.50** ❧ My role isn't to be politically smart. My role is to do what is right under the Constitution.

*Rose Elizabeth Bird, American jurist;*
*chief justice, Supreme Court*
*of California*
Edwin Chen, "Rose Bird Runs for
Her Life," The Nation,
*January 18, 1986*

**34.51** ❧ I'm constitutionally incapable of shutting up.

*Gary Reback, lawyer*
James Daly,
"The Robin Hood of the Rich,"
Wired, *August 1997*

# 35. CONTRACTS

**35.1** ❦ *Caveat emptor.* [Let the buyer beware.]

*Latin legal maxim*

**35.2** ❦ He who derives the advantage ought to sustain the burthen.

*Legal maxim*

**35.3** ❦ No cause of action arises from a bare promise.

*Legal maxim*

**35.4** ❦ To break an oral agreement which is not legally binding is morally wrong.

*Talmud, Bava Metzi'a*

**35.5** ❦ Necessitous men are not, truly speaking, free men, but, to answer a present exigency, will submit to any terms that the crafty may impose upon them.

*Lord Thomas Henley, English jurist*
Vernon v. Bethell *(1762). 2 Eden.*
*110, 113*

**35.6** ❦ The movement of progressive societies has hitherto been a movement from status to contract.

*Sir Henry James Sumner Maine,*
*English jurist and legal historian*
Ancient Law; Its Connection with the
Early History of Society, and Its
Relation to Modern Ideas, *1861*

**35.7** ❦ The law has outgrown its primitive stage of formalism when the precise word was the sovereign talisman, and every slip was fatal. It takes a broader view today. A promise may be lacking, and yet the whole writing may be "instinct with an obligation," imperfectly expressed. . . . If that is so, there is a contract.

*Benjamin N. Cardozo*
Wood v. Lucy, Lady Duff-Gordon,
*1917*

**35.8** ❦ There is grim irony in speaking of the freedom of contract of those who, because of their economic necessities, give their service for less than is needful to keep body and soul together.

*Harlan Fiske Stone*
Morehead v. N.Y. ex rel. Tipaldo,
*298 U.S. 587, 632 (1936)*

**35.9** ❦ A verbal contract isn't worth the paper it's written on.

*Samuel Goldwyn*
*Laurence J. Peter,* Peter's Quotations,
*1977*

# *36.* CORRUPTION

36.1 ❦ There was never anything by the wit of man so well devised, or so sure established, which in continuance of time hath not been corrupted.

*"Concerning the Service,"* Book of Common Prayer

36.2 ❦ King: In the corrupted currents of this world
Offence's gilded hand may shove by justice,
And oft 'tis seen the wicked prize itself
Buys out the law: but 'tis not so above;
There is no shuffling, there the action lies
In his true nature; and we ourselves compell'd
Even to the teeth and forehead of our faults,
To give in evidence.

*Shakespeare*
Hamlet, *III, 3, 1600–1601*

36.3 ❦ Asebia: We never valued right and wrong
But as they serve our cause.
Zelota: Our business was to please the throng,
And court their wild applause.
Asebia: For this we bribed the lawyer's tongue
And then destroyed the laws.

*John Dryden*
Albion and Albanius, *1685*

36.4 ❦ Corruption's not of modern date; It hath been tried in ev'ry state.

*John Gay*
Fables, *1738*

36.5 ❦ Touch but a cobweb in Westminster Hall, and the old spider of the law is out upon you with all his vermin at his heels.

*Henry Fox,* 1705–1774
*Marshall Brown,* Wit and Humor of Bench and Bar, *1899*

36.6 ❦ He that accuses all mankind of corruption ought to remember that he is sure to convict only one.

*Edmund Burke*
Letter to the sheriffs of Bristol, *1777*

36.7 ❦ The time to guard against corruption and tyranny is before they shall have gotten hold of us. It is better to keep the wolf out of the fold than to trust to drawing his teeth and talons after he shall have entered.

*Thomas Jefferson*
Notes on the State of Virginia, *1785*

36.8 ❦ We lost because American justice is corrupted by celebrity.

*Marcia Clark*
Without a Doubt, *written with Teresa Carpenter, 1997*

**36.9** ❦ He is a man of splendid abilities, but utterly corrupt.
He shines and stinks like a rotten mackerel by moonlight.

> *John Randolph, 1773–1833, in an*
> *attack on Edward Livingston*
> *Thad Stem, Jr. and Alan Butler,* Sam
> Ervin's Best Stories, *1973*

**36.10** ❦ There is no odor so bad as that which arises from goodness tainted.

> *Henry David Thoreau*
> Walden, *1854*

**36.11** ❦ "Your laws are ineffective," Wen declared. "Why? Because no system of control will work as long as most of those administering the law against an evil have more than a finger dipped into it themselves."

> *Han Suyin*
> *Chinese physician*
> *and writer*
> Destination Chungking, *1942*

**36.12** ❦ We are born in innocence. . . . Corruption comes later. The first fear is a corruption, the first reaching for a something that defies us. The first nuance of difference, the first need to feel better than the different one, more loved, stronger, richer, more blessed—these are corruptions.

> *Laura Z. Hobson*
> Gentlemen's Agreement, *1946*

**36.13** ❦ "Corruption continues with us beyond the grave," she said, "and then plays merry hell with all ideals. . . ."

> *Daphne du Maurier*
> Mary Anne, *1954*

**36.14** ❦ . . . the accomplice to the crime of corruption is frequently our own indifference.

> *Bess Myerson*
> *Claire Safran, "Impeachment?"*
> Redbook, *April 1974*

# *37.* COURTS

**37.1** ❦ A court may not permit one litigant to sit and compel the other to stand, one to speak all his desires and the other to be brief.

> *Talmud, Shevu'ot*

**37.2** ❦ For friend in court ay better is Than peny in purs, certis.

> *Jean de Meun, French poet, c.1279–?*
> Roman de la Rose

**37.3** ❦ Lo, in this pond be fishe and froggis bothe.

> *Sir Thomas More*
> Fortune, *c.1500*

**37.4** ❦ The place of justice is a hallowed place.

> *Francis Bacon*
> *"Of Judicature,"* Essayes, *1625*

37.5 ❦ The law can take an open purse in
    court,
    while it condemns a less delinquent
    for 't.

*Samuel Butler, 1612–1680*
Miscellaneous Thoughts

37.6 ❦ The charge is prepared; the lawyers
    are met,
    The judges all ranged (a terrible
    show!).

*John Gay*
The Beggar's Opera, *1728*

37.7 ❦ Laws are a dead letter without courts
    to expound and define their true
    meaning and operation.

*Alexander Hamilton*
The Federalist, *1788*

37.8 ❦ The business of the court is to try
    the case, and not the man; and a
    very bad man may have a very right-
    eous cause.

*Anonymous*
Thompson v. Church *(1791),*
*1 Root 312*

37.9 ❦ The man that has no friend at court,
    Must make the laws confine his
    sport;
    But he that has, by dint of flaws,
    May make his sport confine the laws.

*Thomas Chatterton*
The Revenge, *1795*

37.10 ❦ Suitors, whose aching backs do break
    With costs, and penalities, and pains,

We take—at least you'll own—we
    take
Judicial notice that it rains.

*Showell Rogers*
*"Ballade of Judicial Notice," c.1845*

37.11 ❦ Fresh from brawling courts
    And dusty purlieus of the law.

*Tennyson*
In Memoriam, *1850*

37.12 ❦ "[Heaven is] to sit at *nisi prius* all
    day, and play whist all night."

*Francis Butler, English jurist; justice of*
*the King's Bench*
*Marshall Brown,* Wit and Humor of
Bench and Bar, *1899*

37.13 ❦ A revolt of the judiciary is more dan-
    gerous to a government than any
    other, even a military revolt. Now
    and then it uses the military to sup-
    press disorder, but it defends itself
    every day by means of the courts.

*Alexis de Tocqueville, 1805–1859*
*W. H. Auden and Louis Kronenberger,*
The Viking Book of Aphorisms, *1962*

37.14 ❦ The prophecies of what the courts
    will do in fact, and nothing more
    pretentious, are what I mean by
    the law.

*Oliver Wendell Holmes*
*"Path of the Law," 10* Harvard Law
Review *457, 461 (1897)*

37.15 ❦ I know of no duty of the Court
    which it is more important to ob-
    serve, and no powers of the Court

which it is more important to enforce, than its power of keeping public bodies within their rights. The moment public bodies exceed their rights they do so to the injury and oppression of private individuals. . . .

*Nathaniel Lindley, English jurist*
Robert v. Gwyrfai District Council
*(1899), L.R 2 C.D. 614*

37.16 ❦ The decisions of the courts on economic and social questions depend on their economic and social philosophy.

*Theodore Roosevelt, 1858–1919*
*Laurence J. Peter,* Peter's Quotations,
*1977*

37.17 ❦ No court can make time stand still.

*Felix Frankfurter*
Scripps-Howard Radio v. Federal
Communications Commission, *316*
*U.S. 4, 9 (1942)*

37.18 ❦ A court which yields to the popular will thereby license itself to practice despotism, for there can be no assurance that it will not on another occasion indulge its own will.

*Felix Frankfurter*
American Federation of Labor v.
American Sash & Door Co., *335*
*U.S. 538, 557 (1949)*

37.19 ❦ Madrigal: Truth doesn't ring true in a court of law.

*Enid Bagnold, English dramatist*
The Chalk Garden, *1953*

37.20 ❦ The penalty for laughing in a courtroom is six months; if it were not for this penalty the jury would never hear the evidence.

*H. L. Mencken, 1880–1956*
*Kenneth Redden,* Modern Legal
Glossary, *1983*

37.21 ❦ Courtroom: A place where Jesus Christ and Judas Iscariot would be equals, with the betting odds in favor of Judas.

*H. L. Mencken, 1880–1956*
*Laurence J. Peter,* Peter's Quotations,
*1977*

37.22 ❦ If respect for the courts and for their judicial process is gone or steadily weakened, no law can save us as a society. Lawyers, whatever their views on controversial decisions, must inspire respect for the judiciary.

*William T. Gossett, American lawyer:*
*president, American Bar Association*
*Speech, Canadian Bar Association,*
*Ottawa, September 3, 1969*

37.23 ❦ The flagrant disregard in the courtroom of elementary standards of proper conduct should not and cannot be tolerated. We believe trial judges confronted with disruptive, contumacious, stubbornly defiant defendants must be given sufficient discretion to meet the circumstances in each case.

*Hugo L. Black*
New York Times, April 1, 1970

**37.24** ❧ I have nothing but utter contempt for the courts of this land.

*George C. Wallace*
*Plainview (Texas) Daily Herald,*
*September 24, 1971*

**37.25** ❧ The court should be a place where anybody can come—whatever they have in their pocket—and be able to file a complaint in simple fashion and at least have somebody give consideration to it and give them an opportunity to be heard.

*Thomas T. Curtin, American jurist;*
*judge, U.S. District Court*
*New York Times, October 7, 1971*

**37.26** ❧ No one can ever be sure how courts will interpret any new law or amendment.

*Susan C. Ross, American lawyer*
*The Rights of Women, 1973*

**37.27** ❧ The court will even make up or accept a spurious purpose for the law in order to justify differential treatment.

*Susan C. Ross, American lawyer*
*The Rights of Women, 1973*

**37.28** ❧ I do think people are putting too much reliance on courts. I also believe the courts are too prone to take on problems that they have no business getting into. To me, the idea of a court deciding whether or not girls should be permitted to play Little League baseball is ludicrous. Con-

gress too contributes to this glut which I call legal pollution.

*Thomas Ehrlich, American educator;*
*dean, Stanford University School of Law*
*U.S. News & World Report,*
*July 21, 1975*

**37.29** ❧ The courts hold a unique position among our democratic institutions. In a sense, they represent one of our last bastions of participatory democracy, in which disputants go directly before a judge or jury to resolve an issue. In no other governmental context does an individual have the opportunity to take a problem to a decision-maker who represents the full force and power of that particular branch of government. This direct interchange between the individual and the state is at the heart of the democratic process. . . . We must protect this unique heritage and strive to preserve the values it represents.

*Rose E. Bird, American jurist; chief*
*justice, Supreme Court of California*
*Los Angeles Times,*
*November 16, 1977*

**37.30** ❧ We should get away from the idea that a court is the only place in which to settle disputes. People with claims are likely people with pains. They want relief and results and they don't care whether it's in a courtroom with lawyers and judges, or somewhere else.

*Warren E. Burger*
*Address, American Bar Association,*
*New Orleans, reported in the Los*
*Angeles Times,*
*August 27, 1978*

37.31 ❦ If our courts lose their authority and their rulings are no longer respected, there will be no one left to resolve the divisive issues that can rip the social fabric apart. . . . The courts are a safety valve without which no democratic society can survive.

> *Rose E. Bird, American jurist; chief*
> *justice, Supreme Court of California*
> Los Angeles Times,
> *September 11, 1978*

37.32 ❦ The court is a political institution. All of us here were appointed by politicians and none of us can deny we were chosen in part for our political belief. To suggest that doesn't influence our thinking now that we are judges is just naive.

> *William P. Clark. Jr., American jurist;*
> *justice, Supreme Court of California*
> Los Angeles Times,
> *November 23, 1978*

37.33 ❦ The young judge spends the first third of his life in fear that he might be reversed by the court of appeals, the middle third in the conviction that the court of appeals was always wrong and the last third not caring whether it was right or wrong.

> *Patrick Devlin, English jurist*
> The Judge, *1979*

37.34 ❦ The judiciary has been the forum of ultimate resort for individuals and organizations representing almost every position on the political spectrum.

> *Ruth Bader Ginsburg*
> 15 Georgia Law Review 539, *1981*

37.35 ❦ There is a reciprocal relationship between the U.S. Supreme Court and the state courts. As the Supreme Court's own energy flags or it reaches the limits of appropriate Federal judicial activity, it may nonetheless have marked the path that creative state jurists will want to follow. In the long view of history, most of the truly creative developments in the American law have come from the states.

> *Laurence H. Tribe, American educator;*
> *professor, Harvard University*
> New York Times, *May 19, 1982*

37.36 ❦ We must use our courage to ensure a judiciary not governed by the daily polls but by the rules of law, serving not the special interest of the few but the best interest of all, devoted not to self-preservation, but to the preservation of those great Constitutional principles which history has bequeathed to us.

> *Rose E. Bird, American jurist; chief*
> *justice, Supreme Court of California*
> Los Angeles Times, *July 20, 1982*

37.37 ❦ The courts are an easy scapegoat because at a time when everything has to be boiled down to easy slogans, we speak in subtleties.

> *Rose E. Bird, American jurist; chief*
> *justice, Supreme Court of California*
> Newsweek, *August 9, 1982*

37.38 ❦ [The court] is the lengthened shadow of many men.

*C. J. Field*
*Observance of the 250th Anniversary*
*of the Supreme Court*

37.39 ❦ A court victory is important but just the beginning of the process. It must translate into empowerment. It is the people that have the power to give life to those court victories.

*Antonia Hernandez, lawyer, 1991*
*Dawn Bradley Berry,* The 50 Most
Influential Women in American Law,
*1996*

37.40 ❦ A poor man may still get into heaven, but after Reaganization, he may not be able to get into court.

*Jane Bryant Quinn*
Lawyer's Wit and Wisdom, *edited by*
*Bruce Nash, Allan Zullo and compiled*
*by Kathryn Zullo, 1995*

37.41 ❦ Just like in Hollywood, image is everything in the courtroom . . .

*Darlene Ricker*
Lawyer's Wit and Wisdom, *edited by*
*Bruce Nash, Allan Zullo and compiled*
*by Kathryn Zullo, 1995*

37.42 ❦ When it is proper to say in a court of law that a defendant is *entitled* to mislead a jury, you have to wonder.

*Judge Harold J. Rothwax*
Guilty: The Collapse of Criminal
Justice, *1996*

37.43 ❦ It is irresponsible for public officials, especially those who are lawyers, to use our courts as a political football, when they must know that an independent judiciary is essential to our system of justice.

*Barbara Paul Robinson, President of*
*the Association of the Bar*
*of the City of New York*
New York Times *editorial*

# 38. CRIME

38.1 ❦ The greatest crimes are caused by surfeit, not by want. Men do not become tyrants in order that they may not suffer cold.

*Aristotle*
Politics, *c.322* B.C.

38.2 ❦ Crime and intention of crime are equal in their nature.

*Cicero, 106–43* B.C.
*W. Gurney Benham,* Putnam's
Complete Book of Quotations,
Proverbs and Household Words, *1927*

38.3 ❦ No crime is founded upon reason.

*Livy*
History of Rome, *c.10* B.C.

38.4 ❦ Evil booty does not bring good luck.

*Ovid*, 43 B.C.–?A.D. 7
Amores

38.5 ❦ Crime must be safeguarded by crime.

*Seneca*
De Clementia, *c.55*

38.6 ❦ A happy issue makes some crimes honorable.

*Seneca*
Hippolytus, *c.60*

38.7 ❦ There is no crime without a precedent.

*Seneca*
Hippolytus, *c.60*

38.8 ❦ The safe way to crime is always through crime.

*Seneca*, 4 B.C.?–A.D. 65
Agamemnon

38.9 ❦ With a differing fate, men commit the same crimes: one man gets a cross as a reward of villainy, another a crown.

*Juvenal*
Satires, *c.120*

38.10 ❦ What man was ever content with one crime?

*Juvenal*
Satires, *c.120*

38.11 ❦ No crime is rooted out once and for all.

*Tertullian*
The Christian's Defense, *c.215*

38.12 ❦ If little faults, proceeding on
distemper,
Shall not be wink'd at, how shall we
stretch our eye
When capital crimes, chew'd,
swallow'd, and digested,
Appear before us?

*Shakespeare*
Henry V, *II, 2, 1598–1599*

38.13 ❦ Tremble, thou wretch,
That hast within thee undivulged
crimes.
Unwhipp'd of justice.

*Shakespeare*
King Lear, *III, 2, 1605–1606*

38.14 ❦ A deed without a name.

*Shakespeare*
Macbeth, *IV, 1, 1605–1606*

38.15 ❦ The source of every crime is some defect of the understanding, or some error in reasoning, or some sudden force of the passions.

*Thomas Hobbes*
Leviathan, *1651*

**38.16** ❧ If poverty is the mother of crime,
then want of sense is its father.

*Jean de La Bruyère*
Caractères, *1688*

**38.17** ❧ For crime is all the shame of
punishment.

*Daniel Defoe*
Hymn to the Pillory, *1703*

**38.18** ❧ The number of the Malefactors,
authorizes not the Crime.

*Proverb*
*Thomas Fuller,* Gnomologia, *1732*

**38.19** ❧ All, all look up with reverential awe,
at crimes that 'scape, or triumph o'er
the law.

*Alexander Pope*
Epilogue, Satires, *1738*

**38.20** ❧ The history of the great events of
this world is scarcely more than the
history of crimes.

*Voltaire*
Essai sur les moeurs, *1740–1743*

**38.21** ❧ He that carries a small Crime easily,
will carry it on when it comes to be
an ox.

*Benjamin Franklin*
Poor Richard's Almanack, *1758*

**38.22** ❧ Crimes not against forms, but
against those eternal laws of justice,
which are our rule and birthright.

*Edmund Burke*
Impeachment of Warren Hastings,
February 15, *1788*

**38.23** ❧ For you'll ne'er mend your fortunes,
nor help the just cause,
By breaking of windows, or
breaking of laws.

*Hannah More, English writer*
Address to the Meeting in Spa Fields,
*1817*

**38.24** ❧ Nor florid prose, nor honeyed lines
of rhyme,
Can blazon evil deeds, or concen-
trate a crime.

*Lord Byron*
Childe Harold, *1812–1818*

**38.25** ❧ That ill-gotten gain never prospers
is the trite consolation administered
to the easy dupe, when he has been
tricked out of his money or estate.

*Charles Lamb, 1775–1834*
*Bergen Evans,* Dictionary of
Quotations, *1968*

**38.26** ❧ It is worse than a crime, it is a blunder.

Attributed to Talleyrand, *1754–1838*
*William S. Walsh,* International
Encyclopedia of Prose and Poetical
Quotations, *1951*

**38.27** ❧ Petty laws breed great crimes.

*Ouida (pseudonym of Marie Louise De
La Ramée), English writer "Pipistrello"
(1880),* Wisdom, Wit and Pathos,
*1884*

38.28 ❦ An English historian, contrasting the London of his day with the London of the time when its streets, supplied only with oil lamps, were scenes of nightly robberies, says that "the adventurers in gas lights did more for the prevention of crime than the government had done since the days of Alfred."

*John M. Harlan*
New Orleans Gas Light Co. v.
Louisiana Light Mfg. Co., *115 U.S.*
*650, 658 (1885)*

38.29 ❦ The real significance of crime is in its being a breach of faith with the community of mankind.

*Joseph Conrad*
Lord Jim, *1900*

38.30 ❦ Crime is only the retail department of what, in wholesale, we call penal law.

*George Bernard Shaw*
Man and Superman, *1903*

38.31 ❦ Crime is naught but misdirected energy.

*Emma Goldman*
Anarchism, *1910*

38.32 ❦ For de little stealin' dey gits you in jail soon or late. For de big stealin' dey makes you emperor and puts you in de Hall o' Fame when you croaks.

*Eugene O'Neill*
The Emperor Jones, *1920*

38.33 ❦ Crime is contagious. If the Government becomes a lawbreaker, it breeds contempt for law; it invites every man to become a law unto himself; it invites anarchy.

*Louis D. Brandeis*
Olmstead v. United States, *277 U.S.*
*438 (1928)*

38.34 ❦ The more featureless and commonplace a crime is, the more difficult it is to bring it home.

*Sir Arthur Conan Doyle,* 1859–1930
*W. H. Auden and Louis Kronenberger,*
The Viking Book of Aphorisms, *1962*

38.35 ❦ To say that crime brings its own punishment is by way of being a platitude, and yet in my opinion nothing can be truer.

*Agatha Christie*
The Tuesday Club Murders, *1933*

38.36 ❦ It ain't no sin if you crack a few laws now and then, just so long as you don't break any.

*Mae West*
Every Day's a Holiday *(film), 1937*

38.37 ❦ [Coercion:] The unpardonable crime.

*Dorothy Miller Richardson,*
*English writer*
Pilgrimage, *1938*

38.38 ❦ To initiate a war of aggression . . . is not only an international crime; it is the supreme international crime differing only from other war crimes in that it contains within itself the accumulated evil of the whole.

*Judgement,* Trial of the Major War
Criminals Before the International
Military Tribunal, *vol.2,*
*Nürnberg, Germany, 1947*

38.39 ❦ When a man wants to murder a tiger, he calls it sport: when the tiger wants to murder him, he calls it ferocity. The distinction between crime and justice is no greater.

*George Bernard Shaw, 1856–1950*
*W. H. Auden and Louis Kronenberger,*
The Viking Book of Aphorisms, *1962*

38.40 ❦ The duty to disclose knowledge of crime rests upon all citizens.

*Robert H. Jackson*
Stein v. New York, *346 U.S. 156,*
*184 (1953)*

38.41 ❦ I hate this "crime doesn't pay" stuff. Crime in the U.S. is perhaps one of the biggest businesses in the world today.

*Paul Kirk*
Wall Street Journal,
*February 26, 1960*

38.42 ❦ If we were brought to trial for the crimes we have committed against ourselves, few would escape the gallows.

*Paul Eldridge*
Maxims for a Modern Man, *1965*

38.43 ❦ [If crime is increasing nationally], it is due in large part to the fact that waiting in the wings are lawyers willing to go beyond their professional

responsibility, professional rights and professional duty.

*Julius J. Hoffman, American jurist*
*At the trial of the Chicago 7, reported*
*in the* Los Angeles Times,
*February 16, 1970*

38.44 ❦ Premeditated crime: the longer the meditating, the dreaming, the more triumphant the execution!

*Joyce Carol Oates, writer*
Do with Me What You Will, *1970*

38.45 ❦ When is conduct a crime, and when is a crime not a crime? When Somebody Up There—a monarch, a dictator, a Pope, a legislator—so decrees.

*Jessica Mitford, writer*
Kind and Unusual Punishment, *1971*

38.46 ❦ . . . a crime is anything that a group in power chooses to prohibit.

*Freda Adler, American educator*
Sisters in Crime, *1975*

38.47 ❦ Children's bodies aren't like automobiles with the assailant's fingerprints lingering on the wheel. The world of sexual abuse is quintessentially secret. It is the perfect crime.

*Beatrix Campbell*
Unofficial Secrets, *1988*

38.48 ❦ He'd forgotten just how addictive crime can be. Repeat offenders are motivated more by withdrawal symptoms than necessity.

*Sue Grafton*
"H" is for Homicide, *1991*

38.49 ❧ Debates about crime control are rarely sensible. They're ruled by politics and fear and the mindless exchange of attitudes that dominates the worst talk shows, where people never exchange ideas.

*Wendy Kaminer, lawyer and social critic*
It's All the Rage, *1995*

# 39. CRIMINALS

39.1 ❧ Lawmakers ought not to be lawbreakers.

*English proverb*
*Geoffrey Chaucer, "The Man of Law's*
*Tale,"* The Canterbury Tales, *c. 1386*

39.2 ❧ All criminals turn preachers under the gallows.

*Italian proverb*
*H. L. Mencken,* A New Dictionary of Quotations, *1946*

39.3 ❧ The act is not criminal unless the mind is criminal.

*Legal maxim*

39.4 ❧ The wrathful man does not see the law.

*Publilius Syrus, Latin writer,*
1st century B.C.
*W. Gurney Benham,* Putnam's Complete Book of Quotations, Proverbs and Household Words, *1927*

39.5 ❧ It is better that a criminal be not accused than that he be acquitted.

*Livy*
History of Rome, *c.10* B.C.

39.6 ❧ Who breaks no law is subject to no kings.

*George Chapman*
Revenge of Bussy d'Ambois, *1613*

39.7 ❧ A man is not born a knave; there must be time to make him so, nor is he presently discovered after he becomes one.

*Sir John Holt, English jurist;*
*Chief Justice*
Reg. v. Swendson *(1702), 14 How.*
St. Tr. 596

39.8 ❧ Let me remember, when I find myself inclined to pity a criminal, that there is likewise a pity due to the country.

*Sir Matthew Hale*
History of the Pleas of the Crown, *1736*

39.9 ❦ People crushed by law have no hope but from power. If laws are their enemies, they will be enemies to laws; and those who have much to hope and nothing to lose will always be dangerous, more or less.

*Edmund Burke*
*Letter to the Honorable C. J. Fox,*
*October 8, 1777*

39.10 ❦ If there were no bad people there would be no good lawyers.

*Charles Dickens*
The Old Curiosity Shop, *1841*

39.11 ❦ The law's made to take care o' raskills.

*George Eliot*
The Mill on the Floss, *1860*

39.12 ❦ Laws and institutions require to be adapted, not to good men, but to bad.

*John Stuart Mill*
The Subjugation of Women, *1869*

39.13 ❦ When a felon's not engaged in his employment,
Or maturing his felonious little plans,
His capacity for innocent enjoyment
Is just as great as any other man's.

*W. S. Gilbert*
The Pirates of Penzance, *1880*

39.14 ❦ When the enterprising burglar's not a-burgling,
When the cutthroat isn't occupied in crime,

He loves to hear the little brook a-gurgling,
And to listen to the merry village chime.

*W. S. Gilbert*
The Pirates of Penzance, *1880*

39.15 ❦ Whether you're an honest man or Whether you're a thief,
Depends on whose solicitor has given me a brief.

*W. S. Gilbert*
Utopia Limited, *1893*

39.16 ❦ Imagination is the first faculty wanting in those that do harm to their kind.

*Margaret Oliphant, Scottish writer and*
*historian,* 1828–1897
*"Innocent"*

39.17 ❦ Given a child falling into a river, an old person in a burning building, and a woman fainting in the street, a band of convicts would risk their lives to give aid as quickly at least as a band of millionaires.

*Clarence Darrow*
Resist Not Evil, *1903*

39.18 ❦ We have to choose, and for my part I think it a less evil that some criminals should escape than that the Government should play an ignoble part.

*Oliver Wendell Holmes*
Olmstead v. United States, *277 U.S.*
*438, 470 (1928)*

39.19 ❧ It's not the people in prison who worry me. It's the people who aren't.

*Arthur Gore, earl of Arran*
New York Times, *January 7, 1962*

39.20 ❧ There are certain characters who, unable to read a writ from the court of conscience and reason, must be served with one from a court—even though it be inferior—whose language they understand.

*A. B. Smith*
W. H. Auden and Louis Kronenberger,
The Viking Book of Aphorisms, *1962*

39.21 ❧ Americans are solicitous enough concerning the rights of the individual criminal; they need to cultivate regard for the rights of the community.

*Anonymous judge*
Richard O'Connor, Courtroom
Warrior, *1963*

39.22 ❧ Whereas formerly convicts tended to regard themselves as unfortunates whose accident of birth at the bottom of the heap was largely responsible for their plight, today many are questioning the validity of the heap.

*Jessica Mitford, writer*
Kind and Unusual Punishment, *1971*

# 40. CROSS-EXAMINATION

40.1 ❧ When you have no basis for argument, abuse the plaintiff.

*Cicero, 106–43 B.C.*
*Louis Levinson,* Bartlett's Unfamiliar
Quotations, *1971*

40.2 ❧ Then, if at any time you find you have the worst end of the staff, leave off your cause and fall upon the person of your adversary; put it boldly and enough of 't, and somewhat must stick; no matter how true or false, it begets a prejudice to a person, and many times forejudges the cause.

*Christopher North (pseudonym of John*
*Wilson), 1785–1854*
The Cheats

40.3 ❧ Be mild with the mild, shrewd with the crafty, confiding to the honest, rough to the ruffian, and a thunderbolt to the liar. But in all this, never be unmindful of your own dignity.

*David Paul Brown*
*Marshall Brown,* Wit and Humor of
Bench and Bar, *1899*

40.4 ❧ More cross-examinations are suicidal than homicidal.

*Emory R. Buckner*
*Francis Lewis Wellman,* Art of
Cross-Examination, *1936*

40.5 ❧ Never, never, never, on cross-examination ask a witness a question you don't already know the answer to was a tenet I absorbed with my babyfood. Do it, and you'll often get an answer you don't want, an answer that might wreck your case.

*Harper Lee*
To Kill a Mockingbird,
*1960*

40.6 ❦ Challenging an expert and questioning his expertise is the lifeblood of our legal system—whether it is a psychiatrist discussing mental disturbances, a physicist testifying on the environ-

mental impact of a nuclear power plant, or a General Motors executive insisting on the impossiblity of meeting Federal anti-pollution standards by 1975. It is the only way a judge or jury can decide whom to trust.

*David L. Bazelon, American jurist;*
*chief judge, U.S. Court of Appeals*
Dallas Times Herald,
*May 13, 1973*

# 41. CUSTOM

41.1 ❦ Custom makes law.

*English proverb*
*John Wycliffe,* Seven Werkys of
Merely Bodyly, *1382*

41.2 ❦ Custom is held as Law.

*Latin legal phrase*
*W. Gurney Benham,* Putnam's
Complete Book of Quotations,
Proverbs and Household Words, *1927*

41.3 ❦ Custom has the force of law.

*Proverb*
*Rosalind Fergusson,* The Facts On File
Dictionary of Proverbs, *1983*

41.4 ❦ Every land has its own law.

*Proverb*
*Rosalind Fergusson,* The Facts On File
Dictionary of Proverbs,
*1983*

41.5 ❦ With customs we live well, but laws undo us.

*Proverb*
*Rosalind Fergusson,* The Facts On
File Dictionary of Proverbs, *1983*

41.6 ❦ The law follows custom.

*Plautus*
Trinummus, *c.190* B.C.

41.7 ❦ Modesty forbids that to be done which the law does not forbid.

*Seneca*
Hippolytus, *c.60*

41.8 ❦ As laws are necessary that good manners may be preserved, so good manners are necessary that laws may be maintained.

*Machiavelli*
Discourses on Livy, *1513*

41.9 ❦ Custom, that is before all law;
Nature, that is above all art.

*Samuel Daniel, English poet*
*A Defence of Rhyme, 1603*

41.10 ❦ We must not make a scarecrow of
the law,
Setting it up to fear the birds of prey,
And let it keep one shape, till
custom make it
Their perch and not their terror.

*Shakespeare*
Measure for Measure,
*II, 1, 1604–1605*

41.11 ❦ Custom, that unwritten law,
By which the people keep even kings
in awe.

*Sir William Davenant, 1606–1668*
Circe

41.12 ❦ Let the law never be contradictory
to custom: for if the custom be
good, the law is worthless.

*Voltaire*
Philosophical Dictionary, *1764*

41.13 ❦ Laws and customs may be creative of
vice; and should be therefore perpetu-
ally under process of observation and
correction: but laws and customs cannot be creative of virtue. . . .

*Harriet Martineau,*
*American writer and critic*
*"Marriage,"* Society in America, *1837*

41.14 ❦ Custom is never, by her nature, the
handmaid of freedom.

*Maria W. Chapman*
Right and Wrong in Massachusetts,
*1839*

41.15 ❦ There are two kinds of restrictions
upon human liberty—the restraint
of law and that of custom. No written law has ever been more binding
than unwritten custom supported
by popular opinion.

*Carrie Chapman Catt*
Speech, February 8, *1900*

41.16 ❦ Custom controls the sexual impulse
as it controls no other.

*Margaret Sanger*
*Interview,* American Mercury, *1924*

41.17 ❦ . . . when common understanding
and practice have established a way
it is a waste of time to wander in by-
paths of logic.

*Oliver Wendell Holmes*
Ruddy v. Rossi, *248 U.S. 104, 111*
*(1918)*

41.18 ❦ . . . where is the society which does
not struggle along under a dead-
weight of tradition and law inherited from its grandfathers?

*Suzanne LaFollette, American feminist*
*and writer*
*"The Beginnings of Emancipation,"*
Concerning Women, *1926*

41.19 ❦ "Custom is before all law." As soon
as you begin to say "We have always
done things this way—perhaps *that*
might be a better way," conscious
law-making is beginning. As soon as
you begin to say "*We* do things this
way—*they* do things that way—
what is to be done about it?" men
are beginning to feel towards justice,

that resides between the endless jar of right and wrong.

*Helen M. Cam, English historian*
*Lecture, Girton College,*
*February 18, 1956*

41.20 ❦ Custom has furnished the only basis which ethics have ever had.

*Joseph Wood Krutch*
The Modern Temper, *1956*

41.21 ❦ Superfluity, excess of custom, and superstition would climb like a choking vine on the Fence of the Law if skepticism did not continually hack them away to make freedom for purity.

*Cynthia Ozick*
*"The Pagan Rabbi" (1966),* The Pagan Rabbi and Other Stories, *1971*

# *42.* DEATH AND DYING

*42.1* ❦ Nothing can be meaner than the anxiety to live on, to live on anyhow and in any shape; a spirit with any honor is not willing to live except in its own way, and a spirit with any wisdom is not over-eager to live at all.

*George Santayana*
Winds of Doctrine, *1913*

*42.2* ❦ Pray for the dead and fight like hell for the living!

*Mother (Mary Harris) Jones*
Autobiography, *1925*

*42.3* ❦ Into the darkness they go, the wise and the lovely.

*Edna St. Vincent Millay*
*"Dirge Without Music,"*
The Buck in the Snow, *1928*

*42.4* ❦ Death cannot alter facts, only feelings.

*Frances Noyes Hart*
The Crooked Lane, *1933*

*42.5* ❦ If I were dying my last words would be: Have faith and pursue the unknown end.

*Oliver Wendell Holmes,* 1841–1935
*Catherine Drinker Bowen,* Yankee from Olympus, *1944*

*42.6* ❦ Dying seems less sad than having lived too little.

*Gloria Steinem*
Outrageous Acts and Everyday Rebellions, *1983*

*42.7* ❦ If it is permissible to kill the unborn human being for convenience, it surely is permissible to kill those who are thought soon to die for the same reason . . . Humans tend to be inconvenient at both ends of their lives.

*Robert H. Bork*
Inconvenient Lives, *1966*

# *43.* DEBT

*43.1* ❦ He who desireth to sleep soundly, let him buy the bed of a bankrupt.

*English proverb*
John Ray, English Proverbs, *1678*

*43.2* ❦ Thou canst not fly high with borrowed Wings.

*Proverb*
Thomas Fuller, Gnomologia, *1732*

**43.3** ❧ If one wants to know the real value of money he needs but to borrow some from his friends.

*Confucius*
Analects, *c.500* B.C.

**43.4** ❧ He that buildeth his house with
other men's money,
Is as one gathering stones for his
sepulchre.

*Ben Sira*
*Old Testament, Ecclesiasticus 21:8,*
*c.190* B.C.

**43.5** ❧ A trifling debt makes a man your debtor, a large one makes him your enemy.

*Seneca*
Epistulae Morales ad Lucilium *63–65*

**43.6** ❧ Do not borrow, for you will incur the derision of the proverb, "I am unable to carry the goat, so put the ox upon me."

*Plutarch*
*"On Borrowing,"* Moralia, *97*

**43.7** ❧ The man who is once involved in debt remains a debtor all his life, exchanging, like a horse that has once been bridled, one rider for another.

*Plutarch*
*"On Borrowing,"* Moralia, *97*

**43.8** ❧ Neither a borrower nor a lender be:
For loan oft loses both itself and
friend,
And borrowing dulls the edge of
husbandry.

*Shakespeare*
Hamlet, *I, 3, 1600–1601*

**43.9** ❧ He that would have a short Lent, let him borrow money to be repaid at Easter.

*Benjamin Franklin*
Poor Richard's Almanack, *1738*

**43.10** ❧ Creditors have better memories than debtors.

*Benjamin Franklin*
Poor Richard's Almanack, *1758*

**43.11** ❧ Debt is the sort of Bedfellow who is forever pulling all the Covers his way.

*Minna Thomas Antrim*
Don'ts for Bachelors and Old Maids,
*1908*

**43.12** ❧ Never spend your money before you have it.

*Thomas Jefferson, 1743–1826*
*Franklin Pierce Adams, F.P.A.*
Book of Quotations, *1952*

**43.13** ❧ Debt is the prolific mother of folly and of crime.

*Benjamin Disraeli*
Henrietta Temple, *1837*

**43.14** ❧ . . . it is the policy of the law that the debtor be just before he be generous.

*Edward R. Finch, American jurist*
Hearn 45 St. Corp. v. Jano,
*283 N.Y. 139, 142 (1940)*

## 44. DECISIONS

44.1 ❧ Out of thy own mouth I will
judge thee.

*New Testament, Luke*
*19:22*

44.2 ❧ How a good meaning
May be corrupted by a
misconstruction.

*Thomas Middleton*
*The Old Law, 1656*

44.3 ❧ Evil stands the case when it is to be
said of a judicial decree as the saying
goes in the play of the "Two Gentlemen of Verona" . . .
'I have no other but a woman's
reason;
I think him so, because I think
him so.'

*Benjamin N. Cardozo*
*The Nature of the Judicial Process,*
*1921*

44.4 ❧ Lines should not be drawn simply
for the sake of drawing lines.

*Felix Frankfurter*
Pearce v. Commissioner of Internal
Revenue, *314 U.S. 593, 62 S. Ct. 98,*
*86 L.Ed. 479 (1942)*

44.5 ❧ To the somnambulist, sleep-walking
may seem more pleasant and less
hazardous than wakeful walking, but
the latter is the wiser mode of loco-
motion in the congested traffic of a
modern community. It is about time
to abandon judicial somnambulism.

*Jerome Frank*
Law and the Modern Mind, *1963*

## 45. DEFENSE

45.1 ❧ My rule is this, in doubtful cases,
when men are upon their lives,
I had rather hear what is imperti-
nent, than not let them make a
full defence.

*Sir William Scroggs, English jurist;*
*Lord Chief Justice*
Whitehead's Case, *1679*

45.2 ❧ The laws of God and man both give
the party an opportunity to make
his defence, if he has any. I remember to have heard it observed by a
very learned man upon such an occasion, that even God himself did not
pass sentence upon *Adam* before he
was called upon to make his

defence. *Adam* (says God), where art thou? Hast thou eaten of the tree, whereof I commanded thee that thou shouldest not eat? And the same question was put to *Eve* also.

*William Fortescue, English jurist*
The King v. Chancellor, etc. of the University of Cambridge *(1723),*
*1 Str. 566*

45.3 ❦ In the early days of English criminal jurisprudence, when even a trifling larceny was punishable with death, there was reason why the judicial mind should exhaust its ingenuity in aid of the defense, and seize upon every technicality to avert from the prisoner a punishment so disproportionate to his crime. . . . The reason for resorting to mere technicality to enable the criminal to evade the sanctions of the law no longer exists, and the practice to which that reason led should therefore cease.

*Bennet Van Syckel, American jurist*
Patterson v. State, *48 N.J.L. 381,*
*383, 4A. 449, 450 (1886)*

45.4 ❦ The right to be heard would be, in many cases, of little avail if it did not comprehend the right to be heard by counsel.

*George Sutherland, American jurist*
Powell v. Alabama, *287 U.S. 45, 53*
*S.Ct. 55, 77 L.Ed. 158 (1932)*

45.5 ❦ The pair were playing a game that defied intervention; they were matched like reel and rod and there was no unwinding. They juggled in jargon, dabbled in *double-entendres,*

wallowed in each other's witticisms, and all at the expense of the Defendant.

*Daphne du Maurier*
Mary Anne, *1954*

45.6 ❦ It is a lawyer's duty to represent a guilty man, but not to free him.

*Grant B. Cooper, American lawyer*
Los Angeles Times, *April 13, 1969*

45.7 ❦ The insanity defense is a key part of our criminal justice system which is founded on the belief that [people] normally choose whether or not to obey the law.

*Elyce Zenoff, American educator;*
*professor, George Washington University*
U.S. News & World Report,
*July 5, 1982*

45.8 ❦ I am a mercenary. A person who is accused of something comes into my office and he wants me to be his sword, he wants me to protect his rights. I must, if I accept his case, close my eyes to the needs of society and I do what I can to protect him within legal ethics, without any regard to society's needs or anyone else's needs. The fact is that society gains most of all by seeing to it that the rule of law applies to all. It is not tested with the law-abiding middle class, but with the people who need it most.

*Jay Goldberg, American lawyer*
New York Times, *May 24, 1969*

**45.9** ❧ . . . he believed in the justice of his using any legal methods he could improvise to force the other side into compromise or into dismissals of charges, or to lead a jury into the verdict he wanted. Why not? He was a defense lawyer, not a judge or a juror or a policeman or a legislator or a theoretician or an anarchist or a murderer.

*Joyce Carol Oates*
Do with Me What You Will, *1970*

**45.10** ❧ I am not interested in my client's innocence or guilt; I am not interested in seeing that justice is done when I'm the defense attorney. I am interested in seeing them acquitted. It's not the defense attorney's job to do justice. His job is to defend vigorously his client. . . . It's not a happy experience to get people off who are guilty. I don't expect any prizes or plaudits for it. . . . What we do is a necessary evil—a very necessary evil.

*Alan M. Dershowitz*
Los Angeles Herald-Examiner,
*May 26, 1982*

# 46. DELAYS

**46.1** ❧ Delays in the law are hateful.

*Latin legal phrase*
*W. Gurney Benham,* Putnam's
Complete Book of Quotations,
Proverbs and Household Words, *1927*

**46.2** ❧ No delay [in law] is long concerning the death of a man.

*Latin legal phrase*
*W. Gurney Benham,* Putnam's
Complete Book of Quotations,
Proverbs and Household Words, *1927*

**46.3** ❧ For who would bear the whips and
     scorns of time,
The oppressor's wrong, the proud
     man's contumely,
The pangs of dispriz'd love, the law's
     delay,
The insolence of office, and the
     spurns,
That patient merit of the unworthy
     takes,

When he himself might his quietus
     make
With a bare bodkin

*Shakespeare*
Hamlet, *III,*
*1, 1600–1601*

**46.4** ❧ It is not to be imagined that the King will be guilty of vexatious delays.

*Sir Dudley Ryder, English jurist;*
*Lord Chief Justice*
Rex v. Berkley and another *(1754),*
*Sayer's Rep. 124*

**46.5** ❧ Delay will frequently have . . . considerable influence upon the judgment which ought to be formed upon the evidence adduced.

*Frederic Thesiger, 1st Lord Chelmsford,*
*English jurist; Lord Chancellor*
Cuno v. Cuno *(1873), L.R.*
*2 Sc. & D. 302*

46.6 ❧ In any event, mere speed is not a test of justice. Deliberate speed is. Deliberate speed takes time. But it is time well spent.

*Felix Frankfurter*
First Iowa Coop. v. Power Comm'n.,
*328 U.S. 152, 188 (1946)*

46.7 ❧ The judgments below . . . are accordingly reversed and the cases are remanded to the District Courts to take such proceedings and enter such orders and decrees consistent with this opinion as are necessary and proper to admit to public schools on a racially nondiscriminatory basis with all deliberate speed the parties to these cases.

*Earl Warren*
Brown v. Board of Education of
Topeka, *349 U.S.
294, 301 (1955)*

# 47. DEMOCRACY

47.1 ❧ Democracy . . . a charming form of government, full of variety and disorder, and dispensing a sort of equality to equals and unequals alike.

*Plato*
The Republic, *c.370* B.C.

47.2 ❧ If liberty and equality, as is thought by some, are chiefly to be found in democracy, they will be best attained when all persons alike share in the government to the utmost.

*Aristotle*
Politics, *c.322* B.C.

47.3 ❧ Democracy arose from men thinking that if they are equal in any respect they are equal in all respects.

*Aristotle*
Politics, *c.322* B.C.

47.4 ❧ Republics are brought to their ends by luxury, monarchies by poverty.

*de Montesquieu*
The Spirit of the Laws, *1748*

47.5 ❧ The tyranny of a multitude is a multiplied tyranny.

*Edmund Burke*
Letter to Thomas Mercer, *1790*

47.6 ❧ The republican is the only form of government which is not eternally at open or secret war with the rights of mankind.

*Thomas Jefferson, 1743–1826*
*Franklin Pierce Adams, F.P.A. Book of*
Quotations, *1952*

**47.7** ❧ A minority is powerless while it con-
forms to the majority.

*Henry David Thoreau*
Civil Disobedience, *1849*

**47.8** ❧ Any man more right than his neighbors constitutes a majority of one
already.

*Henry David Thoreau*
Civil Disobedience, *1849*

**47.9** ❧ There are nine hundred and ninety-
nine patrons of virtue to one
virtuous man.

*Henry David Thoreau*
Civil Disobedience, *1849*

**47.10** ❧ Among free men there can be no
successful appeal from the ballot to
the bullet.

*Abraham Lincoln, 1809–1865*
*Franklin Pierce Adams, F.P.A.*
Book of Quotations, *1952*

**47.11** ❧ As I would not be a *slave*, so I would
not be a *master*. This expresses my
idea of democracy. Whatever differs
from this, to the extent of the
difference, is no democracy.

*Abraham Lincoln*
*"Fragment on Slavery," August 1, 1858*

**47.12** ❧ . . . ballots are the rightful and peaceful successors of bullets.

*Abraham Lincoln*
Message to Congress, *July 4, 1861*

**47.13** ❧ The ship of Democracy, which has
weathered many storms, may
sink through the mutiny of those
on board.

*Grover Cleveland*
Letter to Wilson S. Bissell, *1894*

**47.14** ❧ It was we, the people; not we, the
white male citizens; nor yet we, the
male citizens; but we the whole people who formed the Union . . . not
to give the blessings of liberty, but to
secure them . . . to the whole
people—women as well as men.

*Susan B. Anthony, 1820–1906*
A Woman's Right to Suffrage

**47.15** ❧ We are thus brought to a conception
of Democracy not merely as a
sentiment which desires the
well-being of all men, nor yet as a
creed which believes in the essential
dignity and equality of all men, but
as that which affords a rule of living
as well as a test of faith.

*Jane Addams*
Introduction, Democracy and
Social Ethics, *1902*

**47.16** ❧ The world must be made safe for
democracy.

*Woodrow Wilson*
Address to Congress, *April 2, 1917*

**47.17** ❧ All the ills of democracy can be
cured by more democracy.

*Alfred E. Smith*
Speech, *June 27, 1933*

47.18 ❧ On the whole, with scandalous exceptions, Democracy has given the ordinary worker more dignity than he ever had.

*Sinclair Lewis*
It Can't Happen Here, *1935*

47.19 ❧ We must be the great arsenal of democracy.

*Franklin Delano Roosevelt*
*Radio address, 1940*

47.20 ❧ People who want to understand democracy should spend less time in the library with Aristotle and more time on the buses and in the subway.

*Simeon Strunsky, American journalist*
*and author*
No Mean City, *1944*

47.21 ❧ Our people do not want barren theories from their democracy, Maury Maverick has expressed very quaintly, but clearly, what they really want when he says: "We Americans want to talk, pray, think as we please-*and eat regular.*"

*Robert H. Jackson, 1892–1954*
"Back to the American Way,"
Unpublished Speeches, *vol. 5, no. 14,*
*as quoted in Eugene C. Gerhart,*
America's Advocate: Robert H.
Jackson, *1958*

47.22 ❧ There is a basic inconsistency between popular government and judicial supremacy.

*Robert H. Jackson, 1892–1954*
*Thomas C. Cochran and Wayne*
*Andrews, eds.,* Concise Dictionary of
American History, *1962*

47.23 ❧ Democracy is no harlot to be picked up in the street by a man with a tommy gun.

*Sir Winston S. Churchill*
*F. B. Czarnomski, ed.,* The Wisdom
of Winston Churchill, *1956*

47.24 ❧ The conception of political equality from the Declaration of Independence to Lincoln's Gettysburg Address, to the Fifteenth, Seventeenth, and Nineteenth Amendments can mean only one thing—one person, one vote.

*William O. Douglas*
Gray v. Sanders, *372 U.S. 368, 381*
*(1963)*

47.25 ❧ Every democratic system evolves its own conventions. It is only the water but the banks which make the river.

*Indira Gandhi, in 1967*
Speeches and Writings, *1975*

47.26 ❧ As there were no black Founding Fathers, there were no founding mothers—a great pity on both counts.

*Shirley Chisholm*
Congressional Record, *Joint*
*Resolution 264, August 10, 1970*

47.27 ❧ Democracy, like any noncoercive relationship, rests on a shared understanding of limits.

*Elizabeth Drew*
Washington Journal, *1975*

47.28 ❧ Democracy is not a spectator sport.

*Marian Wright Edelman*
Families in Peril, *1987*

# *48.* DESIRE

*48.1* ❧ Desire can blind us to the hazards of our enterprises.

> *Marie de France,* 12th century
> Medieval Fables of Marie de France,
> *Jeannette Beer, tr., 1981*

*48.2* ❧ There is only one big thing—desire. And before it, when it is big, all is little.

> *Willa Cather*
> The Song of the Lark, *1915*

# *49.* DISSENT

*49.1* ❧ Dissent, not satisfied with toleration, is not conscience, but ambition.

> *Edmund Burke*
> *Speech on the Acts of Uniformity,*
> *House of Commons, February 1772*

*49.2* ❧ A little rebellion now and then is a good thing.

> *Thomas Jefferson*
> *On the Shays' Rebellion, c.1790*

*49.3* ❧ But freedom to differ is not limited to things that do not matter much. That would be a mere shadow of freedom. The test of its substance is the right to differ as to things that touch the heart of existing order.

> *Robert H. Jackson*
> West Virginia State Board of Education v.
> Barnette, *319 U.S. 624, 642 (1943)*

*49.4* ❧ The whole drift of our law is toward the absolute prohibition of all ideas that diverge in the slightest form from the accepted platitudes, and behind that drift of law there is a far more potent force of growing custom, and under that custom there is a natural philosophy which erects conformity into the noblest of virtues and the free functioning of personality into a capital crime against society.

> *H. L. Mencken, 1880–1956*
> New York Times Magazine,
> *August 9, 1964*

*49.5* ❧ The right to dissent is the only thing that makes life tolerable for a judge of an appellate court.

> *William O. Douglas*
> America Challenged, *1960*

*49.6* ❧ Dissent and dissenters have no monopoly on freedom. They must tolerate opposition. They must accept dissent from their dissent. And they must give it the respect and the latitude which they claim for themselves.

> *Abe Fortas*
> *"The Limits of Civil Disobedience,"*
> New York Times Magazine,
> *May 12, 1968*

**49.7** ❧ The long history of antiobscenity laws makes it very clear that such laws are most often invoked against political and life-style dissidents.

*Gloria Steinem*
*"Gazette News: Obscene?" Ms.,*
*October 1973*

**49.8** ❧ The "flatfoot mentality" insists that any individual or organization that wants to change *anything* in our present system is somehow subversive of "the American way," and should be under continuous surveillance—a task that appears to absorb most of our resources for fighting genuine crime.

*Toni Carabillo, American writer*
*"The 'Flatfoot Mentality,'" Hollywood*
*NOW News, August 1975*

**49.9** ❧ One generation's dissents have often become the rule of law years later.

*Irving Kaufman, American jurist*
*"Keeping Politics Out of the Court,"*
*New York Times, December 9, 1984*

---

# 50. DOUBT

---

**50.1** ❧ How long halt thee between two opinions?

*Old Testament, I Kings 4:25*

**50.2** ❧ To know much is often the cause of doubting more.

*Michel de Montaigne*
*Essais, 1588*

**50.3** ❧ What do I know? What does it matter?

*Michel de Montaigne,*
*1533–1592*
*Motto*

**50.4** ❧ If a man will begin with certainties, he shall end in doubts; but if he will be content to begin with doubts, he shall end in certainties.

*Francis Bacon*
*The Advancement of Learning, 1605*

**50.5** ❧ . . . certaintie is the mother of quietness and repose, and uncertaintie the cause of variance and contentions.

*Sir Edward Coke*
*The Institutes of the Lawes of*
*England, vol. 1, 1628–1641*

**50.6** ❧ Doubt grows with knowledge.

*Goethe*
*Sprüche in Prosa, 1819*

**50.7** ❧ I always thought it better to allow myself to doubt before I decided, than to expose myself to the misery after I had decided, of doubting whether I had decided rightly and justly.

*John Scott, Lord Eldon, 1751–1838*
*Horace Twiss, Life of Lord Eldon,*
*1844*

**50.8** ❧ I may be wrong, and often am, but I never doubt.

> *Sir George Jessel, English jurist, replying*
> *to a question about whether he had any*
> *doubts in reference to the* Alabama
> *claims (1871–1872)*
> *M. Frances McNamara,* Ragbag of
> Legal Quotations, *1960*

**50.9** ❧ . . . all things are presumed to have been rightly done unless there is reasonable ground shown for doubting it.

> *Sir James Hannen, British jurist*
> Woodhouse v. Balfour *(1887), L.R.*
> *13 Pr. D. 4*

**50.10** ❧ A new beatitude I write for thee,/"Blessed are they who are not sure of things."

> *Julia C.R. Dorr*
> *"A New Beatitude,"* Poems,
> *1897*

**50.11** ❧ But certainty is generally illusion, and repose is not the destiny of man.

> *Oliver Wendell Holmes*
> *"The Path of the Law,"*
> *10* Harvard Law Review *457*
> *(1897)*

**50.12** ❧ To have doubted one's own first principles is the mark of a civilized man.

> *Oliver Wendell Holmes*
> *"Ideals and Doubts," 10* Illinois Law
> Review *3 (1915)*

**50.13** ❧ To rest upon a formula is a slumber that, prolonged, means death.

> *Oliver Wendell Holmes*
> *"Ideals and Doubts," 10* Illinois Law
> Review *3 (1915)*

**50.14** ❧ Four be the things I'd been better without:/Love, curiosity, freckles, and doubt.

> *Dorothy Parker*
> *"Inventory,"* Enough Rope, *1926*

**50.15** ❧ An honest man can never surrender an honest doubt.

> *Walter Malone, 1866–1915*
> *Bergen Evans,* Dictionary of
> Quotations, *1968*

**50.16** ❧ . . . in my first years upon the bench. . . . I sought for certainty. I was oppressed and disheartened when I found that the quest for it was futile. I was trying to reach land, the solid land of fixed and settled rules, the paradise of a justice that would declare itself by tokens plainer and more commanding than its pale and glimmering reflections in my own vacillating mind and conscience.

> *Benjamin N. Cardozo*
> The Nature of the Judicial Process,
> *1921*

**50.17** ❧ Just think of the tragedy of teaching children not to doubt.

> *Clarence Darrow, 1857–1938*
> *Franklin Pierce Adams,* F.P.A.
> Book of Quotations, *1952*

50.18 ❦ . . . the old rule of "Give the accused the benefit of the doubt."

*Freeman W. Crofts, Irish mystery writer*
Circumstantial Evidence, *1941*

50.19 ❦ In the absence of eye-witnesses, there's always a shadow of a doubt. The law says "reasonable doubt," but I think a defendant's entitled to the shadow of a doubt. There's always the possibility, no matter how improbable, that he's innocent.

*Harper Lee*
To Kill a Mockingbird, *1960*

50.20 ❦ Increasingly constructive doubt is the sign of advancing civilization. We must put question marks alongside many of our inherited legal dogmas, since they are dangerously out of line with social facts.

*Jerome Frank*
Law and the Modern Mind, *1963*

50.21 ❦ The rather random observations and any tentative conclusions reached in this paper rest on opinion; here, the opinion of one who claims no special competence to observe or judge. Hence the Apologia:
Sage: My son, a man who is absolutely certain of anything is a fool!
Son: Are you sure?
Sage: Positive!

*Laurens Williams*
Toward More Effective Coordination
of the Work of Government
Personnel and Professional Groups in
Tax Legislation, *American Law
Institute, 1964*

# 51. DRUNKENNESS

51.1 ❦ Let us eat and drink, for tomorrow we die.

*New Testament, I Corinthians, 15:32*

51.2 ❦ Let him who sins when drunk, be punished when sober.

*Anonymous*
Kendrick v. Hopkins *(1580), Cary's
Rep. 133*

51.3 ❦ Oons, Sir! do you say that I am drunk? I say, Sir, that I am as sober as a judge; . . .

*Henry Fielding*
Don Quixote in England,
*1734*

51.4 ❦ Men intoxicated are sometimes stunned into sobriety.

*Sir James Mansfield, English jurist;
Chief Justice, 1733–1821*
Rex v. Wilkes *(1769), 4 Burr. Part
IV. 2563*

**51.5**  ❦ There is in all men a demand for the superlative, so much so that the poor devil who has no other way of reaching it attains it by getting drunk.

*Oliver Wendell Holmes*
*"Natural Law," 82* Harvard Law Review *(1918)*

**51.6**  ❦ The prohibition law, written for weaklings and derelicts, has divided the nation, like Gaul, into three parts—wets, drys and hypocrites.

*Florence Sabin, American scientist*
*Speech, February 9, 1931*

**51.7**  ❦ The horse and mule live thirty years
And nothing know of wines and beers;
The goat and sheep at twenty die,
And never taste of Scotch or Rye;
The cow drinks water by the ton
And at eighteen is mostly done;
Without the aid of rum and gin
The dog at fifteen cashes in;
The cat in milk and water soaks,
And then at twelve years old she croaks;
The modest, sober bone-dry hen
Lays eggs for nogs and dies at ten;
All animals are strictly dry;
They sinless live and swiftly die,
While sinful, gleeful rum-soaked men
Survive for three score years and ten.
And some of us—a mighty few—
Stay pickled 'till we're ninety-two.

*Harlan Fiske Stone, 1872–1946*
*Alpheus Thomas Mason,* Harlan Fisk Stone, Pillar of the Law, *1956*

# 52. DUE PROCESS

**52.1**  ❦ No man should be condemned unheard.

*Legal maxim*

**52.2**  ❦ That no man of what estate or condition, shall be put out of land or tenement, nor taken nor imprisoned, nor disinherited, nor put to death, without being brought in answer by due process of law.

*Statute of Westminister, c.13th century*

**52.3**  ❦ Nor shall any person . . . be deprived of life, liberty, or property, without due process of law.

*Constitution of the United States,*
*Fifth Amendment, 1791*

**52.4**  ❦ . . . nor shall any State deprive any person of life, liberty, or property, without due process of law. . . .

*Constitution of the United States,*
*14th Amendment, 1868*

52.5 ❧ Whatever disagreement there may be as to the scope of the phrase "due process of law" there can be no doubt that it embraces the fundamental conception of a fair trial, with opportunity to be heard.

*Oliver Wendell Holmes*
Frank v. Mangum, *237 U.S. 309, 347 (1915)*

52.6 ❧ Due process is a growth too sturdy to succumb to the infection of the least ingredient of error.

*Benjamin Cardozo*
Roberts v. New York, *295 U.S. 264, 278, 79 L.Ed. 1429, 1436, 55 S. Ct. 669 (1935)*

52.7 ❧ Bad men, like good men, are entitled to be tried and sentenced in accordance with law, . . .

*Hugo L. Black*
Green v. United States, *365 U.S. 301, 309–310 (1961)*

52.8 ❧ . . . freedom of personal choice in matters of marriage and family life is one of the liberties protected by the Due Process Clause of the Fourteenth Amendment. . . . That right necessarily includes the right of a woman to decide whether or not to terminate her pregnancy.

*Harry Blackmun*
Roe v. Wade, *410 U.S. 113, 93 S. Ct. 705, 35 L.Ed.2d 147 (1973)*

52.9 ❧ The worse the society, the more law there will be. In Hell there will be nothing but law and due process will be meticulously observed.

*Grant Gilmore*
New York Times,
*February 23, 1977*

# *53.* EDUCATION

**53.1** ❧ Equality! Where is it, if not in education? Equal rights! They cannot exist without equality of instruction.

*Frances Wright, English writer*
*"Of Free Enquiry,"* Course of Popular
Lectures, *1829*

**53.2** ❧ The highest result of education is tolerance.

*Helen Keller*
Optimism, *1903*

**53.3** ❧ . . . with the feminist ideal of education accepted in every home and school, and with all special barriers removed in every field of human activity, there is no reason why women should not become almost a human thing.

*Crystal Eastman, c. 1920*
*Dawn Bradley Berry,*
The 50 Most Influential Women in
American Law, *1996*

**53.4** ❧ The only thing better than education is more education.

*Agnes E. Benedict*
Progress to Freedom, *1942*

**53.5** ❧ Separate educational facilities are inherently unequal.

*Earl Warren*
Brown v. Board of Education
of Topeka,
*May 17, 1954*

**53.6** ❧ To be able to be caught up into the world of thought—that is to be educated.

*Edith Hamilton*
Adventures of the Mind,
*Richard Thruelsen and*
*John Kobler, eds.,* 1st series,
*1959*

# *54.* ENVIRONMENT

**54.1** ❧ Men as a general rule have very little reverence for trees.

*Elizabeth Cady Stanton*
Diary entry, *1900*

**54.2** ❧ A river is more than an amenity; it is a treasure.

*Oliver Wendell Holmes,*
New Jersey v. New York et al.,
*1931*

**54.3** ❦ As crude a weapon as a cave man's club, the chemical barrage has been hurled against the fabric of life.

*Rachel Carson*
Silent Spring, *1962*

**54.4** ❦ The supreme reality of our time is the vulnerability of our planet.

*John F. Kennedy*
Speech, June 28, 1963

# *55.* EQUALITY

**55.1** ❦ What is lawful to Jupiter is not lawful to the ox.

*Latin proverb*
*W. Gurney Benham,* Putnam's Book of Quotations, Proverbs and Household Words, *1927*

**55.2** ❦ The rich break the laws, and the poor are punished for it.

*Spanish proverb*
*Charles Cahier,* Quelques Six Milles Proverbes, *1856*

**55.3** ❦ Obey the law, whoever you be that made the law.

*Pittacus, Greek statesman and sage,*
c.650–570 B.C.
*Maxim*

**55.4** ❦ Would you say that all men are equal in excellence, or is one man better than another?

*Plato*
The Republic, *c.370* B.C.

**55.5** ❦ There is no occupation concerned with the management of social affairs which belongs either to women or to men, as such . . . and every occupation is open to both.

*Plato*
The Republic, *c.370* B.C.

**55.6** ❦ The law for the rich and poor is not the same.

*Plautus*
Cistellaria, *c.200* B.C.

**55.7** ❦ The nets not stretched to catch the hawk,
Or kite, who do us wrong; but laid for those
Who do us none at all.

*Terence*
Phormio, *161* B.C.

**55.8** ❦ The censor absolves the crow, and passes sentence on the dove.

*Juvenal*
Satires, *c.120*

**55.9** ❦ For if all things were equally in all men, nothing would be prized.

*Thomas Hobbes*
Leviathan,
*1651*

**55.10** ❦ It is not true that equality is a law of nature. Nature knows no equality. Its sovereign law is subordination and dependence.

*Marquis de Vauvenargues,*
*French moralist*
Réflexions, *1746*

**55.11** ❦ Law has no power to equalize men in defiance of nature.

*Marquis de Vauvenargues, French moralist, 1715–1747*
*W. Gurney Benham,* Putnam's Complete Book of Quotations, Proverbs and Household Words, *1927*

**55.12** ❦ All men have equal rights to liberty, to their property, and to the protection of the laws.

*Voltaire*
Essay on Manners, *1756*

**55.13** ❦ Laws are always useful to those who possess and vexatious to those who have nothing.

*Jean Jacques Rousseau*
Du Contrat Social, *1762*

**55.14** ❦ We hold these truths to be self-evident; that all men are created equal; that they are endowed by their Creator with certain unalienable rights; that among these are life, liberty, and the pursuit of happiness. . . .

*Declaration of Independence, July 4, 1776*

**55.15** ❦ Virtue can only flourish among equals.

*Mary Wollstonecraft*
A Vindication of the Rights of Men, *1790*

**55.16** ❦ When man, governed by reasonable laws, enjoys his natural freedom, let him despise woman, if she do not share it with him.

*Mary Wollstonecraft*
A Vindication of the Rights of Women, *1792*

**55.17** ❦ One law for the ox and the ass is oppression.

*William Blake, 1757–1827*
*W. H. Auden and Louis Kronenberger,* The Viking Book of Aphorisms, *1962*

**55.18** ❦ We hold these truths to be self-evident, that all men and women are created equal.

*Elizabeth Cady Stanton,* Declaration of Sentiments, *First Women's Rights Convention, Seneca Falls, NY, July 19–20, 1848*

**55.19** ❦ All men are free and equal *in the grave*, if it comes to that.

*Harriet Beecher Stowe*
Uncle Tom's Cabin, *1852*

**55.20** ❦ Has God given one half of his creatures talents and gifts that are but a mockery—wings but not to fly?

*Belva Lockwood, 1830–1917*
*Dawn Bradley Berry,* The 50 Most Influential Women in American Law, *1996*

**55.21** ❦ Four score and seven years ago our fathers brought forth on this continent, a new nation, conceived in Liberty, and dedicated to the proposition that all men are created equal.

*Abraham Lincoln*
Gettysburg Address, November 19, 1863

**55.22** ❦ Equality may be as much as anything equality of misery.

*Rudolph von Jhering, German jurist,*
*1818–1892*
Law as a Means to an End

**55.23** ❦ . . . there never will be complete equality until women themselves help to make laws and elect lawmakers.

*Susan B. Anthony*
*"The Status of Women, Past, Present*
*and Future," The Arena, May 1897*

**55.24** ❦ The law, in its majestic equality, forbids all men to sleep under bridges, to beg in the streets, and to steal bread—the rich as well as the poor.

*Anatole France*
Crainquebille, *1902*

**55.25** ❦ The Procrustean bed is not a symbol of equality.

*Felix Frankfurter*
New York v. United States, *331 U.S.*
*284, 353 (1947)*

**55.26** ❦ It was a wise man who said that there is no greater inequality than the equal treatment of unequals.

*Felix Frankfurter*
Dennis v. United States *339 U.S.*
*162, 184 (1950)*

**55.27** ❦ True equality can only mean the right to be uniquely creative.

*Erik H. Erikson*
The Woman in America, *1965*

**55.28** ❦ If the affluent flagrantly disregard the law, the poor and the deprived will follow their leadership.

*Robert M. Morgenthau*
New York Times, *June 26, 1969*

**55.29** ❦ The brutal fact is that convicted women . . . have not yet won the right to equal treatment in the criminal and juvenile justice system.

*Susan C. Ross, American lawyer*
The Rights of Women, *1973*

**55.30** ❦ The American Republic is now almost 200 years old, and in the eyes of the law women are still not equal with men. The special legislation which will remedy that situation is the Equal Rights Amendment. Its language is short and simple: *Equality of rights under the law shall not be abridged in the United States or by any state on account of sex.*

*Clare Boothe Luce*
Bulletin of the Baldwin School,
*Pennsylvania, September 1974*

**55.31** ❦ My greatest disappointment in all the projects I worked on during the White House years was the failure of the Equal Rights Amendment to be ratified . . . Why all the controversy and why such difficulty in giving women the protection of the Constitution that should have been theirs long ago?

*Rosalyn Carter*
First Lady From Plains, *1984*

**55.32** ❧ A sign that says "men only" looks very different on a bathroom door than a courthouse door.

*Thurgood Marshall*
City of Cleburne v. Cleburne Living
Center, Inc., *473 U.S. 432, 468–69,*
*1985*

**55.33** ❧ . . . it is only the exceptional woman who escapes gender inequality enough to be able to claim that she is injured by it. It seems that we al-

ready have to be equal before we can complain of inequality.

*Catharine A. MacKinnon*
*"On Exceptionality: Women as Women*
*in Law,"* Feminism Unmodified, *1987*

**55.34** ❧ We should focus less on the quest for gender differences and more on the inequality they create.

*Deborah L. Rhode*
Speaking of Sex, *1997*

# *56.* EQUITY

**56.1** ❧ A legal fiction is always consistent with equity.

*Legal maxim*

**56.2** ❧ Equity is that idea of justice, which contravenes the written law.

*Aristotle*
Rhetoric, *c.322* B.C.

**56.3** ❧ The umpire has regard to equity, the judge to law.

*Aristotle*
Rhetoric, *c.322* B.C.

**56.4** ❧ It is difficult, when you desire to assist everyone, to preserve equity, which appertains most especially to justice.

*Cicero*
De Officiis, *c.45–44* B.C.

**56.5** ❧ You wish nothing to be lawful to me, and all things to you.

*Martial, Roman epigrammatist*
Epigrams, *85*

**56.6** ❧ All the sentences of precedent judges that have ever been cannot altogether make a law contrary to natural equity.

*Thomas Hobbes*
Leviathan, *1651*

**56.7** ❧ Equity, in law, is the same that the spirit is in religion: What everyone pleases to make it.

*John Selden, English legal antiquarian*
*and politician, 1584–1654*
*"Equity,"* Table-Talk, *1689*

**56.8** ❧ Equity is a rougish thing. For Law we have to measure, know what to trust to; Equity is according to the conscience of him that is Chancellor, and as that is larger or narrower, so is Equity. 'Tis all one as if they should make the standard for the measure we call a "foot" a Chancellor's foot; what an uncertain measure would this be! One Chancellor has a long foot, another a short foot, a third an indifferent foot. 'Tis the same thing in the Chancellor's conscience.

*John Selden, 1584–1654*
*"Equity," Table-Talk, 1689*

56.9 ❦ Equality is equity.

*Richard Francis*
Maxims of Equity, *1728*

56.10 ❦ There is but one law for all, namely, that law which governs all law, the law of our Creator, the law of humanity, justice, equity—the law of nature and of nations.

*Edmund Burke, on May 28, 1794*
*W. Gurney Benham,*
Putnam's Complete Book of
Quotations, *1927*

56.11 ❦ There are two, and only two, foundations of law . . . equity and utility.

*Edmund Burke, 1729–1797*
Tracts on the Popery Laws

56.12 ❦ Law and equity are two things which God has joined, but which man hath put asunder.

*Charles Caleb Colton*
Lacon, *1820*

56.13 ❦ The flour merchant, the house builder, and the postman charge us no less on account of our sex; but when we endeavor to earn money to pay all these, then, indeed, we find the difference.

*Lucy Stone, Elizabeth Cady Stanton,*
*Susan B. Anthony, and*
*Matilda J. Gage, eds.,*
History of Woman Suffrage,
*vol. 1, 1881*

56.14 ❦ I have determined to make a specialty of equity. It is very interesting to me, and a very nice subject for a lady to pursue.

*Lettie Burlingame, 1859–1890,*
*diary entry*
*Dawn Bradley Berry,*
The 50 Most Influential Women in
American Law, *1996*

56.15 ❦ He who seeks equity must do equity.

*Joseph Story*
Equity Jurisprudence, *1896*

56.16 ❦ When we sum up the columns that make 'success' for the boy on the one hand and the girl on the other, you find the girl has the much longer column to add.

*Mabel Walker Willebrandt*
*"Give Women a Fighting Chance,"*
The Smart Set, *1930*

56.17 ❦ Equity speaks softly and wins in the end.

*Caroline Bird, American writer*
Born Female, *1968*

**56.18** ❦ Tremendous amounts of talent are being lost to our society just because that talent wears a skirt.

*Shirley Chisholm*
Unbought and Unbossed, *1970*

**56.19** ❦ We don't so much want to see a female Einstein become an assistant professor. We want a woman schlemiel to get promoted as quickly as a male schlemiel.

*Bella Abzug, 1977*
*Lois Gordon and Alan Gordon,*
American Chronicle, *1987*

**56.20** ❦ If you play by the rules, you deserve a fair day's pay for a fair day's work.

*Geraldine A. Ferraro*
Ferraro: My Story, *with*
*Linda Bird Franke, 1985*

**56.21** ❦ Women's equality under the law does not effortlessly translate into equal partnership in the legal profession.

*Sandra Day O'Connor*
Speech, *1985*

**56.22** ❦ The ceiling isn't glass; it's a very dense layer of men.

*Alice Jardim*
New Yorker, *1996*

# *57.* ERROR(S)

**57.1** ❦ The cautious seldom err.

*Confucius*
Analects, *c.500* B.C.

**57.2** ❦ I would rather err with Plato than perceive the truth with others.

*Cicero,* 106–43 B.C.
Tusculanae Disputationes

**57.3** ❦ An error is not counted as a crime.

*Seneca*
Hercules Octaeus, *c.60*

**57.4** ❦ The strength of our persuasions is no evidence at all of their own rectitude: crooked things may be as stiff and inflexible as straight: and men may be as positive and peremptory in error as in truth.

*John Locke*
An Essay Concerning Human
Understanding, *1690*

**57.5** ❦ The progress of rivers to the ocean is not so rapid as that of man to error.

*Voltaire*
A Philosophical Dictionary: Rivers,
*1764*

57.6 ❧ I know but of one Being to whom error may not be imputed.

*Edward Law, Lord Ellenborough,*
*English jurist; Chief Justice*
Rex v. Lambert and Perry *(1810),*
*2 Camp. 402*

57.7 ❧ Delay is preferable to error.

*Thomas Jefferson*
*To George Washington, May 16, 1792*

57.8 ❧ Mistakes are the inevitable lot of mankind.

*Sir George Jessel, English jurist*
Tomlin v. Underhay *(1882), L.R. 22*
*C.D. (1883)*

57.9 ❧ Lack of recent information . . . is responsible for more mistakes of judgment than erroneous reasoning.

*Matthew Arnold, 1822–1888*
*Louis D. Brandeis,* "The Living Law,"
The Curse of Bigness, *1935*

57.10 ❧ If someone made a mistake he [Darrow] would drawl, "Hell, that's why they make erasers."

*Clarence Darrow, 1857–1938*
*Irving Stone,* Clarence Darrow for
the Defense, *1941*

57.11 ❧ One utterance of [Oliver Cromwell] has always hung in my mind. It was just before the Battle of Dunbar; he beat the Scots in the end, as you know, after a very tough fight; but he wrote them before the battle, trying to get them to accept a reasonable composition. These were his words: "I beseech ye in the bowels of Christ, think that ye may be mistaken." I should like to have that written over the portals of every church, every school, and every court house, and, may I say, of every legislative body in the United States.

*Learned Hand*
*Irving Dilliard,* The Spirit of Liberty,
*1960*

# 58. ESTATES

58.1 ❧ When a festive occasion our spirit
　　　unbends
　　We should never forget the
　　　profession's best friends.
　　So we'll pass round the wine
　　And a light bumper fill
　　To the jolly testator who makes his
　　　own will.

*Anonymous*
*Jacob M. Brande,* Lifetime Speaker's
Encyclopedia, *1962*

58.2 ❧ Land was never lost for want of an heir.

*English proverb*
*John Ray,* Complete Collection of
English Proverbs, *1670*

**58.3** ❦ All things which are so written in a will as to be unintelligible are to be on that account regarded as though they were not written.

*Latin legal phrase*
*W. Gurney Benham,* Putnam's Complete Book of Quotations, Proverbs and Household Words, *1927*

**58.4** ❦ That which is ill-gotten a third heir hardly ever enjoys.

*Latin phrase*
*Thomas Walsingham,* Historia Anglicana, *c.1422*

**58.5** ❦ No one can be heir during the life of his ancestor.

*Legal maxim*

**58.6** ❦ The bestower of a gift has a right to regulate its disposal.

*Legal maxim*

**58.7** ❦ Dowries and inheritances bring no luck.

*Yiddish proverb*
*Joseph L. Baron,* A Treasury of Jewish Quotations, *1956*

**58.8** ❦ Who comes for the inheritance is often made to pay for the funeral.

*Yiddish proverb*
*Joseph L. Baron,*
A Treasury of Jewish Quotations, *1956*

**58.9** ❦ A lawyer's dream of heaven—every man reclaimed his property at the resurrection, and each tried to recover it from all his forefathers.

*Samuel Butler, 1612–1680*
*W. H. Auden and Louis Kronenberger,* The Viking Book of Aphorisms, *1962*

**58.10** ❦ There is no instance where men are so easily imposed upon, as at the time of their dying under the pretence of charity.

*William Cowper, English jurist;*
*Lord Chancellor*
Attorney-General v. Barnes et uxor *(1707), Gilbert Eq. Ca. 5*

**58.11** ❦ . . . man with all his wisdom, *toils for heirs he knows not who.*

*Andrew Kirkpatrick, American jurist*
William Nevision et al. v. James Taylor, *8 N.J.L. 43, 46 (1824)*

**58.12** ❦ There is an objection to the taxation of the inheritance of personal property of a very serious kind. It is that it is one law for the rich and another for the poor.

*J. E. T. Rogers, English economist*
The Economic Interpretation of History, *1888*

## 59. ETHICS

59.1 ❧ "Virtue down the middle," said the Devil as he sat down between two lawyers.

*Danish proverb*
*H. L. Mencken,*
*A New Dictionary of Quotations,*
*1946*

59.2 ❧ The law often permits what honor forbids.

*Bernard Joseph Saurin,*
*French tragic writer*
Spartacus, *1760*

59.3 ❧ Just to the windward of the law.

*Charles Churchill, English dramatist*
The Ghost,
*1762–1763*

59.4 ❧ . . . the man whose probity consists in merely obeying the laws, cannot be truly virtuous or estimable; for he will find many opportunities of doing contemptible and even dishonest acts, which the laws cannot punish.

*Stephanie Félicité Genlis, French*
*harpist and author*
*"Laws," Tales of the Castle,*
*c.1793*

59.5 ❧ We do not believe the less in astronomy and vegetation because we are writhing and roaring in our beds with rheumatism.

*Walt Whitman*
The Sovereignty of Ethics,
*1878*

59.6 ❧ I will not counsel or maintain any suit or proceeding which shall appear to me to be unjust, nor any defense except such as I believe to be honestly debatable under the law of the land.

*Oath for Candidates for Admission to*
*the Bar, American Bar Association,*
*c.1925*

59.7 ❧ There are . . . many forms of professional misconduct that do not amount to crimes.

*Benjamin N. Cardozo*
People ex rel. Karlin v. Culkin, *248*
*N.Y. 465, 470 (1928)*

59.8 ❧ As to ethics, the parties seem to me as much on a parity as the pot and the kettle.

*Robert H. Jackson*
Mercoid Corporation v.
Mid-Continent Co. *320 U.S. 661,*
*679 (1944)*

59.9 ❧ In civilized life, law floats in a sea of ethics.

*Earl Warren*
New York Times,
*November 12, 1962*

59.10 ❧ We [lawyers] must alter our prime axiom—that we are combat mercenaries available indifferently for any cause or purpose a client is ready to finance. . . . We should all be what I would term "ministers of justice." As such, we would have to reconsider and revise a system of loyalty to clients that results too often in coverups, frauds, and injury to innocent people. A favorite quotation in the legal profession . . . is Lord Brougham's declaration that an advocate "knows but one person in all the world, and that person is his client. . . ." For him Lord Brougham said, the advocate would stand against the world . . . Lord

Brougham was wrong; we should be less willing to fight the world and . . . more concerned to save our own souls. As ministers of justice, we should find ourselves more positively concerned than we now are with the pursuit of truth.

*Marvin E. Frankel, American jurist;*
*judge, U.S. District Court*
Washington Post, *May 7, 1978*

# *60.* EVIDENCE

60.1 ❧ Judge a man not by the words of his mother, but from the comments of his neighbors.

*Jewish folk saying*
*Leo Rosten,*
Treasury of Jewish
Quotations, *1972*

60.2 ❧ The drunkard smells of whiskey—but so does the bartender.

*Jewish folk saying*
*Joseph L. Baron,* A Treasury of Jewish
Quotations, *1956*

60.3 ❧ To assume is to fool one's self.

*Jewish folk saying*
*Joseph L. Baron,* A Treasury of Jewish
Quotations, *1956*

60.4 ❧ Where there is room for question, something is wrong.

*Jewish folk saying*
*Joseph L. Baron,* A Treasury of Jewish
Quotations, *1956*

60.5 ❧ You don't have to see the lion if you see his hair.

*Jewish folk saying*
*Joseph L. Baron,* A Treasury of Jewish
Quotations, *1956*

60.6 ❧ And I would sooner trust the smallest slip of paper for truth, than the strongest and most retentive memory, ever bestowed on mortal man.

*Joseph Henry Lumpkin, American jurist*
Miller and others v. Cotton
and others, 5 Ga. 341, 349
(1848)

60.7 ❧ If a man go into the London Docks sober without means of getting drunk, and comes out of one of the cellars very drunk wherein are a million gallons of wine, I think that would be reasonable evidence that he had stolen some of the wine in that cellar, though you could not prove that any wine was stolen, or any wine was missed.

*Sir William Henry Maule,*
*English jurist*
*Reg. v. Burton (1854), Dearsly's C.C.*
*284*

60.8 ❧ Some circumstantial evidence is very strong, as when you find a trout in the milk.

*Henry David Thoreau,1817–1862*
*W. H. Auden and Louis Kronenberger,*
*The Viking Book of Aphorisms, 1962*

60.9 ❧ Human nature constitutes a part of the evidence in every case.

*Elisha R. Potter, American jurist*
*Green v. Harris, HRI 5, 17 (1875)*

60.10 ❧ But evidence drawn empirically from facts, though it may justify the action of the practical man, is not scientifically conclusive.

*Beatrice Potter Webb, English sociologist*
*and social reformer*
*"The Economics of Factory Legislation,"*
*Socialism and National Minimum,*
*1909*

60.11 ❧ My friend—had to save him. The evidence of a woman devoted to him would not have been enough—you hinted as much yourself. But I know something of the psychology of crowds. Let my evidence be wrung from me, as an admission, damning me in the eyes of the law, and a reaction in favor of the prisoner would immediately set in.

*Agatha Christie*
*Witness for the Prosecution, 1924*

60.12 ❧ It is for ordinary minds, and not for psychoanalysts, that our rules of evidence are framed.

*Benjamin N. Cardozo*
*Shepard v. United States, 290 U.S.*
*96, 104 (1933)*

60.13 ❧ Chemists employed by the police can do remarkable things with blood. They can find it in shreds of cloth, in the interstices of floor boards, on the iron of a heel, and can measure it and swear to it and weave it into a rope to hang a man.

*Margery Allingham, English writer*
*The Tiger in the Smoke, 1952*

60.14 ❧ . . . the allowance of the privilege to withhold evidence that is demonstrably relevant in a criminal trial would cut deeply into the guarantee of due process of law and gravely impair the basic function of the courts.

*Warren E. Burger*
*United States v. Nixon, 418 U.S.*
*683, 94 S. Ct. 3090, 41 L.Ed.2d*
*1039 (1974)*

## *61.* EVIL

**61.1**  That which is evil is soon learn't.
*English proverb*
*John Ray,* English Proverbs, *1670*

**61.2**  Virtue and vice divide the world;
but vice has got the greater share.
*German proverb*
*Thomas Fuller,* Gnomologia, *1732*

**61.3**  Better suffer a great evil than do little one.
*Proverb*
*H. G. Bohn,* Handbook of Proverbs,
*1855*

**61.4**  Why does the way of the wicked prosper?
*Old Testament, Jeremiah 12:1*

**61.5**  Evil deeds never prosper.
*Homer*
Odyssey, *c.8th century* B.C.

**61.6**  It is not noble to return evil for evil; at no time ought we do an injury to our neighbors.
*Plato*
Crito, *c.350* B.C.

**61.7**  To a good man nothing that happens is evil.
*Plato, 427–347* B.C.
Apology

**61.8**  One evil flows from another.
*Terence*
Eunuchus, *c.160* B.C.

**61.9**  He who is bent on doing evil can never want occasion.
*Publilius Syrus, Latin writer*
Sententiae, *c.43* B.C.

**61.10**  An evil life is a kind of death.
*Ovid*
Epistulae ex Ponto, *c.5*

**61.11**  The evil best known is the most tolerable.
*Livy*
History of Rome, *c.10*

**61.12**  It is not goodness to be better than the worst.
*Seneca*
Epistulae Morales ad Lucilium,
*c.63–65*

**61.13**  Justice has but one form, evil has many.
*Moses Ben Jacob Meir Ibn Ezra,*
*Spanish-Hebrew poet and philosopher,*
*c.1070–1130*
Shirat Yisrael, *1924*

**61.14**  Of two evils we should always choose the less.
*Thomas Kempis*
Imitation of Christ, *c.1420*

**61.15** There are three all-powerful evils:
lust, anger and greed.

*Tulsī Dās, Hindu poet*
Rāmāyan, *1574*

**61.16** All evils become equal when they are
extreme.

*Pierre Corneille, French dramatist*
Horace, *1639*

**61.17** There are men of whom we can
never believe evil without having
seen it. Yet there are few in whom
we should be surprised to see it.

*La Rochefoucauld*
Maximes, *1665*

**61.18** Where two evils [are] present, a wise
administration, if there be room for
an option, will choose the least.

*Sir Michael Foster, English jurist*
Case of Pressing Mariners *(1743), 18*
*How. St. Tr. 1330*

**61.19** No evil without its advantages.

*William Hone*
Every-Day Book, *1827*

**61.20** I think the old, sound, and honest
maxim that "*you shall not do evil that
good may come,*" is applicable in law
as well as in morals.

*Sir Alexander James Edmund*
*Cockburn, British jurist;*
*Lord Chief Justice*
Reg. v. Hicklin and another *(1868),*
*11 Cox, C.C. 27; S.C. 3 L.R.Q.B. 372*

**61.21** There is in many, if not in all men, a
constant inward struggle between
the principles of good and evil; and
because a man has grossly fallen, and
at the time of his fall added the guilt
of hypocrisy to another sort of
immorality, it is not necessary, therefore, to believe that his whole life
has been false, or that all the good
which he ever professed was
insincere or unreal.

*Roundell Palmer, 1st earl of Selborne,*
*British jurist; Lord Chancellor*
Symington v. Symington
*(1875),*
*L.R. 2 Sc. & D. 428*

**61.22** It is a sin to believe evil of others,
but it is seldom a mistake.

*H. L. Mencken,*
A Book of Burlesques, *1916*

**61.23** Evil becomes an operative motive far
more easily than good. . . .

*Simone Weil, French philosopher*
L'Enracinement, *1949*

**61.24** They did not know . . . that the
same force that had made him toler-
ant, was now the force that made
him ruthless—that the justice which
would forgive miles of innocent
errors of knowledge, would not
forgive a single step taken in
conscious evil.

*Ayn Rand*
Atlas Shrugged, *1957*

61.25 ❧ Evil is not something superhuman, it's something less than human.

*Agatha Christie*
The Pale Horse, *1961*

61.26 ❧ It is by the promise of an occult sense of power that evil often attracts the weak.

*Eric Hoffer, American philosopher*
*W. H. Auden and Louis Kronenberger,*
The Viking Book of Aphorisms, *1962*

61.27 ❧ The banality of evil.

*Hannah Arendt*
Eichmann in Jerusalem, *1963*

61.28 ❧ Evil is obvious only in retrospect.

*Gloria Steinem*
Outrageous Acts and Everyday
Rebellions, *1983*

61.29 ❧ Here's a rule I recommend. Never practice two vices at once.

*Tallulah Bankhead, 1903–1968*

61.30 ❧ When choosing between two evils, I always like to try the one I've never tried before.

*Mae West, 1892–1980*

# *62.* FACTS

62.1 ❦ We should not investigate facts by the light of arguments, but arguments by the light of facts.

> *Myson, of Chen, one of the Seven Sages,*
> c.600 B.C.
> *Burton Stevenson,* Home Book of
> Proverbs, Maxims and Familiar
> Phrases, *1948*

62.2 ❦ When speculation has done its worst, two and two still make four.

> *Samuel Johnson*
> The Idler, *c.1758*

62.3 ❦ Facts are apt to alarm us more than the most dangerous principles.

> *Junius, unidentified English letter writer*
> *A letter to the* Public Advertiser, *1769*

62.4 ❦ There is nothing more horrible than the murder of a beautiful theory by a brutal gang of facts.

> *La Rochefoucauld,*
> *1747–1827*

62.5 ❦ Facts are stubborn things.

> *Ebenezer Elliott, 1781–1849*
> Field Husbandry

62.6 ❦ The state of a man's mind is as much fact as the state of his digestion.

> *Charles Bowen, English jurist*
> Edgington v. Fitzmaurice *(1884),*
> *29 L.R., Ch. Div. 459, 483*

62.7 ❦ Fact and fancy look alike across the years that link the past with the present.

> *Helen Keller*
> The Story of My Life, *1903*

62.8 ❦ This is not a matter for polite presumptions; we must look facts in the face.

> *Oliver Wendell Holmes*
> Frank v. Mangum, *237 U.S. 309,*
> *347 (1915)*

62.9 ❦ No law, apart from a Lawgiver, is a proper object of reverence. It is merely a brute fact.

> *William Temple, English clergyman;*
> *archbishop of Canterbury*
> Nature, Man, and God, *1934*

62.10 ❦ No facts however indubitably detected, no effort of reason however magnificently maintained, can prove that Bach's music is beautiful.

> *Edith Hamilton*
> Witness to the Truth,
> *1948*

62.11 ❦ . . . take as your motto this thought from Huxley: "God give me strength to face a fact though it slay me."

> *Bernard Baruch*
> A Philosophy for
> Our Time, *1954*

*62.12* ✣ "... facts are like cows. If you look them in the face hard enough they generally run away."

Dorothy L. Sayers
Clouds of Witness, *1956*

*62.13* ✣ While it is not always profitable to analogize "fact" to "fiction," La Fontaine's fable of the crow, the cheese, and the fox demonstrates that there is a substantial difference between holding a piece of cheese in the beak and putting it in the stomach.

Felix Frankfurter
Alleghany Corp. v. Breswick & Co.,
*353 U.S. 151, 170 (1957)*

*62.14* ✣ ... I fear that the American people are ahead of their leaders in realism and courage—but behind them in knowledge of the facts because the facts have not been given to them.

Margaret Chase Smith
Speech to U.S. Senate,
*September 21, 1961*

*62.15* ✣ We want the facts to fit the preconceptions. When they don't, it is easier to ignore the facts than to change the preconceptions.

Jessamyn West, American writer
The Quaker Reader, *1962*

*62.16* ✣ Facts do not cease to exist because they are ignored.

Aldous Huxley, 1894–1963
A Note on Dogma

*62.17* ✣ The ends of criminal justice would be defeated if judgements were to be founded on a partial or speculative presentation of the facts. The very integrity of the judicial system and public confidence in the system depend on full disclosure of all the facts, within the framework of the rules of evidence.

Warren E. Burger
United States v. Nixon, *418 U.S.
683, 94 S. Ct. 3090, 41 L.Ed.2d
1039 (1974)*

*62.18* ✣ [A lawyer's] performance in the courtroom is responsible for about 25 percent of the outcome; the remaining 75 percent depends on the facts.

Melvin Belli
U.S. News & World Report,
*September 20, 1982*

*62.19* ✣ There's a world of difference between truth and facts. Facts can obscure the truth.

Maya Angelou
Brian Lanker, I Dream a World, *1989*

*62.20* ✣ If it does not fit, then you must acquit.

Johnnie L. Cochran
Journey to Justice, *with Tim Rutten,
1996*

## *63.* FALSEHOOD

**63.1**  ❦ No law for lying.

> *Proverb*
> *Rosalind Fergusson,* The Facts On File
> Dictionary of Proverbs, *1983*

**63.2**  ❦ A hair perhaps divides the false
and true.

> *Omar Khayyám, 1048–1122*
> The Rubáyiát

**63.3**  ❦ This is a false, perjured, and for-
sworn man.

> *Inscription on a paper put over the head of a*
> *man set up in the pillory in the marketplace,*
> *Canterbury, England, 1524*

**63.4**  ❦ As false as dicers' oaths.

> *Shakespeare*
> Hamlet, *III, 4, 1600–1601*

**63.5**  ❦ Sin has many tools, but a lie is the
handle which fits them all.

> *Oliver Wendell Holmes*
> The Autocrat of the Breakfast Table,
> *1858*

**63.6**  ❦ There are three kinds of lies: lies,
damned lies, and statistics.

> *Benjamin Disraeli*
> *Franklin Pierce Adams,* F.P.A. Book of
> Quotations, *1952*

**63.7**  ❦ When Falsehood saw he had no legs,
he made himself wings.

> *Simchah Ben Zion, Hebrew translator*
> Luah Achiasaf, *1897*

**63.8**  ❦ To have no occasion for lying does
not yet mean to be honest.

> *Arthur Schnitzler*
> Buch der Sprüche und Bedenken,
> *1927*

**63.9**  ❦ I know the face of Falsehood and
her tongue
Honeyed with unction, plausible
with guile. . . .

> *Edna St. Vincent Millay*
> *"Fatal Interview,"* Fatal Interview,
> *1931*

## *64.* FAMILY

**64.1**  ❦ They wish to know the family secrets and to be feared accordingly.

> *Juvenal*
> Satire III, *113*

**64.2**  ❦ I have assisted in drawing a grand
and petit jury, deposited a ballot,
and helped canvass the voters after
the electing, and in performing all
those duties I do not know as I have

neglected my family any more than in ordinary shopping.

*Esther McQuigg Morris, in the*
Laramie Sentinel, *1871*
*Dawn Bradley Berry,* The 50 Most
Influential Women in American Law,
*1996*

64.3 ❧ If the hogs of the nation are ten times more important than the children, it is high time that women should make their influence felt.

*Jeannette Rankin*
*Campaign speech on federal government*
*appropriation of $300,000 to study*
*fodder for hogs and only $30,000 to*
*study children's needs, 1916*

64.4 ❧ Pluck from under the family all the props which religion and morality have given it, strip it of the glamour, true or false, cast round it by romance, it will still remain a prosaic, indisputable fact, that the whole business of begetting, bearing and rearing children, is the most essential of all the nation's businesses.

*Eleanor F. Rathbone*
*English politician, suffragist*
The Disinherited Family, *1924*

64.5 ❧ Being a mother is a noble status, right? So why does it change when you put "unwed" or "welfare" in front of it?

*Florynce Kennedy*
*Gloria Steinem, "The Verbal Karate of*
*Florynce Kennedy, Esq." Ms., 1973*

64.6 ❧ Women who pack lunch for their kids, or take the early bus to work, or stay out late at the PTA, or spend every spare minute tending to their aging parents do not need lectures from Washington about values.

*Hillary Rodham Clinton*
*Commencement Speech, Wellesley*
*College, May 29, 1992*

64.7 ❧ It is a national shame that many Americans are more thoughtful about planning their weekend entertainment than about planning their families.

*Hillary Rodham Clinton*
It Takes a Village and Other Lessons
Children Teach Us,
*1996*

64.8 ❧ All mothers, married or not, are affected by how the law treats married women with children.

*Edward J. McCaffery*
Taxing Women, *1997*

# 65. FEES

**65.1**  ❦ A lawyer and a wagon-wheel must be well greased.

> *German proverb*
> *H. L. Mencken,*
> A New Dictionary
> of Quotations, *1946*

**65.2**  ❦ Doctors purge the body, preachers the conscience, lawyers the purse.

> *German proverb*
> *Charles Cahier*
> Quelques Six Mille Proverbes, *1856*

**65.3**  ❦ A lawyer's opinion is worth nothing unless paid for.

> *Proverb*
> *Rosalind Fergusson,* The Facts On File
> Dictionary of Proverbs, *1983*

**65.4**  ❦ Lawyers' houses are built on the heads of fools.

> *Proverb*
> *Thomas Fuller,* Gnomologia, *1732*

**65.5**  ❦ Law's costly: tak' a pint and 'gree.

> *Scottish proverb*
> *W. Gurney Benham,* Putnam's
> Complete Book of Quotations,
> Proverbs and Household Words, *1927*

**65.6**  ❦ No fee, no law.

> *Gabriel Harvey, English writer*
> Works, *1597*

**65.7**  ❦ Agree, for the law is costly.

> *William Camden, English antiquarian*
> *and historian*
> Remains, *1605*

**65.8**  ❦ 'Tis like the breath of an unfee'd lawyer;
> you gave me nothing for 't.

> *Shakespeare*
> King Lear, *I, 4, 1605–1606*

**65.9**  ❦ A man may as well as open an oyster without a knife, as a lawyer's mouth without a fee.

> *Barten Holyday, English writer*
> Technogamia, *1618*

**65.10**  ❦ Litigious terms, fat contentions and flowing fees.

> *John Milton*
> Tractate on Education, *1644*

**65.11**  ❦ If you simply buy a house,
> He will take note of every interview,
> And charge you for receiving your instructions,
> Charge you likewise for drawing up the same—
> Eight folio pages with a world of margin;
> Charge you likewise for copying the same,
> Charge you likewise for reading you the same,
> And reading of it to the other party;
> Charge you likewise for reading long reply
> From Finden, lawyer, with a draft agreement;

Charge you likewise perusing said
draft;
Charge you likewise transmitting
draft agreement.

*James Hurnard*
*"The Setting Sun," 1871*

65.12 ❦ First, I charge a retainer; then I
charge a reminder; next I charge a re-
fresher; and then I charge a finisher.

*Judah P. Benjamin, 1811–1884*
*P. J. Clark,* Great Sayings by Great
Lawyers, *1926*

65.13 ❦ Go to the court o' last resort
For the sake o' your poor family!
The Lord sustain! My client's gane,
He's ruined—but I've got my fee!

*George Outram*
Legal and Other Lyrics, *1888*

65.14 ❦ The old judge had a picture, promi-
nently displayed, of an English barrister flourishing an oyster on a fork
as two countrymen, holding the
shells, looked on agape. Underneath
was the couplet:
A pearly shell for you and me;
The oyster is the lawyer's fee.

*Harvey O'Connor,*
Mellon's Millions, The Biography
of a Fortune,
*1933*

65.15 ❦ I dislike sending in professional
charges to friendly people, but we
have a saying here that offices like individuals have to live.

*Reginald L. Hine, American jurist*
Confessions of an Un-Common
Attorney, *1945*

65.16 ❦ When there's a rift in the lute, the
business of a lawyer is to widen the
rift and gather the loot.

*Arthur Garfield Hays, American*
*lawyer, 1881–1954*
*Leonard Lewis Levinson,* Bartlett's
Unfamiliar Quotations, *1971*

65.17 ❦ I get paid for seeing that my clients
have every break the law allows. I
have knowingly defended a number
of guilty men. But the guilty never
escape unscathed. My fees are sufficient punishment for anyone.

*F. Lee Bailey*
Los Angeles Times,
*January 9, 1972*

65.18 ❦ I don't charge by the hour or by the
day. I'm not a mechanic. I'm an artist. If you are going to use the time
to be a bookkeeper, you can't be a
trial lawyer.

*Percy Foreman*
Dallas Times Herald,
*May 12, 1972*

65.19 ❦ . . . lawyers do not unfairly charge
their clients. Rather, they simply do
not dispense legal services efficiently.

*James D. Fellers, American lawyer;*
*president, American Bar Association*
Los Angeles Times,
*May 30, 1975*

65.20 ❦ For many middle-income people, using a lawyer is like going to a dentist. They only go when they have
to, because the costs of legal services

prevent their using lawyers for preventive services.

*Philip J. Murphy, American lawyer*
New York Times, *January 18, 1976*

65.21 ❧ The cost of rendering legal services today has become so high that in modest matters lawyers cannot afford to undertake the work and prospective clients cannot afford to retain lawyers.

*Justin A. Stanley, American lawyer;*
*president, American Bar Association*
New York Times, *May 2, 1976*

65.22 ❧ The legal profession has indicated in its operative canons of ethics that the principal responsibility for the representation of people unable to afford legal fees ought to be placed on the profession itself. . . . The bar has a fundamental responsibility to undertake that which its own set of ethics imposes. And we do think it somewhat troublesome that a bar whose members' total gross income

now substantially exceeds $20 billion a year needs to lobby for a wholly Federally funded program in order to exercise its own responsibility.

*Michael J. Horowitz, American lawyer*
New York Times, *June 28, 1981*

65.23 ❧ The [legal] fees are outrageous. With the cost of litigation these days, I think clients would often be better off if they just met in the halls and threw dice. Certainly it would be cheaper.

*Walter McLaughlin, American jurist;*
*Chief Justice, Supreme Court*
*of Massachusetts*
Time, *July 27, 1981*

65.24 ❧ Lawyers like to leave no stone unturned, provided they can charge by the stone.

*Deborah L. Rhode*
*"Ethical Perspectives on Legal Practice,"*
Stanford Law Review, *January 1985*

# 66. FRAUD

66.1 ❧ He is not deemed to give consent who is under a mistake.

*Latin legal phrase*
W. Gurney Benham, Putnam's
Complete Book of Quotations,
Proverbs and Household Words, *1927*

66.2 ❧ No one can bring an action upon his own fraud.

*Latin legal phrase*
W. Gurney Benham, Putnam's
Complete Book of Quotations,
Proverbs and Household Words, *1927*

66.3 ❧ Frauds are not frauds, unless you make a practice of deceit.

*Plautus, 254?–184* B.C.
Captivi

66.4 ❧ Fraud and deceit abound in these days more than in former times.

*Sir Edward Coke*
Twyne's Case, *1602*

66.5 ❧ Fraud may consist as well in the suppression of what is true as in the representation of what is false.

*Justice Heath, English jurist*
Tapp v. Lee *(1803), 3 Bos. & Pull, 371*

66.6 ❧ The strongest mind cannot always contend with deceit and falsehood.

*Sir William Draper Best, Lord*
*Wynford, British jurist; Chief Justice*
Blackford v. Christian *(1829),*
*1 Knapp, 77*

66.7 ❧ Fraud includes the pretense of knowledge when knowledge there is none.

*Benjamin Cardozo*
Ultramares Corporation v. Touche,
*255 N.Y. 170, 179 (1931)*

66.8 ❧ Laws are made to protect the trusting as well as the suspicious.

*Hugo L. Black*
Federal Trade Commission v.
Standard Education Society, *302 U.S.*
*112, 116 (1937)*

66.9 ❧ . . . nobody wants a prosaic explanation of fraud and greed.

*Margery Allingham, English writer*
The Villa Marie Celeste, *1960*

66.10 ❧ Secrecy is the badge of fraud.

*Sir John Chadwick, British judge*
Independent, *London, July 26, 1990*

# 67. FREEDOM

67.1 ❧ Slavery and freedom, when excessive, are evils; but when moderate are altogether good.

*Plato, 427–347* B.C.
Epistle 8

67.2 ❧ Law alone can give us freedom.

*Goethe, 1749–1832*
*W. Gurney Benham,* Putnam's
Complete Book of Quotations,
Proverbs and Household Words, *1927*

67.3 ❧ In every human breast, God has implanted a principle, which we call love of freedom; it is impatient of oppression and pants for deliverance.

*Phyllis Wheatley*
The Boston Post-Boy, *1774*

67.4  ❦  The law will never make men free; it is men who have got to make the law free.

*Henry David Thoreau*
Slavery in Massachusetts, *1854*

67.5  ❦  In giving freedom to the slave we assure freedom to the free—honorable alike in what we give and what we preserve.

*Abraham Lincoln*
Annual message to Congress, *1862*

67.6  ❦  . . . true emancipation begins neither at the polls nor in courts. It begins in women's soul.

*Emma Goldman*
*"The Tragedy of Women's Emancipation,"* Anarchism and Other Essays, *1911*

67.7  ❦  It is necessary to grow accustomed to freedom before one may walk in it sure-footedly.

*Suzanne LaFollette*
Concerning Women, *1926*

67.8  ❦  . . . sunlight is the best of disinfectants. . . .

*Louis D. Brandeis, 1856–1941*
New York Times,
*February 15, 1984*

67.9  ❦  Liberty cannot be caged into a charter and handed on ready made to the next generation. Each generation must re-create liberty for its own times. Whether or not we establish freedom rests with ourselves.

*Florence Ellinwood Allen*
This Constitution of Ours, *1940*

67.10  ❦  None who have always been free can understand the terrible fascinating power of the hope of freedom to those who are not free.

*Pearl S. Buck*
What America Means to Me,
*1943*

67.11  ❦  The mark of a truly civilized man is confidence in the strength and security derived from the inquiring mind.

*Felix Frankfurter*
Dennis v. United States, *341 U.S. 494, 556 (1951)*

67.12  ❦  Freedom is not a luxury that we can indulge in when at last we have security and prosperity and enlightenment; it is, rather, antecedent to all of these, for without it we can have neither security nor prosperity nor enlightenment.

*Henry Steele Commager*
Freedom, Loyalty, Dissent, *1954*

67.13  ❦  Each freedom gained in theory is balanced by one lost in fact.

*C. Northcote Parkinson*
New York Law Journal,
*December 19, 1963*

67.14  ❦  The essence of a free life is being able to choose the style of living you prefer free from exclusion and without the compulsion of conformity or law.

*Eleanor Holmes Norton*
Commencement address, Barnard
College, June 6, 1972

67.15 ❧ [A]nyone with an ounce of political analysis should know that freedom before equality, freedom before justice, will only further liberate the power of the powerful and will never free what is most in need of expression.

*Catharine A. MacKinnon*
*Introduction,* Feminism Unmodified,
*1987*

67.16 ❧ The function of freedom is to free somebody else.

*Toni Morrison, 1931–*

67.17 ❧ Freedom means the right to assemble, organize, and debate openly. It means not taking citizens away from their loved ones and jailing them, mistreating them, or denying them their freedom or dignity because of peaceful expression of their ideas and opinions.

*Hillary Rodham Clinton*
*Speech, Fourth World Conference on*
*Women, Beijing, China, Sept. 5, 1995*

# *68.* GOD'S LAW

68.1 ❧ . . . he that keepeth the law, happy
is he.

*Old Testament, Proverbs, 29:18*

68.2 ❧ But his delight is in the law of the
Lord; and in his law will he exercise
himself day and night.

*Old Testament, Psalms 1:2*

68.3 ❧ But the fruit of the Spirit is love, joy,
peace, longsuffering, gentleness,
goodness, faith.
Meekness, temperance: against such
there is no law.

*New Testament, Galatians 5:22–23*

68.4 ❧ If ye then, being evil, know how to
give good gifts unto your children,
how much more shall your Father
which is in heaven give good things
to them that ask him?
Therefore all things whatsoever ye
would that men should do to you,
do ye even so to them: for this is the
law and the prophets.

*New Testament, Matthew 7:11–12*

68.5 ❧ Jesus said unto him, Thou shalt love
the Lord thy God with all thy heart,
and with all thy soul, and with all
thy mind.
This is the first and great commandment.
And the second is like unto it, Thou
shalt love thy neighbor as
thyself.
On these two commandments
hang all the law and the prophets.

*New Testament, Matthew 22:37–40*

68.6 ❧ For when the Gentiles, which have
not the law, do by nature the
things contained in the law, these,
having not the law, are a law unto
themselves.

*New Testament, Romans 2:14*

68.7 ❧ Render therefore to all their dues:
tribute to whom tribute is due; custom to whom custom; fear to whom
fear, honour to whom honour.
Owe no man any thing but to
love one another: for he that loveth
another hath fulfilled the law.

*New Testament, Romans 13:7–8*

68.8 ❧ Just as it is forbidden to permit that
which is prohibited, so it is forbidden to prohibit that which should
be permitted.

*Talmud, Terumot*

68.9 ❧ Charity itself fulfills the law.

*Shakespeare*
*Love's Labour's Lost, I, 3, 1594–1595*

*68.10* ❦ Who sees not, that whosoever ministers to the poor, ministers to God? as
it appears in that solemn sentence of
the last day, Inasmuch as you did
feed, clothe, lodge the poor, you did
it unto me.

*Sir Henry Hobart, English jurist;*
*Chief Justice*
*Pits v. James (1614), Lord Hobart's*
*Rep. 125*

*68.11* ❦ The wildest scorner of his Maker's
laws
Finds in a sober moment time to
pause.

*William Cowper, 1731–1800*
*Tirocinium*

*68.12* ❦ Be just—not like man's law, which
seizes on one isolated fact, but like
God's judging angel, whose clear,
sad eye saw all the countless canker-
ing days of this man's life. . . .

*Rebecca Harding Davis, American*
*social critic and writer*
*"Life in the Iron Mills," Atlantic*
*Monthly, April 1861*

*68.13* ❦ But men never violate the laws of
God without suffering the consequences, sooner or later.

*Lydia M. Child*
*American abolitionist and editor*
*"Toussaint L'Ouverture," The*
*Freedman's Book, 1865*

*68.14* ❦ A difficult form of virtue is to try in
your own life to obey what you
believe to be God's will.

*John Duke Coleridge, English jurist;*
*Lord Chief Justice*
*Reg. v. Ramsey (1883), 1 Cababé and*
*Ellis's Q.B.D. Rep. 145*

*68.15* ❦ Once early in the morning . . . when
the master was asleep, the books in
the library began to quarrel with
each other as to which was the king
of the library. The dictionary con-
tended quite angrily that he was the
master of the library because without words there would be no communication at all. The book of
science argued stridently that he was
the master of the library for without
science there would have been no
printing press or any of the other
wonders of the world. The book of
poetry claimed that he was . . . the
master of the library, because he
gave surcease and calm to his master
when he was troubled. The books of
philosophy, the economic books, all
put in their claims, and the clamor
was great and the noise at its height
when a small low voice was heard
from an old brown book lying in
the center of the table and the voice
said, "The Lord is my shepherd, I
shall not want." And all of the noise
and the clamor in the library ceased,
and there was a hush in the library,
for all of the books knew who the
real master of the library was.

*Louis Nizer*
*"Ministers of Justice," Tennessee Law*
*Review, Fall 1963*

# *69.* GOVERNMENT

**69.1** ❦ The makers of laws are the majority who are weak; they make laws and distribute praises and censures with a view to themselves and to their own interests; and they terrify the stronger sort of men, and those who are able to get the better of them, in order that they may not get the better of them.

*Plato*
Gorgias, *c.360* B.C.

**69.2** ❦ A good government produces citizens distinguished for courage, love of justice, and every other good quality; a bad government makes them cowardly, rapacious, and the slaves of every foul desire.

*Dionysius of Halicarnassus*
Antiquities of Rome, *c.20* B.C.

**69.3** ❦ . . . governments rather depend upon men than men upon governments.

*William Penn*
Preface to Pennsylvania's Frame of
Government, 1682–1684

**69.4** ❦ . . . an Act of Parliament can do no wrong, though it may do several things that look pretty odd; . . .

*Sir John Holt, English jurist;*
*Chief Justice*
City of London v. Wood *(1701), 12*
*Mod. 669, 687*

**69.5** ❦ If men be good, government cannot be bad.

*William Penn, 1644–1718*
Fruits of Solitude

**69.6** ❦ Governments derive their just powers from the consent of the governed.

*Declaration of Independence, 1776*

**69.7** ❦ Laws always lose in energy what the government gains in extent.

*Immanuel Kant*
Perpetual Peace, *1795*

**69.8** ❦ And having looked to Government for bread, on the first scarcity they will turn and bite the hand that fed them.

*Edmund Burke, 1729–1797*
Thoughts and Details on Scarcity

**69.9** ❦ Though in a state of society some must have greater luxuries and comforts than others, yet all should have the necessaries of life; and if the poor cannot exist, in vain may the rich look for happiness or prosperity. The legislature is never so well employed as when they look to the interests of those who are at a distance from them in the ranks of society. It is their duty to do so; religion calls for it; humanity calls for it; and if there are hearts who are not awake to either of those feelings, their own interests would dictate it.

> *Sir Lloyd Kenyon, English jurist;*
> *Lord Chief Justice*
> Rex v. Rusby *(1800),*
> *Peake's N.P. Cases 192*

**69.10** ⚘ The will of the people is the only legitimate foundation of any government, and to protect its free expression should be our first object.

> *Thomas Jefferson*
> *First inaugural address, March 4, 1801*

**69.11** ⚘ A single good government is a blessing to the whole earth.

> *Thomas Jefferson*
> *Letter to George Flower, 1817*

**69.12** ⚘ Self-government is the natural government of man.

> *Henry Clay*
> *Speech, 1818*

**69.13** ⚘ That one hundred and fifty lawyers should do business together ought not to be expected.

> *Thomas Jefferson, 1743–1826,*
> *referring to the Congress of the*
> *United States*
> Autobiography, *1853*

**69.14** ⚘ The spirit of resistance to government is so valuable on certain occasions that I wish it to be always kept alive.

> *Thomas Jefferson, 1743–1826*
> *To Abigail Adams*

**69.15** ⚘ The whole of government consists in the art of being honest.

> *Thomas Jefferson, 1743–1826*
> *Letter to John Adams*

**69.16** ⚘ Were we directed from Washington when to sow, and when to reap, we should soon want bread.

> *Thomas Jefferson, 1743–1826*
> Autobiography, *1853*

**69.17** ⚘ Government is a trust, and the officers of the government are trustees; and both the trust and the trustees are created for the benefit of the people.

> *Henry Clay*
> *Speech, 1829*

**69.18** ⚘ Any people anywhere being inclined and having the power have the right to rise up and shake off the existing government, and form a new one that suits them better. This is a most valuable, a most sacred right—a right which we hope and believe is to liberate the world.

> *Abraham Lincoln*
> *Speech, Congress, January 12, 1848*

**69.19** ⚘ Why does [the government] always crucify Christ, and excommunicate Copernicus and Luther, and pronounce Washington and Franklin rebels?

> *Henry David Thoreau*
> Civil Disobedience, *1849*

**69.20** ⚘ The people's government, made for the people, made by the people, and answerable to the people.

> *Daniel Webster, 1782–1852*
> *Franklin Pierce Adams,* F.P.A.
> Book of Quotations, *1952*

69.21 ❦ . . . no man is good enough to govern another man without that
other's consent.

*Abraham Lincoln*
*Speech, Peoria, Illinois,*
*October 16, 1854*

69.22 ❦ "A house divided against itself cannot stand."* I believe this government cannot endure permanently
half-slave and half-free.

*Abraham Lincoln*
*Speech, Republican State Convention,*
*Springfield, Illinois, June 16, 1858*

69.23 ❦ The decisions of the House of Lords
are binding on me and upon all the
Courts except itself.

*Sir John Romilly, English jurist*
Attorney-General v. The Dean and
Canons of Windsor *(1858), 24 Beav.*
*715*

69.24 ❦ The only government that I recognize . . . is that power that establishes justice in the land, never that
which establishes injustice.

*Henry David Thoreau*
John Brown's Body, *1859*

69.25 ❦ While the people retain their virtue
and vigilance, no administration, by
any extreme of wickedness or folly,
can very seriously injure the government in the short space of four years.

*Abraham Lincoln*
*First Inaugural Address, March 4, 1861*

69.26 ❦ . . . that this nation, under God,
shall have a new birth of freedom,
and that government of the people,
by the people, for the people, shall
not perish from the earth.

*Abraham Lincoln*
*Gettysburg Address,*
*November 19, 1863*

69.27 ❦ You can fool some of the people all
of the time, and all of the people
some of the time, but you cannot
fool all of the people all of the time.

*Abraham Lincoln, 1809–1865*

69.28 ❦ The divine right of kings may have
been a plea for feeble tyrants, but
the divine right of government is the
keystone of human progress, and
without it government sinks into police and a nation into a mob.

*Benjamin Disraeli*
Preface, Lothair, *1870*

69.29 ❦ The government's like a mule, it's
slow and it's sure; it's slow to turn,
and it's sure to turn the way you
don't want it.

*Ellen Glasgow*
The Voice of the People, *1900*

69.30 ❦ The government is us; we are the
government, you and I.

*Theodore Roosevelt*
*Speech, 1902*

*New Testament, Mark 3:25

**69.31** ❧ Men must turn square corners when they deal with the Government.

*Oliver Wendell Holmes*
Rock Island C. R. R. v.
United States, *254*
*U.S. 141, 143*
*(1920)*

**69.32** ❧ At the foundation of our civil liberty lies the principle which denies to government officials an exceptional position before the law and which subjects them to the same rules of conduct that are commands to the citizen.

*Louis D. Brandeis*
Burdeau v. McDowell,
*256 U.S. 465, 477*
*(1921)*

**69.33** ❧ Experience should teach us to be most on our guard to protect liberty when the Government's purposes are beneficent.

*Louis D. Brandeis*
Olmstead v. United States, *277*
*U.S. 438, 478*
*(1928)*

**69.34** ❧ If the law is upheld only by government officials, then all law is at an end.

*Herbert Hoover*
*Message to Congress, 1929*

**69.35** ❧ That government which thinks in terms of humanity will continue.

*Franklin Delano Roosevelt*
*Campaign speech,*
*1936*

**69.36** ❧ I can retain neither respect nor affection for a Government which has been moving from wrong to wrong in order to defend its immorality.

*Mohandas Gandhi*, 1869–1948
*Franklin Pierce Adams,*
F.P.A. Book of Quotations, *1952*

**69.37** ❧ . . . all power tends to develop into a government in itself. Power that controls the economy should be in the hands of elected representatives of the people, not in the hands of an industrial oligarchy. Industrial power should be decentralized. It should be scattered into many hands so that the fortunes of the people will not be dependent on the whim or caprice, the political prejudices, the emotional stability of a few self-appointed men.

*William O. Douglas*
United States v. Steel Co., *334*
*U.S. 495, 536*
*(1948)*

**69.38** ❧ You had the famous American maxim, "Governments derive their just powers from the consent of the governed," and we both noticed that the world was divided into peoples that owned the governments and governments that owned the peoples.

*Winston Churchill*
*Speech, 1949*

**69.39** ❧ Government is like fire. If it is kept within bounds and under the control of the people, it contributes to the welfare of all. But if it gets out of place, if it gets too big and out of

control, it destroys the happiness
and even the lives of the people.

*Harold E. Stassen, 1907–*
*Franklin Pierce Adams,*
F.P.A. Book of Quotations,
*1952*

69.40 ❦ Thought control is a copyright of
totalitarianism, and we have no
claim to it. It is not the function of
our Government to keep the citizen
from falling into error; it is the function of the citizen to keep the Government from falling into error.

*Robert H. Jackson*
American Communications Assn. v.
Douds, *339 U.S. 382, 442–43 (1950)*

69.41 ❦ Government can easily exist without
law, but law cannot exist without
government.

*Bertrand Russell*
*"Ideas That Have Helped Mankind,"*
Unpopular Essays, *1951*

69.42 ❦ The task of law is to maintain an
ever-readjusted balance between the
needful restraint on the powers of
government and the needful exercise
of the powers of government.

*Leon Jaworski Address, American Bar*
*Association, New York, reported in the*
Boston Globe, *July 5, 1971*

69.43 ❦ I am working for the time when unqualified blacks, browns and women
join the unqualified men in running
our government.

*Sissy Farenthold, 1974*
Power Quotes *by Daniel B. Baker,*
*1992*

69.44 ❦ Under current law, it is a crime for a
private citizen to lie to a government

official, but not for the government
to lie to the people.

*Donald M. Fraser*
Laurence J. Peter, Peter's Quotations,
*1977*

69.45 ❦ The single most exciting thing you
encounter in government is competence, because it's so rare.

*Daniel Patrick Moynihan*
New York Times, *March 2, 1976*

69.46 ❦ Personal virtue is a good in itself,
but it is not a sufficient means to
the end of good government.

*Jeane Kirkpatrick*
*Speech, Washington, D.C.,*
*September 29, 1982*

69.47 ❦ Those who attempt to capture the
daily counseling, oversight, common sense, and vision of my grandparents in a governmental program
are engaging in sheer folly. Government cannot develop individual
responsibility.

*Clarence Thomas, U.S. Supreme Court*
*associate justice*
*Speech at the Heritage Foundation,*
*1987*

69.48 ❦ Government is a tool, like a hammer. You can use a hammer to build
with or you can use a hammer to
destroy.

*Molly Ivins*
Fort Worth Star-Telegram, *1992*

69.49 ❦ It's all very well to run around saying regulation is bad, get the government off our backs, etc. Of course our lives are regulated. When you come to a stop sign, you stop; if you want to go fishing, you get a license; if you want to shoot ducks, you can shoot only three ducks. The alternative is dead bodies at intersections, no fish and no ducks.

*Molly Ivins*
*Fort Worth Star-Telegram, 1995*

69.50 ❦ Let us use government as we have in the past, to further the common good.

*Hillary Rodham Clinton*
*It Takes a Village and Other Lessons*
*Children Teach Us, 1996*

69.51 ❦ As a matter of principle, I don't feel that the government should be in the position of market-testing its arguments.

*Marcia Clark*
*Without a Doubt, with*
*Teresa Carpenter, 1997*

# 70. GUILT

70.1 ❦ Nothing is more wretched than the mind of a man conscious of guilt.

*Plautus, c.254–184 B.C.*
*Mostellaria*

70.2 ❦ Queen: So full of artless jealousy is guilt,
It spills itself in fearing to be spilt.

*Shakespeare*
*Hamlet, IV, 5, 1600–1601*

70.3 ❦ The pot calls the kettle black.

*Cervantes*
*Don Quixote, 1605*

70.4 ❦ Sire, we have little defense against the opinion of a monarch, and even the most innocent man who ever lived will begin to be guilty if the king thinks him so.

*Pierre Corneille, French poet*
*and dramatist*
*Horace, 1640*

70.5 ❦ Guilt has very quick ears to accusation.

*Henry Fielding*
*Amelia, 1752*

70.6 ❦ Ah! it is well for the unfortunate to be resigned, but for the guilty there is no peace.

*Mary Wollstonecraft Shelley*
*Frankenstein, 1818*

70.7 ❦ Give him rope enough and he will hang himself.

*Charlotte Brontë*
Shirley, *1849*

70.8 ❦ *. . . if we see cruelty or wrong that we have the power to stop, and do nothing, we make ourselves sharers in the guilt.*

*Anna Sewell, British writer*
Black Beauty, *1877*

70.9 ❦ . . . the twofold aim [of criminal justice] is that guilt shall not escape or innocence suffer.

Berger v. United States, *295 U.S. 78 (1935)*

70.10 ❦ Now, if any fundamental assumption underlies our system, it is that guilt is personal not inheritable.

*Robert H. Jackson*
Korematsu v. United States, *323 U.S. 214 (1944)*

70.11 ❦ In former days, everyone found the assumption of innocence so easy; today we find fatally easy the assumption of guilt.

*Amanda Cross*
Poetic Justice, *1970*

70.12 ❦ Guilt: the gift that keeps on giving.

*Erma Bombeck*
Time, *July 2, 1984*

70.13 ❦ A trial is a minefield, and any judicial misstep—or even a perceived misstep—can lead to a reversal of the verdict, with no consideration of whether the defendant is guilty or not.

*Judge Harold J. Rothwax*
Guilty: The Collapse of Criminal Justice, *1996*

# 71. HATE

71.1 ❦ Hate is like fire—it makes even light rubbish deadly.

*George Eliot*
*Scenes of Clerical Life, 1857*

# 72. HEALTH

72.1 ❦ If men could get pregnant, abortion would be a sacrament.

*Florynce Kennedy,*
*Gloria Steinem, "The Verbal Karate of*
*Florynce Kennedy, Esq.,"*
*Ms., March 1973*

72.2 ❦ The emphasis must not be on the right to abortion but on the right to privacy and reproductive control.

*Ruth Bader Ginsburg*
*Susan Edmiston, "Portia Faces*
*Life—The Trials of Law School," Ms.,*
*April 1974*

72.3 ❦ Like the effects of industrial pollution and the new system of global financial markets, the AIDS crisis is evidence of a world in which nothing important is regional, local, limited; in which everything that can circulate does and every problem is, or is destined to become, worldwide.

*Susan Sontag*
*AIDS and Its Metaphors, 1983*

72.4 ❦ We currently have a system for taking care of sickness. We do not have a system for enhancing and promoting health.

*Hillary Rodham Clinton*
*Speech, 1993*

# 73. HOMOSEXUALITY

73.1 ❧ If homosexuality were the normal way, God would have made Adam and Bruce.

*Anita Bryant*
New York Times, *1977*

73.2 ❧ We know that priorities are amiss in the world when a man gets a military medal of honor for killing another man and a dishonorable discharge for loving one.

*Charlotte Bunch*
*"Speaking Out, Reaching Out,"*
Passionate Politics, *1987*

73.3 ❧ No government has the right to tell its citizens when or whom to love. The only queer people are those who don't love anybody.

*Rita Mae Brown*
At the Gay Olympics, *1982*

# 74. HUMAN NATURE

74.1 ❧ No man is so exquisitely honest or upright in living but that ten times in his life he might not lawfully be hanged.

*Michel de Montaigne*
Essais, *1588*

74.2 ❧ Those who fear men like laws.

*Marquis de Vauvenargues,*
*French moralist*
Réflexions, *1746*

74.3 ❧ For behaviour, men learn it, as they take diseases, one of another.

*Francis Bacon*
The Advancement of Learning, *1605*

74.4 ❧ Nature never deceives us; it is always we who deceive ourselves.

*Jean-Jacques Rousseau*
Emile, *1762*

74.5 ❧ Every law which the state enacts indicates a fact in human nature.

*Ralph Waldo Emerson*
*"History,"* Essays, *1899*

74.6 ❧ Man may be a little lower than the angels, but he has not yet shaken off the brute. . . . His path is strewn with carnage, murder lurks always not far beneath, to break out from time to time, peace resolution to the contrary notwithstanding.

*Learned Hand*
*"Democracy! Its Presumptions and*
*Realities," 1* Federal Bar Association
Journal *2 (1932)*

*74.7*  ✌  I wish I loved my fellow men more than I do, but to love one's neighbor as oneself, taken literally, would mean to realize all his impulses as one's own, which no one can, and which I humbly think would not be desirable if one could.

*Oliver Wendell Holmes, 1841–1935*
*Harry C. Shriver, ed.,* Justice Oliver Wendell Holmes: His Book Notices and Uncollected Letters and Papers, *1936*

*74.8*  ✌  Possibly gaiety is the miasmic mist of misery.

*Oliver Wendell Holmes, 1841–1935*
*Mark De Wolfe Howe,*
Holmes-Pollock Letters, *1946*

*74.9*  ✌  Neither Law nor Human Nature is an exact science.

*George W. Keeton, ed.,* Harris's Hints on Advocacy, *1943*

*74.10*  ✌  . . . [government employees] are subject to that very human weakness, especially displayed in Washington, which leads men to "crook the pregnant hinges of the knee where thrift may follow fawning."

*Robert H. Jackson*
Frazier v. United States, *335 U.S. 497, 515 (1948)*

*74.11*  ✌  Law is born from despair of human nature.

*José Ortega y Gasset, 1883–1955*
*W. H. Auden and Louis Kronenberger.*
The Viking Book of Aphorisms, *1962*

*74.12*  ✌  But Corwin's Law was established in advice he gave a budding speaker "Never make people laugh. If you would succeed in life, you must be solemn, solemn as an ass. All the great monuments are built over solemn asses."

*Thomas Corwin, American politician*
*Clayton Fritchey, "A Politician Must Watch His Wit,"* New York Times Magazine, *July 3, 1960*

# 75. IGNORANCE

*75.1* ❦ Ignorance of the law does not prevent the losing lawyer from collecting his bill.

*Anonymous*
*Laurence J. Peter,* Peter's Quotations,
*1977*

*75.2* ❦ Ignorance of the law excuses no man; not that all men know the law, but because 'tis an excuse every man will plead, and no man can tell how to refute him.

*John Selden* 1584–1654
*"Law,"* Table-Talk, *1689*

*75.3* ❦ Ignorance is preferable to error; and he is less remote from the truth who believes nothing, than he who believes what is wrong.

*Thomas Jefferson*
Notes on the State of Virginia, *1785*

*75.4* ❦ Ignorance of the law is not excuse in any country. If it were, the laws would lose their effect, because it can always be pretended.

*Thomas Jefferson*
*To M. Limozin,*
*December 22, 1787*

*75.5* ❦ If a nation expects to be ignorant and free, in a state of civilization, it expects what never was and never will be.

*Thomas Jefferson*
*Letter to Charles Yancy,*
*January 6, 1816*

*75.6* ❦ Lawyers are the only persons in whom ignorance of the law is not punished.

*Ascribed to Jeremy*
*Bentham,1748–1832*
*Wolfe D. Goodman, "Sole Practice,*
*Partnership or Merger,"* 9 Canadian
Bar Journal *3 (June 1966)*

*75.7* ❦ To be conscious that you are ignorant is a great step to knowledge.
*Benjamin Disraeli*
Sybil, *1845*

*75.8* ❦ And there comes a point where this Court should not be ignorant as judges of what we know as men.
*Felix Frankfurter*
Watts v. Indiana, *338 U.S. 49, 52*
*(1949)*

# *76.* IMPRISONMENT

**76.1**   ❦ Golden fetters.

*Diogenes, c.*4th century B.C.
*William S. Walsh,* International
Encyclopedia of Prose and
Poetical Quotations, *1968*

**76.2**   ❦ No freeman shall be taken or imprisoned or disseised or exiled or in any
way destroyed, nor will we go upon
him nor will we send upon him, except by the lawful judgment of his
peers or by the law of the land.

*Magna Carta 1215*

**76.3**   ❦ A foole I doe him firmly hold, That
loves his fetters, though they were of
gold.

*Edmund Spenser*
Fairie Queene, *1589*

**76.4**   ❦ Experience hath shewn, that
between the prisons and the graves
of princes, the distance is very small.

*Sir Michael Foster, English jurist*
Foster's Crown Case, *(1762),*
Discourse I. c. 1, s. 3

**76.5**   ❦ Durance vile.

*W. Kendrick, British dramatist*
Falstaff's Wedding, *1776*

**76.6**   ❦ A learned county court judge told
me that at first he used to make orders of committal for a short time
and he found that the people went
to prison. He then lengthened the
period, and he found that fewer people went to prison; and he found
that the longer the period for which

he committed people to prison for
not paying, the shorter was the total
amount of imprisonment suffered
by debtors, because when they were
committed for the whole six weeks
they moved heaven and earth
among their friends to get the funds
and pay; whereas if the term was a
short one, they underwent the punishment.

*Lord William Bramwell, English jurist*
Stonor v. Fowle *(1887),*
L.R. 13 Ap. Ca. 28

**76.7**   ❦ I know not whether Laws be right,
Or whether Laws be wrong;
All that we know who lie in gaol
Is that the wall is strong;
And that each day is like a year,
A year whose days are long.

*Oscar Wilde*
The Ballad of Reading Gaol, *1898*

**76.8**   ❦ You have put me in here [jail] a cub,
but I will come out roaring like a
lion, and I will make all hell howl!

*Carry Nation*
*Carleton Beals,*
Cyclone Carry, *c.1901*

**76.9**   ❦ Whilst we have prisons, it matters
little which of us occupy the cells.

*George Bernard Shaw, 1856–1950*
*W. H. Auden and Louis Kronenberger,*
The Viking Book of Aphorisms, *1962*

**76.10**   ❦ No doubt like schools, old-age
homes, mental hospitals, and other
closed institutions that house the

powerless, prisons afford a very special opportunity to employees at all
levels for various kinds of graft and
thievery.

*Jessica Mitford, writer*
*Kind and Unusual Punishment, 1971*

76.11 ❧ . . . if you think only terrible people
go to prison, that solves that
problem.

*Alta, American poet*
*Untitled Poem, 1972*

76.12 ❧ Jails and prisons are designed to
break human beings, to convert the
population into specimens in a

zoo—obedient to our keepers, but
dangerous to each other.

*Angela Davis*
*Angela Davis An Autobiography,*
*1974*

76.13 ❧ More than half of the jail population have never been convicted of
anything, yet they languish in
those cells.

*Angela Davis*
*Angela Davis: An Autobiography,*
*1974*

# 77. INJUSTICE

77.1 ❧ Woe to him who builds his house
by . . . injustice, who uses his neighbor's services without wages.

*Old Testament, Jeremiah 22:13*

77.2 ❧ If it were not for injustice, men
would not know justice.

*Heraclitus, c.540–c.480 B.C.*
*Marjorie P. Katz and Jean S. Arbeiter,*
*Pegs to Hang Ideas On, 1973*

77.3 ❧ Is not injustice the greatest of all
threats of the state?

*Plato*
*The Republic, c.370 B.C.*

77.4 ❧ To do evil to men differs in no respect from injustice.

*Plato*
*Crito, c.350 B.C.*

77.5 ❧ Extreme law is often extreme
injustice.

*Terence*
*The Self-Tormentor, 163 B.C.*

77.6 ❧ How lightly do we sanction a law
unjust to ourselves.

*Horace*
*Satires, 35 B.C.*

*77.7* ❦ A good man should and must
Sit rather down with loss,
Than rise unjust.

*Ben Jonson*
Sejanus, *1603*

*77.8* ❦ When one has been threatened with
a great injustice, one accepts a
smaller as a favour.

*Jane Welsh Carlyle, Scottish woman of*
*letters and diarist*
*Journal entry, November 21, 1855,*
Letters and Memorials, *1883 ff.*

*77.9* ❦ Nothing can be permanently useful
which is unjust.

*Leone Levi, English jurist and*
*statistician*
International Law, *1888*

*77.10* ❦ A fruitful parent of injustice is the
tyranny of concepts.

*Benjamin N. Cardozo, 1870–1938*
*"The Paradoxes of Legal Science,"*
Selected Writings of Benjamin
Nathan Cardozo, *edited by*
*Margaret E. Hall, 1947*

*77.11* ❦ . . . justice can never be done in the
midst of injustice.

*Simone de Beauvoir*
The Second Sex, *1953*

*77.12* ❦ An unrectified case of injustice has
a terrible way of lingering restlessly,
in the social atmosphere like an
unfinished question.

*Mary McCarthy*
*"My Confession,"* On The Contrary,
*1961*

*77.13* ❦ One had better die fighting against
injustice than die like a dog or a rat
in a trap.

*Ida B. Wells*
Lawyer's Wit and Wisdom, *edited by*
*Bruce Nash, Allan Zullo and compiled*
*by Kathryn Zullo, 1995*

# *78.* INNOCENCE

*78.1* ❦ He who is free from fever does not
fear to eat watermelons.

*Chinese proverb*
*William Scarborough,* Chinese
Proverbs, *1875*

*78.2* ❦ God will not cast away an
innocent man.

*Old Testament, Job 8:20*

*78.3* ❦ When innocence is frightened
The judge is condemned.

*Publilius Syrus, Latin writer*
Sententiae, *c.43* B.C.

*78.4* ❦ The next best to guiltless hands is ignorance of guilt itself.

*Seneca, 4* B.C.–A.D. *65*
Hercules Furens

*78.5* ❧ I should, indeed, prefer twenty guilty men to escape death through mercy, than one innocent to be condemned unjustly.

> *Sir John Fortescue, English jurist;*
> *Chief Justice*
> De Laudibus Legum Angliae, *c.1470*

*78.6* ❧ Innocence has more power than all the deceits of an evil man.

> *Giambattista Battista Giraldi*
> *(aka Cinthio)*
> Selene, *c.1549*

*78.7* ❧ Innocence is not nearly so well shielded as crime.

> *La Rochefoucauld*
> Maximes, *1665*

*78.8* ❧ It is better to risk saving a guilty man than to condemn an innocent one.

> *Voltaire*
> Zadig, *1747*

*78.9* ❧ It is better that ten guilty persons escape than one innocent suffer.

> *Sir William Blackstone*
> Commentaries on the Laws of
> England, *1765–1769*

*78.10* ❧ In England a man is presoomed to be innicent till he's proved guilty an' they take it f'r granted he's guilty. In this counthry a man is presoomed to be guilty ontil he's proved guilty an' afther that he's presoomed to be innicent.

> *Finley Peter Dunne, 1867–1936*
> *Edward J. Bander, ed.,* Mr. Dooley on
> the Choice of Law, *1963*

*78.11* ❧ Our national nostrum, "Not Proven" . . . a verdict which has been construed by the profane to mean "Not Guilty, but don't do it again."

> *William Roughead*
> The Art of Murder, *1943*

*78.12* ❧ [U]nless you're O.J. Simpson you're not presumed to be innocent but believed to be guilty the minute people start calling you "the defendant."

> *Leslie Abramson*
> The Defense Is Ready,
> *with Richard Flaste,*
> *1997*

# *79.* JUDGES

79.1 ❦ The judge is nothing but the law speaking.

*Aphorism*
*Benjamin Whichcote,* Moral and Religious Aphorisms, *1753*

79.2 ❦ It is the duty of a judge to administer the law, not to make it.

*Latin legal phrase*
*W. Gurney Benham,* Putnam's Complete Book of Quotations, Proverbs and Household Words, *1927*

79.3 ❦ It is the duty of a judge to judge according to what things are alleged and what things are proved.

*Latin legal phrase*
*W. Gurney Benham,* Putnam's Complete Book of Quotations, Proverbs and Household Words, *1927*

79.4 ❦ The best law leaves the least discretion to the judge.

*Latin proverb*
*H. L. Mencken,* A New Dictionary of Quotations, *1946*

79.5 ❦ A good judge conceives quickly, judges slowly.

*Proverb*
*Rosalind Fergusson,* The Facts On File Dictionary of Proverbs, *1983*

79.6 ❦ A judge knows nothing unless it has been explained to him three times.

*Proverb*
*Rosalind Fergusson,* The Facts On File Dictionary of Proverbs, *1983*

79.7 ❦ A judge and a stomach do their asking in silence.

*Russian proverb*
*H. L. Mencken,* A New Dictionary of Quotations, *1946*

79.8 ❦ Tell God the truth but give the judge money.

*Russian proverb*
*H. L. Mencken,* A New Dictionary of Quotations, *1946*

79.9 ❦ A judge who accepts bribes brings terror into the world.

*Talmud, Bava Batra*

79.10 ❦ Woe to the generation that judges its judges.

*Talmud, Bava Batra*

79.11 ❦ A habitual borrower is unfit to be a judge.

*Talmud, Ketubot*

79.12 ❦ A judge is disqualified for a case involving one he loves or hates.

*Talmud, Ketubot*

79.13 ❦ As Rabbi Samuel was boarding a ferry, a man rushed up to help him; the rabbi asked why he was so attentive, and the man said, "Because I have a lawsuit that will come up in your court." To which Rabbi Samuel replied, "Then I am forbidden to be your judge."

*Talmud, Ketubot*

79.14 ❦ When a court has pronounced a sentence of death, its members [judges] should taste nothing for the rest of that day.

*Talmud, Sanhedrin*

79.15 ❦ When a judge sits in judgment over a fellow man, he should feel as if a sword is pointed at his own heart.

*Talmud, Sanhedrin*

79.16 ❦ Disaster comes because of the kind of judges we have.

*Talmud, Shabbat*

79.17 ❦ I cannot try the case of one of my students, because I love him as myself, and no one can see a fault in himself.

*Talmud, Shabbat*

79.18 ❦ Four things belong to a judge: to hear courteously, to answer wisely, to consider soberly, and to decide impartially.

*Socrates, 470–399* B.C.
*Franklin Pierce Adams, F.P.A. Book of Quotations, 1952*

79.19 ❦ A judge should not be a youth, but old.

*Plato*
*The Republic, c.370* B.C.

79.20 ❦ The Judge should not be young; he should have learned to know evil, not from his own soul, but from late and long observance of the nature of evil in others: knowledge should be his guide, not personal experience.

*Plato*
*The Republic, c.370* B.C.

79.21 ❦ Ye judges who give judgments by law, ought to be obedient to the laws.

*Cicero, 106–43* B.C.
*W. Gurney Benham, Putnam's Complete Book of Quotations, Proverbs and Household Words, 1927*

79.22 ❦ He makes speed to repentance who judges hastily.

*Publilius Syrus, Latin writer,* 1st century B.C.
In Judicando

79.23 ❦ First he [Radamanthus, the judge of Hell] punished before he heard, and when he had heard his denial, he compelled the party accused by torture to confess.

*Virgil*
Aeneid, *c.19* B.C.

79.24 ❦ A good and faithful judge prefers what is right to what is expedient.

*Horace*
Carmina, *c.13* B.C.

79.25 ❧ It is the duty of a judge to enquire not only into the matter but into the circumstances of the matter.

*Ovid*
Tristia, *c.9–17*

79.26 ❧ A judge is unjust who hears but one side of a case, even though he decide it justly.

*Seneca,* 4 B.C.–A.D. 65
Medea

79.27 ❧ No one is ever innocent when his opponent is the judge.

*Lucan, Roman poet, 39–65*
Pharsalia

79.28 ❧ A judge must bear in mind that when he tries a case he is himself on trial.

*Philo*
Special Laws, *1st century*

79.29 ❧ Judges are best in the beginning; they deteriorate as time passes.

*Tacitus*
Annals, *c.110*

79.30 ❧ There must always be a goodly number of judges, for few will always do the will of the few.

*Machiavelli*
Discorsi, *1531*

79.31 ❧ Portia: To offend, and judge, are distinct offices,
And of opposed natures.

*Shakespeare*
The Merchant of Venice, *II, 9,*
*1596–1597*

79.32 ❧ Jacques: And then the justice
In fair round belly with good capon lined.

*Shakespeare*
As You Like It, *II, 7, 1599–1600*

79.33 ❧ Angelo: Thieves for their robbery have authority.
When judges steal themselves.

*Shakespeare*
Measure for Measure, *II, 2,*
*1604–1605*

79.34 ❧ Look with thine ears: see how yond justice rails upon yond simple thief. Hark, in thine ear: change places; and, handy-dandy, which is the justice, which is the thief.

*Shakespeare*
King Lear, *IV, 3, 1605–1606*

79.35 ❧ . . . a corrupt judge offendeth not so highly as a facile.

*Francis Bacon*
The Advancement of Learning, *1605*

79.36 ❧ He who has the judge for his father goes into court with an easy mind.

*Cervantes*
Don Quixote, *1615*

**79.37** ❦ When a judge departs from the letter of the law he becomes a law-breaker.

*Francis Bacon*
De Argumentis Scientiarum, *1623*

**79.38** ❦ Judges must beware of hard constructions and strained influences; for there is no worse torture than the torture of laws: specially in the case of laws penal, they ought to have care, that that which was meant for terror be not turned into rigor.

*Francis Bacon*
*"Of Judicature,"* Essayes, *1625*

**79.39** ❦ You should be a light to jurors to open their eyes, but not a guide to lead them by their noses.

*Lord Bacon's advice to Justice Hutton*
*Marshall Brown,* Wit and Humor of Bench and Bar, *1899*

**79.40** ❦ When he [a judge] put on his robes, he put off his relation to any; and . . . becomes without pedigree.

*Thomas Fuller*
Holy State, *1642*

**79.41** ❦ When by a pardon'd murd'rer blood is spilt,
The judge that pardon'd hath the greatest guilt.

*Sir John Denham, English poet,*
*1615–1669*
On Justice

**79.42** ❦ The most just man in the world may still not act as judge in his own case.

*Pascal*
Pensées, *1670*

**79.43** ❦ A popular judge is a deformed thing, and plaudits are fitter for players than for magistrates.

*George Savile, 1st marquess of Halifax,*
*English politician, 1633–1695*
*W. H. Auden and Louis Kronenberger,*
The Viking Book of Aphorisms, *1962*

**79.44** ❦ The duty of a judge is to render justice; his art is to delay it.

*Jean de La Bruyère, 1645–1696*

**79.45** ❦ Tis but half a judge's task to know.

*Alexander Pope*
Essay on Criticism, *1711*

**79.46** ❦ God forbid that Judges upon their oath should make resolutions to enlarge jurisdiction.

*William Cowper, English jurist;*
*Lord Chancellor*
Reeves v. Buttler *(1715),*
*Gilbert, Eq. Ca. 196*

**79.47** ❦ Judges . . . are picked out from the most dexterous lawyers, who are grown old or lazy, and having been biased all their lives against truth and equity, are under such a fatal necessity of favoring fraud, perjury, and oppression, that I have known several of them refuse a large bribe from the side where justice lay, rather than injure the faculty by doing any thing unbecoming their nature or their office.

*Jonathan Swift*
Gulliver's Travels, *1726*

79.48 ❧ Laws should be made by legislators, not by judges.

*Cesare Beccaria*
Trattato dei delitti e delle pene, *1764*

79.49 ❧ Set the sternest of judges to plead in his own case and then see how he expounds the law!

*Pierre-Augustin Caron*
*de Beaumarchais*
Marriage of Figaro, *1784*

79.50 ❧ Next to permanency in office, nothing can contribute more to the independence of the judges than a fixed provision for their support.

*Alexander Hamilton*
The Federalist, *1788*

79.51 ❧ To vindicate the policy of the law is no necessary part of the office of a judge.

*Gustavus Scott, American jurist*
Evans v. Evans, *1790*

79.52 ❧ The cold neutrality of an impartial judge.

*Edmund Burke,* 1729–1797
Works

79.53 ❧ Knowing that religion does not furnish grosser bigots than law, I expect little from old judges.

*Thomas Jefferson*
Letter to Thomas Cooper, *1810*

79.54 ❧ It is the judges . . . that make the common law. . . . When your dog does anything you want to break him of, you wait till he does it, and then beat him for it. This is the way you make laws for your dog; and this is the way the judges make law for you and me.

*Jeremy Bentham*
Truth v. Ashhurst *(1823), 5 Works*
*233, 235*

79.55 ❧ That part of the law of every country which was made by judges has been far better made than the part which consists of statutes enacted by the legislature.

*John Austin*
Austin's Jurisprudence, *1832*

79.56 ❧ The acme of judicial distinction means the ability to look a lawyer straight in the eyes for two hours and not to hear a damned word he says.

*John Marshall,* 1755–1835
*Albert J. Beveridge,* The Life of John Marshall, *1919*

79.57 ❧ It is the duty of a Judge to make it disagreeable to counsel to talk non-sense.

*John Singleton Copley, the younger, 1st*
*baron Lyndhurst, English jurist;*
*Lord Chancellor*
*John Campbell,* Lives of Lord Chancellors, *1849*

79.58 ❧ Judges, like *Caesar's* wife, should be above suspicion.

*Charles Bowen, English jurist*
Leeson v. General Council of Medical Education and Registration *(1889), L.R. 43 C.D. 385*

79.59 ❦ Credulity is not esteemed a paramount virtue of the judicial mind.

*Joseph Waldo Huston, American lawyer*
Rankin v. Jauman, *4 Idaho, 394, 401*
*(1895)*

79.60 ❦ There is a story of a Vermont justice of the peace before whom a suit was brought by one farmer against another for breaking a churn. The justice took time to consider, and then said that he had looked through the statutes and could find nothing about churns, and gave judgment for the defendant. The same state of mind is shown in all our common digests and textbooks.

*Oliver Wendell Holmes*
*"The Path of the Law" (address), 1897*

79.61 ❦ "If I had me job to pick out," said Mr. Dooley, "I'd be a judge. I've looked over all th' others an that's the on'y wan that suits. I have th' judicyal timperamint. I hate wurruk."

*Finley Peter Dunne*
Observations by Mr. Dooley: The
Law's Delays, *1906*

79.62 ❦ Judges are apt to be naif, simple-minded men, and they need something of Mephistopheles. We too need education in the obvious— to learn to transcend our own convictions and to leave room for much that we hold dear to be done away with short of revolution by the orderly change of law.

*Oliver Wendell Holmes*
*"Law and the Court," 1913,* Collected
Legal Papers, *1920*

79.63 ❦ But even judges sometimes progress.

*Emma Goldman*
*"The Social Aspects of Birth Control,"*
Mother Earth, *April 1916*

79.64 ❦ There are no more reactionary people in the world than judges.

*Lenin*
Political Parties and the Proletariat,
*1917*

79.65 ❦ . . . a judge of the United States is expected to be a man of ordinary firmness of character.

*Oliver Wendell Holmes*
Toledo Newspaper Co. v. United
States, *247 U.S. 402, 424 (1918)*

79.66 ❦ The great tides and currents which engulf the rest of men do not turn aside in their course, and pass the judges by.

*Benjamin N. Cardozo*
The Nature of the Judicial Process,
*1921*

79.67 ❦ Judges commonly are elderly men, and are more likely to hate at sight any analysis to which they are not accustomed, and which disturbs repose of mind, than to fall in love with novelties.

*Oliver Wendell Holmes*
Law in Science—Science in Law,
*1921*

79.68 ❦ We rate the judge who is only a lawyer higher than the judge who is only a philosopher.

*Cuthbert W. Pound, American jurist*
*"Defective Law—Its Cause and*
*Remedy,"* New York State Bar
Bulletin, *1929*

79.69  ❧  I venture to believe that it is important to a judge called upon to pass on a question of Constitutional law, to have at least a bowing acquaintance with Acton and Maitland, with Thucydides, Gibbon and Carlyle, with Homer, Dante, Shakespeare and Milton, with Machiavelli, Montaigne and Rabelais, with Plato, Bacon, Hume and Kant. . . . Men do not gather figs of thistles, nor supple institutions from judges whose outlook is limited by parish or class.

*Learned Hand*
*"Sources of Tolerance," 79* University of Pennsylvania Law Review *1, 12 (1930)*

79.70  ❧  I could carve out of a banana a judge with more backbone than that.

*Oliver Wendell Holmes,* 1841–1935
New York Times, *February 23, 1984*

79.71  ❧  . . . one's final judge and only rival is oneself.

*Oliver Wendell Holmes,* 1841–1935
*Catherine Drinker Bowen,* Yankee from Olympus, *1944*

79.72  ❧  No judge writes on a wholly clean slate.

*Felix Frankfurter*
The Commerce Clause, *1937*

79.73  ❧  A judge rarely performs his functions adequately unless the case before him is adequately presented.

*Louis D. Brandeis,* 1856–1941
*B. Donovan James,* Strangers on a Bridge, *1964*

79.74  ❧  The position of a judge has been likened to that of an oyster anchored in one place, unable to take the initiative, unable to go out after things, restricted to working on and digesting that which the fortuitous eddies and currents of litigation may bring his way.

*Louis D. Brandeis,* 1856–1941
*Felix Frankfurter,* Mr. Justice Brandeis, *1932*

79.75  ❧  I do not know whether it is the view of the Court that a judge must be thick-skinned or just thickheaded, but nothing in my experience or observation confirms the idea that he is insensitive to publicity. Who does not prefer good to ill report of his work? And if fame—a good public name–is, as Milton said, the "last infirmity of noble mind," it is frequently the first infirmity of a mediocre one.

*Robert H. Jackson*
Craig v. Harney, *331 U.S. 367, 396 (1947)*

79.76  ❧  It has not been unknown that judges persist in error to avoid giving the appearance of weakness and vacillation.

*Felix Frankfurter*
Craig v. Harney, *331 U.S. 367, 392 (1947)*

79.77  ❧  When my father became a Judge I said to him, "Be kind to the *young lawyers.*" When I became a Judge, he said to me, "Be kind to the *old lawyers.*"

*Claude McColloch, American jurist*
Notes of a District Judge, *1948*

79.78 ❧ After all is said and done, we cannot deny the fact that a judge is almost of necessity surrounded by people who keep telling him what a wonderful fellow he is. And if he once begins to believe it, he is a lost soul.

*Harold R. Medina, American jurist*
*"Some Reflections on the Judicial*
*Function: A Personal Viewpoint," 38*
American Bar Association Journal
*107, 108 (1952)*

79.79 ❧ What becomes decisive to a Justice's functioning on the Court . . . is his general attitude toward law, the habits of mind that he has formed or is capable of unforming, his capacity for detachment, his temperament or training for putting his passion behind his judgment instead of in front of it. The attitudes and qualities which I am groping to characterize are ingredients of what compendiously might be called dominating humility.

*Felix Frankfurter*
*Forward,* Columbia Law Review,
*April 1955*

79.80 ❧ A society whose judges have taught it to expect complaisance will exact complaisance; and complaisance under the pretense of interpretation is rottenness. If judges are to kill this thing they love, let them do it, not like cowards with a kiss, but like brave men with a sword.

*Learned Hand*
*Irving Dilliard,*
The Spirit of Liberty, *1960*

79.81 ❧ A judge is not supposed to know anything about the facts of life until they have been presented in evidence and explained to him at least three times.

*Lord Chief Justice Parker, British judge*
Observer, *London, March 12, 1961*

79.82 ❧ . . . a Judge who is both stupid and industrious is without question an unqualified disaster.

*Dana Porter, Canadian jurist; Chief*
*Justice, Province of Ontario*
*"What Once the Fleeting Hour Has*
*Brought," 33* New York State Bar
Journal *4 (August 1961)*

79.83 ❧ I'm important in the County
I'm a Justice of the Peace
And I disbelieve Defendants
When they contradict the P'lice.

*John A. Nordberg*
*"Farewell to Illinois J.P.'s—A Lesson*
*from History," 44* Chicago Bar Record
*10*
*(September 1963)*

79.84 ❧ You see a court of appeals judge has a sort of intermediate status. It is the duty of a judge of a district court to be quick, courteous and wrong, but it must not be supposed from that that the court of appeals must be slow, crapulous and right, for that would be to usurp the functions of the supreme court.

*Editorial comment*
Yearbook of the Canadian Bar
Association, *1963*

79.85 ❧ I found the compliments very disturbing; when a judge compliments you, it usually means you have lost.

*James B. Donovan*
*Strangers on a Bridge, 1964*

79.86 ❧ The judge who does not agonize before passing a sentence is a criminal.

*John Ciardi*
*Saturday Review, February 13, 1965*

79.87 ❧ It is upon their seats that judges shine most.

*Sir Gerald Dodson, recorder, Old Bailey*
*Criminal Court, 1884–1966*
*New York Times, November 5, 1966*

79.88 ❧ Our Chief Justices have probably had more profound and lasting influence on their times and on the direction of the nation than most presidents have had.

*Richard M. Nixon*
*Television broadcast, May 21, 1969*

79.89 ❧ When we put our judges in an ivory tower, you put justice in an ivory tower.

*Bernard G. Segal, American lawyer;*
*president, American Bar Association*
*Speech, American Bar Association,*
*August 15, 1969*

79.90 ❧ What most impresses us about great jurists is not their tenacious grasp of fine points, honed almost to invisibility; it is the moment when we are suddenly aware of the sweep and direction of the law, and its place in the lives of men.

*Irving R. Kaufman*
*Speech, Institute of Judicial*
*Administration,*
*August 26, 1969*

79.91 ❧ Like generals who have [had] no wars for a generation are out of practice, we judges have perhaps been sluggish in responding to the new ways of trying legal and factual issues. But in time we do respond . . . It would be foolhardy not to be concerned about the turmoil and strife and violence we witness, much of it mindless and devoid of constructive ends. But concern must not give way to panic.

*Warren E. Burger*
*Speech, American Law Institute,*
*Washington, D.C., as reported in the*
*Washington Observer,*
*May 25, 1970*

79.92 ❧ What a judge does with his time while he is not on the bench is of great interest to the public. It is absolutely necessary that the clear light of day should illuminate any off-the-bench activity by a judge—and particularly any money he makes off of it.

*Roger J. Traynor, American jurist;*
*Chief Justice, California Supreme Court*
*New York Times, August 9, 1970*

79.93 ❧ It's easier to be cynical than to be correct. I know that from the judging business. It's easier to write a stinging dissent than a persuasive majority opinion.

*Harry A. Blackmun*
*San Francisco Examiner, July 12, 1971*

79.94 ❧ A great intellectual doesn't make a great trial judge. A man who's been a trial lawyer is a better judge of human nature than Professor X at Harvard, who's probably never been in the well of a courtroom. . . . The important question is whether a judge is honest and does he have the courage of his convictions to do what is right at the moment.

*John J. Sirica*
*New York Times Magazine,*
*November 4, 1973*

79.95 ❧ Old magistrate to young lawyer: "Young man, quit jumping up and saying 'I object. You are not proceeding according to law.' I'll have you understand I am running this court, and the law hasn't got a damn thing to do with it!"

*Sam Ervin*
*Thad Stem, Jr. and Alan Butler* Sam
*Ervin's Best Stories, 1973*

79.96 ❧ There is always a tendency to judicialize everything that goes wrong in our criminal justice system. The judge has one pill in his little black bag: it is called judicialization. The trouble with that is that solutions are stuck into these problems, but no one ever examines why the problems arose in the first place.

*Donald Cressey, American educator;*
*professor, University of California,*
*Santa Barbara*
*Center Magazine,*
*November–December 1975*

79.97 ❧ If the judiciary is to be the primary agency for social reform, shouldn't we be more concerned about the quality of the people we choose for judges? For the most part, judges are narrow-minded lawyers with little

background for making social judgments.

*Philip B. Kurland, American educator;*
*professor, University of*
*Chicago Law School*
*U.S. News & World Report,*
*January 19, 1976*

79.98 ❧ Judges are the weakest link in our system of justice, and they are also the most protected.

*Alan Dershowitz*
*Newsweek, February 20, 1978*

79.99 ❧ The more the courts are asked to handle political issues, the more their fragility is exposed. To some extent, the questioning of the courts is simply part of the increased attention that has been paid to all our institutions over the past several years. What concerns me is that the focus of this questioning of the courts seems to be not on matters of substance but rather on points of prejudice and personal pique. A judge's integrity, fairness, temperament, and knowledge of the law are all pertinent areas for public inquiry. However, what is happening instead is that judges are being perceived as easy targets and are being portrayed in a manner calculated to create prejudice in the public mind.

*Rose E. Bird, American jurist;*
*Chief Justice, California State*
*Supreme Court*
*San Francisco Examiner & Chronicle,*
*October 22, 1978*

*79.100* ❦ The most important [judicial qualities are]: quality and competence and temperament and character and diligence.

> *Potter Stewart*
> Washington Post,
> *June 20, 1981*

*79.101* ❦ We must never forget that the only real source of power that we as judges can tap is the respect of the people.

> *Thurgood Marshall*
> Chicago Tribune, *August 15, 1981*

*79.102* ❦ . . . has the judiciary's perception of right and wrong gone so far out of the mainstream of that society that people are concerned and alarmed? If they are, they should be able to express it through the ballot box. They [justices] cannot become some kind of priesthood beyond the reach of people in a democratic society.

> *Gideon Kanner, American educator;*
> *professor, Loyola University*
> Christian Science Monitor,
> *October 13, 1982*

*79.103* ❦ Judges are, in many respects, like parents. You have to give them a good enough reason to do what you want.

> *Darlene Ricker*
> Lawyer's Wit and Wisdom, *edited by*
> *Bruce Nash, Allan Zullo and compiled*
> *by Kathryn Zullo, 1995*

*79.104* ❦ A judge steps out of the proper judicial role most conspicuously and dangerously when he or she flinches from a decision that is legally right because the decision is not the one the home crowd wants.

> *Ruth Bader Ginsburg*
> *Dawn Bradley Berry,* The 50 Most
> Influential Women in American Law,
> *1996*

*79.105* ❦ Once you put on a robe, the male-female distinction disappears, at least as far as the people who appear before you are concerned. They don't see you as either male or female.

> *Cecilia Goetz, judge*
> *Dawn Bradley Berry,* The 50 Most
> Influential Women in American Law,
> *1996*

*79.106* ❦ What we needed was someone who would be temperate but decisive. Someone who would be consistent. Someone who knew enough law and had enough confidence to rule from the bench. We needed the ump of all umps. A square-jawed, rock-ribbed referee with heuvos of steel.

> *Marcia Clark*
> Without a Doubt, *with Teresa*
> *Carpenter, 1997*

*79.107* ❦ It's not unusual for a D.A. to be tweaked by a judge's day-to-day rulings, only to recall him as a fine and thoughtful jurist when the outcome is favorable.

> *Marcia Clark*
> Without a Doubt, *with Teresa*
> *Carpenter, 1997*

# *80.* JUDGMENT

*80.1* ❧ If a wicked man and a pious man are before you in court, do not say: I will turn judgment against the wicked.

*Anonymous*
Joseph L. Baron, A Treasury of Jewish Quotations, *1956*

*80.2* ❧ Only judge when you have heard all.

*Greek proverb*
Robert and Mary Collison, The Dictionary of Foreign Quotations, *1980*

*80.3* ❧ Before you start up a ladder, count the rungs.

*Jewish folk saying*
Joseph L. Baron, A Treasury of Jewish Quotations, *1956*

*80.4* ❧ Don't try to fill a sack that's full of holes.

*Jewish folk saying*
Joseph L. Baron, A Treasury of Jewish Quotations, *1956*

*80.5* ❧ Usage is the best interpreter of things.

*Legal maxim*

*80.6* ❧ Give every man the benefit of the doubt.

*Sayings of the Fathers*
Joseph L. Baron, A Treasury of Jewish Quotations, *1956*

*80.7* ❧ Just as you listen to the poor man, listen to the rich man, for it is written, "Ye shall not favor persons in judgment."

*Rabbi Nathan*
Midrash, Aboth de Rabbi Nathan

*80.8* ❧ He who passes judgment on fools is himself judged a fool.

*Midrash*

*80.9* ❧ Judgment delayed is judgment voided.

*Talmud, Sanhedrin*

*80.10* ❧ Judge every man charitably.

*Joshua, the Son of Perachyah*
Aboth: Sayings of the Fathers, *c.200*
Joseph L. Baron, A Teasury of Jewish Quotations, *1956*

*80.11* ❧ O mortal men, be wary how ye judge.

*Dante*
Paradiso, *1320*

*80.12* ❧ A man had need of tough ears to hear himself judged.

*Michel de Montaigne*
Essais, *1588*

**80.13** ❦ The law is not exact upon the subject, but leaves it open to a good man's judgment.

*Hugo Grotius, 1583–1645*
*W. Gurney Benham,* Putnam's
Complete Book of Quotations,
Proverbs and Household Words, *1927*

**80.14** ❦ The greatest of all gifts is the power to estimate things at their true worth.

*La Rochefoucauld*
Maximes, *1665*

**80.15** ❦ Sir, as a man advances in life, he gets what is better than admiration— judgment, to estimate things at their true value.

*Samuel Johnson*
*James Boswell,* The Life of Samuel
Johnson, *1791*

**80.16** ❦ Nothing is so easy as to be wise after the event.

*Chief Justice Jervis*
*c.1859*

**80.17** ❦ The state trial judges are being asked to make moral judgments. On abortion. On the question of when death occurs. These shouldn't be a judge's decisions. These should be scientific or theological decisions.

*Jack P. Etheridge, American jurist;*
*judge, Senior Circuit Court, Georgia*
Christian Science Monitor,
*November 27, 1978*

# *81.* JURIES

**81.1** ❦ Let the judge answer on the question of law; the jury on the question of fact.

*Latin legal phrase W. Gurney Benham,*
Putnam's Complete Book of
Quotations, Proverbs and
Household Words, *1927*

**81.2** ❦ A fox should not be of the jury at a goose's trial.

*Proverb*
*Thomas Fuller,* Gnomologia, 1732

**81.3** ❦ Keep your fellows' counsels and your own.

*Shakespeare*
*Oath administered to a Grand Jury,*
Much Ado About Nothing, *III, 3,*
*1598–1599*

**81.4** ❦ The jury, passing on the prisoner's life,
May in the sworn twelve have a thief or two
Guiltier than him they try.

*Shakespeare*
Measure for Measure,
*II, 1, 1604–1605*

**81.5** ❧ Wilt make haste to give up thy
verdict because thou wilt not lose
thy dinner.

*Thomas Middleton*
*A Trick to Catch the Old One,*
*c.1604–1611*

**81.6** ❧ As the law does think fit
No butchers shall on juries sit.

*Charles Churchill*
*The Ghost, 1762–1763*

**81.7** ❧ Twelve good honest men shall
decide in our cause,
And be judges of fact though not
judges of law.

*William Pulteney, earl of Bath,*
*1684–1764*
*"The Honest Jury" (song)*

**81.8** ❧ Every new tribunal, erected for the
decision of facts, without the
intervention of a jury . . . is a step
towards establishing aristocracy, the
most oppressive of absolute
governments.

*Sir William Blackstone*
*Commentaries on the Laws of*
*England, 1765–1769*

**81.9** ❧ There is no distinction between a
good jury and a common jury.

*Charles Butler, English jurist*
*King v. Perry (1793), 5 T.R. 460*

**81.10** ❧ In truth, it is better to toss up cross
and pile [heads or tails] in a cause
than to refer it to a judge whose
mind is warped by any motive

whatever, in that particular case. But
the common sense of twelve honest
men gives still a better chance of just
decision than the hazard of cross
and pile.

*Thomas Jefferson, 1743–1826*
*Saul K. Padover,* The Complete
Jefferson, *1943*

**81.11** ❧ In my mind, he was guilty of no error, he was chargeable with no exag-
geration, he was betrayed by his
fancy into no metaphor, who once
said that all we see about us, kings,
lords, and Commons, the whole machinery of the State, all the apparatus of the system, and its varied
workings, end in simply bringing
twelve good men into a box.

*Henry Peter Brougham, English jurist;*
*Lord Chancellor*
*"Present State of the Law" (speech),*
*February 7, 1828*

**81.12** ❧ Juries, above all civil juries, help
every citizen to share something of
the deliberations that go on in the
judge's mind; and it is these very
deliberations which best prepare the
people to be free.

*Alexis de Tocqueville*
*Democracy in America, 1835–1840*

**81.13** ❧ Juries . . . have the effect . . . of
placing the law in the hands of those
who would be most apt to abuse it.

*James Fenimore Cooper*
*The Redskins, 1846*

**81.14** ❦ A jury too frequently have at least one member more ready to hang the panel than hang the traitor.

*Abraham Lincoln*
*Letter to Erastus Corning et al,*
*June 12, 1863*

**81.15** ❦ I confess that in my experience I have not found juries specially inspired for the discovery of the truth . . . they will introduce into their verdict a certain amount—a very large amount, so far as I have observed—of popular prejudice, and thus keep the administration of the law in accord with the wishes and feelings of the community.

*Oliver Wendell Holmes*
*Address, January 17, 1899*

**81.16** ❦ Th' lawyers make th' law, th' judges make th' errors, but th' editors make th' juries.

*Finley Peter Dunne*
*American Magazine, October 1906*

**81.17** ❦ The jury has the power to bring in a verdict in the teeth of both law and facts.

*Oliver Wendell Holmes*
*Horning v. District of Columbia, 249*
*U.S. 596, 39 S. Ct. 386, 63 L. Ed.*
*794 (1920)*

**81.18** ❦ Trial by jury is a rough scales at best; the beam ought not to tip for motes and straws.

*Learned Hand*
*United States v. Brown, 79F (2d)*
*321, 326 (1935)*

**81.19** ❦ And how, milord, can we expect these twelve poor mutts on the jury—
The Judge: What is a mutt?
Sir Ethelred: Milord, a mutt—
The Judge: Sir Ethelred, no doubt you know best the lines of advocacy most likely to advance the interests of your clients; but is it quite wise to describe the jury as 'mutts', which, though I am not familiar with it, I judge instinctively to be a term of depreciation?
Sir Ethelred: Milord, 'mutt' is a relative term. The Prime Minister, if he were requested to transpose a musical composition in A flat major into the key of E minor would readily confess himself a mutt in relation to that particular task.
The Judge: Very well, Sir Ethelred. Proceed.
Sir Ethelred (turning to the jury): How, I say, can you poor mutts be expected to get a grip of this colossal conundrum *without the assistance of any documents at all?*

*A. P. Herbert*
*Uncommon Law, 1936*

**81.20** ❦ But juries are not bound by what seems inescapable logic to judges.

*Robert H. Jackson*
*Morissette v. United States, 342 U.S.*
*246, 276 (1952)*

**81.21** ❦ Jury service honorably performed is as important in the defense of our country, its Constitution and laws, and the ideals and standards for which they stand, as the service that is rendered by the soldier on the field of battle in time of war.

*George H. Boldt, American jurist*
United States v. Beck *(1959)*

81.22 ❧ A jury verdict is a quotient of the prejudices of twelve people.

*Kenneth P. Grubb, American jurist*
*"False Fears,"* Insurance Counsel
Journal, *October 1959*

81.23 ❧ Gentlemen, a court is no better than each man of you sitting before me on this jury. A court is only as sound as its jury, and a jury is only as sound as the men who make it up.

*Harper Lee*
To Kill a Mockingbird, *1960*

81.24 ❧ A jury consists of 12 persons chosen to decide who has the better lawyer.

*Robert Frost,* 1874–1963
*Kenneth Redden,* Modern Legal
Glossary, *1983*

81.25 ❧ The classic adversary system in the United States not only encourages, it demands that each lawyer attempt to empanel the jury most likely to understand his argument, or least likely to understand that of his opponent. You don't approach a case with the philosophy of applying abstract justice. You go in to win.

*Percy Foreman*
New York Times, *February 3, 1969*

81.26 ❧ The day of manipulating a jury is absolutely gone, if there ever was such a day. Cases are won through preparation, dragging the facts into the courtroom. The lawyer excavates the facts, and the more he digs, the more certain is he to win; and then he can pound upon the facts and an emotional appeal—that's the way of persuasion. But to play clever with a jury when you don't have the facts leaves them cold. They resent it.

*Louis Nizer*
San Francisco Examiner,
*May 29, 1974*

81.27 ❧ Percy Foreman and I once had an argument as to which one of us had picked the most stupid jury. I think I won with one that returned a verdict which amounted to "Not guilty with a recommendation of clemency because of reasonable doubt."

*F. Lee Bailey*
Lawyer's Wit and Wisdom, *edited by*
*Bruce Nash, Allan Zullo and compiled*
*by Kathryn Zullo, 1995*

81.28 ❧ If the district attorney wanted, a grand jury would indict a ham sandwich.

*Sydney Biddle Barrows*
Lawyer's Wit and Wisdom, *edited by*
*Bruce Nash, Allan Zullo and compiled*
*by Kathryn Zullo,*
*1995*

81.29 ❧ As proud as we trial lawyers are of our abilities, the fact is that none of our skills, however polished, and none of our evidence, however convincing, necessarily amounts to anything, if we don't have a jury that is willing to listen.

*Johnnie L. Cochran*
Journey to Justice, *with Tim Rutten,*
*1996*

81.30 ❦ Why did we wind up with the jury pool from hell?

*Marcia Clark*
Without a Doubt, *with Teresa*
*Carpenter, 1997*

# *82.* JUSTICE

82.1 ❦ Justice delayed is worse than injustice.

*Jewish folk saying*
*Joseph L. Baron,* A Treasury of Jewish
Quotations, *1956*

82.2 ❦ A just balance preserves justice.

*Latin proverb*
*W. Gurney Benham,* Putnam's
Complete Book of Quotations,
Proverbs and Household Words, *1927*

82.3 ❦ There is no wrong without a remedy.

*Legal maxim*

82.4 ❦ Be just before you are generous.

*Proverb*
*Bergen Evans,* Dictionary of
Quotations, *1968*

82.5 ❦ Much law, but little justice.

*Proverb*
*Rosalind Fergusson,* The Facts On File
Dictionary of Proverbs, *1983*

82.6 ❦ Justice pleaseth few in their own house.

*Proverb*
*George Herbert,* Outlandish Proverbs,
*1639*

82.7 ❦ Justice, justice shall you pursue.

*Old Testament, Deuteronomy 16:20*

82.8 ❦ Eye for eye, tooth for tooth, hand for hand, foot for foot.

*Old Testament, Exodus 21:24*

82.9 ❦ Just balances, just weights . . . shall ye have: . . .

*Old Testament, Leviticus 19:36*

82.10 ❦ Abraham said to God: "If you want the world to exist, you cannot insist upon complete justice; if it is complete justice you want, the world cannot endure."

*Midrash, Genesis Rabba*

**82.11** ❦ Justice is but the interest of the stronger.

*Plato*
The Republic, c.370 B.C.

**82.12** ❦ It were to be wished that those who are at the head of the common-wealth were like the laws, which are moved to punish, not by anger, but by justice.

*Cicero*
De Officiis, 45–44 B.C.

**82.13** ❦ The foundations of justice are that no one shall be harmed, and next that the common weal be served.

*Cicero,* 106–43 B.C.
*William S. Walsh,* International Encyclopedia of Prose and Poetical Quotations, 1968

**82.14** ❦ The people become more subservi-ent to justice . . . when they see the author of a law obeying it himself.

*Claudian (Claudius Claudianus)*
Panegyricus de Quarto Consulatu Honorii Augusti, 398

**82.15** ❦ If you see wicked men perverting jus-tice, do not say: "Since they are many, I must follow after them."

*Rashi (Rabbi Solomon Ben Isaac),*
1040–1105
Commentaries on the Pentateuch

**82.16** ❦ To no one will we sell, to no one will we refuse or delay, right or justice.

*Magna Carta, 1215*

**82.17** ❦ Kings gain greater riches through justice than do tyrants by rapacity.

*St. Thomas Aquinas*
On Princely Government, 1266

**82.18** ❦ Let justice be done though the world perish.

*Ferdinand I, emperor of the Holy Roman Empire,* 1558–1564
*Motto*

**82.19** ❦ Law hath certain lawful fictions upon which it groundeth the truth of justice.

*Michel de Montaigne*
Essais, 1588

**82.20** ❦ I beseech your Majesty, let me have Justice, and I will then trust the law.

*Elizabeth Hoby Russell, English diarist and courtier*
*Spoken to King James I, 1603*

**82.21** ❦ Duke: . . . our decrees,
Dead to infliction, to themselves are dead;
And liberty plucks Justice by the nose.

*Shakespeare*
Measure for Measure, I, 3, 1604–1605

**82.22** ❦ Lear: Plate sin with gold,
And the strong lance of justice hurtless breaks;
Arm it in rags, a pigmy's straw doth pierce it.

*Shakespeare*
King Lear, IV, 6, 1605–1606

82.23 ❦ Justice may wink a while, but see
at last.

*Thomas Middleton*
The Mayor of Quinborough, *1606*

82.24 ❦ The weakest arm is strong enough
that strikes,
With the sword of justice.

*John Webster*
The Dutchess of Malfi, *c.1614*

82.25 ❦ Fresh justice is the sweetest.

*Francis Bacon, on taking his seat as*
*Lord Keeper*
Speech, May 7, *1617*

82.26 ❦ . . . it is the worst oppression, that is
done by colour of justice.

*Sir Edward Coke*
The Institutes of the Lawes of
England, *vol. 2, 1628–1641*

82.27 ❦ Where the fault springs, there let justice fall.

*Robert Herrick*
Hesperides, *1648*

82.28 ❦ Justice is blind, he knows nobody.

*John Dryden,*
The Wild Gallant, *1663*

82.29 ❦ Justice, while she winks at crimes,
Stumbles on innocence sometimes.

*Samuel Butler*
Hudibras, *1663–1678*

82.30 ❦ The love of justice is simply, in the
majority of men, the fear of suffering injustice.

*La Rochefoucauld*
Maximes, *1665*

82.31 ❦ Justice is what is established; and
thus all our established laws will be
regarded as just, without being
examined, since they are established.

*Pascal*
Pensées, *1670*

82.32 ❦ Justice is lame as well as blind,
amongst us.

*Thomas Otway*
Venice Preserved, *1682*

82.33 ❦ A prince's favours but on few can
fall,
But justice is a virtue shar'd by all.

*John Dryden, 1631–1700*
Britannia Rediviva

82.34 ❦ "There, take," says Justice, "take you
each a shell.
We thrive at Westminster on fools
like you.
'Twas a fat oyster—Live in peace—
Adieu!"

*Nicolas Boileau-Despréaux,*
*1636–1711*
*W. Gurney Benham,* Putnam's
Complete Dictionary of Quotations,
Proverbs and Household Words, *1927*

82.35 ❦ Hard is the task of justice, where
distress
Excites our mercy, yet demands
redress.

*Colley Cibber*
The Heroik Daughter, *1718*

82.36 ❦ Poetic Justice, with her lifted scale,
Where in nice balance truth with
gold she weighs,
And solid pudding against empty
praise.

*Alexander Pope*
The Dunciad, *1728–1743*

82.37 ❦ A good person once said that where
mystery begins religion ends.
Cannot I say, as truly at least, of
human laws, that where mystery
begins, justice ends?

*Edmund Burke*
A Vindication of Natural Society,
*1761*

82.38 ❦ Amongst the sons of men how few
are known
Who dare be just to merit not their
own?

*Charles Churchill*
Epistle to W. Hogarth, *July 1763*

82.39 ❦ Justice, that in the rigid paths of law,
would still some drops from Pity's
fountain draw.

*John Langhorne, American poet*
The Country Justice, *c.1766*

82.40 ❦ Let justice be done though the
heavens fall.

*Sir James Mansfield, English jurist;*
*Chief Justice*
Rex v. Wilkes *(1769), 4 Burr. Part*
*IV., p. 2549*

82.41 ❦ It looks to me to be narrow and pe-
dantic to apply the ordinary ideas of
criminal justice to this great public
contest. I do not know the method

of drawing up an indictment against
a whole people.

*Edmund Burke*
*Speech on moving his resolutions for*
*conciliation with the Colonies,*
*March 22, 1775*

82.42 ❦ I tremble for my country when I
reflect that God is just; that his
justice cannot sleep forever; that
considering numbers, nature, and
natural means only, a revolution of
the wheel of fortune, an exchange of
situation, is among possible events;
that it may become probable by
supernatural interference! The
Almighty has no attribute which can
take side with us in such a contest.

*Thomas Jefferson*
Notes on Virginia, *1785*

82.43 ❦ There is one universal law that has
been formed or at least adopted . . .
by the majority of mankind. That
law is justice. Justice forms the cornerstone of each nation's law.

*Alexis de Tocqueville*
Democracy in America, *1835*

82.44 ❦ Justice first, then after that the law.

*Esther McQuigg Morris, first female*
*judge in the U.S.*
*Dawn Bradley Berry,* The 50 Most
Influential Women in American Law,
*1996*

82.45 ❦ Justice is truth in action.

*Benjamin Disraeli*
*Speech, House of Commons,*
*February 11, 1851*

82.46 ❦ The law does not generate justice.
The law is nothing but a declaration
and application of what is
already just.

> *Pierre Joseph Proudhon*
> De la justice dans la révolution, *1858*

82.47 ❦ It costs us nothing to be just.

> *Henry David Thoreau*
> John Brown's Body, *1859*

82.48 ❦ Justice is like the Kingdom of
God—it is not without us as a fact,
it is within us as a great yearning.

> *George Eliot*
> Romola, *1862–1863*

82.49 ❦ Justice travels with a leaden heel, but
strikes with an iron hand.

> *Jeremiah S. Black, American jurist*
> *Warning after the decision in the*
> *Hayes-Tilden presidential election count*
> *of 1876*

82.50 ❦ Whoever fights, whoever falls, Justice conquers evermore.

> *Ralph Waldo Emerson,* 1803–1882
> Voluntaries

82.51 ❦ We love justice greatly, and just men
but little.

> *Joseph Roux*
> Meditations of a Parish Priest, *1886*

82.52 ❦ But the sunshine aye shall light the
sky,
As round and round we run;
And the truth shall ever come upper-
most.
And justice shall be done.

> *Charles Mackay, Scottish writer,*
> 1814–1889
> Eternal Justice

82.53 ❦ Of relative justice law may know
something; of expediency it knows
much; with absolute justice it does
not concern itself.

> *Oliver Wendell Holmes, American*
> *physician and author*
> The Works of Oliver Wendell
> Holmes, *1891*

82.54 ❦ The hope of all who suffer,
The dread of all who wrong.

> *John Greenleaf Whittier,* 1807–1892
> Mantle of St. John De Matha

82.55 ❦ The attainment of justice is the highest human endeavor.

> *Florence Ellinwood Allen,* 1884–1966
> *Dawn Bradley Berry,* The 50 Most
> Influential Women in American Law,
> *1996*

82.56 ❦ We are the whirlwinds that winnow
the West—
We scatter the wicked like straw!
We are the Nemeses, never at rest—
We are Justice, and Right, and
the Law!

> *Margaret Ashmun*
> *"The Vigilantes,"* Pacific Monthly,
> *1907*

82.57 ❦ Crime takes but a moment but
justice an eternity.

> *Ellen O'Grady*
> *Djuna Barnes, "Woman Police Deputy*
> *Is Writer of Poetry,"* New York
> Sun Magazine, *1918*

*82.58* ❦ Injustice is relatively easy to bear;
what stings is justice.

> *H. L. Mencken*
> Prejudices: Third series, *1922*

*82.59* ❦ Justice is not to be taken by storm.
She is to be wooed by slow advances.

> *Benjamin N. Cardozo*
> The Growth of the Law, *1924*

*82.60* ❦ There is a justice, but we do not always see it. Discreet, smiling, it is
there, at one side, a little behind injustice, which makes a big noise.

> *Jules Renard*
> Journal, *1925–1927*

*82.61* ❦ No system of justice can rise above
the ethics of those who administer it.

> Report of the National (Wickersham)
> Commission on Law Observance and
> Law Enforcement, *1929*

*82.62* ❦ There is no such thing as justice—in
or out of court.

> *Clarence Darrow*
> New York Times, *April 19, 1936*

*82.63* ❦ Justice is not a cloistered virtue:
she must be allowed to suffer the
scrutiny and respectful, even
though outspoken, comments of
ordinary men.

> *James Richard Atkin, 1st baron of*
> *Aberdovey*
> Ambard v. Attorney General for
> Trinidad *(1936), A.C. 322, 335*

*82.64* ❦ Justice, though due to the accused,
is due to the accuser also.

> *Benjamin N. Cardozo, 1870–1938*
> *Kenneth Redden,* Modern Legal
> Glossary, *1983*

*82.65* ❦ Why should there be not a patient
confidence in the ultimate justice of
the people?

> *Inscription over the main door of the*
> *Manhattan Criminal Court Building,*
> *1939*

*82.66* ❦ Justice is not a prize tendered to the
good-natured, nor is it to be with-
held from the ill-bred.

> *Charles L. Aarons*
> Hach v. Lewinsky et al., *(1945)*

*82.67* ❦ Justice, I think, is the tolerable accommodation of the conflicting interests of society, and I don't believe
there is any royal road to attain such
accommodations concretely.

> *Learned Hand*
> Life, *November 4, 1946*

*82.68* ❦ If we are to keep our democracy,
there must be one commandment:
Thou shalt not ration justice.

> *Learned Hand*
> Address, Legal Aid Society of New York,
> *February 16, 1951*

*82.69* ❦ Justice is too good for some people
and not good enough for the rest.

> *Norman Douglas, 1868–1952*
> *Laurence J. Peter,* Peter's Quotations,
> *1977*

82.70 ❦ Justice has been described as a lady who has been subject to so many miscarriages as to cast serious reflections upon her virtue.

*William L. Prosser, American educator;*
*dean, University of California Law*
*School*
The Judicial Humorist, *1952*

82.71 ❦ We should not permit tolerance to degenerate into indifference.

*Margaret Chase Smith*
*Raymond Swing, ed.,* This I Believe: 2,
*1954*

82.72 ❦ One must always be ready to change sides with justice, that fugitive from the winning camp.

*Simone Weil*
*Peter Viereck,* The Unadjusted Man,
*1956*

82.73 ❦ Swift justice demands more than just swiftness.

*Potter Stewart*
Time, *Oct. 20, 1958*

82.74 ❦ Fairness is what justice really is.

*Potter Stewart*
Time, *October 20, 1958*

82.75 ❦ The justice of the law is, therefore, a "statistical" justice, an average justice, a kind of rationed goods preserving all from want but sufficient for no one.

*Moshe Silberg*
*"Law and Morals in Jewish*
*Jurisprudence," 75* Harvard Law
Review *306, 316 (1961)*

82.76 ❦ "Look here," Furii said. "I never promised you a rose garden. I never promised you perfect justice. . . ."

*Hannah Green, American writer*
I Never Promised You a Rose
Garden, *1964*

82.77 ❦ They call it the Halls of Justice because the only place you get justice is in the halls.

*Lenny Bruce, 1926–1966*
*Kenneth Redden,* Modern Legal
Glossary, *1983*

82.78 ❦ Justice at its best is love correcting everything that stands against love.

*Martin Luther King, Jr.*
Where Do We Go from Here: Chaos
or Community?, *1967*

82.79 ❦ Justice delayed is not only justice denied—it is also justice circumvented, justice mocked and the system of justice undermined.

*Richard M. Nixon*
New York Times, *March 12, 1971*

82.80 ❦ Ideas, ideals and great conceptions are vital to a system of justice, but it must have more than that—there must be delivery and execution. Concepts of justice must have hands and feet or they remain sterile abstractions. The hands and feet we need are efficient means and methods to carry out justice in every case in the shortest possible time and at the lowest possible cost. This is the challenge to every lawyer and judge in America.

*Warren E. Burger*
*Address, American Bar Association,*
*San Francisco, reported in* Vital
Speeches, *October 1, 1972*

*82.81* ❧ The law is not the private property of lawyers, nor is justice the exclusive province of judges and juries. In the final analysis, true justice is not a matter of courts and law books, but of a commitment in each of us to liberty and mutual respect.

> *Jimmy Carter*
> Dallas Times-Herald, *April 26, 1978*

*82.82* ❧ Justice is: JUST US.

> *Richard Pryor*
> *In performance*

*82.83* ❧ Pride is never sinful when it is Justice.

> *Barbara Chase-Riboud*
> Echo of Lions, *1989*

*82.84* ❧ When it comes to justice, I take no prisoners and I don't believe in compromising.

> *Mary Frances Berry*
> Lawyer's Wit and Wisdom,
> *edited by Bruce Nash,*
> *Allan Zullo and compiled by*
> *Kathryn Zullo, 1995*

*82.85* ❧ I have a saying—there's no justice in the law.

> *Ellen Morphonios*
> Lawyer's Wit and Wisdom, *edited by*
> *Bruce Nash, Allan Zullo and compiled*
> *by Kathryn Zullo, 1995*

*82.86* ❧ It is the zealous defense of the individual—however unpopular, however revolting the alleged crime—that guarantees the right of the peace-loving majority to live secure in its freedom. It is this unyielding commitment to equal and indivisible justice for all—no matter what the personal cost—that makes a defense attorney more than just a profiteer of pain.

> *Johnnie L. Cochran*
> Journey to Justice, *with Tim Rutten,*
> *1996*

*82.87* ❧ Americans dislike the fact that legal access is for sale, but they also dislike efforts to remedy it. Justice is what we proclaim on courthouse entrances, not in redistributed policies. As a result, most Americans end up with all—and only—the justice money can buy.

> *Deborah L. Rhode*
> Lawyers, *in press*

# *83.* LAW

83.1 ❧ Even as there are laws of poetry, so there is poetry in law.

*Anonymous*
*Joseph L. Baron*, A Treasury of Jewish Quotations, *1956*

83.2 ❧ The glorious uncertainty of the law.

*English phrase*

83.3 ❧ Worse people worse laws.

*English proverb*
*George England and A. W. Pollard,* Towneley Plays, *1897*

83.4 ❧ Good laws come from lewd lives.

*French or English proverb*
*James Howell*, Proverbs, *1659*

83.5 ❧ The law has a wax nose.

*French proverb*
*H. L. Mencken*, A New Dictionary of Quotations, *1946*

83.6 ❧ When a law is made the way to avoid it is found out.

*Italian proverb*
*W. Gurney Benham,* Putnam's Book of Quotations, Proverbs and Household Words, *1927*

83.7 ❧ Without law, civilization dies.

*Jewish folk saying*
Leo Rosten's Treasury of Jewish Quotations, *1972*

83.8 ❧ The disposition of law is more decisive and powerful than that of men.

*Latin legal phrase*
*W. Gurney Benham,* Putnam's Complete Book of Quotations, Proverbs and Household Words, *1927*

83.9 ❧ The law aims at perfection.

*Latin legal phrase*
*W. Gurney Benham,* Putnam's Complete Book of Quotations, Proverbs and Household Words, *1927*

83.10 ❧ The law effects injustice to no one; and does injury to no one.

*Latin legal phrase*
*W. Gurney Benham,* Putnam's Book of Quotations, Proverbs and Household Words, *1927*

83.11 ❧ Laws are made by the conqueror, and accepted by the conquered.

*Latin proverb*
*H. L. Mencken*, A New Dictionary of Quotations, *1946*

83.12 ❦ Like King, like law; like law, like people.

*Portuguese proverb*
*W. Gurney Benham,* Putnam's Complete Book of Quotations, Proverbs and Household Words, *1927*

83.13 ❦ Be you never so high, the law is above you.

*Proverb*
*Thomas Fuller,* Gnomologia, *1732*

83.14 ❦ Every law has a loophole.

*Proverb*
*Rosalind Fergusson,* The Facts On File Dictionary of Proverbs, *1983*

83.15 ❦ Ill Kings make many good laws.

*Proverb*
*Thomas Fuller,* Gnomologia, *1732*

83.16 ❦ Law governs man and reason the law.

*Proverb*
*Thomas Fuller,* Gnomologia, *1732*

83.17 ❦ Laws catch flies but let hornets go free.

*Proverb*
*Rosalind Fergusson,* The Facts On File Dictionary of Proverbs, *1983*

83.18 ❦ Many lords, many laws.

*Proverb*
*Rosalind Fergusson,* The Facts On File Dictionary of Proverbs, *1983*

83.19 ❦ New lords, new laws.

*Proverb*
*Rosalind Fergusson,* The Facts On File Dictionary of Proverbs, *1983*

83.20 ❦ New laws, new frauds.

*Proverb*
*W. Gurney Benham,* Putnam's Complete Book of Quotations, Proverbs and Household Words, *1927*

83.21 ❦ The law is not the same at morning and at night.

*Proverb*
*Rosalind Fergusson,* The Facts On File Dictionary of Proverbs, *1983*

83.22 ❦ The more laws, the more offenders.

*Proverb*
*Rosalind Fergusson,* The Facts On File Dictionary of Proverbs, *1983*

83.23 ❦ Wrong laws make short governance.

*Proverb*
*Rosalind Fergusson,* The Facts On File Dictionary of Proverbs, *1983*

83.24 ❦ A penny-weight of love is worth a pound of law.

*Scottish proverb*
*James Kelly,* Complete Collection of Scottish Proverbs, *1721*

83.25 ❦ Show me the man, and I shall show you the law.

*Scottish proverb*
*W. Gurney Benham,* Putnam's Book of
Quotations, Proverbs and
Household Words, *1927*

83.26 ❦ Ye shall have one manner of law, as well for the stranger, as for one of your own country. . . .

*Old Testament, Leviticus 24:22*

83.27 ❦ . . . the law is light. . . .

*Old Testament, Proverbs 6:23*

83.28 ❦ All things are lawful for me, but all things are not expedient: all things are lawful for me, but all things edify not.

*New Testament, 1 Corinthians 10:23*

83.29 ❦ . . . the letter killeth, but the spirit giveth life.

*New Testament, 2 Corinthians 3:6*

83.30 ❦ Is it not lawful for me to do what I will with mine own? Is thine eye evil, because I am good?

*New Testament, Matthew 20:15*

83.31 ❦ . . . where no law is, there is no transgression.

*New Testament, Romans 4:15*

83.32 ❦ But now we are delivered from the law, that being dead wherein we were held; that we should serve in newness of spirit, and not in the oldness of the letter.

*New Testament, Romans 7:6*

83.33 ❦ . . . the law is good, if a man use it lawfully.

*New Testament, 1 Timothy 1:8*

83.34 ❦ The law of the state is one law.

*Talmud, Gittin*

83.35 ❦ Taking the law into one's own hands.

*Aesop,* c.620–560 B.C.
Fables

83.36 ❦ The more mandates and laws are enacted, the more there will be thieves and robbers.

*Lao-tze,* 604?–?531 B.C.
Tao-te-ching

83.37 ❦ The people should fight for the law as for their city wall.

*Heraclitus,* 6th–5th century B.C.
*W. H. Auden and Louis Kronenberger,*
The Viking Book of Aphorisms, *1962*

83.38 ❦ Law, lord of all, mortals and immortals, carries everything with a high hand.

*Pindar*
Fragments, *c.480* B.C.

83.39 ❦ Law can never issue an injunction binding on all which really embodies what is best for each; it cannot prescribe with perfect accuracy what is good and right for each member of the community at any one time. The differences of human personality, the variety of men's activities and the inevitable unsettlement attending all human experience make it impossible for any act whatsoever to issue unqualified rules holding good on all questions at all times.

*Plato,* 427?–347 B.C.
*Politicus*

83.40 ❦ Law, being a tyrant, compels many things to be done contrary to nature.

*Plato*
*Protagoras, c.389* B.C.

83.41 ❦ Every law is the invention and gift of the gods.

*Demosthenes,* 385?–322 B.C.
*W. Gurney Benham,* Putnam's Complete Book of Quotations, Proverbs and Household Words, *1927*

83.42 ❦ Even when laws have been written down, they ought not always to remain unaltered.

*Aristotle*
*Politics, c.322* B.C.

83.43 ❦ Good law means good order.

*Aristotle*
*Politics, c.322* B.C.

83.44 ❦ Law is a pledge that citizens of a state will do justice to one another.

*Aristotle*
*Politics, c.322* B.C.

83.45 ❦ The best laws should be constructed as to leave as little as possible to the decision of the judge.

*Aristotle*
*Rhetoric, c.322* B.C.

83.46 ❦ The law is reason free from passion.

*Aristotle,* 384–322 B.C.
*Laurence J. Peter,* Peter's Quotations, *1977*

83.47 ❦ Accept the law which you yourself make.

*Cato*
*"Prologus,"* Distichia, *c.175* B.C.

83.48 ❦ A people can be strong where the laws are strong.

*Publilius Syrus, Latin writer,* 1st century B.C.
*W. Gurney Benham,* Putnam's Complete Book of Quotations, Proverbs and Household Words, *1927*

83.49 ❦ The universal law is that which ordains that we are to be born and to die.

*Publilius Syrus, Latin writer,* 1st century B.C.
*W. Gurney Benham,* Putnam's Complete Book of Quotations, Proverbs and Household Words, *1927*

**83.50** ❦ Law is the highest reason, implanted
in Nature, which commands what
ought to be done and forbids the
opposite.

*Cicero*
De Legibus, *52* B.C.

**83.51** ❦ The magistrate is a speaking law, but
the law is a silent magistrate.

*Cicero*
De Legibus, *52* B.C.

**83.52** ❦ The laws put the safety of all above
the safety of one.

*Cicero*
De Finibus, *c.50* B.C.

**83.53** ❦ These laws being removed, the right
appear wrong.

*Cicero,* 106–43 B.C.
*W. Gurney Benham,* Putnam's
Complete Book of Quotations,
Proverbs and Household Words, *1927*

**83.54** ❦ How rashly we sanction a law unfair
to ourselves.

*Horace*
Satires, *35* B.C.

**83.55** ❦ He gives laws to the peoples, and
makes for himself a way to the
heavens.

*Virgil*
Georgics, *30* B.C.

**83.56** ❦ Time is the best interpreter of every
doubtful law.

*Dionysius of Halicarnassus*
Antiquities of Rome, *c.20* B.C.

**83.57** ❦ No law perfectly suits the convenience of every member of the community; the only consideration is,
whether upon the whole it be profitable to the greater part.

*Livy*
History of Rome, *c.10* B.C.

**83.58** ❦ Laws were made that the stronger
might not in all things have his way.

*Ovid*
Fasti, *c.8*

**83.59** ❦ The purpose of law is to prevent the
strong always having their way.

*Ovid*
Fasti, *c.8*

**83.60** ❦ Law has bread and butter in it.

*Petronius*
Satyricon, *c.60*

**83.61** ❦ It is right that a law should be short
in order that it may be the more
easily grasped by the unlearned.

*Seneca*
Epistulae Morales ad Lucilium, *63–65*

**83.62** ❦ Some [laws] are good, some are
middling, the most are bad.

*Martial*
Epigrams, *85*

83.63 ❧ The prince is not above the laws, but the laws above the prince.

*Pliny the Younger*
Panegyricus Traianus, *100*

83.64 ❧ As physicians are the preservers of the sick, so are the laws of the injured.

*Epictetus*
Encheiridion, *c.110*

83.65 ❧ Good men need no laws, and bad men are not made better by them.

*Ascribed to Demonax of Cyprus,*
*Cynic philosopher, 70–170*
*H. L. Mencken,* A New Dictionary
of Quotations, *1946*

83.66 ❧ Laws are spiders' webs, which stand firm when any light and yielding object falls upon them, while a larger thing breaks through them and escapes.

*Solon*
*Diogenes Laërtius,* Lives of Eminent
Philosophers, *3rd Century*

83.67 ❧ Good laws are produced by bad manners.

*Macrobius, Latin writer and*
*philosopher, fl.* c.400
Saturnalia

83.68 ❧ The precepts of the law are these: to live honorably, to injure no other man, to render every man his due.

*Justinian I*
Institutes, *c.533*

83.69 ❧ The law is lordly.

*William Langland*
The Vision of William Concerning
Piers the Plowman, *c.1362–c.1390*

83.70 ❧ Forthy [therefore] men seyn [say] ech contree hath his laws.

*Chaucer*
Troilus and Criseyde, *c.1385*

83.71 ❧ Do law away, what is a King? Where is the right of any thing?

*John Gower*
Confessio Amantis, *c.1390*

83.72 ❧ And nowadays the law is ended as a man is friended.

*Henry D. Brinklow*
Henry Brinklow's Complaynt of
Roderyck Mors, *c.1542*

83.73 ❧ It would be better to have no laws at all than it is to have so many as we have.

*Michel de Montaigne*
Essais, *1588*

83.74 ❧ There is no one law governing all things.

*Giordano Bruno*
De Monade, numero, et figura, *1591*

83.75 ❧ I have, perhaps, some shallow spirit of judgment;
But in these nice sharp quillets of the law,
Good faith, I am no wiser than a daw.

*Shakespeare*
*1* Henry VI, *II, 4, 1591–1592*

83.76 ❧ Law, Logic and Switzers may be hired to fight for anybody.

*Thomas Nashe*
Christ's Tears, *1593*

83.77 ❦ When law can do no right,
    Let it be lawful that law bar no wrong.

*Shakespeare*
*King John, III, 1, 1596–1597*

83.78 ❦ Portia: The brain may devise laws
        for the blood;
    but a hot temper leaps o'er a cold
        decree!

*Shakespeare*
*The Merchant of Venice, I, 2,*
*1596–1597*

83.79 ❦ There is no worse torture than the
    torture of laws.

*Francis Bacon*
*"Of Judicature," Essayes, 1597*

83.80 ❦ . . . old father antic the law?

*Shakespeare*
*1 Henry IV, I, 2, 1597–1598*

83.81 ❦ First Clown: Argal, he that is not
        guilty of his own death shortens
        not his own life.
    Second Clown: But is this law?
    First Clown: Ay, marry is't;
        crowner's quest law.

*Shakespeare*
*Hamlet, V, 1, 1600–1601*

83.82 ❦ Still you keep o' th' windy side of
    the law.

*Shakespeare*
*Twelfth Night, III, 4, 1601–1602*

83.83 ❦ The law hath not been dead, though
    it hath slept.

*Shakespeare*
*Measure for Measure, II, 2,*
*1604–1605*

83.84 ❦ Duke: The bloody book of law
    You shall yourself read in the bitter
        letter
    After your own sense.

*Shakespeare*
*Othello, I, 3, 1604–1605*

83.85 ❦ Some say men on the back of law
    May ride and rule it like a patient
        ass,
    And with a golden bridle in the
        mouth
    Direct it into anything they please.

*Nathaniel Field*
*A Woman Is a Weathercock, c.1610*

83.86 ❦ The law obliges us to do what is
    proper, not simply what is just.

*Hugo Grotius*
*De Jure Belli ac Pacis, 1625*

83.87 ❦ Law is the safest helmet.

*Sir Edward Coke*
*Inscription, on rings that he gave to*
*friends, c.1630*

83.88 ❦ The good needs fear no law,
    It is his safety and the bad man's awe.

*Phillip Massinger, 1583–1640*
*The Old Law*

83.89 ❦ Law is King.

*Samuel Rutherford, Scottish clergyman*
*Lex Rex, 1644*

83.90 ❦ Law is a pickpurse.

*James Howell, Welsh writer*
*Familiar Letters, 1645–1655*

83.91 ❦ Unnecessary laws are not good laws,
but traps for money.

> *Thomas Hobbes*
> Leviathan, *1651*

83.92 ❦ Ill Manners occasion Good laws, as
the Handsome Children of Ugly
Parents.

> *Thomas Fuller*
> The History of the University of
> Cambridge, *1655*

83.93 ❦ Possession is nine points of the law.

> *Thomas Fuller, 1608–1661*
> Holy War

83.94 ❦ So many Laws argue so many sins.

> *John Milton*
> Paradise Lost, *1667*

83.95 ❦ Old laws have not been suffered to
be pointed,
To leave the sense at large the more
disjointed,
And furnish lawyers, with the
greater ease,
To turn and wind them any way
they please.

> *Samuel Butler, 1617–1680*
> Miscellaneous Thoughts

83.96 ❦ No written laws can be so plain,
so pure,
But wit may gloss and malice may
obscure.

> *John Dryden*
> The Hind and
> the Panther, *1687*

83.97 ❦ For in all the states of created beings, capable of laws, where there is
no law there is no freedom.

> *John Locke*
> Two Treatises on Civil Government,
> *1690*

83.98 ❦ Shall free-born men, in humble awe,
Submit to servile shame;
Who from consent and custom draw
The same right to be ruled by law,
Which kings pretend to reign?

> *John Dryden, 1631–1700*
> On the Young Statesman

83.99 ❦ All voice of nations and the course
of things
Allow that laws superior are to kings.

> *Daniel Defoe*
> The True-Born Englishman, *1701*

83.100 ❦ Laws are the sovereigns of sovereigns.

> *Louis XIV, 1638–1715*

83.101 ❦ Where carcasses are, eagles will
gather,
And where good laws are, much
people flock thither.

> *Benjamin Franklin*
> Poor Richard's Almanack, *1734*

83.102 ❦ Law [is] licensed breaking of the peace.

> *Matthew Green, English poet*
> The Spleen, *1737*

83.103 ❦ Laws too gentle are seldom obeyed;
too severe, seldom executed.

> *Benjamin Franklin*
> Poor Richard's Almanack, *1756*

83.104 ❧ The law is a sort of hocus-pocus science, that smiles in yer face while it
picks yer pocket.

*Charles Macklin, English actor and*
*dramatist*
*Love à la Mode, 1759*

83.105 ❧ Good laws lead to the making of better ones; bad ones bring in worse.

*Jean-Jacques Rousseau*
*Du contrat social, 1762*

83.106 ❧ Laws grind the poor, and rich men
rule the law.

*Oliver Goldsmith*
*The Traveller, 1764*

83.107 ❧ How small, of all that human hearts
endure,
That part which laws or kings can
cause or cure.

*Oliver Goldsmith*
*The Traveller, 1764*

83.108 ❧ Let all the laws be clear, uniform and
precise; to interpret laws is
almost always to corrupt them.

*Voltaire*
*Philosophical Dictionary, 1764*

83.109 ❧ What is the law, if those who make it
Become the forwardest to break it?

*James Beattie*
*The Wolf and the Shepherds, 1776*

83.110 ❧ The laws of a nation form the most
instructive portion of its history. . . .

*Edward Gibbon*
*The Decline and Fall of the Roman*
*Empire, 1776*

83.111 ❧ Bad laws are the worst sort of
tyranny.

*Edmund Burke*
*Speech at Bristol, 1780*

83.112 ❧ Law is law—law is law; and as in
such, and so forth, and hereby, and
aforesaid, provided always, nevertheless, and notwithstanding. Law is
like a country dance: people are led
up and down it till they are tired.
Law is like a book of surgery: there
are a great many desperate cases in
it. It is also like physic: they that
take least of it are best off. Law is
like a homely gentlewoman: very
well to follow. Law is also like a
scolding wife: very bad when it follows us. Law is like a new fashion:
people are bewitched to get into it;
it is also like bad weather: most people are glad when they get out of it.

*George Stevenson, ?–1784*
*Marshall Brown,* Wit and Humor of
Bench and Bar, *1899*

83.113 ❧ The sober second thought of people
shall be the law.

*Fisher Ames, American politician*
*Congressional Speech, 1788*

83.114 ❧ And sovereign Law, that State's
collected will,
O'er thrones and globes elate,
Sits Empress, crowning good,
repressing ill.

*Sir William Jones, English Orientalist*
*and jurist,*
*1746–1794 Ode in Imitation*
*of Alcaeus*

*83.115* ❦ Laws, like houses, lean on one another.

> *Edmund Burke, 1729–1797*
> Tracts on the Popery Laws

*83.116* ❦ . . . three things are always favoured in law—life, liberty and dower.

> Dumsday v. Hughes *(1803), 3 Bos.*
> *and Pull. 456*

*83.117* ❦ . . . but we find the law, as well as many other pursuits, requires much perseverance and patience to obtain the object; it is well for us that we do not always foresee the degree that it is necessary. . . .

> *Susannah Farnum Copley,*
> *American-English letter writer*
> *Letter to her daughter, March 15, 1805*

*83.118* ❦ "That sounds like nonsense, my dear."
"Maybe so, my dear; but it may be very good law for all that."

> *Sir Walter Scott*
> Guy Mannering, *1815*

*83.119* ❦ The laws are with us and God is on our side.

> *Robert Southey*
> *"Popular Disaffection,"* Essays, *c.1820*

*83.120* ❦ Laws were made to be broken.

> *Christopher North (pseudonym*
> *of John Wilson)*
> Noctes Ambrosianae, *1830*

*83.121* ❦ Law alone can give us freedom.

> *Goethe, 1749–1832*
> *W. Gurney Benham,* Putnam's Book of
> Quotations, Proverbs and
> Household Words, *1927*

*83.122* ❦ Sancho: Me care for te laws when te laws care for me.

> *Joanna Baillie,*
> *Scottish poet and dramatist*
> The Alienated Manor, *1836*

*83.123* ❦ Law is whatever is boldly asserted and plausibly maintained.

> *Aaron Burr, 1756–1836*
> *Burton Stevenson,* Home Book of
> Proverbs, Maxims and Familiar
> Phrases, *1948*

*83.124* ❦ Let reverence for the laws be breathed by every American mother to the lisping babe that prattles on her lap; let it be taught in schools, in seminaries, and in colleges; let it be written in primers, spelling-books, and in almanacs; let it be preached from the pulpit, proclaimed in legislative halls, and enforced in courts of justice. And, in short, let it become the political religion of the nation; and let the old and the young, the rich and the poor, the grave and the gay of all sexes and tongues and colors and conditions, sacrifice unceasingly upon its altars.

> *Abraham Lincoln*
> Address before the Young Men's
> Lyceum of Springfield, Illinois,
> January 27, 1837

*83.125* ❦ "If the law supposes that," said Mr. Bumble, "the law is a ass, a idiot."

> *Charles Dickens*
> Oliver Twist, *1838*

*83.126* ❦ Let a man keep the law,—any law,—and his way will be strewn with satisfaction.

> *Ralph Waldo Emerson*
> *"Prudence,"* Essays: First Series, *1841*

83.127 ❧ The mere repetition of the *Cantilena* [lyric melody] of the lawyers cannot make it law.

> *Sir Thomas Denman, English jurist;*
> *Lord Chief Justice*
> O'Connell v. The Queen,
> *September 4, 1844*

83.128 ❧ Any laws but those we make for ourselves are laughable.

> *Ralph Waldo Emerson*
> "Politics," Essays: Second Series, *1844*

83.129 ❧ The law is only a memorandum.

> *Ralph Waldo Emerson*
> "Politics," Essays: Second Series, *1844*

83.130 ❧ "Laws and principles are not for the times when there is no temptation: they are for such moments as this, when body and soul rise in mutiny against their rigour; stringent are they; inviolate they shall be. If at my individual convenience I might break them, what would be their worth?"

> *Charlotte Brontë*
> Jane Eyre, *1847*

83.131 ❧ 'T is best to make the Law our friend.

> *Emma Hart Willard*
> Harry Guy, *1848*

83.132 ❧ Law never made men a whit more just.

> *Henry David Thoreau*
> Civil Disobedience, *1849*

83.133 ❧ The law is for the protection of the weak more than the strong.

> *Sir William Erle, English jurist;*
> *Chief Justice*
> Reg. v. Woolley *(1850), 4 Cox,*
> *C.C. 196*

83.134 ❧ Ring out a slowly dying cause,
And ancient forms of party strife;
Ring in the nobler modes of life,
With sweeter manners, purer laws.

> *Tennyson*
> In Memoriam, *1850*

83.135 ❧ The best use of good laws is to teach men to trample bad laws under their feet.

> *Wendell Phillips*
> Speech, *April 12, 1852*

83.136 ❧ "The law will admit of no rival. . . ." but I will say, that it is a jealous mistress, and requires a long and constant courtship. It is not to be won by trifling favors, but by lavish homage.

> *Joseph Story*
> The Miscellaneous Writings of
> Joseph Story, *1852*

83.137 ❧ Are laws to be enforced simply because they were made?

> *Henry David Thoreau*
> John Brown's Body, *1859*

83.138 ❧ To make laws that man cannot, and will not obey, serves to bring all law into contempt.

> *Elizabeth Cady Stanton*
> Address, *1861*

83.139 ❦ Law is not a science, but is essentially empirical.

*Oliver Wendell Holmes*
*"Codes, and the Arrangement of the*
*Law," 5* American Law Review *1*
*(1870)*

83.140 ❦ Laws are like medicines: they usually cure the disease only by setting up another that is lesser or more transient.

*Otto von Bismarck*
*Speech in the Prussian Upper House,*
*March 6, 1872*

83.141 ❦ All law has for its object to confirm and exalt into a system the exploitation of the workers by a ruling class.

*Mikhail Bakunin, 1814–1876*
*Kenneth Redden,* Modern
Legal Glossary, *1983*

83.142 ❦ Men would be great criminals did they need as many laws as they make.

*Charles John Darling, 1st baron,*
*English jurist*
Scintillae Juris, *1877*

83.143 ❦ Law is an alliance of those who have farsight and insight against the shortsighted.

*Rudolf von Jhering, German jurist*
Der Zweck im Recht, *1877*

83.144 ❦ The life of the law has not been logic; it has been experience.

*Oliver Wendell Holmes*
The Common Law, *1881*

83.145 ❦ The standards of the law are standards of general application. The law takes no account of the infinite varieties of temperament, intellect, and education which make the internal character of a given act so different in different men. It does not attempt to see men as God sees them. . . .

*Oliver Wendell Holmes*
The Common Law, *1881*

83.146 ❦ God's blood! is law for man's sake made, or man
For law's sake only, to be held in bonds?

*Algernon Charles Swinburne*
Mary Stuart, *1881*

83.147 ❦ . . . we must not be guilty of taking the law into our own hands, and converting it from what it really is to what we think it ought to be.

*John Duke Coleridge, English jurist;*
*Lord Chief Justice, 1820–1894*
Regina v. Ramsey *(1883), 1 C. &*
*E. 126, 136*

83.148 ❦ Around the ancient track marched, rank on rank,
The army of unalterable law.

*George Meredith*
Lucifer in Starlight, *1883*

83.149 ❦ Now the law steps in, bigwigg'd, voluminous-jaw'd.

*Charles Stuart Calverley,*
*English writer, 1831–1884*
The Cock and the Bull

*83.150* ❦ Laws only bind when they are in accordance with right reason, and
hence with the eternal law of God.

*Leo XIII, Pope*
Rerum Novarum, *1891*

*83.151* ❦ To take Macaulay's instance, it is
against the law for an apple-woman
to stop up the street with her cart; it
is not against the law for a miser to
allow the benefactor to whom he
owes his whole success to die in the
poorhouse.

*John Chipman Gray, American lawyer,*
*1839–1915*
*"Some Definitions and Questions in*
*Jurisprudence," 6* Harvard Law
Review *21 (1893)*

*83.152* ❦ To succeed in other trades, capacity
must be shown; in the law, conceal-
ment will do.

*Mark Twain*
Following the Equator, *1897*

*83.153* ❦ The attempt to guard adult man by
law is a bad education for the battle
of life.

*William Edward Hartpole Lecky,*
*British historian, 1838–1903*
Democracy and Liberty

*83.154* ❦ It's not possible to make a bad law. If
it is bad, it is not a law.

*Carry Nation*
The Use and Need of the Life of
Carry A. Nation, *1904*

*83.155* ❦ No man has yet been hanged for
breaking the spirit of the law.

*Grover Cleveland, 1837–1908*

*83.156* ❦ *Law:* Simply a matter of the length
of the judge's ears.

*Elbert Hubbard*
Book of Epigrams, *1910*

*83.157* ❦ When I am sick, then I believe
in law.

*Anna Wickham, English poet*
*"Self-Analysis,"* The Contemplative
Quarry, *1915*

*83.158* ❦ . . . no great idea in its beginning
can ever be within the law. How
can it be within the law? The law is
stationary. The law is fixed. The
law is a chariot wheel which binds
us all regardless of conditions or
place or time.

*Emma Goldman*
*"Address to the Jury,"* Mother Earth,
*July 1917*

*83.159* ❦ One with the law is a majority.

*Calvin Coolidge*
Speech, *July 27, 1920*

*83.160* ❦ It is perfectly proper to regard and
study the law simply as a great an-
thropological document.

*Oliver Wendell Holmes*
*"Law in Science and Science in Law,"*
Collected Legal Papers, *1921*

*83.161* ❦ Law must be stable, and yet it cannot stand still.

*Roscoe Pound*
Introduction to the Philosophy of
Law, *1922*

83.162 ❦ Law does not mean then whatever people usually do, or even what they think to be right. Certainly it does not mean what only the most enlightened individuals usually do or think right. It is the conduct which the government, whether it is a king, or a popular assembly, will compel individuals to conform to. . . .

*Learned Hand*
*Radio address, May 14, 1933*

83.163 ❦ . . . the law is not the place for the artist or the poet. The law is the calling of thinkers.

*Oliver Wendell Holmes*
*"The Profession of the Law," Speeches,*
*1934*

83.164 ❦ We must not read either law or history backwards.

*Helen M. Cam, English historian*
*H. D. Hazeltine, G. Lapsley, and P. H.*
*Winfield, eds., Introduction, Selected*
*Essays of F. W. Maitland, 1936*

83.165 ❦ Leave to live by no man's leave, underneath the Law. . . .

*Rudyard Kipling, 1865–1936*
*"The Old Issue"*

83.166 ❦ When there is such a degree of probability as to lead to a reasonable assurance that a given conclusion ought to be and will be reduced to a judgment, we speak of that conclusion as the law.

*Benjamin N. Cardozo, 1870–1938*
*Kenneth Redden, Modern Legal*
*Glossary, 1983*

83.167 ❦ Yet law-abiding scholars write:
Law is neither wrong or right:
Law is only crimes
Punished by places and by times. . . .

*W. H. Auden*
*"Law Like Love," 1939*

83.168 ❦ It would be a narrow conception of jurisprudence to confine the notion of "laws" to what is found written on the statute books.

*Felix Frankfurter*
*Nashville, Chattanooga and St. Louis*
*Railway v. Browning, 310 U.S. 362,*
*369 (1940)*

83.169 ❦ Law as it exists in the modern community may be conveniently, although perhaps not comprehensively, defined as the sum total of all those rules of conduct for which there is state sanction.

*Harlan Fiske Stone, 1872–1946*
*Kenneth Redden, Modern Legal*
*Glossary, 1983*

83.170 ❦ A man is allowed by law to be a fool, if he likes.

*Arthur Lehmann Goodhart*
*Five Jewish Lawyers of the Common*
*Law, 1949*

83.171 ❦ A law is something which must have a moral basis, so that there is an inner compelling force for every citizen to obey.

*Chaim Weizmann*
*Trial and Error, 1949*

*83.172* ❦ Liberty is not the mere absence of restraint, it is not a spontaneous product of majority rule, it is not achieved merely by lifting underprivileged classes to power, nor is it the inevitable by-product of technological expansion. It is achieved only by a rule of law.

> *Robert H. Jackson*
> The Supreme Court in the American
> System of Government, *1955*

*83.173* ❦ Law offers a guiding thread to us . . . one of purpose—and a purpose infinitely worthwhile, for in the long view it is more important that human beings should learn to get on with each other than that they should be more comfortable materially and safer physically.

> *Helen M. Cam, English historian*
> *Lecture, "Law as It Looks to a*
> *Historian," Girton College,*
> *February 18, 1956*

*83.174* ❦ The law is not an end in itself, nor does it provide ends. It is preeminently a means to serve what we think is right.

> *William J. Brennan, Jr.*
> Roth v. United States, *1957*

*83.175* ❦ The law's final justification is in the good it does or fails to do the society of a given place and time.

> *Albert Camus, 1913–1960*
> *Laurence J. Peter, Peter's Quotations,*
> *1977*

*83.176* ❦ Law is experience developed by reason and applied continually to further experience.

> *Roscoe Pound*
> Christian Science Monitor,
> *April 24, 1963*

*83.177* ❦ Certain other societies may respect the rule of force—we respect the rule of law.

> *John F. Kennedy*
> New York Times, *May 19, 1963*

*83.178* ❦ [Law] liberates the desire to build and subdues the desire to destroy. And if war can tear us apart, law can unite us—out of fear, or love, or reason, or all three. Law is the greatest human invention. All the rest give man mastery over his world. Law gives him mastery over himself.

> *Lyndon B. Johnson*
> Time, *September 24, 1965*

*83.179* ❦ It is the capacity to command free assent that makes law a substitute for power. The force of legitimacy—and conversely the habit of voluntary compliance—is the foundation of the law's civilizing and liberalizing influence. Indeed . . . law in this sense is the very fabric of a free society. There is no alternative short of the millennium.

> *Archibald Cox, Mark De Wolfe Howe,*
> *and J. R. Wiggins*
> Civil Rights, the Constitution, and
> the Courts, *1967*

**83.180** ❧ One can always legislate against specific acts of human wickedness: but one can never legislate against the irrational itself.

*Morton Irving Seiden, American*
*educator; professor, Brooklyn College*
A Paradox of Hate: A Study in Ritual
Murder, *1967*

**83.181** ❧ If there isn't a law there will be.

*Harold Farber*
New York Times Magazine,
*March 17, 1968*

**83.182** ❧ Law is the backbone which keeps man erect.

*S. C. Yuter*
Bulletin of Atomic Scientists,
*October 1969*

**83.183** ❧ You have to have respect for the law. But you can't respect the law when the law is not respectable.

*Ramsey Clark*
Before the Senate Judiciary Committee,
*November 5, 1969*

**83.184** ❧ An Irish attorney was making the best of a rather shaky case when the judge interrupted him on a point of law. "Surely," he asked, "your clients are aware of the doctrine *de minimis non curat lex?*" "I assure you, my lord," came the suave reply, "that, in the remote and inhospitable hamlet where my clients have their humble abode, it forms the sole topic of conversation."

*Walter Bryan*
The Improbable Irish, *1969*

**83.185** ❧ I know the law. It is used to oppress those who threaten the ruling class.

The judicial decree has replaced the assassin. . . . I stay with the law only because the law is maneuverable, it can be manipulated.

*William M. Kunstler*
Human Events, *February 12, 1972*

**83.186** ❧ It's a terrible American weakness to believe that if you've got a problem all you have to do is pass a law.

*Kingman Brewster, Jr.*
Dallas Times-Herald, *June 15, 1972*

**83.187** ❧ Law then is not a preordained set of doctrines, applied rigidly and unswervingly in every situation. Rather, law is molded from the arguments and decisions of thousands of persons. It is very much a human process, a game of trying to convince others . . . that your view of what the law requires is correct.

*Susan C. Ross*
The Rights of Women, *1973*

**83.188** ❧ The law is above the law, you know.

*Dorothy Salisbury Davis*
*American writer*
The Little Brothers, *1973*

**83.189** ❧ In commercial law, the person duped was too often a woman. In a section on land tenure, one 1968 textbook explains that "land, like women, was meant to be possessed."

*Ruth Bader Ginsburg*
Susan Emiston, "Portia Faces
Life—The Trials of Law School,"Ms.
Magazine, *April 1974*

**83.190** ❧ The contempt for law and the contempt for the human consequences of lawbreaking go from the bottom to the top of American society.

*Margaret Mead*
*Claire Safran, "Impeachment?"*
Redbook, *April 1974*

83.191 ❦ The law can never make us as secure as we are when we do not need it.

*Alexander M. Bickel*
The Morality of Consent, *1975*

83.192 ❦ Law is not everything in society. . . . The public, the press, the academic community, the artists, all by their assertions and conduct inform and develop the law.

*Edward H. Levi*
Los Angeles Times, *May 23, 1975*

83.193 ❦ . . . I cannot accept the idea of law as merely repressive or punitive. It can be expressive and conducive to the development of social values.

*June L. Tapp, American psychologist*
*Gordon Berman, "The Notion of*
*Conspiracy Is Not Tasty to Americans,"*
Psychology Today, *May 1975*

83.194 ❦ Unnecessary laws are bad laws, if for no other reason than they substitute legal coercion for freedom of choice.

*Thomas A. Murphy, American business*
*executive; chairman, General Motors*
*Corporation*
New York Times,
*January 31, 1976*

83.195 ❦ The law has to encourage a kind of reasoning together. That is going to be hard for some people who don't regard the law as a reasoning device.

They say use it as a weapon and go as far as you can.

*Edward H. Levi*
Time,
*December 20, 1976*

83.196 ❦ Fidelity to the public requires that the laws be as plain and explicit as possible, that the less knowing may understand, and not be ensnared by them, while the artful evade their force.

*Samuel Cooke*
*Laurence J. Peter,* Peter's Quotations,
*1977*

83.197 ❦ If you love the law and you love good sausage, don't watch either of them being made.

*Betty Talmadge, U.S. meat broker,*
*cookbook writer*
The Reader, *November 25, 1977*

83.198 ❦ Laws that are not enforced . . . are bad laws.

*Lionel J. Castillo, American*
*government official; commissioner, U.S.*
*Immigration & Naturalization Service*
Los Angeles Herald Examiner,
*March 24, 1978*

83.199 ❦ Your lordships will be glad to hear that I shall present a point of law un-corrupted by any merits.

*Patrick Devlin*
The Judge, *1979*

83.200 ❦ America is a nation of laws. . . . The law is not always an easy friend, be-cause the law does not play favor-

ites. But for those who seek justice
in a society of responsible citizens,
the law will always be an ally.

*Edward I. Koch*
Los Angeles Times, *September 8, 1981*

83.201 ❦ Lawyering is within the relatively
narrow category of occupations
where borderline dishonesty is fairly
lucrative. In many instances, the
very art of the lawyer is a sort of calculated disregard of the law or at
least of ordinary notions of morality.

*Eric Schnapper*
*Kenneth Redden,* Modern Legal
Glossary, *1983*

83.202 ❦ Particularly in its upper reaches,
much of what has passed for feminism in law has been the attempt to
get for men what little has been re-
served for women or to get for some
women some of the plunder that
some men have previously divided
(unequally) among themselves.

*Catharine A. MacKinnon*
*Introduction,* Feminism Unmodified,
*1987*

83.203 ❦ For purposes of sex discrimination
law, to be a woman means either to
be like a man, or to be like a lady.
We have to meet either the male
standards for males or the male
standards for females.

*Catharine A. MacKinnon*
*"On Exceptionality: Women as Women
in Law,"* Feminism Unmodified,
*1987*

83.204 ❦ A law can be both economic folly
and constitutional.

*Antonin Scalia, concurring opinion,*
*April 21, 1987*
*Daniel B. Baker,* Power Quotes,
*1992*

83.205 ❦ Laws are ways that society makes
sense of things.

*Mary Ann Glendon*
*lawyer, Harvard professor*
*Bill Moyers,* A World of Ideas, *1989*

83.206 ❦ [T]he law draws force from the clarity of its command and the certainty
of its application.

*Clarence Thomas*
Dogget v. United States, *112 S. Ct.*
*2686 (1992)*

83.207 ❦ Laws are felt only when the individual comes into conflict with them.

*Suzanne La Follette*
Lawyer's Wit and Wisdom, *edited by*
*Bruce Nash, Allan Zullo and compiled*
*by Kathryn Zullo, 1995*

83.208 ❦ The law is so phallic! It doesn't leave
much room for sensitivity, which
must be why so many guys are
happy in it.

*Alyson Singer*
Lawyer's Wit and Wisdom, *edited by*
*Bruce Nash, Allan Zullo and compiled*
*by Kathryn Zullo, 1995*

83.209 ❧ The public seems, in fact, to have a
love-hate relationship with law. It
sees law as a bag of tricks, a bottomless pit of artifice and legalism; but it
also sees law as a shining sword of
justice, a powerful weapon of public
purpose. Law is, indeed, one of the
very foundation stones of liberty.

*Lawrence M. Friedman*
Civilization, *April/May 1997*

# *84.* LAW AND ORDER

84.1 ❧ Fish die when they are out of
water, and people die without law
and order.

*Talmud, Avoda zara*

84.2 ❧ Law is a form of order, and good law
must necessarily mean good order.

*Aristotle*
Politics, *c.322* B.C.

84.3 ❧ I am of his mind that said, "Better it
is to live where nothing is lawful,
than where all things are lawful."

*Francis Bacon*
Apophthagmes, *1625*

84.4 ❧ Revolt and terror pay a price.
Order and law have a cost.

*Carl Sandburg*
The People, Yes!, *1936*

84.5 ❧ Our defense is not in armaments,
nor in science, nor in going under-
ground. Our defense is in law and
order.

*Albert Einstein*
*"The Real Problem Is in the Hearts of
Men,"* New York Times Magazine,
*June 23, 1946*

84.6 ❧ In the whole history of law and
order the longest step forward was
taken by primitive man when, as if
by common consent, the tribe sat
down in a circle and allowed only
one man to speak at a time.

*Derek Curtis Bok, American educator*
*"If We Are to Act Like Free Men . . . ,"*
Saturday Review, *February 13, 1954*

84.7 ❧ The image created by the beatniks
and by most of their predecessors
back to the 19th century bohemians
has led us to suppose that people of
high originality are somehow lawless. But the truly creative man is

not an outlaw but a lawmaker. Every great creative performance since the initial one has been in some measure a bringing of order out of chaos.

*John W. Gardner*
*"Thoughts," Think, May–June 1966*

84.8 ❦ A man's respect for law and order exists in precise relationship to the size of his paycheck.

*Adam Clayton Powell, Jr.*
*Keep the Faith, Baby! 1967*

# 85. LAW ENFORCEMENT

85.1 ❦ It is not the thief who is hanged, but one who was caught stealing.

*Czech proverb*
H. L. Mencken, A New Dictionary of Quotations, *1946*

85.2 ❦ Highest law, highest cross.

*Latin phrase*
W. Gurney Benham, Putnam's Complete Book of Quotations, Proverbs and Household Words, *1927*

85.3 ❦ Fear is the beadle of the law.

*Proverb*
Thomas Fuller, Gnomologia, *1732*

85.4 ❦ Laws can never be enforced unless fear supports them.

*Sophocles*
Ajax, *c.450* B.C.

85.5 ❦ Nobody has a more sacred obligation to obey the law than those who make the law.

*Sophocles, 496?–406* B.C.
Laurence J. Peter, Peter's Quotations, *1977*

85.6 ❦ If human society cannot be carried on without lawsuits, it cannot be carried on without penalties.

*Aristotle, 384–322* B.C.
*W. H. Auden and Louis Kronenberger,*
The Viking Book of Aphorisms, *1962*

85.7 ❦ A law observed is merely Law; broken, it is law and executioner.

*Menander*
Fragments, *c.300* B.C.

85.8 ❦ It becometh a law-maker not to be a law-breaker.

*Francis Meres*
*English divine and author*
Nicholas Ling, Politeuphuia, *1597*

85.9 ❦ Let him have all the rigour of the law.

*Shakespeare*
2 Henry VI, I, 3, *1589–1591*

*85.10* ❦ It is the crime which makes the shame and not the scaffold.

> *Corneille*
> Comte de Essex, *c.1650*

*85.11* ❦ When justice on offenders is not done,
Law, government, and commerce are o'erthrown.

> *Sir John Denham, English poet*
> Of Justice, *c.1668*

*85.12* ❦ Xenophanes being jeered for refusing to play a forbidden game, answered. . . . "They that make laws, must keep them."

> *William Penn*
> No Cross, No Crown, *1669*

*85.13* ❦ The first intent of laws
Was to correct the effect, and check the cause,
And all the ends of punishment
Were only future mischiefs to prevent.
But justice intervened, when
Those engines of the law,
Instead of pinching vicious men,
Keep honest ones in awe.

> *Daniel Defoe*
> Hymn to the Pillory, *1703*

*85.14* ❦ . . . the *Law* shows her teeth, but dares not bite.

> *Edward Young, English poet,*
> *1683–1765*
> Love of Fame, *1725*

*85.15* ❦ The atrocity of the laws prevents their execution.

> *de Montesquieu, 1689–1755*
> *W. Gurney Benham,* Putnam's
> Complete Book of Quotations,
> Proverbs and Household Words, *1927*

*85.16* ❦ What is law, if those who make it
Become the forwardest to break it?

> *James Beattie*
> The Wolf and the Shepherds, *1776*

*85.17* ❦ No man e'er felt the halter draw
With good opinion of the law.

> *John Trumbull, American poet*
> *and jurist*
> M' Fingal, *1782*

*85.18* ❦ The execution of the laws is more important than the making of them.

> *Thomas Jefferson*
> *Letter to the Abbé Arnond, 1789*

*85.19* ❦ He who holds no laws in awe,
He must perish by the law.

> *Lord Byron*
> *"A Very Mournful Ballad on the Siege*
> *and Conquest of Alhambra," c.1810*

*85.20* ❦ Laws exist in vain for those who have not the courage and the means to defend them.

> *Thomas Babington Macaulay*
> *"Burleigh and His Times,"* Edinburgh
> Review, *April 1832*

*85.21* ❦ To render a people obedient and keep them so, savage laws inefficiently enforced are less effective than mild laws enforced by an efficient administration regularly, automatically, as it were, every day and on all alike.

*Alexis de Tocqueville, 1805–1859*
*W. H. Auden and Louis Kronenberger,*
The Viking Book of Aphorisms, *1962*

85.22 ☙ I know no method to secure the repeal of bad or obnoxious laws so effective as their stringent execution.

*Ulysses S. Grant*
Inaugural address, March 4, 1869

85.23 ☙ A citizen of the United States . . . is not bound to cringe to any superior, or to pray for any act of grace, as a means of enjoying all the rights and privileges enjoyed by other citizens. And when the spirit of lawlessness, mob violence, and sectional hate can be so completely repressed as to give full practical effect to this right, we shall be a happier nation, and a more prosperous one than we now are.

*Joseph P. Bradley*
Slaughter-House Cases, *83 U.S. (16 Wall.) 36, 112–13 (1872)*

85.24 ☙ A crowded police court docket is the surest of all signs that trade is brisk and money plenty.

*Mark Twain*
Roughing It, *1872*

85.25 ☙ After all, the eleventh commandment (thou shalt not be found out) is the only one that is virtually impossible to keep in these days.

*Bertha Buxton, English writer*
Jenny of the Princes, *1879*

85.26 ☙ Ah, take one consideration with another
A policeman's lot is not a happy one.

*W. S. Gilbert*
The Pirates of Penzance, *1879*

85.27 ☙ We enact many laws that manufacture criminals, and then a few that punish them.

*Benjamin R. Tucker, American journalist and anarchist*
Instead of a Book, *1893*

85.28 ☙ The speedy arm of justice was never known to fail;
The gaol supplied the gallows, the gallows thinned the gaol,
And sundry wise precautions the sages of the law
Discreetly framed whereby they aimed to keep the rogues in awe.

*John W. Smith*
Selection of Leading Cases on Various Branches of the Law, *1896*

85.29 ☙ Enormous offences call for a greater axe.

*Sir Frederick Pollock, English jurist*
The Expansion of the Common Law, *1904*

85.30 ☙ There's a lot of law at the end of a nightstick.

*Grover Whalen, American law enforcement official; police commissioner, New York City, 1928–1930*
*M. Francis McNamara, 2000 Famous Legal Quotations, 1967*

85.31 ❧ Criminals do not die by the hands of the law. They die by the hands of other men.

*George Bernard Shaw, 1856–1950*
*W. H. Auden and Louis Kronenberger,*
The Viking Book of Aphorisms, *1962*

85.32 ❧ He didn't know the right people. That's all a police record means.

*Raymond Chandler, 1888–1959*
*Laurence J. Peter,* Peter's Quotations,
*1977*

85.33 ❧ One reason for our high crime rate is that the long arm of the law is often shorthanded.

*Hal Chadwick*
Reader's Digest, *March 1960*

85.34 ❧ . . . coercion can be mental as well as physical, and . . . the blood of the accused is not the only hallmark of an unconstitutional inquisition.

Blackburn v. Alabama, *361 U.S. 199*
*(1960)*

85.35 ❧ In the age of modern advanced technology, when the criminal can avail himself of every new invention, law-enforcement officers are denied even the simplest of electronic devices, even though they will be under the supervision of the Courts. The result is like asking a champion boxer to fight a gorilla and insisting that the boxer abide by the Marquis of Queensbury Rules, while the gorilla is limited only by the law of the jungle.

*Miles F. McDonald, American lawyer*
*"Law Enforcement—Have We Gone*
*Too Far in Protecting the Accused?" 39*
New York State Bar Journal *5*
*(October 1967)*

85.36 ❧ If law is not made more than a policeman's nightstick, American society will be destroyed.

*Arthur Goldberg*
*Speech, reported in the* New York
Times, *June 22, 1969*

85.37 ❧ Who will protect the public when the police violate the law?

*Ramsey Clark*
*Laurence J. Peter,* Peter's Quotations,
*1977*

85.38 ❧ This won't be the first time I've arrested somebody and then built my case afterward.

*James Garrison, New Orleans*
*district attorney*
*Laurence J. Peter,*
Peter's Quotations, *1977*

85.39 ❧ I'm not *against* the police; I'm just afraid of them.

*Alfred Hitchcock*
*Laurence J. Peter,* Peter's Quotations,
*1977*

85.40 ❧ Laws not enforced cease to be laws, and rights not defended may wither away.

*Thomas E. Moriarty,*
*American educator*
*Laurence J. Peter,* Peter's Quotations,
*1977*

85.41 ❧ Police efficiency must yield to constitutional rights.

*John Minor Wisdom, American jurist*
*Laurence J. Peter,* Peter's Quotations, *1977*

*85.42* ❦ [T]he policeman on the street is the single most powerful person in the entire American system of criminal justice.

*Johnnie L. Cochran*
Journey to Justice, *with Tim Rutten, 1996*

*85.43* ❦ The weapons of war are now being used against American citizens for civilian law enforcement, and the casualties of this war are the constitutional rights of the innocent.

*John Henry Hingson III*
*Mark Hansen, "No Place to Hide,"*
ABA Journal, *August 1997*

# 86. LAWYERS

*86.1* ❦ A lawyer must first get on, then get honor, then get honest.

*Anonymous*
*H. L. Mencken,* A New Dictionary of Quotations, *1946*

*86.2* ❦ The animals are not so stupid as is thought: they have no lawyers.

*Anonymous*
*H. L. Mencken,* A New Dictionary of Quotations, *1946*

*86.3* ❦ You can always tell a barber
By the way he parts his hair;
You can always tell a dentist
When you're in the dentist's chair;
And even a musician—
You can tell him by his touch;
You can always tell a lawyer,
But you cannot tell him much.

*Anonymous*
*Jacob M. Braude,* Lifetime Speaker's Encyclopedia, *1962*

*86.4* ❦ Who taught me first to litigate,
My neighbor and my brother hate,

And my own rights overrate?
It was my lawyer.

*Anonymous*
*Jacob M. Braude,* Lifetime Speaker's Encyclopedia, *1962*

*86.5* ❦ Now, then, all ye black guards that isn't lawyers, out ye go!

*Crier at Ballinloe when ordered to clear*
*the court by the judge*

*86.6* ❦ God save us from a lawyer's et cetera.

*French proverb*
*H. L. Mencken,* A New Dictionary of Quotations, *1946*

*86.7* ❦ Only painters and lawyers can change white to black.

*Japanese proverb*
*Louis Levinson,* Bartlett's Unfamiliar Quotations, *1971*

*86.8* ❦ Every business has its own best season. That is why they say June is the best month of the year for preachers. Lawyers have the other eleven.

*Popular saying*

**86.9** ❧ It is hard to say whether the doctors of law or divinity have made the greater advances in the lucrative business of mystery.

*Popular saying*

**86.10** ❧ Lawyers: Persons who write a 10,000 word document and call it a brief.

*Popular saying*

**86.11** ❧ There are two kinds of lawyers: those who know the law and those who know the judge.

*Popular saying*

**86.12** ❧ There's no better way of exercising the imagination than the study of law.

*Popular saying*

**86.13** ❧ A good lawyer, an evil neighbor.

*Proverb*
*Rosalind Fergusson,* The Facts On File
Dictionary of Proverbs, *1983*

**86.14** ❧ A good lawyer must be a great liar.

*Proverb*
*Rosalind Fergusson,* The Facts On File
Dictionary of Proverbs, *1983*

**86.15** ❧ Kick an attorney downstairs and he'll stick to you for life.

*Proverb*
*Rosalind Fergusson,* The Facts On File
Dictionary of Proverbs, *1983*

**86.16** ❧ Two attorneys can live in a town, when one cannot.

*Proverb*
*Rosalind Fergusson,* The Facts On File
Dictionary of Proverbs, *1983*

**86.17** ❧ Go not for every grief to the physician, nor for every quarrel to the lawyer, nor for every thirst to the pot.

*Proverb*
*George Herbert,* Outlandish Proverbs,
*1639*

**86.18** ❧ A peasant between two lawyers is like a fish between two cats.

*Spanish proverb*
*H. L. Mencken,* A New Dictionary of
Quotations, *1946*

**86.19** ❧ Hide nothing from thy minister, physician, and lawyer.

*Scottish or English proverb*
*John Ray,* Compleat Collection of
English Proverbs, *1670*

**86.20** ❧ It's an ill cause that the lawyer thinks shame o'.

*Scottish proverb*
*H. L. Mencken,* A New Dictionary of
Quotations, *1946*

**86.21** ❧ . . . the Pharisees and lawyers rejected the counsel of God. . . .

*New Testament, Luke 7:30*

**86.22** ❧ And he said, Woe unto you also, ye lawyers! for ye lade men with burdens grievous to be borne, and ye yourselves touch not the burdens with one of your fingers.

*New Testament: Luke 11:46*

86.23 ❧ Woe unto you, lawyers! for ye have taken away the key of knowledge: ye entered not in yourselves, and them that were entering in ye hindered.

*New Testament, Luke 11:52*

86.24 ❧ The lawyer is always in a hurry.

*Plato*
Theaetetus, *c.360* B.C.

86.25 ❧ For the house of a great lawyer is assuredly the oracular seat of the whole community.

*Cicero*
De Oratore, *55* B.C.

86.26 ❧ Ulysses was not beautiful, but he was eloquent.

*Ovid*
Ars Armatoria, *c.1* B.C.

86.27 ❧ He lets out to hire his anger and words.

*Seneca, 4* B.C.?–A.D. *65*
Hercules Furens

86.28 ❧ A serjeant of the law, wary and wise,
There was also, full rich of
    excellence,
Discreet he was, and of great
    reverence.

*Chaucer Prologue,*
The Canterbury Tales, *c.1380*

86.29 ❧ [The serjeant of the law.] He rode but homely in a medley coat.

*Chaucer*
Prologue, The Canterbury Tales,
*c.1380*

86.30 ❧ Amongst the learned, the lawyers claim first place, the most self-satisfied class of people, as they roll their rock of Sisyphus and string together six hundred laws in the same breath, no matter whether relevant or not . . .

*Desiderius Erasmus, 1509*
Civilization, *April/May 1997*

86.31 ❧ One thing I supplicate your majesty: that you will give orders, under a great penalty, that no bachelors of law should be allowed to come here [the New World] (sic); for not only are they bad themselves, but they also make and contrive a thousand inquiries.

*Vasco Nuñez de Balboa, 1513*

86.32 ❧ Such poor folk as to law do go are
    driven oft to curse:
But in mean while, the Lawyer
    thrives,
the money in his purse.

*Isabella Whitney, English poet*
"The 104. Flower," A Sweet Nosegay
or Pleasant Posye Containing
a Hundred and Ten
Phylosophicall Flowers, *1573*

86.33 ❧ For lawyers and their pleading,
They 'steem it not a straw;
They think that honest meaning
Is of itself a law.

*William Byrd, English composer*
"The Herdman's Happy Life," Sonnets
and Songs of Sadness and Pietie,
made into musicke of five parties,
*1588*

86.34 ❧ The first thing we do, let's kill all the lawyers.

*Shakespeare*
2 King Henry IV, *2, 1589–1591*

*86.35* ❦ Duch: Why should calamity be full
of words?
Q. Eliz: Windy attorneys to their
client woes,
Airy succeeders of intestate joys,
Poor breathing orators of miseries,
Let them have scope! though what
they will impart
Help nothing else, yet do they ease
the heart.

*Shakespeare*
Richard III, *IV, 4, 1592–1593*

*86.36* ❦ Isabella: O perilous mouths,
That bear in them one and the
self-same tongue,
Either of condemnation or aproof!
Bidding the law make court'sy to
their will,
Hooking both right and wrong to
the appetite,
To follow as it draws.

*Shakespeare*
Measure for Measure, *III, 4,*
*1604–1605*

*86.37* ❦ Few lawyers die well,
few physicians live well.

*William Camden*
Remains, *1605*

*86.38* ❦ I oft have heard him say how he
admir'd
Men of your large profession, that
could speak
To every cause, and things mere
contraries,
Till they were hoarse again, yet all
be law.

*Ben Jonson*
Volpone, *1605*

*86.39* ❦ He who loves the law dies either
mad or poor.

*Thomas Middleton*
The Phoenix, *c.1607*

*86.40* ❦ Our wrangling lawyers . . . are so litigious and busy here on earth, that I
think they will plead their clients'
causes hereafter, some of them in
hell.

*Robert Burton*
The Anatomy of Melancholy, *1621*

*86.41* ❦ He that with injury is grieved
And goes to law to be relieved,
Is sillier than a scottish chouse[*]
Who, when a thief has robbed his
house,
Applies himself to cunning men
To help him to his goods again.

*Samuel Butler*
Hudibras, *1663–1678*

*86.42* ❦ Lawyers, of whose art the basis
Is raising feuds and splitting cases.

*Samuel Butler*
Hudibras, *1663–1678*

*86.43* ❦ With books and money placed for
show
Like nest-eggs to make clients lay,
And for his false opinion pay.

*Samuel Butler*
Hudibras, *1663–1678*

*86.44* ❦ These [the lawyers] are the mounte-
banks of the State,

[*]Dupe

Who by the sleight of tongues can crimes create.

*Daniel Defoe*
Hymn to the Pillory, *1703*

86.45 ❧ . . . very many men among us were bred up from their youth in the art of proving by words multiplied for the purpose that white is black, and black is white, according as they are paid.

*Jonathan Swift*
Gulliver's Travels, *1726*

86.46 ❧ The toils of law, What dark and insidious men
Have cumbrous added to perplex the truth,
And lengthen simple justice into trade.

*James Thomson*
"Winter," The Seasons, *1726*

86.47 ❧ I know you lawyers can, with ease, Twist words and meanings as you please;
That language, by your skill made pliant,
Will bend to favour every client;
That 'tis the fee directs the sense
To make out either side's pretence.

*John Gay,* 1685–1732
*William Andrews,* The Lawyer in History, Literature and Humour, *1896*

86.48 ❧ Lawyers, preachers, and tomtit's eggs, there are more of them hatched than come to perfection.

*Benjamin Franklin*
Poor Richard's Almanack, *1734*

86.49 ❧ Lawyers are always more ready to get a man into troubles than out of them.

*Oliver Goldsmith*
The Good-Natur'd Man, *1768*

86.50 ❧ Boswell: But, Sir, does not affecting a warmth when you have no warmth, and appearing to be clearly of one opinion when you are in reality of another opinion, does not such dissimulation impair [a lawyer's] honesty? . . .
　　Johnson: Why no, Sir. Everybody knows you are paid for affecting warmth for your client; and it is, therefore, properly no dissimulation: the moment you come from the bar, you resume your usual behaviour. Sir, a man will no more carry the artifice of the bar into the common intercourse of society, than a man who is paid for tumbling upon his hands will continue to tumble upon his hands when he should walk on his feet.

*James Boswell*
The Life of Samuel Johnson, *1791*

86.51 ❧ ". . . he did not care to speak ill of any man behind his back, but he believed the gentleman was an attorney."

*Samuel Johnson*
*James Boswell,*
The Life of Samuel Johnson, *1791*

86.52 ❧ Then, shifting his side (as a lawyer knows how). . . .

*William Cowper,* 1731–1800
The Report of an Adjudged Case

*86.53* ❦ It would (to use a Yankee phrase) puzzle a dozen Philadelphia lawyers *to unriddle the conduct of the democrats.*

> *Anonymous*
> The Balance, *November 15, 1803*

*86.54* ❦ Who calls a lawyer rogue, may find, too late,
On one of these depends his whole estate.

> *George Crabbe*
> "The Gentleman Farmer," Tales, *1812*

*86.55* ❦ I think we may class lawyers in the natural history of monsters.

> *John Keats,* 1795–1821
> *Kenneth Redden,* Modern Legal Glossary, *1983*

*86.56* ❦ The New England folks have a saying that three Philadelphia lawyers are a match for the very devil himself.

> *Anonymous*
> Salem Observer, *March 13, 1824*

*86.57* ❦ The end aim of a lawyer is duplex, first, to know, and second to appear to know—the latter brings clients and the former holds them.

> *Roger North, English lawyer*
> On the Study of Laws, *1824*

*86.58* ❦ It's the trade of lawyers to question everything, yield nothing, and to talk by the hour.

> *Thomas Jefferson,* 1743–1826
> *Louis Levinson,* Bartlett's Unfamiliar Quotations, *1971*

*86.59* ❦ He is no lawyer who cannot take two sides.

> *Charles Lamb,* 1775–1834
> *W. H. Auden and Louis Kronenberger,*
> The Viking Book of Aphorisms, *1962*

*86.60* ❦ Lawyers, I suppose, were children once.

> *Charles Lamb,* 1775–1834
> *W. H. Auden and Louis Kronenberger,*
> The Viking Book of Aphorisms, *1962*

*86.61* ❦ He saw a lawyer killing a viper
On a dunghill hard by his own stable;
And the Devil smiled, for it put him in mind
Of Cain and his brother Abel.

> *Samuel Taylor Coleridge*
> The Devil's Thoughts, *c.1834*

*86.62* ❦ . . . I cannot believe that a republic could subsist at the present time if the influence of lawyers in public business did not increase in proportion to the power of the people.

> *Alexis de Tocqueville*
> Democracy in America, *1835–1840*

*86.63* ❦ In America there are no nobles or literary men, and the people are apt to mistrust the wealthy; lawyers consequently form the highest political class and the most cultivated portion of society. . . . If I were asked where I place the American aristocracy, I should reply without hesitation that . . . it occupies the judicial bench and the bar.

> *Alexis de Tocqueville*
> Democracy in America, *1835–1840*

86.64 ❦ The more that we reflect upon all
that occurs in the United States the
more we shall be persuaded that
the lawyers as a body form the most
powerful, if not the only, counter-
poise to the democratic element.

*Alexis de Tocqueville*
Democracy in America, *1835–1840*

86.65 ❦ After twenty-five years' observation,
I can give it as the condensed history
of most, if not all, good lawyers, that
they lived well and died poor.

*Daniel Webster*
*Address, Charleston, South Carolina,*
*Bar, May 10, 1847*

86.66 ❦ An eminent lawyer cannot be a
dishonest man.

*Daniel Webster*
Address, Charleston, South Carolina,
Bar, May 10, 1847

86.67 ❦ And through the heat of conflict
keeps the law
In calmness made.

*William Wordsworth, 1770–1850*
*"Character of the Happy Lawyer"*

86.68 ❦ Resolve to be honest at all events:
and if in your judgment you cannot
be an honest lawyer, resolve to be
honest without being a lawyer.
Choose some other occupation.

*Abraham Lincoln*
*Notes for a lecture, 1850*

86.69 ❦ Self-defense is the clearest of all
laws; and for this reason—the
lawyers didn't make it.

*Douglas Jerrold, English humorist and*
*playwright, 1803–1851*
*Marshall Brown,* Wit and Humor of
Bench and Bar, *1899*

86.70 ❦ The sharp employ the sharp; verily, a
man may be known by his attorney.

*Douglas Jerrold, English humorist and*
*playwright, 1803–1851*

86.71 ❦ Who's a great lawyer? He, who aims
to say
The least his cause requires, not all
he may.

*William Wetmore Story*
Life and Letters of Joseph Story, *1852*

86.72 ❦ Most men can counsel others; few
themselves.

*Christopher North (pseudonym of*
*John Wilson), 1785–1854*
The Cheats

86.73 ❦ I don't want to be a doctor, and live
by men's diseases; nor a minister to
live by their sins; nor a lawyer to live
by their quarrels.

*Nathaniel Hawthorne, 1804–1864*
*Remark to his mother*

86.74 ❦ Whom does any body trust so
implicitly as he trusts his own attorney? And yet is it not the case that
the body of attorneys is supposed
to be the most roguish body in
existence?

*Anthony Trollope*
Miss Mackenzie, *1865*

**86.75** ❧ Weary lawyers with endless tongues.

> *John Greenleaf Whittier*
> Maud Muller, *1867*

**86.76** ❧ A lawyer is a learned gentleman who rescues your estate from your enemies and keeps it for himself.

> *Henry Brougham, English jurist; Lord*
> *Chancellor, 1778–1868*
> *Kenneth Redden,* Modern Legal
> Glossary, *1983*

**86.77** ❧ All lawyers, be they knaves or fools,
> Know that a seat is worth the
>    earning,
> Since Parliament's astounding rules
> Vouch for their honour and their
>    learning.

> *James Edwin Thorold Rogers,*
> *English political economist*
> On the Eagerness
> of Lawyers to obtain
> Seats in the House, *1876*

**86.78** ❧ The fact that a lawyer advised such foolish conduct, does not relieve it of its foolishness. . . .

> *Lucilius A. Emery, American jurist*
> Hanscom v. Marston, *82 Me. 288,*
> *298 (1890)*

**86.79** ❧ The farther I go west, the more convinced I am that the wise men came from the east.

> *Joseph Jeckell, English lawyer and*
> *politician,* fl. early 18th century
> *Marshall Brown,* Wit and Humor of
> Bench and Bar, *1899*

**86.80** ❧ Lawyers have been known to wrest from reluctant juries triumphant verdicts of acquittal for their clients, even when those clients, as often

happens, were clearly and unmistakably innocent.

> *Oscar Wilde,* 1854–1900
> *Kenneth Redden,* Modern Legal
> Glossary, *1983*

**86.81** ❧ A law, Hennessy, that might look like a wall to you or me would look like a triumphal arch to the experienced eye of a lawyer.

> *Finley Peter Dunne*
> "Mr. Dooley on the Power of the Press,"
> American Magazine, *no. 62, 1906*

**86.82** ❧ . . . a written document makes lawyers of us all. . . .

> *Woodrow Wilson*
> Constitutional Government in the
> United States, *1908*

**86.83** ❧ [*Lawyer:*] One skilled in circumvention of the law.

> *Ambrose Bierce*
> The Devil's Dictionary, *1906*

**86.84** ❧ "An Honest Lawyer"—book just
>    out—
> What can the author have to say?
> Reprint perhaps of ancient tome—
> A work of fiction anyway.

> *Grace Hibbard, American writer and*
> *poet,* 1870?–1911
> *"Books Received"*

**86.85** ❧ I don't want a lawyer to tell me what I cannot do; I hire him to tell me how to do what I want to do.

> *J. P. Morgan,* 1837–1913
> *Kenneth Redden,* Modern Legal
> Glossary, *1983*

*86.86* ❧ But Benjamin [Disraeli] shied at the prospect of being buried in lawyer's chambers. "The Bar: pooh! law and bad tricks till we are forty, and then, with the most brilliant success, the prospect of gout and a coronet. Besides, to succeed as an advocate, I must be a great lawyer, and to be a great lawyer, I must give up my chance of being a great man."

*André Maurois*
Disraeli, *1930*

*86.87* ❧ The minute you read something you can't understand, you can almost be sure it was drawn up by a lawyer.

*Will Rogers,* 1879–1935
*Laurence J. Peter,* Peter's Quotations, *1977*

*86.88* ❧ About half the practice of a decent lawyer consists in telling would-be clients that they are damned fools and should stop.

*Elihu Root,* 1845–1937
*Martin Mayer,* The Lawyers, *1967*

*86.89* ❧ Your law may be perfect, your ability to apply it great, and yet you cannot be a successful adviser unless your advice is followed. . . .

*Louis D. Brandeis,* 1856–1941
*Thomas Alpheus Mason,* Brandeis: A Free Man's Life, *1946*

*86.90* ❧ Holmes divided lawyers into kitchen knives, razors, and stings. Brandeis, he said, was a sting.

*Catherine Drinker Bowen*
Yankee from Olympus, *1944*

*86.91* ❧ I shall not rest until every German sees that it is a shameful thing to be a lawyer.

*Adolf Hitler,* 1889–1945
*Kenneth Redden,* Modern Legal Glossary, *1983*

*86.92* ❧ . . . advocates, including advocates for States, are like managers of pugilistic and election contestants in that they have a propensity for claiming everything.

*Felix Frankfurter*
First Iowa Hydro-Electric Cooperative v. Federal Power Commission, *328 U.S. 152, 187 (1946)*

*86.93* ❧ Why is there always a secret singing
When a lawyer cashes in?
Why does a hearse horse snicker
Hauling a lawyer away?

*Carl Sandburg*
*"The Lawyers Know Too Much,"* Complete Poems, *1950*

*86.94* ❧ As to setting forth the outstanding qualities of an advocate. . . . There is no doubt that Daniel Webster named the principal quality when he said, "The power of clear statement is the great power at the bar."

*John W. Davis, American educator*
Letter to Eugene Gerhart, May 8, 1951

*86.95* ❧ There, but for the grace of God, goes God.

*Sir Winston Churchill, referring to Sir Stafford Cripps (1889–1952)*
*Clayton Fritchey, "A Politician Must Watch His Wit,"* New York Times Magazine, *July 3, 1960*

*86.96* ❦ The late George Haight, a giant of the Chicago bar, was once asked "What makes a good lawyer?" His short reply deserves to be remembered: "Lots of scar tissue."

*George Haight, 1878–1955*
*Milton B. Pollock, "Some Practical*
*Aspects of Appellate Advocacy,"*
New York State Bar Bulletin,
*February 1959*

*86.97* ❦ "Lawyers enjoy a little mystery, you know. Why, if everybody came forward and told the truth, the whole truth, and nothing but the truth straight out, we should all retire to the workhouse."

*Dorothy L. Sayers*
Clouds of Witness, *1956*

*86.98* ❦ . . . lawyers better remember they are human beings, and a human being who hasn't his periods of doubts and distresses and disappointments must be a cabbage, not a human being.

*Felix Frankfurter*
*"Proceedings in Honor of Mr. Justice*
*Frankfurter and*
*Distinguished Alumni,"*
Occasional Pamphlet, *No. 3,*
*Harvard Law School, 1960*

*86.99* ❦ A lawyer starts life giving five hundred dollars' worth of law for five dollars, and ends giving five dollars' worth for five hundred dollars.

*Benjamin H. Brewster, American*
*business executive, 1900–1961*
*Laurence J. Peter,* Peter's Quotations,
*1977*

*86.100* ❦ Most lawyers who win a case advise their clients "We have won," and when justice has frowned upon their cause . . . "*You* have lost."

*Louis Nizer*
My Life in Court, *1960*

*86.101* ❦ . . . the Congress is predominantly a lawyers' body.

*Felix Frankfurter* Callanan v. United
States, *364 U.S. 587, 594 (1961)*

*86.102* ❦ "Old Bull" Warren at Harvard was right when he said that one didn't need brains to be a lawyer, only a cast-iron bottom.

*Edward Lamb, American lawyer*
No Lamb for Slaughter, *1963*

*86.103* ❦ In the professional sense we are all descendants of Demosthenes and Pericles. Greece had no lawyers but a person forced to appear before the jury in the Agora could have the assistance of someone to write out his speech of defense and an adviser. The classic illustration is the adviser to a beautiful girl accused of some morals offense.

*Reginald Heber Smith*
*American lawyer*
*"Selected Readings on the Legal*
*Profession," 7* Boston Bar Journal *1*
*(1963)*

*86.104* ❦ The trouble with lawyers is they convince themselves that their clients are right.

*Charles W. Ainey*
*dean of the Susquehanna,*
*Pennsylvania Bar Association*
To Eugene Gerhart, *August 25, 1963*

**86.105** ✥ Obviously, the whole purpose of a police investigation is frustrated if a suspect is entitled to have a lawyer during preliminary questioning, for any lawyer worth his fee will tell him to keep his mouth shut.

*Frank S. Hogan*
New York Times, *December 2, 1965*

**86.106** ✥ Next to the confrontation between two highly trained, finely honed batteries of lawyers, jungle warfare is a stately minuet.

*Bill Veeck*
The Hustler's Handbook, *1965*

**86.107** ✥ When the lawyers are through, what is there left? . . . Can a mouse nibble at it and find enough to fasten a tooth in?

*Carl Sandburg, 1878–1967*
*Kenneth Redden,* Modern Legal
Glossary, *1983*

**86.108** ✥ The American Bar Association formula of a lawyer for hire specifically excludes those who most need legal help—the vast army of the poor.

*William M. Kunstler*
Quote, *August 2, 1970*

**86.109** ✥ The law does not exist just for the lawyers though there are some of us who seem to think that it does. The law is for all the people and the lawyers are only its ministers.

*Robert A. Leflar, American jurist;*
*Arkansas Supreme Court Address,*
*American Judicature Society,*
*reported in the* Wall Street Journal,
*May 27, 1971*

**86.110** ✥ [The law] is designed to protect the power and privilege of those who write the law and to ward off any values or vision that threatens it.

*Andrew Young*
New York Times, *August 7, 1976*

**86.111** ✥ Lawyers are . . . operators of toll bridges across which anyone in search of justice must pass.

*Jane Bryant Quinn*
Newsweek, *October 9, 1978*

**86.112** ✥ I don't think it's useful to talk about percentages when discussing lawyer competency. It depends on one's standards for competency. If the standard is that of lawyers who shouldn't be practicing at all, the incompetency rate is, maybe, five percent. If the standard is room for improvement, that would include 99 percent of all lawyers and 99.9 percent of all judges.

*Anthony G. Amsterdam*
*American educator*
Los Angeles Times, *November 5, 1978*

**86.113** ✥ We [lawyers] shake papers at each other the way primitive tribes shake spears.

*John Jay Osborn, Jr., American lawyer*
The Associates, *1979*

**86.114** ✥ A lawyer's job is to manipulate the skeletons in other people's closets.

*Sol Stein*
*American publisher and writer*
Other People, *1979*

86.115 ❦ If war is too important to be left to the generals, surely justice is too important to be left to the lawyers.

*Robert McKay, American educator;*
*dean, New York University Law School*
*Kenneth Redden,* Modern Legal
Glossary, *1983*

86.116 ❦ It is a secret worth knowing that lawyers rarely go to law themselves.

*Moses Crowell Kenneth Redden,*
Modern Legal Glossary, *1983*

86.117 ❦ How in God's name could so many lawyers get involved in something like Watergate.

*John Dean*
*Kenneth Redden,* Modern Legal
Glossary, *1983*

86.118 ❦ Apologists for the profession contend that lawyers are as honest as other men, but this is not very encouraging.

*Ferdinand Lundberg, American author*
*Kenneth Redden,* Modern Legal
Glossary, *1983*

86.119 ❦ Castles in the air are the only property you can own without the intervention of lawyers.

*J. Feidor Rees, English writer*

86.120 ❦ Lawyers earn a living by the sweat of their browbeating.

*James Gibbons Hanneker*

86.121 ❦ Lawyers considering whether anything can be done for a woman who is damaged in ways that make her less than the perfect case rarely conclude that they should confront or change the law. They look at cases the way surfers look at waves.

*Catharine A. MacKinnon*
*Introduction,* Feminism Unmodified,
*1987*

86.122 ❦ A lawyer's relationship to justice and wisdom . . . is on a par with a piano tuner's relationship to a concert. He neither composes the music, nor interprets it—he merely keeps the machinery running.

*Lucille Kallen*
Lawyer's Wit and Wisdom, *edited by*
*Bruce Nash, Alla Zullo and compiled*
*by Kathryn Zullo, 1995*

86.123 ❦ I'm not an ambulance chaser. I'm usually there before the ambulance.

*Melvin Belli*
Lawyer's Wit and Wisdom, *edited by*
*Bruce Nash, Allan Zullo and compiled*
*by Kathryn Zullo, 1995*

86.124 ❦ Female attorneys today still face the paradox that traits considered most desirable in a male attorney— self-assurance, a competitive and aggressive nature, and high ambition—are considered by many to be "unfeminine."

*Dawn Bradley Berry, J.D.*
50 Most Influential Women in
American Law, *1996*

86.125 ❧ I understand that some black prose-cutors have a name for the pressure they feel from those in the community who criticize them for standing up and convicting black criminals. They call it the "Darden Dilemma."

*Christopher Darden*
*In Contempt, with Jess Walter, 1996*

86.126 ❧ I suppose I could have stayed home and baked cookies and had teas, but what I decided to do is fulfill my profession.

*Hillary Rodham Clinton*
*The Unique Voice of Hillary*
*Rodham Clinton, Claire G. Osborne,*
*1997*

86.127 ❧ Young lawyers are wined and dined, then worked to death.

*Deborah L. Rhode*
*Lawyers, in press*

# 87. LEGAL ETIQUETTE

87.1 ❧ The lawyers' contribution to the civilizing of humanity is evidenced in the capacity of lawyers to argue furiously in the courtroom, then sit down as friends over a drink or dinner. This habit is often interpreted by the layman as a mark of their ultimate corruption. In my opinion, it is their greatest moral achievement; it is a characteristic of human tolerance that is most desperately needed at the present time.

*John R. Silber, American educator;*
*president, Boston University*
*Wall Street Journal, March 16, 1972*

87.2 ❧ A truly qualified advocate—like every genuine professional—resembles a seamless garment, in the sense that legal knowledge, forensic skills, professional ethics, courtroom etiquette and manners are blended in the total person. There are some lawyers who scoff at the idea that manners and etiquette form any part of the necessary equipment of the courtroom advocate. Yet if one were to undertake a list of the truly great advocates of the past 100 years, I suggest he would find a common denominator: They were all intensely individualistic but each was a lawyer for whom courtroom manners were a key weapon in his arsenal. Whether engaged in the destruction of adverse witnesses or undermining damaging evidence or in final argument, the performance was characterized by coolness, poise, and graphic clarity, without shouting or ranting, without baiting witnesses, opponents or the judge.

*Warren E. Burger*
*Lecture, Fordham University Law School,*
*reported in the Los Angeles Times,*
*December 28, 1973*

# *88.* LEGAL PROCESS

**88.1** ❦ Sunday is not a day for judicial or legal proceedings.

*Legal maxim*

**88.2** ❦ Whatever was required to be done, the Circumlocation Office was beforehand with all the public departments in the art of perceiving *HOW NOT TO DO IT.*

*Charles Dickens*
Little Dorrit, *1857*

**88.3** ❦ You cannot imagine the beauty of an intricate, mazy law process, embodying the doubts and subtleties of generations of men. I say, looked at that way, there is something picturesque in an Act of Parliament.

*Sir Arthur Helps*
*English historian and writer*
Friends in Council, *1847–1859*

**88.4** ❦ The judicial process is one of compromise, a compromise between paradoxes, between certainty and uncertainty, between the liberalism that is the exaltation of the written word and the nihilism that is destructive of regularity and order.

*Benjamin N. Cardozo,* 1870–1938
Selected Writings of Benjamin
Nathan Cardozo, *1947*

**88.5** ❦ To be effective, judicial administration must not be leaden-footed.

*Felix Frankfurter*
Cobbledick v. United States, *309*
U.S. 323, 325 (1940)

**88.6** ❦ The time has come to eliminate slow-motion justice in America. Nothing is more difficult to explain about American institutions to the intelligent inquiring layman than why a man accused of robbing a fellow citizen at the point of a gun can stall the process for two years before facing the day of punishment.

*Edward Bennett Williams*
Salt Lake Tribune, *May 29, 1971*

**88.7** ❦ The law will never move as rapidly as a bullet, nor will its dispositions ever be as demolishing as a bomb. Justice should be reasoned, and reasoning takes a certain length of time.

*Edward L. Wright, American lawyer;*
*president, American Bar Association*
Plainview *(Texas)* Daily Herald,
*July 13, 1971*

**88.8** ❦ There is no finality in the law any more. To move a case to trial we first have to run an obstacle course of motions. . . . Many are made merely to gain delay. They are frivolous. They are not intended to gain a legitimate remedy but as a weapon in a war of attrition to exhaust the prosecution in hope that the case will fade away, or at worst, that the prosecution will finally settle for a lesser plea.

*Frank S. Hogan*
*Los Angeles Times, August 14, 1972*

88.9 ❦ Procrastination is a sin of lawyers, trial judges, reporters, appellate judges, in brief, everyone connected with the machinery of criminal law.

*Macklin Fleming, American jurist*
*Los Angeles Times, July 24, 1974*

88.10 ❦ The harsh truth is that unless we devise substitutes for the courtroom processes, we may be on our way to a society overrun by hordes of lawyers hungry as locusts and brigades of judges never before contemplated. . . . The notion that

people want black-robed judges, well-dressed lawyers and fine-paneled courtrooms as the setting to resolve their disputes is not correct. People with problems, like people with pains, want relief, and they want it as quickly and inexpensively as possible.

*Warren E. Burger*
*Address, American Bar Association,*
*New York, reported in the* Los Angeles
Times, *May 28, 1977*

88.11 ❦ The legal process, because of its un-bridled growth, has become a cancer which threatens the vitality of our forms of capitalism and democracy.

*Laurence Silberman, American lawyer;*
*U.S. deputy attorney general*
*Kenneth Redden,* Modern Legal
Glossary, *1983*

# *89.* LEGAL PROFESSION

89.1 ❦ He that loves law will get his fill of it.

*Scottish proverb*
Complete Collection of Scottish
Proverbs, *1721*

89.2 ❦ It is a slight thing to be good according to law.

*Seneca,* 4 B.C.?–A.D. 65
*W. Gurney Benham,* Putnam's
Complete Book of Quotations,
Proverbs and Household Words, *1927*

89.3 ❦ He hath in great perfection the three chief qualifications of a lawyer: boldness, boldness, boldness.

*Anonymous, referring to an*
*English judge*
Hatton Correspondence,
*c. late 16th century*

89.4 ❦ I hold every man a debtor to his profession.

*Francis Bacon*
The Elements of the Common Lawes
of England, *1630*

89.5 ❧ . . . these men of Law and their con-
federates . . . the caterpillars of this
Kingdom, who with their uncon-
trolled exactions and extortions, eat
up the free-born people of this Nation. . . .

*Bathsua Makin, English scholar and author*
*The Malady . . . and Remedy of*
*Vexations and Unjust Arrests and*
*Actions, 1646*

89.6 ❧ This house, where once a lawyer
dwelt,
Is now a smith's. Alas!
How rapidly the iron age
Succeeds the age of brass!

*John Erskin, 1695–1768, alluding to the*
*removal of a distinguished counsellor*
*from a house in Red Lion Square,*
*and an ironmonger becoming its occupant*
*Marshall Brown,* Wit and Humor of
Bench and Bar, *1899*

89.7 ❧ But what his common sense came
short,
He ekèd out wi' law, man.

*Robert Burns, 1759–1796*
*In the Court of Session, Edinburgh*

89.8 ❧ I will not say with Lord Hale, that
"The Law will admit of no rival" . . .
but I will say that it is a jealous mistress, and requires a long and constant courtship. It is not to be won
by trifling favors, but by lavish homage.

*Joseph Story*
The Value and Importance
of Legal Studies,
*August 5, 1829*

89.9 ❧ . . . daily drudgery of a precarious
profession.

*Sir Walter Scott, 1771–1832*
*William Andrews,* The Lawyer in
History, Literature, and Humour,
*1896*

89.10 ❧ There was no great love between us,
and it pleased Heaven to decrease it
on further acquaintance.

*Sir Walter Scott, speaking of himself*
*and the law, 1771–1832*
*"Merry Wives"*

89.11 ❧ The profession of the law is the only
aristocratic element that can be
amalgamated without violence with
the natural elements of democracy
and be advantageously and permanently combined with them.

*Alexis de Tocqueville*
Democracy in America, *1835–1840*

89.12 ❧ Eight points of the law:
1. A good cause;
2. A good purse;
3. An honest and skillful attorney;
4. An upright judge;
5. Good evidence;
6. Able counsel;
7. An upright judge;
8. Good luck

*Attributed to Charles James Fox,*
*English statesman*
*John Campbell,* Lives of the Lord
Chancellors, *1845–1847*

89.13 ❧ At the top of my street[*] the
attorneys abound,
And down at the bottom the barges
are found;

[*]Craven Street, The Strand, London

Fly, Honesty, fly to some safer
  retreat,
For there's craft in the river, and
craft in the street.

> *James Smith, English author and*
> *humorist, 1775–1859*
> *Marshall Brown,* Wit and Humor of
> Bench and Bar, *1882*

**89.14** ❦ The devil makes his Christmas-
pies of lawyers' tongues and
clerks' fingers.

> *Thomas Adams*
> *American clergyman and poet*
> *Sermons, 1862*

**89.15** ❦ YOURS OF THE 10TH
RECEIVED. First of all, he has a wife
and a baby; together they ought to
be worth $500,000 to any man.
Secondly, he has an office in which
there is a table worth $1.50 and three
chairs worth, say, $1. Last of all, there
is in one corner a large rathole,
which will bear looking into.
Respectfully,
A. Lincoln

> *Abraham Lincoln, 1809–1865*
> *Letter to a New York firm inquiring for*
> *recommendations*

**89.16** ❦ It is not the saints of the world
who chiefly give employment to our
profession.

> *Edward G. Ryan, American jurist*
> *Motion to Admit Miss Lavinia*
> *Goodell to the Bar, 1875*

**89.17** ❦ The glory of lawyers, like that of
men of science, is more corporate
than individual.

> *Oliver Wendell Holmes*
> *Answer to Resolution of the Bar on*
> *Daniel S. Richardson, April 15, 1890*

**89.18** ❦ Every calling is great when greatly
pursued.

> *Oliver Wendell Holmes*
> *"The Law," Speeches, 1913*

**89.19** ❦ The practice of law is more than a
mere trade or business, and . . .
those who engage in it are the
guardians of ideals and traditions to
which it is right that they should
from time to time dedicate themselves anew.

> *Hugh Patterson MacMillan,*
> *Scottish lawyer*
> *"The Ethics of Advocacy" (address)*
> *1916*

**89.20** ❦ The office of the lawyer . . . is too
delicate, personal and confidential
to be occupied by a corporation.

> *Robert H. Jackson*
> *"Functions of the Trust Company in*
> *the Field of Law," 52* Report of the
> New York State Bar Association, *142,*
> *144 (1929)*

**89.21** ❦ Was there ever such a profession as
ours, anyhow? We speak of ourselves
as practicing law, as teaching it, as
deciding it; and not one of us can
say what law means.

> *Benjamin N. Cardozo, 1870–1938*
> Selected Writings of Benjamin
> Nathan Cardozo, *1947*

89.22  ❦ Historically, there are three ideas involved in a profession, organization, learning, and a spirit of public service. These are essential. The remaining idea, that of gaining a livelihood, is incidental.

*Roscoe Pound*
*"What Is a Profession," 19* Notre
Dame L. *203, 204 (1944)*

89.23  ❦ The United States is the greatest law factory the world has ever known.

*Charles Evans Hughes,* 1862–1948
*Laurence J. Peter,* Peter's Quotations,
*1977*

89.24  ❦ The law is the only profession which records its mistakes carefully, exactly as they occurred, and yet does not identify them as mistakes. . . .

*Eliot Dunlap Smith, American jurist*
*Louis M. Brown, "Legal Autopsy,"*
Journal of the American Judicial
Society, *November 1954*

89.25  ❦ If you think that you can think about a thing, inextricably attached to something else, without thinking of the thing it is attached to, then you have a legal mind.

*Thomas Reed Powell, American*
*educator,* 1880–1955
*Laurence J. Peter,* Peter's Quotations,
*1977*

89.26  ❦ Getting ahead in a big law firm means a hefty amount of evening and weekend work. . . . Wall Street lawyers still like to recall an anecdote about the late Hoyt A. Moore, a partner in Cravath, Swaine & Moore. A colleague once told Moore that the firm ought to hire more associates because the staff was overworked.

"That's silly," Partner Moore replied. "No one is under pressure. There wasn't a light on when I left at 2 o'clock this morning."

Time, *January 24, 1964*

89.27  ❦ Our civilization must go through a period of far reaching and rapid change to survive the transition to a world that is nuclear dominated, automated, over populated and under employed; . . . An occasion may arise when, confronted by authority, the stark choice before a profession becomes either acquiescence or the necessity to say "No." The challenge must be met on the basis of humanist principle—not self-interest. Only thus may the integrity of a profession be preserved.

*A. A. Klass*
*"Professional Integrity and the State," 8*
The Canadian Bar Journal *2*
*(April 1965)*

89.28  ❦ [Law] is not a profession at all, but rather a business service station and repair shop.

*Adlai E. Stevenson,* 1900–1965
*Walter Johnson and Carol Evans,*
The Papers of Adlai Stevenson, *1972*

89.29  ❦ You will all remember the famous saying that war is far too serious a matter to be left to generals. We in England think that it is possibly also true that law reform is far too serious a matter to be left to the legal profession.

*Leslie Scarman, English lawyer*
*"The Role of the Legal Profession in*
*Law Reform," Association of the Bar of*
*the City of New York* Record,
*vol. 21, no. 1, January 1966*

89.30 ❧ Edmund Burke is supposed to have said, "Law sharpens the mind by narrowing it." It seems to me that the words were meant less in praise of the profession than in warning to it. . . . To the extent that the judicial profession becomes the daily routine of deciding cases on the most secure precedents and the narrowest grounds available, the judicial mind atrophies and its perspective shrinks. What most impresses us about great jurists is not their tenacious grasp of fine points, honed almost to invisibility; it is the moment when we are suddenly made aware of the sweep and direction of the law, and its place in the lives of men.

*Irving R. Kaufman, American jurist;*
*chief judge, U.S. Court of Appeals*
*Speech, Institute of Judicial*
*Administration, August 26, 1969*

89.31 ❧ Don't go into the legal profession if you want social change.

*Warren E. Burger Melvin Belli,*
*Los Angeles Herald-Examiner,*
*September 3, 1972*

89.32 ❧ The practice of law in most courtrooms today is about as modern as performing surgery in a barbershop.

*Gordon D. Schaber, American*
*educator; dean, University of Pacific*
*Law School*
*San Francisco Examiner,*
*March 9, 1973*

89.33 ❧ We inherit the tradition of seven or eight centuries of continuous concern for the institutions and

aspirations . . . that make for a free and civilized society. It is not the age of the profession that matters . . . what matters most is that, through the centuries men of law have been persistently concerned with the resolution of disputes . . . in ways that enable society to achieve its goals with a minimum of force and maximum of reason.

*Archibald Cox*
*New York Times, May 29, 1974*

89.34 ❧ When dictators and tyrants seek to destroy the freedoms of men, their first target is the legal profession and through it the rule of law.

*Leon Jaworski*
*Dallas Times Herald, July 5, 1974*

89.35 ❧ We are coming into the Golden Age of Law. . . . It is the new breed of lawyers, the young kids fresh out of law school, who are bringing this refreshing change. In the old days it was the thing to join the "respected" Establishment law firm. Today, the reverse is true. The young attorney won't join anything unless he knows his prospective employer is involved in cost-free, diligent community and minority group activity.

*Melvin Belli*
*San Francisco Examiner &*
*Chronicle, October 4, 1974*

89.36 ❧ [Law is] an odd profession that presents its greatest scholarship in student-run publications.

*Morton J. Horwitz, American educator*
*Newsweek, September 15, 1975*

89.37 ❧ The legal profession is a business with a tremendous collection of egos. Few people who are not strong egoistically gravitate to it. If they do, they wind up in the archives or doing tax returns, or they stay as junior partners in a law firm for the rest of their lives. To get ahead you have got to assert yourself. That's the lawyer's stock in trade.

*F. Lee Bailey*
U.S. News & World Report,
*September 14, 1981*

89.38 ❧ We may be well on our way to a society overrun by hordes of lawyers, hungry as locusts, and brigades of judges in numbers never before contemplated.

*Warren E. Burger*
*Kenneth Redden,* Modern Legal
Glossary, *1983*

89.39 ❧ We have the heaviest concentration of lawyers on earth—one for every 500 Americans. That is three times more than in England, four times more than in Germany, 21 times more than in Japan. We have more litigation but I am not sure we have more justice. No resource of talent and training in our society, not even medical care, is more wastefully or unfairly distributed than legal skills. Ninety percent of our lawyers serve 10% of our people.

*Jimmy Carter*
*Kenneth Redden,* Modern Legal
Glossary, *1983*

89.40 ❧ The entire legal profession— lawyers, judges, law teachers— has become so mesmerized with the stimulation of the courtroom contest that we tend to forget that we ought to be healers of conflicts. Doctors, in spite of astronomical medical costs, still retain a high degree of public confidence because they are perceived as healers. Should lawyers not be healers? Healers, not warriors? Healers, not procurers? Healers, not hired guns?

*Warren E. Burger*
*Address, American Bar Association, Las
Vegas, reported in the* New York
Times, *February 2, 1984*

89.41 ❧ Instead of resisting the trend toward popular marketing of professional services . . . [we] should encourage and shape it. The public needs the professional equivalent of Chevrolets as well as Cadillacs.

*Doug Harlan, American lawyer*
U.S.A. Today, *February 2, 1984*

89.42 ❧ The average lawyer is essentially a mechanic who works with a pen instead of a ball-peen hammer. Machinists' unions require an apprenticeship, not an advanced degree.

*Bob Schmitt, American jurist*
Americans for Legal Reform, *Vol. 4,
No. 3, Spring 1984*

89.43 ❧ The key thing that makes national law firms work is synergy; with the right combination, one and one make three.

*Steven Kumble, American lawyer*
New York Times, *October 4, 1984*

**89.44** ❧ Like Sisyphus . . . women have long been pushing for equal integration into the profession.

*Laurel Bellows*
Perspectives, *Winter 1995*

**89.45** ❧ In the early '70s, we had a real sense that women would humanize the legal profession . . . how law was practiced and how law firms were structured. Not only has the legal profession not gotten to be more humane and a better place, it has become worse and harder to maintain a law practice and have a full and well-rounded life.

*Honorable Martha Craig Daughtrey*
*"Back to the Future,"* Perspectives,
*Fall 1997*

**89.46** ❧ I hope we're moving not toward focusing more on how women can conform to the profession as it exists, but how we can bring women's characteristics and qualities to better the profession.

*Judy Perez Martinez*
*"Back to the Future,"* Perspectives,
*Fall 1997*

**89.47** ❧ Highly competitive markets are no fun for most sellers. Law is not an exception and fun is not the only casualty.

*Deborah L. Rhode*
Lawyers, *in press*

# 90. LEGAL SYSTEM

**90.1** ❧ The law will not in its executive capacity work a wrong.

*Legal maxim*

**90.2** ❧ Things established by law are done away with by an opposite law.

*Legal maxim*

**90.3** ❧ We are all servants of the laws to the end that it may be possible for us to be free.

*Cicero*
Pro Cluentio, *66* B.C.

**90.4** ❧ The gladsome light of Jurisprudence.

*Sir Edward Coke*
The Institutes of the Lawes of
England, *Vol. 1, 1628–1641*

**90.5** ❧ Where there's no law there's no bread.

*Benjamin Franklin*
Poor Richard's Almanack, *1744*

**90.6** ❧ Former President Taft, after a discussion with President Hoover on the legal machinery, said: "Hoover thinks it really is machinery."

*William Howard Taft, c.1930*
*Dean Acheson,* Among Friends:
Letters of Dean Acheson, *1980*

90.7 ❦ Legal concepts are supernatural entities which do not have a verifiable existence except to the eyes of faith.

*Felix S. Cohen, American lawyer*
Transcendental Nonsense and the
Functional Approach, *1935*

90.8 ❦ The sacredness of human life is a formula that is good only inside a system of law.

*Oliver Wendell Holmes,* 1841–1935
*W. H. Auden and Louis Kronenberger,*
The Viking Book of Aphorisms, *1962*

90.9 ❦ . . . bureaucracy, the rule of no one, has become the modern form of despotism.

*Mary McCarthy*
*"The Vita Activa,"* New Yorker,
*October 18, 1958*

90.10 ❦ . . . we have never been a tightly disciplined people and, reflecting this, our legal structure has been more relaxed than that of many other societies. If this has negative aspects, it also gives us a resiliency to tide us over and enable us to meet any crisis as it arises. We will respond slowly, but that is the nature of a democratic society.

*Warren E. Burger*
*Speech, American Law Institute,*
*Washington, D.C.,*
*May 19, 1970*

90.11 ❦ The legal system isn't working. It is like a scarecrow in the field that doesn't scare the crows anymore because it is too beaten and tattered—and the crows are sitting on the arms and cawing their contemptuous defiance.

*Edward Bennett Williams*
U.S. News & World Report,
*September 21, 1970*

90.12 ❦ The greatest weakness of our judicial system is that it has become clogged and does not function in a fluent fashion resulting in prompt determination of the guilt or innocence of those charged with crime.

*Earl Warren*
*Speech, Johns Hopkins University,*
*reported in the* San Francisco
Examiner & Chronicle,
*November 15, 1970*

90.13 ❦ Foremost among the stabilizing factors, more enduring than customs, manners and traditions, are the legal systems that regulate our life in the world and our daily affairs with each other.

*Hannah Arendt*
*"Civil Disobedience,"* Crises of the
Republic, *1972*

90.14 ❦ . . . it is quite possible to have too many laws and regulations . . . the whole legal apparatus of government may collapse from its own weight; and . . . too many laws and regulations may paralyze society so that we have a condition approximating anarchy. Too much may be the equivalent of none at all.

*Lee Loevinger, American lawyer*
*Lecture, New York University,*
*December 15, 1978*

**90.15** ❦ I have spent all my life under a Communist regime, and I will tell you that a society without any objective legal scale is a terrible one indeed. But a society with no other scale but the legal one is also less than worthy of man.

*Alexandr I. Solzhenitsyn*
*Address, Harvard University, September 1, 1983*

**90.16** ❦ The law is a very mischievous system designed not to achieve but to frustrate the truth.

*Abraham Pomerantz, American lawyer*
*Kenneth Redden*, Modern Legal Glossary, *1983*

# 91. LEGAL TRAINING

**91.1** ❦ Much knowledge does not teach wisdom.

*Heraclitus, 6th–5th century* B.C.
*James Bryce*, Modern Democracies, *1921*

**91.2** ❦ Books must follow sciences, and not sciences books.

*Francis Bacon, 1561–1626*
A Proposal for Amending the Laws of England

**91.3** ❦ A Little Learning *misleadeth*, and a great deal often *stupifieth* the Understanding.

*George Savile, 1st marquess of Halifax, English politician, 1633–1695*
*"False Learning,"* The Complete Works of George Savile, First Marquess of Halifax, *1912*

**91.4** ❦ The system of competitive examination is a sad necessity. Knowledge is wooed for her dowry, not her diviner charms.

*Charles Bowen, English jurist 1835–1894*
*Edward William Donoghue Manson, "Lecture on Education,"* Builders of Our Law *113 L.T. 356 (1902)*

**91.5** ❦ To know is not less than to feel.

*Oliver Wendell Holmes, 1841–1935*
*Catherine Drinker Bowen,* Yankee from Olympus, *1944*

**91.6** ❦ The greatest bores in the world are the come-outers who are cock-sure of a dozen nostrums. The dogmatism of a little education is hopeless.

*Oliver Wendell Holmes, 1841–1935*
*Mark De Wolfe Howe,* Holmes-Pollock Letters, *1946*

*91.7* ❧ . . . a lawyer who has not studied economics and sociology is very apt to become a public enemy.

*Louis D. Brandeis,* 1856–1941
*Samuel J. Konefsky,* The Legacy of Holmes and Brandeis, *1956*

*91.8* ❧ "In university they don't tell you that the greater part of the law is learning to tolerate fools."

*Doris Lessing*
Martha Quest, *1952*

*91.9* ❧ . . . defeat is education. It is a step to something better.

*Louis Nizer,* My Life in Court, *1960*

*9.10* ❧ There is a story of an applicant for admission to a famous graduate school, who, when asked by the Dean of Admissions whether he had graduated in the upper half of his college class—replied with great pride: "Sir, I belong to that section of the class which makes the upper half of the class possible."

*Julius Cohen, American educator*
*"An Evening with Three Legal Philosophers, "*Journal of Legal Education, *1962*

*91.11* ❧ The idea that we should spend all our time in law school teaching people how to win instead of how to settle is very damaging in this day and age.

*Michael I. Sovern, American educator;*
*president, Columbia University*
Time, *April 20, 1970*

*91.12* ❧ Today, lawyers are educated and licensed as if they could eventually do everything which constitutes the practice of law. The myth of omni-competence is precisely that—a myth. Our economic and social life is far too complex to support such a reality.

*Robert W. Meserve, American lawyer;*
*president, American Bar Association*
*Address, New York Bar Association,*
*reported in the* National Observer,
*February 17, 1973*

*91.13* ❧ . . . in spite of all the bar examinations and better law schools, we are more casual about qualifying the people we allow to act as advocates in the courtroom than we are about licensing electricians. The painful fact is that the courtrooms of America all too often have Piper-Cub advocates trying to handle the controls of Boeing 747 litigation.

*Warren E. Burger*
*Lecture, Fordham University Law School, reported in the*
Los Angeles Times,
*December 28, 1973*

*91.14* ❧ Law students can learn more from knowing how to ask good questions than from studying appellate briefs. To be able to make split-second decisions, they have to feel the law in their bones.

*Anthony G. Amsterdam*
*American educator*
Time, *March 14, 1977*

*91.15* ❧ If law school graduates, like cars, could be recalled for failure to meet commercial standards, the recall rate would be very high on those who go into courts without substantial added training. . . . We must require some form of internship before lawyers claim a right to represent clients in the trial courts.

*Warren E. Burger*
*Address, American Bar Association,*
*New Orleans, reported in* U.S. News
& World Report, *August 21, 1978*

91.16 ❧ The study of law is the search for justice, for the equitable resolution of conflict, for tolerance. The search for justice is not easy. That's why the study of law cannot and should not be easy; that is why we ask more questions than we know the answers to.

*Thomas Buergenthal, American*
*educator; dean, American University*
Washington Post, *August 30, 1981*

91.17 ❧ There can be no question that law schools must train advocates. [Yet] the most rigorous standards of professional education are satisfied only when we teach the substance of law, and when lawyers state it as precisely as they can, being fair and

clear about where their own preferences come into play.

*Gerhard Gasper, American educator;*
*dean, University of Chicago Law School*
Wall Street Journal,
*April 13, 1982*

91.18 ❧ To be a lawyer you have to learn to work off of precedents and to explore statutory ambiguities. But you should also understand that the law is not a disciplined set of rules. The landscape in which the law exists is changing, and so should the law school curriculum.

*Charles R. Halpern, American*
*educator; dean, City University of New*
*York Law School at Queens College*
New York Times, *September 14, 1982*

91.19 ❧ Issues of entry, both in the law schools and in the practice of law, are largely behind us.

*William G. Paul*
*"Back to the Future,"* Perspectives,
*1997*

# 92. LIBERTY

92.1 ❧ Liberty is the power of doing
What is allowed by law.

*Latin legal phrase*
*W. Gurney Benham,* Putnam's
Complete Book of Quotations,
Proverbs and Household Words, *1927*

92.2 ❧ Liberty is the Mistress of Mankind, she hath powerful Charms which do so dazzle us, that we find Beauties in

her which perhaps are not there, as we do in other Mistresses; yet if she was not a Beauty, the World would not run mad for her. . . .

*George Savile, 1st marquess of Halifax,*
*English politician, 1633–1695*
*"The Trimmer's Opinion of The Laws*
*and Government,"* The Complete
Works of George Savile, First
Marquess of Halifax, *1912*

92.3 ✥ Is life so dear, or peace so sweet, as to be purchased at the price of chains and slavery? Forbid it, Almighty God! I know not what course others may take, but as for me, give me liberty or give me death!

*Patrick Henry, 1736–1799*
*Speech, Virginia Revolutionary*
*Council, Richmond, 1775*

92.4 ✥ Corruption, the most infallible symptom of constitutional liberty.

*Edward Gibbon*
The Decline and Fall of the Roman
Empire, *1776*

92.5 ✥ What signify a few lives lost in a century or two? The tree of liberty must be refreshed from time to time with the blood of patriots and tyrants. It is its natural manure.

*Thomas Jefferson*
*Letter to W. S. Smith,*
*November 13, 1787*

92.6 ✥ The effect of liberty to individuals is that they may do what they please: we ought to see what it will please them to do, before we risk congratulations, which may be soon turned into complaints. Prudence would dictate this in the case of separate, insulated, private men; but liberty, when men act in bodies, is *power.*

*Edmund Burke*
Reflections on the Revolution in
France, *1790*

92.7 ✥ It is liberty alone that fits men for liberty.

*William Gladstone, 1809–1898*

92.8 ✥ [*Liberty:*] One of Imagination's most precious possessions.

*Ambrose Bierce*
The Devil's Dictionary, *1906*

92.9 ✥ Excess of liberty contradicts itself. In short there is no such thing; there is only liberty for one and restraint for another.

*Leonard T. Hobhouse, English*
*philosopher and sociologist*
Social Evolution and Political Theory,
*1911*

92.10 ✥ Liberty in the most literal sense is the negation of law, for law is restraint, and the absence of restraint is anarchy.

*Benjamin N. Cardozo, 1870–1938*
*"The Paradoxes of Legal Science," in*
Selected Writings of Benjamin
Nathan Cardozo, *edited by*
*Margaret E. Hall, 1947*

92.11 ✥ What then is the spirit of liberty? I cannot define it; I can only tell you my own faith. The spirit of liberty is the spirit which is not too sure that it is right; the spirit of liberty is the spirit which seeks to understand the minds of other men and women; the spirit of liberty is the spirit which weighs their interests alongside its own without bias; the spirit of liberty remembers that not even a sparrow falls to earth unheeded; the spirit of liberty is the spirit of Him who, near two thousand years ago, taught mankind that lesson it has never learned, but has never quite forgotten; that there may be a kingdom where the least shall be heard and considered side by side with the greatest.

*Learned Hand*
*"I Am an American Day" (speech),*
*1944*

92.12 ❦ Liberty is too priceless to be forfeited through the zeal of an administrative agent.

*Frank Murphy*
Oklahoma Press Publishing Co. v. Walling, *327 U.S. 186, 219 (1946)*

92.13 ❦ It is a fair summary of history to say that the safeguards of liberty have frequently been forged in controversies involving not very nice people.

*Felix Frankfurter*
United States v. Rabinowitz, *339 U.S. 56, 69 (1950)*

92.14 ❦ We can afford no liberties with liberty itself.

*Robert H. Jackson*
United States v. Spector, *343 U.S. 169, 180 (1952)*

92.15 ❦ There is no such thing as an achieved liberty; like electricity, there can be no substantial storage and it must be generated as it is enjoyed, or the lights go out.

*Robert H. Jackson*
*"The Task of Maintaining our Liberties:*
*The Role of the Judiciary," 39*
American Bar Association Journal,
*961, 962 (1953)*

92.16 ❦ Not every defeat of authority is a gain for individual freedom, nor every judicial rescue of a convict a victory for liberty.

*Robert H. Jackson*
*"The Task of Maintaining Our*
*Liberties," 39* American Bar
Association Journal *964 (1953)*

92.17 ❦ "The price of freedom is eternal vigilance." It was a lawyer who first used those words.

*Alfred Denning,*
*English jurist*
The Road to Justice, *1955*

92.18 ❦ Liberty Is Always Unfinished Business.

*American Civil Liberties Union*
Title of annual report, *1955–56*

92.19 ❦ I often wonder whether we do not rest our hopes too much upon constitutions, upon laws and upon courts. These are false hopes; believe me, these are false hopes. Liberty lies in the hearts of men and women; when it dies there, no constitution, no law, no court can save it. . . .

*Learned Hand*
*Irving Dilliard,*
The Spirit of Liberty, *1960*

92.20 ❦ What is the spirit of moderation? It is the temper which does not press a partisan advantage to its bitter end, which can understand and will respect the other side, which feels a unity between all citizens—real and not the factitious product of propaganda—which recognizes their common fate and their common aspirations—in a word, which has faith in the sacredness of the individual.

*Learned Hand*
*Irving Dilliard,*
The Spirit of Liberty, *1960*

92.21 ❦ It is a myth that today's Americans are a sturdy, self-reliant folk who will fight any officious interference with their liberties.

*Robert H. Bork*
*"Addicted to Health,"* National Review, *July 28, 1997*

# *93.* LIES

93.1 ❦ Particular lies may speak a general truth.

*George Eliot*
The Spanish Gypsy, *1868*

93.2 ❦ She lied with fluency, ease and artistic fervor.

*Agatha Christie*
They Came to Baghdad, *1951*

93.3 ❦ That's not a lie, it's a terminological inexactitude.

*Alexander Haig*
*TV interview, 1983*

93.4 ❦ I believe in the dull lie—make your story boring enough and no one will question it.

*Sara Paretsky*
Blood Shot, *1988*

# *94.* LIFE

94.1 ❦ To everyone his own life is dark.

*Latin proverb*
*W. Gurney Benham,* Putnam's Complete Book of Quotations, Proverbs and Household Words, *1927*

94.2 ❦ Life is like an artichoke, each day, week, month, year, gives you one little bit which you nibble off—but precious little compared with what you throw away.

*Oliver Wendell Holmes*
*Letter from Holmes to Pollock,*
*January 17, 1887*

94.3 ❦ Life is painting a picture, not doing a sum.

*Oliver Wendell Holmes*
*"Class of '61,"* Speeches, *1913*

94.4 ❦ . . . the world needs the flower more than the flower needs life.

*Oliver Wendell Holmes*
*"The Use of Law Schools,"* Speeches, *1913*

*94.5* ❦ Life is an end in itself, and the only question as to whether it is worth living is whether you have enough of it.

*Oliver Wendell Holmes*
*Speech, Bar Association of Boston,*
Speeches, *1913*

*94.6* ❦ . . . all life is an experiment. Every year if not every day we have to wager our salvation upon some prophesy based upon imperfect knowledge.

*Oliver Wendell Holmes, 1841–1935*
*Quoted by Henry Steel Commager,*
New York Times, *November 20, 1985*

*94.7* ❦ We have to think of how to live before we can learn to die.

*Richard Burdon Haldane*
An Autobiography, *1929*

*94.8* ❦ I abhor averages. I like the individual case. A man may have six meals one day and none the next, making an average of three meals per day, but that is not a good way to live.

*Louis D. Brandeis, 1856–1941*
*A. T. Mason,* Brandeis: A Free
Man's Life, *1946*

*94.9* ❦ This is life and all there is of life; to play the game, to play the cards we get; play them uncomplainingly and play them to the end. The game may not be worth the while. The stakes may not be worth the winning. But the playing of the game is the forgetting of self, and we should be game sports and play it bravely to the end.

*Clarence Darrow, 1857–1938*
*Arthur and Lila Weinberg,* Verdicts
Out of Court, *1963*

*94.10* ❦ Life has never been completely charted and as long as change is one of the great facts of life, it never will be; and law, we must always remember, is but one aspect of life.

*Arthur T. Vanderbilt, American jurist*
*"A Report on Prelegal Education,"* New
York University Law Review, *vol. 25,*
*April 1950*

# *95.* LITIGATION

*95.1* ❦ Win your lawsuit and lose your money.

*Chinese proverb*
*Rosalind Fergusson,* The Facts On File
Dictionary of Proverbs, *1983*

*95.2* ❦ He'll go to law for the wagging of a straw.

*English proverb*
*John Ray,* English Proverbs, *1670*

95.3 ❦ From litigation you can never recover your losses.

*Jewish folk saying*
*Joseph L. Baron,* A Treasury of Jewish
Quotations, *1956*

95.4 ❦ Go to law for a sheep and lose
your cow.

*Proverb*
*Rosalind Fergusson,* The Facts On File
Dictionary of Proverbs, *1983*

95.5 ❦ He that goes to law holds a wolf by
the ear.

*Proverb*
*Robert Burton,* The Anatomy of
Melancholy, *1621*

95.6 ❦ Law is a bottomless pit.

*Proverb*
*Rosalind Fergusson,* The Facts On File
Dictionary of Proverbs, *1983*

95.7 ❦ Litigation . . . merely continues
conflict and offends nature; it does
not heal.

*Confucius, c.500* B.C.
*Joseph I. Lieberman "Confucius's Lesson
to Litigants"* The New York Times,
*July 9, 1984*

95.8 ❦ You know what a ticklish thing it is
to go to law.

*Plautus*
Mostellaria, *c.220* B.C.

95.9 ❦ As a man is friended so the law is
ended.

*William Camden*
Remains, *1605*

95.10 ❦ Men are never wise but returning
from law.

*John Wodroephe*
The Spared Houres of a Soldier, *1623*

95.11 ❦ The worst of law is that one suit
breeds twenty.

*George Herbert, 1593–1633*
Jacula Prudentum, *1640*

95.12 ❦ A man must not go to law because
the musician keeps false time with
his foot.

*Jeremy Taylor*
The Worthy Communicant, *1660*

95.13 ❦ The oyster is for the judge, the shells
are for the litigants.

*Jean La Fontaine*
Fables, *1668*

95.14 ❦ That litigious pettifogger.

*Anonymous*
The Plain Dealer, *1677*

95.15 ❦ Those who come into court to seek
justice must come with clean hands.

*Sir Lloyd Kenyon, English jurist; Lord
Chief Justice*
Petrie v. Hennay, *1789*

95.16 ☙ [*Litigation:*] A machine which you go into as a pig and come out as a sausage.

*Ambrose Bierce*
The Devil's Dictionary, *1906*

95.17 ☙ [*Litigant:*] A person about to give up his skin for the hope of retaining his bone.

*Ambrose Bierce*
The Devil's Dictionary, *1906*

95.18 ☙ [*Litigation:*] A form of hell whereby money is transferred from the pockets of the proletariat to that of lawyers.

*Elbert Hubbard,* 1856–1915
*Eugene E. Brussell,* Dictionary of Quotable Definitions, *1970*

95.19 ☙ We hear of those to whom a lawsuit is an agreeable relaxation, a gentle excitement. One of this class, when remonstrated with, retorted, that while one friend kept dogs, and another horses, he, as he had a right to do, kept a lawyer; and no one had a right to dispute his taste.

*Isabella Beeton*
The Book of Household Management, *1861*

95.20 ☙ Litigation is the pursuit of practical ends, not a game of chess.

*Felix Frankfurter*
Indianapolis v. Chase National Bank, Trustee, *314 U.S. 63, 62 S. Ct. 15, 86 L.Ed. 47, reh den 314 U.S. 714, 62 S. Ct. 355, 356, 86 L.Ed. 569 (1941)*

95.21 ☙ The tactics here employed resemble somewhat the military tactics which Marshall Foch is said to have urged on younger officers. He advised them to watch the movement of a parrot in its cage, which progresses by reaching out one claw, grasping firmly, and pausing before bringing the other claw into position— grasp, pause, grasp, pause, was his description of successful forward movement, and whatever its application to modern warfare, it is not a bad motto for constitutional litigation.

*Paul A. Freund, American educator*
On Understanding the Supreme Court, *1949*

95.22 ☙ All litigation is inherently a clumsy, time-consuming business.

*Warren E. Burger*
U.S. News & World Report, *December 14, 1970*

95.23 ☙ We have created here in America the most litigious society in the history of mankind.

*Lewis F. Powell, Jr.*
Washington Post, *April 12, 1973*

95.24 ☙ All of us have heard the term "crisis" used frequently in the past years with reference to the courts and the process of litigation. . . . The pressures from the law explosion are severe, and the courts may not be equal to the task. Important rights may be lost. Defendants charged with crime may go free on bail, some to commit other crimes. Defendants convicted of crime may be free on bail pending delayed appeals. Business controversies may go unresolved because of the lack of a forum. Hapless plaintiffs with meritorious claims may go unpaid because of delay in trial and appellate courts.

*Griffin B. Bell*
*Address, American Bar Association,*
*reported in the* Washington Post,
*November 30, 1977*

95.25 ❦ I believe the system is out of balance. Litigation has come to be regarded as the natural order of things, as though it were the only way to go. It's not just lawyers who think this way; it's their clients too. Often people don't even seek legal counsel until a dispute has gone so far that the gladiators have to fight it out in court. Litigation should be a last resort, not a knee-jerk reflex.

*Irving S. Shapiro, American lawyer,*
*chairman, E. I. Du Pont de Nemours*
*& Company*
Christian Science Monitor,
*December 5, 1978*

95.26 ❦ I have never met a litigator who did not think that he was winning the case right up to the moment when the guillotine came down.

*William F. Baxter, American lawyer;*
*assistant U.S. attorney general*
Washington Post, *April 18, 1982*

95.27 ❦ Litigation takes the place of sex at middle age.

*Gore Vidal*
*Kenneth Redden,* Modern Legal
Glossary, *1983*

95.28 ❦ In the strange heat all litigation brings to bear on things, the very process of litigation fosters the most profound misunderstandings in the world.

*Renata Adler*
Lawyer's Wit and Wisdom, *edited by*
*Bruce Nash, Allan Zullo and compiled*
*by Kathryn Zullo, 1995*

95.29 ❦ Wasting limited assets by encouraging protracted litigation is a cause of, not a cure for, the feminization of poverty.

*Sandra W. Jacobson*
*"Restricting Divorce Hurts Children*
*and Women,"* New York Times,
*February 21, 1996*

95.30 ❦ There's got to be an easier way of making a living than litigating against monopolists and the government.

*Gary Reback, lawyer*
*James Daly, "The Robin Hood of the*
*Rich,"* Wired, *August 1997*

95.31 ❦ We have disputes that are too big for the courts, disputes that are too small, and disputes that should not have been disputes at all.

*Deborah L. Rhode*
Lawyers, *in press*

# 96. LOVE

*96.1* ❧ Mortal love is but the licking of honey from thorns.

> *Anonymous woman at the court of*
> *Eleanor of Aquitane, 1198*
> *Helen Lawrenson,* Whistling Girl,
> *1978*

*96.2* ❧ I have an inalienable constitutional and natural right to love whom I may, to love as long or as short a period as I can, to change that love every day if I please!

> *Victoria Claflin Woodhull*
> Woodhull and Claflin's Weekly,
> *Nov. 20, 1871*

*96.3* ❧ By the time you swear you're his,/Shivering and sighing,/And he vows his passion is/Infinite, undying—/Lady, make a note of this:/One of you is lying.

> *Dorothy Parker*
> *"Unfortunate Coincidence,"*
> Enough Rope, *1926*

# *97.* MARRIAGE AND DIVORCE

*97.1*  ❦ A divorce lawyer is the man who referees the fight and winds up with the purse.

> *Anonymous*
> *Leonard Louis Levinson,* Bartlett's
> Unfamiliar Quotations, *1971*

*97.2*  ❦ Consent makes marriage.

> *Latin legal phrase*
> *W. Gurney Benham,* Putnam's
> Complete Book of Quotations,
> Proverbs and Household Words, *1927*

*97.3*  ❦ A Roman divorced from his wife, being highly blamed by his friends, who demanded, "Was she not chaste? Was she not fair? Was she not fruitful?" holding out his shoe, asked them whether it was not new and well made. "Yet," added he, "none of you can tell where it pinches me."

> *Plutarch, 46?–?120*
> Lives

*97.4*  ❦ When people understand that they *must* live together, except for a very few reasons known to the law, they learn to soften by mutual accommodation that yoke which they know they cannot shake off; they become good husbands, and good wives, from the necessity of remaining husbands and wives; for necessity is a powerful master in teaching the duties which it imposes. If it were once understood, that upon mutual disgust married persons might be legally separated, many couples, who now pass through the world with mutual comfort, with attention to their common offspring and to the moral order of civil society, might have been at this moment living in a state of mutual unkindness—in a stage of estrangement from their common offspring—and in a state of the most licentious and unreserved immorality.

> *Sir William Scott, English jurist*
> Evans v. Evans *(1790), 1 Hagg.*
> Con. Rep. 36, 37

*97.5*  ❦ It is but the name of wife I hate.

> *Lady Caroline Lamb*
> Glenarvon, *1816*

*97.6*  ❦ Love, the quest; marriage, the conquest; divorce, the inquest.

> *Helen Rowland, American humorist*
> Reflections of a Bachelor Girl, *1903*

*97.7*  ❦ Husband and wife are one, and that one is the husband.

> *Professor Loring*
> *Theron G. Strong,* Joseph H. Choate,
> *1917*

*97.8*  ❦ Courtship is a republic; marriage, a monarchy; divorce, a soviet.

> *Helen Rowland, American humorist*
> *"Personally Speaking," in* The Book of
> Diversion, *edited by F. P. Adams, D.*
> *Taylor and J. Bechdolt, 1925*

97.9 ❦ So many persons who think divorce a panacea for every ill find out, when they try it, that the remedy is worse than the disease.

*Dorothy Dix*
*Dorothy Dix, Her Book, 1926*

97.10 ❦ ... where divorce is allowed at all ... society demands a specific grievance of one party against the other. ... The fact that marriage may be a failure spiritually is seldom taken into account.

*Suzanne LaFollette, American*
*feminist and writer*
*"The Beginnings of Emancipation,"*
*Concerning Women, 1926*

97.11 ❦ The claim for alimony ... implies the assumption that a woman is economically helpless. ...

*Suzanne LaFollette, American*
*feminist and writer*
*"Women and Marriage," Concerning*
*Women, 1926*

97.12 ❦ ... when one hears the argument that marriage should be indissoluble for the sake of children, one cannot help wondering whether the protagonist is really such a firm friend of childhood. ...

*Suzanne LaFollette, American*
*feminist and writer*
*"Women and Marriage," Concerning*
*Women, 1926*

97.13 ❦ While the husband is still declared by statute to be the head of the family, he, like the King of England, is largely a figurehead.

*Reginald L. Hine, American jurist*
*Curtis v. Ashworth, 165 Ga.*
*782, 787 (1928)*

97.14 ❦ At the end of one millennium and nine centuries of Christianity, it remains an unshakable assumption of the law in all Christian countries and of the moral judgment of Christians everywhere that if a man and woman, entering a room together, close the door behind them, the man will come out sadder and the woman wiser.

*H. L. Mencken, 1880–1956*
*Bergen Evans, Dictionary of*
*Quotations, 1968*

97.15 ❦ What a holler would ensue if people had to pay the minister as much to marry them as they have to pay a lawyer to get them a divorce.

*Claire Trevor*
*New York Journal-American,*
*October 12, 1960*

97.16 ❦ A lawyer is never entirely comfortable with a friendly divorce, any more than a good mortician wants to finish the job and then have the patient sit up on the table.

*Jean Kerr, American playwright*
*Time, April 14, 1961*

97.17 ❦ With children no longer the universally accepted reason for marriage, marriages are going to have to exist on their own merits.

*Eleanor Holmes Norton*
*"For Sadie and Maude," in Robin*
*Morgan, ed., Sisterhood Is Powerful,*
*1970*

97.18 ☙ It's illegal in England to state in print that a wife can and should derive sexual pleasure from intercourse.

*Bertrand Russell, 1872–1970*
*Laurence J. Peter, Peter's Quotations, 1977*

97.19 ☙ Some of us are becoming the men we wanted to marry.

*Gloria Steinem*
*Speech, Yale University, 1981*

97.20 ☙ What has the women's movement learned from (Geraldine Ferraro's) candidacy for vice president? Never get married.

*Gloria Steinem*
*Boston Globe, May 14, 1987*

97.21 ☙ *Holy Deadlock*

*Sir Alan Patrick Herbert, English author and politician, 1890-1971*
*Title of a novel satirizing English divorce laws*

# 98. MERCY

98.1 ☙ [Mercy:] A virtue of the weak.

*Anonymous*
*Eugene E. Brussell, ed., Dictionary of Quotable Definitions, 1970*

98.2 ☙ Every dog is allowed one bite.

*Proverb*

98.3 ☙ The law is relaxed when the judge shows pity.

*Publilius Syrus, Latin writer*
*Sententiae, c.43 B.C.*

98.4 ☙ The quality of mercy is not strained,
It droppeth as the gentle rain from heaven
Upon the plain beneath:

\* \* \*

And earthly power doth then show like God's
When mercy seasons justice.

*Shakespeare*
*The Merchant of Venice, IV, 1, 1596–1597*

98.5 ☙ No ceremony that to great ones 'longs,
Not the King's crown, nor the deputed sword,
The marshal's truncheon nor the judge's robe,
Become them with one half so good a grace,
As mercy does.

*Shakespeare*
*Measure for Measure, II, 2, 1604–1605*

98.6 ☙ Yet shall I temper so
Justice with mercy.

*Milton*
*Paradise Lost, 1667*

98.7 ☙ Reason to rule, Mercy to forgive:
The first is law, the last perogative.

*John Dryden*
*The Hind and the Panther, 1687*

98.8 ❧ He only judges right who weighs,
    compares,
And, in the sternest sentence which
    his voice
Pronounces, ne'er abandons Charity.

*William Wordsworth*
*Ecclesiastical Sonnets, 1822*

98.9 ❧ We hand folks over to God's mercy,
and show none ourselves.

*George Eliot*
*Adam Bede, 1859*

98.10 ❧ Gentlemen of the jury, think of his
poor mother—his only mother.

*Irish barrister, defending a prisoner*
*Marshall Brown,* Wit and Humor of
Bench and Bar, *1899*

98.11 ❧ He reminds me of the man who
murdered both his parents, and
then, when sentence was about to be
pronounced, pleaded for mercy on
the grounds that he was an orphan.

*Attributed to Abraham Lincoln,*
*1809–1865*
*Franklin Pierce Adams,* F.P.A. Book of
Quotations, *1952*

98.12 ❧ If truth and justice were the rule,
there would be no need for mercy.

*Mendele Mocher Sforim*
*Di Kliatche, 1873*

98.13 ❧ [*Mercy:*] An attribute beloved of
detected offenders.

*Ambrose Bierce*
The Devil's Dictionary, *1906*

98.14 ❧ I can forgive, but if you ask me to
forget, you ask me to give up
experience.

*Louis Brandeis*
*Harlan Phillips,*
Felix Frankfurter Reminisces, *1960*

# 99. MINORITIES

99.1 ❧ All, too, will bear in mind this sacred principle, that though the will
of the majority is in all cases to prevail, that will, to be rightful, must be
reasonable; that the minority possess
their equal rights, which equal laws
must protect, and to violate which
would be oppression.

*Thomas Jefferson*
*First inaugural address, 1801*

99.2 ❧ Our progress in degeneracy appears
to me to be pretty rapid. As a nation
we began by declaring that "*all men
are created equal.*" We now practically read it "all men are created
equal, *except negroes.*" When the
Know-nothings get control, it will
read "all men are created equal, except negroes *and foreigners and
Catholics.*" When it comes to this,

I shall prefer emigrating to some country where they make no pretense of loving liberty,—to Russia, for instance, where despotism can be taken pure, and without the base alloy of hypocrisy.

*Abraham Lincoln*
*Letter to J. F. Speed, August 24, 1855*

99.3 ❧ Persecution is a very easy form of virtue.

*John Duke Coleridge, English jurist;*
*Lord Chief Justicee*
Reg. v. Ramsey *(1883), 1 Cababe and*
*Ellis's Q.B.D. Rep. 145*

99.4 ❧ To protect those who are not able to protect themselves is a duty which every one owes to society.

*Edward Macnaghten, 1st baron,*
*English jurist*
Jenoure v. Delmege *(1890), 60 L.J.*
*Rep. (N.S.) Q.B. 13*

99.5 ❧ Experience tells us that sometimes, when minorities insist on their rights, they ultimately prevail.

*Robert George Kekewich, English jurist*
Young v. South African &c. Syndicate
*(1896), L.R. 2 C.D. (1896), p. 278*

99.6 ❧ History teaches us that there have been but few infringements of personal liberty by the state which have not been justified. . . . in the name of righteousness and the public good, and few which have

not been directed, as they are now, at politically helpless minorities.

*Harlan F. Stone*
Minersville School District v.
Gobitis, *310 U.S. 586, 604 (1940)*

99.7 ❧ There is room here for men of any race, of any creed, or any condition in life, but not for Protestant-Americans, or Catholic-Americans, or Jewish-Americans, nor for German-Americans, Irish-Americans, or Russian-Americans.

*Louis D. Brandeis, 1856–1941*
*Alpheus Thomas Mason, Brandeis:*
A Free Man's Life, *1946*

99.8 ❧ The difference between *de jure* and *de facto* segregation is the difference between open, forthright bigotry and the shamefaced kind that works through unwritten agreements between real estate dealers, school officials, and local politicians.

*Shirley Chisholm*
Unbought and Unbossed, *1970*

99.9 ❧ The experience of Negroes in America has been different in kind, not just in degree, from that of other ethnic groups. It is not merely the history of slavery alone but also that a whole people were marked as inferior by the law. And that mark has endured.

*Thurgood Marshall*
University of California v. Bakke,
*438 U.S. 265, 98 S. Ct. 2733, 57*
*L.Ed.2d 750 (1978)*

*99.10* ❦ When you have majority rule, often you are protecting the rights of people who are unpopular. It is always the minorities who aren't part of the mainstream, who define what the limits of the majority, are going to be.

*Rose Elizabeth Bird, American jurist; Chief Justicee, Supreme Court of California Edwin Chen, "Rose Bird Runs for Her Life,"* The Nation, *January 18, 1986*

# *100.* MISCELLANEOUS

*100.1* ❦ They that once begin first to trouble the water, seldom catch the fish.

*George Jeffreys*
Trial of William Sacheverell and *others (1684), 10 How. St. Tr. 92*

*100.2* ❦ I am by no means sure that if a man kept a tiger, and lightning broke his chain, and he got loose and did mischief, that the man who kept him would not be liable.

*Lord William Bramwell, English jurist*
Nichols v. Marsland *(1875), L.R. 10 Ex. 260*

*100.3* ❦ Masterly inactivity may be prudence to one man, desperate rashness to another.

*Robert George Kekewich, English jurist*
In re Liverpool Household Stores Association *(1890), 59 L.J. Rep. C.D. 618*

*100.4* ❦ Danger invites rescue.

*Benjamin N. Cardozo*
Wagner v. International Ry. Co., *232 N.Y. 13, 25 (1926)*

*100.5* ❦ The hand once set to a task may not always be withdrawn with impunity though liability would fail if it had been applied at all.

*Benjamin N. Cardozo, 1928*

*100.6* ❦ Nothing conduces to brevity like a caving in of the knees.

*Oliver Wendell Holmes, 1841–1935*
*Catherine Drinker Bowen,* Yankee from Olympus, *1944*

*100.7* ❦ Every age is modern to those who are living in it.

*Benjamin N. Cardozo, 1870–1938*
*"Paradoxes of Legal Science,"* Selected writings of Benjamin Nathan Cardozo, *1947*

*100.8* ❧ The whole, though larger than any of its parts, does not necessarily obscure their separate identities.

*William O. Douglas*
United States v. Powers, *307 U.S. 214, 218 (1939)*

*100.9* ❧ I abhor averages. I like the individual case. A man may have six meals one day and none the next, making an average of three meals per day, but that is not a good way to live.

*Louis D. Brandeis,* 1856–1941
*A. T. Mason,* Brandeis: A Free Man's Life, *1946*

*100.10* ❧ He who must search a haystack for a needle is likely to end up with the attitude that the needle is not worth the search.

*Robert H. Jackson*
Brown v. Allen, *344 U.S. 443, 537 (1953)*

*100.11* ❧ There is always the danger that if you speak a language that recognizes only individual rights, you will become a people that can think only about individuals.

*Mary Ann Glendon, lawyer,*
*Harvard professor*
*Bill Moyers,* A World of Ideas, *1989*

# *101.* MONEY

*101.1* ❧ Little money, little law.

*Anonymous*
The Parliament of Byrdes, *c. 1550*

*101.2* ❧ She [Money] is the Sovereign Queen of all delights;
For her the Lawyer pleads, the Soldier fights.

*Richard Barnfield, English poet*
The Encomion of Lady Pecunia, *1598*

*101.3* ❧ Unnecessary laws are not good laws, but traps for money.

*Thomas Hobbes*
Leviathan, *1651*

*101.4* ❧ They who are of opinion that Money will do everything, may very well be suspected to do everything for Money.

*George Savile, 1st marquess of Halifax,*
*English politician,* 1633–1695
*"Of Money,"* The Complete Works of George Savile, First Marquess of Halifax, *1912*

*101.5* ❧ But the rich man . . . is always sold to the institution which makes him rich. Absolutely speaking, the more money, the less virtue.

*Henry David Thoreau*
Civil Disobedience, *1849*

*101.6* ❧ One cannot help regretting that where money is concerned, it is so much the rule to overlook moral obligations.

*Sir Richard Malins, English jurist*
Ellis v. Houston *(1878), L.R. 10 C.D. 240*

**101.7** ❦ To an imagination of any scope the most far-reaching form of power is not money, it is the command of ideas.

> *Oliver Wendell Holmes "The Path of the Law,"* Collected Legal Papers, *1921*

**101.8** ❦ When a man keeps hollering, 'It's the principle of the thing,' he's talking about the money.

> *Kin Hubbard (pseudonym of Frank McKinney Hubbard), American humorist, 1868–1930*
> *Thad Stem, Jr. and Alan Butler,* Sam Ervin's Best Short Stories, *1973*

**101.9** ❦ Men are more often bribed by their loyalties and ambitions than by money.

> *Robert H. Jackson*
> United States v. Wunderlich, *342 U.S. 98, 96 L.Ed. 113, 72 S. Ct. 154 (1951)*

**101.10** ❦ Money speaks sense in a language all nations understand.

> *Aphra Behn*
> The Rover, *1681*

**101.11** ❦ There are many excuses for the persons who made the mistake of confounding money and wealth. Like many they mistook the sign for the thing signified.

> *Millicent Garrett Fawcett*
> Political Economy for Beginners, *1870*

**101.12** ❦ Money is not everything, but it is better than having one's health.

> *Woody Allen*
> Without Feathers, *1975*

**101.13** ❦ If you know how much you've got, you probably haven't got much.

> *Imelda Marcos*
> Sixty Minutes *with Diane Sawyer, September 21, 1986*

**101.14** ❦ No one would remember the Good Samaritan if he'd only had good intentions. He had money as well.

> *Margaret, Lady Thatcher*
> The Times, *London, 1986*

# 102. MORALS

**102.1** ❦ Of what avail are empty laws if we lack principle?

> *Horace*
> Odes, *23* B.C.

**102.2** ❦ Good men must not obey the laws too well.

> *Ralph Waldo Emerson*
> *"Self-Reliance,"* Essays, *1844*

*102.3* ❧ Absolute morality is the regulation of conduct in such a way that pain shall not be inflicted.

*Herbert Spencer, English philosopher,*
*1820–1903*
Essays: Scientific, Political and
Speculative, *1863*

*102.4* ❧ This Court does not sit as a Court of morality, to inflict punishment against those who offend against the social law.

*Sir Francis Henry Jeune, Baron St.*
*Helier, English jurist*
Evans v. Evans *(1899), L.R. Prob.*
*Div. [1899], p. 202*

*102.5* ❧ You will see that international law is revolutionized by putting morals into it.

*Woodrow Wilson*
*Address at Pueblo, 1919*

*102.6* ❧ Morality is simply another means of living but the saints make it an end in itself.

*Oliver Wendell Holmes,* 1841–1935
*Franklin Pierce Adams,* F.P.A. Book of
Quotations, *1952*

*102.7* ❧ I have often thought morality may perhaps consist solely in the courage of making a choice.

*Léon Blum*
*Charles P. Curtis, Jr. and Ferris*
*Greenslet, eds.,* The Practical
Cogitator, *1945*

*102.8* ❧ Morals are three-quarters manners.

*Felix Frankfurter*
*Harlan Phillips,* Felix Frankfurter
Reminiscences, *1960*

*102.9* ❧ When morality comes up against profit, it is seldom that profit loses.

*Shirley Chisholm*
Unbought and Unbossed, *1970*

*102.10* ❧ It is seldom appropriate for one group within society to seek to insert their moral beliefs, however profoundly held, into a document designed for people of fundamentally differing views.

*Robert Drinan, "On Supreme Court*
*Ruling on Abortion,"*
American Herald, *March 25, 1974*

*102.11* ❧ The code of morality is to do unto others as you would have them do unto you. If you make that the central theme of your morality code, it will serve you well as a moral individual.

*Barbara Jordan*
*Malcolm Boyd, "Where Is Barbara*
*Jordan Today?"* Parade,
*February 16, 1986*

*102.12* ❧ There is an ancient Indian saying: "We do not inherit the earth from our ancestors; we borrow it from our children." If we use this ethic as a moral compass, then our rendezvous with reality can also become a rendezvous with opportunity.

*Patricia Schroeder*
Ms. Magazine, *February 1989*

*102.13* ❦ The punters know that the horse named Morality rarely gets past the post, whereas the nag named Self-Interest always runs a good race.

*Gough Whitlam, Australian Labor politician, prime minister*
Daily Telegraph, *London, October 19, 1989*

*102.14* ❦ The bar's ethical code miscasts professional self-interests as moral necessities.

*Deborah L. Rhode "Ethical Perspectives on Legal Practice," 37* Stanford Law Review *589 (Jan. 1985)*

# *103.* MOTIVES

*103.1* ❦ The act does not constitute a criminal unless the mind is criminal.

*Latin legal phrase*
*W. Gurney Benham,* Putnam's Complete Book of Quotations, Proverbs and Household Words, *1927*

*103.2* ❦ Acts indicate the intention.

*Legal maxim*

*103.3* ❦ An act against my will is not my act.

*Legal maxim*

*103.4* ❦ Outward actions are a clue to hidden secrets.

*Legal maxim*

*103.5* ❦ *Cui bono?* [To whose good?]

*Cicero*
Pro Sistio, *c.50* B.C.

*103.6* ❦ The intention ought to be subservient to the laws, not the laws to the intention.

*Sir Edward Coke, 1552–1634*
*W. Gurney Benham,* Putnam's Complete Book of Quotations, Proverbs and Household Words, *1927*

*103.7* ❦ The *end* directs and sanctifies the *means.*

*Sir John Eardley Wilmot, English jurist; Chief Justicee*
Collins v. Blantern *(1767), 2 Wils. Rep. 351*

*103.8* ❦ What passes in the mind of man is not scrutable by any human tribunal; it is only to be collected from his acts.

*Sir John Willes, English jurist*
King v. Shipley *(1784), 3 Doug. 177*

*103.9* ❧ Men's feelings are as different as their faces.

> Sir Nash Grose, English jurist
> Good v. Elliott *(1790), 3 T.R. 701*

*103.10* ❧ It is a principle of law, that a person intends to do that which is the natural effect of what he does.

> Edward Law, Lord Ellenborough,
> English jurist; Chief Justice
> Beckwith v. Wood and another
> *(1817), 2 Starkie, 266*

*103.11* ❧ A man may have as bad a heart as he chooses, if his conduct is within the rules.

> Oliver Wendell Holmes
> The Common Law, *1881*

*103.12* ❧ Philosophy does not furnish motives, but it shows men that they are not fools for doing what they already want to do.

> Oliver Wendell Holmes
> "Natural Law," Collected Legal
> Papers, *1921*

# *104.* MURDER

*104.1* ❧ Thou shalt not kill.

> Old Testament, Exodus 20:13

*104.2* ❧ The guilt of murder is the same, whether the victim be renowned or whether he be obscure.

> Cicero
> Pro Milone, *52* B.C.

*104.3* ❧ He who slayeth one man is as guilty as if he killed the whole human race.

> Muhammad
> Koran, c.622

*104.4* ❧ Mordre wol out, that see we day by day.

> Chaucer
> "The Nun's Priest's Tale," Canterbury
> Tales, c.1380

*104.5* ❧ Ghost: Murder most foul, as in the best it is;
But this most foul, strange and unnatural.

> Shakespeare Hamlet, I, 5 1600–1601

*104.6* ❧ The law against witches does not prove there be any; but it punishes the malice of those people that use such means to take away men's lives.

> John Selden, 1584–1654
> Table-Talk, *1689*

*104.7* ❧ The fashion of poisoning people is getting too common.

> Charlotte-Elisabeth, Duchesse d'Orléans
> Referring to three deaths by poison at
> court, 1690, in Life and Letters of
> Charlotte Elizabeth, *1889*

*104.8* ❦ Gentlemen of the jury, the charge against the prisoner is murder, and the punishment is death; and that simple statement is sufficient to suggest the awful solemnity of the occasion which brings you and me face to face.

*John Inglis*
A Complete Report of the Trial of
Miss Madeline Smith, *1857*

*104.9* ❦ Every murderer is probably somebody's old friend.

*Agatha Christie*
The Mysterious Affair at Styles, *1920*

*104.10* ❦ Other sins only speak,
Murder cries out.

*Anne Hocking, British mystery writer*
Death Loves a Shining Mark, *1943*

*104.11* ❦ Clarissa: Oh dear, I never realized what a terrible lot of explaining one has to do in a murder!

*Agatha Christie*
Spider's Web, *1956*

*104.12* ❦ Murder is not only an offense against an individual; it's an offense against the social order.

*Wendy Kaminer, lawyer & social critic*
It's All the Rage, *1995*

*104.13* ❦ You're no less dead if your killer is fifteen or fifty.

*Judy Sheindlin with Josh Getlin*
Don't Pee on My Leg and Tell Me
It's Raining, *1996*

# 105. NATURAL LAW

**105.1** ❦ Only such decrees should be issued which the majority of a community can endure.

*Midrash, Psalms*

**105.2** ❦ See how people act, and that is the Law.

*Talmud, Berakhot*

**105.3** ❦ What is hateful to you, do not to your fellow: that is the whole Law; all the rest is interpretation.

*Hillel*
*Talmud, Shabbat*

**105.4** ❦ The commands of the law are conventional and have no root in nature.

*Antiphon, Greek orator*
Orations, *c.*435 B.C.

**105.5** ❦ In every matter the consensus of opinion among all nations is to be regarded as the law of nature.

*Cicero*
Tusculanarum Disputationum, *45* B.C.

**105.6** ❦ Through love every law is broken.

*Chaucer*
Troilus and Criseyde, *1385*

**105.7** ❦ Lust of love exceeds law.

*John Gower*
Confessio Amantis, *1393*

**105.8** ❦ Love has no law.

*John Lydgate*
*"Virtues,"* The Minor Poems of
John Lydgate, *1449*

**105.9** ❦ There are in nature certain foundations of justice, whence all civil laws are derived but as streams.

*Francis Bacon*
The Advancement of Learning, *1605*

**105.10** ❦ Oh wearisome condition of
  humanity!
Born under one law, to another
  bound.

*Fulke Greville, 1st baron Brooke,*
*English author and statesman*
Mustapha, *1609*

**105.11** ❦ The first and fundamental law of Nature . . . is "to seek peace and follow it." The second, the sum of the right of Nature . . . is, "by all means we can to defend ourselves."

*Thomas Hobbes*
Leviathan, *1651*

**105.12** ❦ Law and conscience are one and the same.

*Justice Bacon, English jurist*
Watson v. Watson *(1670),*
*Style's Reports 56*

**105.13** ❦ That grounded maxim,
So rife and celebrated in the mouths
Of wisest men, that to the public
  good

Against the law of nature, law of
nations.

*John Milton*
*Samson Agonistes, 1671*

105.14 ❦ Self-defense is nature's eldest law.

*John Dryden*
*Absalom and Achitophel, 1681–1682*

105.15 ❦ The law of heaven and earth is life
for life.

*Lord Byron, 1788–1824*
*"The Curse of Minerva"*

105.16 ❦ When men are pure, laws are
useless; when men are corrupt,
laws are broken.

*Benjamin Disraeli*
*Contarini Fleming, 1832*

105.17 ❦ Nature's rules have no exceptions.

*Herbert Spencer*
*Social Statics, 1851*

105.18 ❦ The law of the past cannot be
eluded,
The law of the present and future
cannot be eluded,
The law of the living cannot be
eluded—it is eternal.

*Walt Whitman*
*"To Think of Time," 1855*

105.19 ❦ That very law which molds a tear,
And bids it trickle from its source,
That law preserves the earth a sphere,
And guides the planets in their
course.

*Samuel Rogers, 1763–1855*
*"In a Tear"*

105.20 ❦ It would not be correct to say that
every moral obligation involves a legal duty; but every legal duty is
founded on a moral obligation.

*John Duke Coleridge, English jurist;*
*Lord Chief Justice*
*The Queen v. Instan (1893), L. R. 1*
*Q. B. (1893), p. 453*

105.21 ❦ The law that will work is merely the
summing up in legislative form of
the moral judgement that the community has already reached.

*Woodrow Wilson*
*Address,*
*December 20, 1915*

105.22 ❦ The laws of God, the laws of man
He may keep that will and can;
Not I; let God and man decree
Laws for themselves and not for me.

*A. E. Housman*
*Last Poems, 1922*

105.23 ❦ The real law in the modern State is
the multitude of little decisions
made daily by millions of men.

*Walter Lippmann*
*A Preface to Morals, 1929*

105.24 ❦ The natural law always buries its un-
dertakers.

*Heinrich Rommen, German lawyer,*
*paraphrasing Etienne Gilson, French*
*philosopher, Natural Law, 1947*

105.25 ❦ There are no natural laws. There are
only temporary habits of nature.

*Alfred North Whitehead*
*Dialogues of Alfred North*
*Whitehead, 1954*

105.26 ❦ There is no such thing as "natural rights"; there are only adjustments of conflicting claims.

*Aldous Huxley*
Music at Night, *1931*

# *106.* NEED

106.1 ❦ Inability suspends the law.

*Latin legal phrase*
*W. Gurney Benham,* Putnam's
Complete Book of Quotations,
Proverbs and Household Words, *1927*

106.2 ❦ No one is held bound to the impossible.

*Latin legal phrase*

106.3 ❦ The law does not seek to compel a man to do that which he cannot possibly perform.

*Legal maxim*

106.4 ❦ Need makes a wise man do evil.

*Proverb*
*E. Gordon Duff, ed.,* Salomon and
Marcolphus, *1492*

106.5 ❦ Necessity has no law.

*St. Augustine*
Soliloquiorum: Animae ad Deum,
*c.410*

106.6 ❦ Need has no law.

*William Langland*
The Vision of William Concerning
Piers the Plowman, *1362–1390*

106.7 ❦ It is necessity which makes laws, and force which makes them observed.

*Voltaire*
"Des Lois," Dictionnaire
Philosophique, *1764*

106.8 ❦ Necessity creates the law,—it supersedes rules; and whatever is reasonable and just in such cases is likewise legal.

*Sir William Scott, Lord Stowell,*
*English jurist*
"The Gratitude" *(1801), 3 Rob.*
*Adm. Rep. 240*

106.9 ❦ Law is mighty, necessity is mightier.

*Goethe, 1749–1832*
*W. Gurney Benham,* Putnam's
Complete Book of Quotations,
Proverbs and Household Words, *1927*

# *107.* OBEDIENCE

**107.1** ❧ 'Tis best to keep the established laws, even to life's end.

*Sophocles*
*Antigone, c.441* B.C.

**107.2** ❧ If you cannot reconcile yourself to the law, remain in the cradle.

*Pedro Calderón de la Barca,*
*1600–1681*
La vida es sueño

**107.3** ❧ The least of our servitudes is to the law.

*Marquis de Vauvenargues,*
*French moralist*
Réflexions, *1746*

**107.4** ❧ A strict observance of the written laws is doubtless *one* of the high duties of a good citizen, but it is not *the highest*. The laws of necessity, of self preservation, of saving our country when in danger, are of a higher obligation. . . . To lose our country by a scrupulous adherence to written law would be to lose the law itself, with life, liberty, property and all those who are enjoying them with us; thus absurdly sacrificing the ends to the means.

*Thomas Jefferson*
*Letter to J. B. Colvin,*
*September 20, 1780*

**107.5** ❧ On great occasions every good officer must be ready to risk himself in going beyond the strict line of the law, when the public preservation requires it; his motives will be a justification.

*Thomas Jefferson*
*Letter to W. C. Claiborne,*
*February 3, 1807*

**107.6** ❧ I am beginning to think . . . that "the people have nothing to do with the laws but to obey them."

*Edgar Allan Poe*
*"Fifty Suggestions,"* Graham's
Magazine, *May–June 1845*

**107.7** ❧ Now these are the Laws of the Jungle, and many and mighty are they; But the head and the hoof of the Law and the haunch and the hump is— Obey!

*Rudyard Kipling*
*"The Law of the Jungle,"* The Second
Jungle Book, *1895*

**107.8** ❧ No man is above the law and no man is below it; nor do we ask any man's permission when we require him to obey it. Obedience to the law is demanded as a right; not asked as a favor.

*Theodore Roosevelt*
*Third annual message,*
*December 7, 1903*

**107.9** ❧ Those who are too lazy and comfortable to think for themselves and be their own judges obey the laws. Others sense their own laws within them.

*Hermann Hesse*
Demian, *1919*

107.10 ❧ Of the contrivances which mankind has devised to lift itself from savagery there are few to compare with the habit of assent, not to a factitious common will, but to the law as it is.

*Learned Hand*
*"Is There a Common Will?"* 28
Michigan Law Review *46, 52 (1929)*

107.11 ❧ It seems to me that the only law which there is any merit obeying is the one you do not agree with either because you think it is mistaken or because you think it operates against your interest; and the only law which there is any merit enforcing is the law which at least somebody would not obey if it were not enforced.

*Lord Hailsham*
Los Angeles Times, *April 23, 1972*

# *108.* OPINIONS

108.1 ❧ Do we admit the existence of opinion?
Undoubtedly.
Then I suppose that opinion appears to you to be darker than knowledge, but lighter than ignorance?
Both; and in no small degree.

*Plato*
The Republic, *c.370* B.C.

108.2 ❧ As many opinions as there are men; each a law to himself.

*Terence*
Phormio, *161* B.C.

108.3 ❧ My brothers differ from me in opinion, and they all differ from one another in the reasons of their opinion; but not withstanding their opinion, I think the plaintiff ought to recover.

*Sir John Holt, English jurist;*
*Chief Justice*
Ashby v. White *(1703),*
*2 Ld. Raym. 938, 950*

108.4 ❧ An opinion is huddled up in conclave, perhaps by a majority of one, delivered as if unanimous, and with the silent acquiescence of lazy or timid associates, by a crafty chief judge. . . .

*Thomas Jefferson,* 1743–1826
*Andrew A. Lipscomb,* The Writings of Thomas Jefferson, *1903*

108.5 ❧ Every opinion tends to become a law.

*Oliver Wendell Holmes*
Lochner v. New York, *198 U.S. 45,*
*75 (1905)*

**108.6** ⬧ In this court dissents have gradually become majority opinions.

> *Felix Frankfurter*
> Graves v. New York ex rel. O'Keefe,
> *360 U.S. 466, 83 L.Ed. 927, Sup. Ct.*
> *595 (1939)*

**108.7** ⬧ Our opinions are at best provisional hypotheses.

> *Learned Hand*
> *"Learned Hand and the Interpretation*
> *of Statutes," 60* Harvard Law Review
> *370, 393 (1947)*

**108.8** ⬧ How I dislike writing opinions! I prefer arguments—and let someone else have the responsibility of decision.

> *Charles Evans Hughes, 1862–1948,*
> *reflecting on his appointment to the*
> *World Court*
> *Merlo Pusey,* Charles Evans Hughes, *1951*

**108.9** ⬧ It is true of opinions as of other compositions that those who are seeped in them, whose ears are sensitive to literary nuances, whose antennae record subtle silences, can gather from their contents meaning beyond the words.

> *Felix Frankfurter*
> *"'The Administrative Side' of Chief*
> *Justice Hughes," 63* Harvard Law
> Review *1, 2 (1949)*

**108.10** ⬧ It is disheartening to find so much that is right in an opinion which seems to me so fundamentally wrong.

> *Frank Murphy*
> Wolf v. Colorado, *388 U.S. 25 (1949)*

**108.11** ⬧ Lord Westbury . . . it is said, rebuffed a barrister's reliance upon an earlier opinion of his Lordship: "I can only say that I am amazed that a man of my intelligence should have been guilty of giving such an opinion." If there are other ways of gracefully and good naturedly surrendering former views to a better considered position, I invoke them all.

> *Robert H. Jackson*
> McGrath v. Kristensen, *340 U.S.*
> *162, 177–78 (1950)*

**108.12** ⬧ When blithe to argument I come,
Though armed with facts, and merry,
May Providence protect me from
   The fool as adversary,
Whose mind to him a kingdom is
   Where reason lacks dominion,
Who calls conviction prejudice
   And prejudice opinion.

> *Phyllis McGinley*
> *"Moody Reflections,"* Times Three:
> 1932–1960, *1960*

**108.13** ⬧ Chief Justice Hennessey of the Massachusetts Supreme Judicial Court in a speech related the time that an attorney rushed into the Superior Court Judge Donahue's chamber to notify the judge that the Supreme Judicial Court had affirmed one of his opinions. The acerbic judge looked up from his papers and said, "I still think I was right."

> *Edward F. Hennessey, American jurist*
> Kenneth Redden, Modern Legal
> Glossary, *1983*

# *109.* PLEAS

*109.1* ❦ An ill plea should be well pleaded.

*Proverb*
*H. G. Bohn,* Handbook of Proverbs,
*1855*

*109.2* ❦ Abr: Do you bite your thumb at us,
sir?
Sam: Is the law on our side if
I say ay?

*Shakespeare*
Romeo and Juliet, *I, 1, 1594–1595*

*109.3* ❦ The world is still deceived with
ornament.
In law, what plea so tainted and
corrupt
But, being seasoned with a gracious
voice,
Obscures the show of evil?

*Shakespeare*
The Merchant of Venice, *III, 1,
1596–1597*

*109.4* ❦ Pleading is an exact setting forth of
the truth.

*Sir Robert Atkyns, English jurist*
Trial of Sir Edward Hales *(1686),
11 How. St. Tr. 1243*

*109.5* ❦ I am sorry when any man is tripped
by a formal objection.

*Justice Park, British jurist*
Aked v. Stocks *(1828), 4 Bing. 509*

*109.6* ❦ In law it is a good policy never to
plead what you need not, lest you
oblige yourself to prove what you
cannot.

*Abraham Lincoln*
Letter to Usher F. Linder,
*February 20, 1848*

*109.7* ❦ If criminals wanted to grind justice
to a halt, they could do it by band-
ing together and all pleading not
guilty. It's only because we have plea-
bargaining that our criminal justice
system is still in motion. That
doesn't say much for the quality of
justice.

*Dorothy Wright Wilson, American
educator; dean, University of Southern
California Law Center*
Los Angeles Times, *August 11, 1974*

*109.8* ❦ Because of plea-bargaining, I guess
we can say, "Gee, the trains run on
time." But do we like where they are
going?

*Franklin E. Zimring, American
educator; professor, University
of Chicago*
Time, *August 28, 1978*

# *110.* POLITICS

**110.1** ❧ You will do very well to refuse offices; for a man seldom fails to give offense in them.

*St. Catherine of Siena, 1376*
St. Catherine of Siena as Seen in Her
Letters, *Vida D. Scudder, ed., 1905*

**110.2** ❧ The Parish makes the Constable, and when the Constable is made, he governs the Parish.

*John Selden,* 1584–1654
Table-Talk, *1689*

**110.3** ❧ Political arguments, in the fullest sense of the word, as they concern the government of a nation, must be, and always have been, of great weight in the consideration of the Court.

*Philip Yorke, 1st earl of Hardwicke,*
*English jurist; Lord Chancellor*
The Earl of Chesterfield v. Janssen
*(1750), 1 Atk. 352,* id. *2 Ves. Sen. 153*

**110.4** ❧ The Constitution does not allow reasons of State to influence our judgments: God forbid it should!

*Sir William Murray, Lord Mansfield,*
*English jurist; Chief Justice*
Case of John Wilkes *(1770),*
*19 How. St. Tr. 1112*

**110.5** ❧ If I could not go to heaven but with a party, I would not go there at all.

*Thomas Jefferson*
*Letter to Francis Hopkinson,*
*March 13, 1789*

**110.6** ❧ Ministers [are] the better for being now and then a little peppered and salted.

*Unknown British politician*
*Quoted by Lord Kenyon,* Holt's Case
*(1793), 22 How. St. Tr. 1234*

**110.7** ❧ One cannot look too closely at and weigh in too golden scales the acts of men hot in their political excitement.

*Sir Henry Hawkins, English jurist*
Ex parte Castioni *(1890), 60 L.J.*
*Rep. (N.S.) Mag. Cas. 33*

**110.8** ❧ God is a politician; so is the devil.

*Carry Nation*
The Use and Need of the Life of
Carry A. Nation, *1904*

**110.9** ❧ More lawyers (considering the number who play the game intensively) have been ruined by politics than by liquor, women, or the stock market.

*Arthur Garfield Hays, American lawyer*
City Lawyer, *1942*

**110.10** ❧ One must bear in mind that the expansion of federal activity is a form of eating for politicians.

*William F. Buckley, Jr.*
National Review, *September 8, 1964*

**110.11** ❧ Some members of Congress are the best actors in the world.

*Shirley Chisholm*
Unbought and Unbossed, *1970*

*110.12* ❦ [Politics] is a beautiful fraud that has been imposed on the people for years, whose practitioners exchange gilded promises for the most valuable thing their victims own: their votes. And who benefits most? The lawyers.

*Shirley Chisholm*
Unbought and Unbossed, *1970*

*110.13* ❦ In politics, if you want anything said, ask a man. If you want anything done, ask a woman.

*Margaret, Lady Thatcher*
People, *September 15, 1975*

*110.14* ❦ Politics is the art of looking for trouble, finding it everywhere, diagnosing it incorrectly, and applying the wrong remedies.

*Groucho Marx*
*Recalled on his death, August 19, 1977*

*110.15* ❦ I must say acting was good training for the political life which lay ahead for us.

*Nancy Reagan*
Nancy, *1980*

*110.16* ❦ Party organization matters. When the door of a smoke-filled room is closed, there's hardly ever a woman inside.

*Millicent Fenwick*
60 Minutes, CBS-TV,
*February 1, 1981*

*110.17* ❦ Politics can be an ugly game . . .

*Geraldine A. Ferraro, with Linda*
*Bird Francke*
Ferraro, *1985*

*110.18* ❦ (Democrats) can't get elected unless things get worse—and things won't get worse unless they get elected.

*Jeane J. Kirkpatrick*
Time, *June 17, 1985*

*110.19* ❦ A politician is required to listen to humbug, talk humbug, condone humbug. The most we can hope for is that we don't actually believe it.

*P. D. James*
A Taste for Death, *1986*

*110.20* ❦ In the past few decades American institutions have struggled with the temptations of politics. Professions and academic disciplines that once possessed a life and structure of their own have steadily succumbed, in some cases almost entirely, to the belief that nothing matters beyond politically desirable results, however achieved. . . .

*Robert Bork*
The Tempting of America, *1990*

*110.21* ❦ You do the policy, I'll do the politics.

*Dan Quayle, to aide*
International Herald Tribune, *Paris,*
*January 13, 1992*

*110.22* ❦ We need to be against brain-dead politics wherever we find it!

*Hillary Rodham Clinton*
*Claire G. Osborne,* The Unique Voice
of Hillary Rodham Clinton, *1997*

110.23 ❦ We shouldn't leave the work of
politics to people who run for
public office.

*Hillary Rodham Clinton*
*Claire G. Osborne,* The Unique Voice
of Hillary Rodham Clinton, *1997*

110.24 ❦ Although women have had the fran-
chise now for over seventy-five years,
few feminists (indeed perhaps few

women) would conclude that
women as a group have experienced
the full measure of their potential
political power.

*Tracey E. Higgins*
*"Democracy and Feminism," 110*
Harvard Law Review 8, *1997*

# *111.* POVERTY

111.1 ❦ Wealth covers sin—the poor/are na-
ked as a pin.

*Kassia, "Epigrams," 9th century*
*Joanna Bankier and Deirdre Lashgari, eds.,*
Women Poets of the World, *1983*

111.2 ❦ Art thou so bare and full of
wretchedness
And fear'st to die? Famine is in
thy cheeks,
Need and oppression starveth in
thine eyes,
Contempt and beggary hang upon
thy back,
The world is not thy friend, nor the
world's law;
The world affords no law to make
thee rich;
Then be not poor, but break it.

*Shakespeare*
Romeo and Juliet, V, 1, *1594–1595*

111.3 ❦ All crimes are safe but hated poverty.
This, only this, the rigid law pursues.

*Samuel Johnson*
*"London," 1738*

111.4 ❦ The rich rob the poor and the poor
rob one another.

*Attributed to Sojourner Truth*

111.5 ❦ Poverty sets a reduced price on
crime.

*Sébastien Roch Nicolas Chamfort,*
*French writer, 1740–1794*
*W. H. Auden and Louis Kronenberger,*
The Viking Book of Aphorisms, *1962*

111.6 ❦ His poverty, not his will, consented
to the danger.

*Sir Henry Hawkins, English jurist*
Thrussell v. Handyside and Co.
*(1888), 20 Q.B.D. 359, 364*

**111.7** ⯈ Poverty and immorality are not synonymous.

> *James F. Byrnes*
> Edwards v. California, *314 U.S. 160,*
> *177 (1941)*

**111.8** ⯈ The mere state of being without funds is a neutral fact—constitutionally an irrelevance, like race, creed, or color.

> *Robert H. Jackson*
> Edwards v. California, *314 U.S. 160,*
> *184 (1941)*

**111.9** ⯈ [L]aw benefits and protects landlords over tenants, creditors over debtors, lenders over borrowers, and the poor are seldom among the favored parties.

> *John N. Turner, Canadian lawyer;*
> *attorney general of Canada*
> *Speech, Canadian Bar Association,*
> *December 7, 1969*

**111.10** ⯈ Hungry people cannot be good at learning or producing anything, except perhaps violence.

> *Pearl Bailey*
> Pearl's Kitchen, *1973*

**111.11** ⯈ Bread, bread, bread! No more preachers, no more politicians, no more lawyers, no more gods, no more heavens, no more promises! Bread!

> *Voltairine de Cleyre*
> *Paul Avrich,*
> An American Anarchist, *1978*

**111.12** ⯈ We think of poverty as a condition simply meaning a lack of funds, no money, but when one sees fifth, sixth, and seventh generation poor, it is clear that poverty is as complicated as high finance.

> *Alice Childress*
> A Hero Ain't Nothin' But a
> Sandwich, *1973*

**111.13** ⯈ We must be careful that the people who make $5000 a year are not pitted against those that make $25,000 a year by those that make $900,000.

> *Barbara A. Mikulski*
> *Speech, 1974*

**111.14** ⯈ It's going to take an act of Congress to deal with poverty . . . We have the resources but we don't have the will.

> *Coretta Scott King*
> *Alice Walker,* In Search of Our
> Mothers' Gardens, *1983*

**111.15** ⯈ The poor have been sent to the front lines of a federal budget deficit reduction war that few other groups were drafted to fight.

> *Marian Wright Edelman*
> Families in Peril, *1987*

# *112.* POWER

*112.1* ❧ Power delegated cannot exceed that which was its origin.

*Legal maxim*

*112.2* ❧ And he who rejoices at the destruction of human life is not fit to be entrusted with power in the world.

*Lao-tzu, c.604?–?531 B.C.*
*Tao te Ching*

*112.3* ❧ No power ought to be above the laws.

*Cicero*
*Paraphrase of* De Domo Sua, *57 B.C.*

*112.4* ❧ Even false becomes true when the chief says so.

*Publilius Syrus, Latin writer*
*Maxims, 42 B.C.*

*112.5* ❧ . . . knowledge itself is power. . . .

*Francis Bacon*
*Meditationes Sacrae, 1597*

*112.6* ❧ Bidding the law make curtsey to their will.

*Shakespeare*
*Measure for Measure, II, 4,*
*1604–1605*

*112.7* ❧ The conscience of a people is their power.

*John Dryden*
*The Duke of Guise, 1683*

*112.8* ❧ Power and Liberty are like Heat and Moisture; where they are well mixt, everything prospers; where they are single, they are destructive.

*First Marquess of Halifax*
*Maxims of State, 1700*

*112.9* ❧ Law is but a heathen word for power.

*Daniel Defoe*
*The History of the Kentish Petition,*
*1701*

*112.10* ❧ I am more and more convinced that man is a dangerous creature; and that power, whether vested in many or a few, is ever grasping, and, like the grave, cries "Give, give."

*Abigail Adams, to her husband,*
*John Adams, 1775*
*Letters of Mrs. Adams, 1848*

*112.11* ❧ . . . a power over a man's subsistence amounts to a power over his will.

*Alexander Hamilton*
*The Federalist Papers, 1787–1788*

*112.12* ❧ Law and arbitrary power are in eternal enmity.

*Edmund Burke*
*Speech on the impeachment of Warren*
*Hastings, February 15, 1788*

112.13 ❧ What do I care about the law?
Hain't I got the power?

> *Cornelius Vanderbilt,* 1794–1877
> *Laurence J. Peter,* Peter's Quotations,
> *1977*

112.14 ❧ Power tends to corrupt and absolute
power corrupts absolutely.

> *Lord Acton*
> *Letter to Bishop Mandell Creighton,*
> *April 5, 1887*

112.15 ❧ The prize of the general is not a
bigger tent, but command.

> *Oliver Wendell Holmes*
> *"Law and the Court,"* Speeches, *1913*

112.16 ❧ We fear to grant power and are
unwilling to recognize it when it
exists.

> *Oliver Wendell Holmes*
> Tyson & Brothers v. Banton, *273*
> *U.S. 418, 445 (1927)*

112.17 ❧ I am the law.

> *Frank Hague, American politician;*
> *mayor, Jersey City,*
> *New Jersey,* 1917–1947
> *New York Times,*
> *November 11, 1937*

112.18 ❧ Government of limited power need
not be anemic government.
Assurance that rights are secure
tends to diminish fear and jealousy
of strong government, and by
making us feel safe to live under it
makes for its better support.

> *Robert H. Jackson*
> West Virginia State Board of
> Education v. Barnette, *319 U.S. 624,*
> *87 L.Ed. 1628, 63 Sup. Ct. 1178*
> *(1943)*

112.19 ❧ No one will question that this [war]
power is the most dangerous one to
free government in the whole
catalogue of powers.

> *Robert H. Jackson*
> Woods v. Miller, *333 U.S. 138, 92*
> *L.Ed. 596, 68 Sup. Ct. 421 (1948)*

112.20 ❧ All executive power—from the reign
of ancient kings to the rule of
modern dictators—has the outward
appearance of efficiency.

> *William O. Douglas*
> Youngstown Sheet & Tube Co. v.
> Sawyer, *343 U.S. 579 (1952)*

112.21 ❧ Power is the great aphrodisiac.

> *Henry Kissinger*
> New York Times, *January 19, 1971*

112.22 ❧ The revolutionaries are those who
know when power is lying in the
street and when they can pick it up.

> *Hannah Arendt*
> *"Thoughts on Politics and Revolution,"*
> Crises of the Republic, *1972*

112.23 ❧ [P]ower constructs the appearance
of reality by silencing the voices of
the powerless, by excluding them
from access to authoritative
discourse.

> *Catharine A. MacKinnon*
> *"Francis Biddle's Sister: Pornography:*
> *Civil Rights and Speech,"* Feminism
> Unmodified, *1987*

112.24 ❧ There is the continuing problem of
client generation. Money talks.

Without the power, we cannot make
the calls and the plays.

*Linda A. Cinciotta*
*"Back to the Future,"* Perspectives,
*Fall 1997*

112.25 ❧ . . . power is something of which I
am convinced there is no innocence
this side of the womb. . . .

*Nadine Gordimer, South African writer*

# 113. PRECEDENTS

113.1 ❧ Judgment should be according to
the laws, not according to the
precedents.

*Latin legal phrase*

113.2 ❧ Don't use the conduct of a fool as a
precedent.

*Talmud, Shabbat*

113.3 ❧ All things which are now regarded as
of great antiquity were once new,
and that which we maintain today
by precedents will be among the
precedents.

*Tacitus*
Annals, *c.110*

113.4 ❧ Portia: It must not be; there is no
power in Venice
Can alter a decree established:
'Twill be recorded for a precedent;
And many an error by the same
example
Will rush into the state.

*Shakespeare*
The Merchant of Venice, *IV, 1,*
*1596–1597*

113.5 ❧ Every precedent had first a
commencement.

*Sir Thomas Egerton, Baron Ellesmere,*
*English jurist and statesman;*
*Lord Chancellor*
Case of Proclamations *(1611), 2*
How. St. Tr. 723, 72J

113.6 ❧ It is dangerous to make a precedent,
an innovation.

*Sir John Pratt, English jurist;*
*Chief Justice*
Layer's Case *(1722), 16 How.*
St. Tr. 267

113.7 ❧ It is a maxim among lawyers that
whatever hath been done before may
be done again: and therefore they
take special care to record all the
decisions formerly made against
common justice and the general
reason of mankind. These, under
the name of *precedents,* they produce
as authorities to justify the most
iniquitous opinions; and the judges
never fail of directing accordingly.

*Jonathan Swift*
Gulliver's Travels, *1726*

*113.8* ❦ There is no magic in parchment or in wax.

> *William Henry Ashhurst, English jurist*
> Master v. Miller *(1763), 4 T.R. 320*

*113.9* ❦ No degree of antiquity can give sanction to a usage bad in itself.

> *Yates and Austin, English jurists*
> Leach v. Three of the Kings
> Messengers *(1765), 19 How.*
> *St. Tr. 1027*

*113.10* ❦ The doctrine of the law then is this: that precedents and rules must be followed, unless flatly absurd or unjust; for though their reason be not obvious at first view, yet we owe such a deference to former times as not to suppose that they acted wholly without consideration.

> *Sir William Blackstone*
> Commentaries on the Laws of
> England, *1765–1769*

*113.11* ❦ One precedent creates another. They soon accumulate and constitute law. What yesterday is fact, today is doctrine.

> *Junius, (pseudonym of*
> *unidentified English letter writer)*
> *"Dedication to the English Nation,"*
> The Letters of Junius, *1772*

*113.12* ❦ Precedent, though it be evidence of law, is not law in itself.

> *William Murray, 1st earl of Mansfield,*
> *English jurist; Chief Justice*
> Jones v. Randall *(1774),*
> *Lofft. 383, 385*

*113.13* ❦ To follow foolish precedents, and wink with both our eyes, is easier than to think.

> *William Cowper*
> Tirocinium, *1785*

*113.14* ❦ A precedent embalms a principle.

> *Attributed to Sir William Scott,*
> *English jurist*
> *Opinion, while advocate general, 1788*

*113.15* ❦ Every law which originated in ignorance and malice, and gratifies the passions from which it sprang, we call the wisdom of our ancestors.

> *Sydney Smith, English clergyman*
> *and writer*
> Peter Plymley's Letters, *1807*

*113.16* ❦ Laws are inherited like diseases.

> *Goethe*
> Faust, *1808*

*113.17* ❦ When a judge challenged Rufus Choate, the famous Massachusetts lawyer, to cite a precedent for his argument before the court, he replied: "I will look, your honor, and endeavor to find a precedent if you require it; though it would seem a pity that the court should lose the distinction of being the first to establish so just a rule."

> *Rufus Choate, 1799–1859*
> *Ed Bander,* The Path of
> the Law, *1980*

*113.18* ❦ Mastering the lawless science of our
>     law,
>   That codeless myriad of precedent,
>   That wilderness of single instances,
>   Through which a few, by wit or
>     fortune led,

May beat a pathway out to wealth
and fame.

> *Tennyson*
> Aylmer's Field, *1864*

**113.19** ✎ The acts of today may become the
precedents of tomorrow.

> *Farrer Herschell, English jurist;*
> *Lord Chancellor*
> Speech, May 23, *1878*

**113.20** ✎ But as precedents survive like the
clavicle in the cat, long after the use
they once served is at an end, and
the reason for them has been
forgotten, the result of following
them must often be failure and
confusion from the merely logical
point of view.

> *Oliver Wendell Holmes*
> *"Common Carriers and the Common*
> *Law,"* 13 American Law Review,
> *608, 630 (1879)*

**113.21** ✎ The life of the law has not been
logic; it has been experience.

> *Oliver Wendell Holmes*
> The Common Law, *1881*

**113.22** ✎ Practically . . . the law . . . is all
*ex post facto.*

> *John Chipman Gray, American lawyer*
> The Nature and Sources of Law, *1909*

**113.23** ✎ The forms of action we have buried
but they rule us from their graves.

> *Frederic W. Maitland*
> The Forms of Action at Common
> Law, *1909*

**113.24** ✎ . . . historic continuity with the past
is not a duty, it is only a necessity.

> *Oliver Wendell Holmes*
> *"Learning and Science,"* Speeches,
> *1913*

**113.25** ✎ There is no superstitious sanctity at-
taching to a precedent. . . . Courts
can only maintain their authority by
correcting their errors to accord with
justice and the advance and progress
of each age.

> *Walter Clark, American jurist*
> State v. Falkner, *1921*

**113.26** ✎ The repetition of a catchword can
hold analysis in fetters for fifty years
and more.

> *Benjamin N. Cardozo*
> *Mr. Justice Holmes,* 44 Harvard Law
> Review 682, 689 *(March 1931)*

**113.27** ✎ If mankind had continued to be the
slave of precedent we should still be
living in the caves and subsisting on
shellfish and wild berries.

> *Philip Snowden, British statesman,*
> *1864–1937*
> *Laurence J. Peter,* Peter's Quotations,
> *1977*

**113.28** ✎ The tendency to disregard
precedents . . . has become so
strong . . . as . . . to shake
confidence in the consistency of
decision and leave the courts below
on an uncharted sea of doubt and
difficulty without any confidence
that what was said yesterday will
hold good tomorrow.

> *Owen J. Roberts*
> Mahnich v. Southern Steamship Co.,
> *321 U.S. 96, 64 S. Ct. 455, 88 L.Ed.*
> *561 (1944)*

*113.29* ❧ . . . constitutional precedents . . . have a mortality rate almost as high as their authors.

> *Robert H. Jackson*
> *"The Task of Maintaining Our*
> *Liberties: The Role of the Judiciary," 39*
> American Bar Association Journal
> *962 (1953)*

*113.30* ❧ Every lawyer of experience comes to know (more or less unconsciously) that in the great majority of cases, the precedents are none too good as bases of prediction. Somehow or other, there are plenty of precedents to go around.

> *Jerome Frank*
> Law and the Modern Mind, *1953*

*113.31* ❧ I don't follow precedent, I establish it.

> *Fanny Holtzman, lawyer,* 1903–1980
> *Dawn Bradley Berry,* The 50 Most
> Influential Women in American Law,
> *1996*

*113.32* ❧ An old lawyer in St. Louis made a speech sometime ago in which he said, "Do not waste your time looking up the law in advance, because you can find some Federal district court that will sustain any proposition you make."

> *Sam Ervin, Jr.*
> *At Senate Watergate Hearings, reported*
> *in the* Dallas Times Herald,
> *June 20, 1973*

*113.33* ❧ Fred Rodell . . . once compared the law to the Killy-loo bird, a creature that he said insisted on flying backward because it didn't care where it was going but was mightily interested in where it had been.

> *Fred Rodell, American educator;*
> *professor, Yale Law School*
> *Paraphrase in the* New York Times,
> *June 27, 1984*

*113.34* ❧ On the theory of the tobacco precedent, car manufacturers should be liable for deaths caused by speed . . .

> *Robert H. Bork*
> *"Addicted to Health,"* National
> Review, *July 28, 1997*

# *114.* PREJUDICE

*114.1* ❧ It is sometimes difficult to get rid of first impressions.

> *Sir Lloyd Kenyon, English jurist;*
> *Lord Chief Justice*
> Withnell v. Gartham *(1795),*
> *6 T.R. 396*

*114.2* ❧ No man can see his own prejudices.

> *Frances Wright*
> A Few Days in Athens, *1822*

114.3 ❦ . . . we can't abolish prejudice through laws . . .

*Belva Lockwood, American lawyer and feminist*, 1830–1917
*Mary Virginia Fox,* Lady for the Defense, *1975*

114.4 ❦ They called me the lady lawyer—a dainty sobriquet—which enabled me to maintain a dainty manner as I browbeat my way through the marshes of ignorance and prejudice.

*Clara Shortridge Foltz, first female member of the California Bar, 1915*

114.5 ❦ Deep-seated preferences cannot be argued about—you cannot argue a man into liking a glass of beer—and therefore, when differences are sufficiently far-reaching, we try to kill the other man rather than let him have his way. But that is perfectly consistent with admitting that, so far as appears, his grounds are just as good as ours.

*Oliver Wendell Holmes*
"Natural Law," Collected Legal Papers, *1921*

114.6 ❦ . . . most of our so-called reasoning consists in finding arguments for going on believing as we already do.

*James Harvey Robinson*
The Mind in the Making, *1921*

114.7 ❦ . . . we must be ever on our guard, lest we erect our prejudices into legal principles.

*Louis D. Brandeis*
New State Ice Co. v. Liebmann, *285 U.S. 262, 311 (1932)*

114.8 ❦ . . . any man who says he is impartial about any subject on which he speaks is either ignorant or a liar. . . .

*Oliver Wendell Holmes*, 1841–1935
Labor Law Journal, *November 1949*

114.9 ❦ Everyone is a prisoner of his own experiences. No one can eliminate prejudices—just recognize them.

*Edward R. Murrow*
News commentary, *December 31, 1955*

114.10 ❦ There are only two ways to be quite unprejudiced and impartial. One is to be completely ignorant. The other is to be completely indifferent. Bias and prejudice are attiitudes to be kept in hand, not attitudes to be avoided.

*Charles P. Curtis, American lawyer*
A Commonplace Book, *1957*

114.11 ❦ Law is a reflection and a source of prejudice. It both enforces and suggests forms of bias.

*Diane B. Schulder, American lawyer and educator*
"Does the Law Oppress Women?"
Sisterhood Is Powerful, *edited by Robin Morgan, 1970*

*114.12* ⚘ You've got to remember to put the law before your own prejudices.

> *Gerhard A. Gesell, American jurist*
> Los Angeles Times, *June 13, 1974*

*114.13* ⚘ I had the benefit of people who knew they had to walk a straighter line, climb a taller mountain, and carry a heavier load. They took all that segregation and prejudice would allow them and at the same time fought to remove those awful barriers.

> *Clarence Thomas*
> Speech, Savannah State College,
> *June 9, 1985*

*114.14* ⚘ Reason transformed into prejudice is the worst form of prejudice, because reason is the only instrument for liberation from prejudice.

> *Allan Bloom, U.S. educator; author*
> The Closing of the American Mind,
> *1987*

*114.15* ⚘ I was raised to survive under the totalitarianism of segregation, not only without the active assistance of government but with its active opposition.

> *Clarence Thomas*
> Speech, Heritage Foundation, *1987*

# *115.* PRESS

*115.1* ⚘ Give me six lines written by the most honorable man, and I will find an excuse in them to hang him.

> *Cardinal Richelieu*
> Miramé, *1641*

*115.2* ⚘ The press is like the air, a chartered libertine.

> *William Pitt*
> To Lord Grenville, *c.1757*

*115.3* ⚘ A writer's fame will not be the less, that he has bread, without being under the necessity of prostituting his pen to flattery or party, to get it.

> *Sir John Willes, English jurist*
> Millar v. Taylor *(1768), 4 Burr. Part*
> *IV., p. 2335*

*115.4* ⚘ Ideas are free. But while the author confines them to his study, they are like birds in a cage, which none but he can have a right to let fly: for till he thinks proper to emancipate them, they are under his own dominion.

> *Sir Joseph Yates, English jurist*
> Millar v. Taylor *(1769), 4 Burr. Part*
> *IV., p. 2379*

*115.5* ⚘ The liberty of the Press is the Palladium of all the civil, political, and religious rights of an Englishman.

> *Junius (pseudonym of unidentified*
> *English letter writer)*
> *"Dedication to the English Nation,"*
> The Letters of Junius, *1772*

**115.6** ⬙ As for the freedom of the press, I will tell you what it is: the liberty of the press is that a man may print what he pleases without license. As long as it remains so, the liberty of the press is not restrained.

*William Murray, 1st earl of Mansfield,*
*English jurist; Chief Justice*
*Charge to the jury in the trial of*
*H. W. Woodfall, 1772*

**115.7** ⬙ Thou god of our idolatry, the Press.

*William Cowper*
*The Progress of Error, 1782*

**115.8** ⬙ . . . were it left to me to decide whether we should have a government without newspapers, or newspapers without a government, I should not hesitate a moment to prefer the latter.

*Thomas Jefferson*
*Letter to Edward Carrington,*
*January 16, 1787*

**115.9** ⬙ The legislature of the United States shall pass no law on the subject of religion nor touching or abridging the liberty of the press.

*Charles Pinckney*
*Resolution offered in The*
*Constitutional Convention, 1787*

**115.10** ⬙ A man may publish anything which twelve of his countrymen think not blamable.

*Sir Lloyd Kenyon, English jurist;*
*Lord Chief Justice*
*Cuthell's Case (1799), 27 How. St.*
*Tr. 675*

**115.11** ⬙ Where vituperation begins, the liberty of the press ends.

*Sir William Draper Best, Lord*
*Wynford, British jurist*
*King v. Burdett (1820), 1 St. Tr.*
*(n.s.) 120*

**115.12** ⬙ No government ought to be without censors; and where the press is free none ever will.

*Thomas Jefferson, 1743–1826*
*Writings, 1853*

**115.13** ⬙ I am myself a gentleman of the Press, and I bear no other scutcheon.

*Benjamin Disraeli*
*Speech in the House of Commons,*
*February 18, 1863*

**115.14** ⬙ Why the devil they have to put on that 'girly-girly' tea party description every time they tell anything a professional woman does is more than I can see.

*Mabel Walker Willebrandt, lawyer,*
*1889–1963*
*Dawn Bradley Berry, The 50 Most*
*Influential Women in*
*American Law, 1996*

**115.15** ⬙ A free press stands as one of the great interpreters between the government and the people. To allow it to be fettered is to fetter ourselves.

*George Sutherland, American jurist*
*Grosjean v. American Press Co., 297*
*U.S. 233, 250 (1936)*

*115.16* ❧ Did you ever hear anyone say "that work had better be banned because I might read it and it might be very damaging to me"?

*Joseph Henry Jackson, American journalist; editor,* San Francisco Chronicle; *1894–1946*

*115.17* ❧ People everywhere confuse what they read in newspapers with news.

*A. J. Liebling*
*"A Talkative Something or Other,"* New Yorker, *April 7, 1956*

*115.18* ❧ I won't say that the papers misquote me, but I sometimes wonder where Christianity would be today if some of those reporters had been Matthew, Mark, Luke and John.

*Barry M. Goldwater*
*Speech, Washington, D.C.,*
*August 10, 1964*

*115.19* ❧ A free press is not a privilege but [a] necessity in a great society.

*Walter Lippmann*
*Syndicated column, May 27, 1965*

*115.20* ❧ Newspapers, television networks, and magazines have sometimes been outrageously abusive, untruthful, arrogant, and hypocritical. But it hardly follows that elimination of a strong and independent press is the way to eliminate abusiveness, untruth, arrogance, or hypocrisy from government itself.

*Potter Stewart*
*Speech, Yale University Law School,*
*1974*

*115.21* ❧ Minimum information given with maximum politeness.

*Jacqueline Kennedy, guidelines for dealing with the press*
*Ralph G. Martin,* A Hero for Our Time, *1983*

*115.22* ❧ In Czechoslovakia there is no such thing as freedom of the press. In the United States there is no such thing as freedom from the press.

*Martina Navratilova*
*Lee Green,* Sportswit, *1984*

*115.23* ❧ The American press is extraordinarily free and vigorous, as it should be. It should be, not because it is free of inaccuracy, oversimplification and bias, but because the alternative to that freedom is worse than those failings.

*Robert Bork, American jurist; judge,*
*U.S. Court of Appeals*
New York Times, *April 11, 1985*

*115.24* ❧ I always cheer up immensely if an attack is particularly wounding because I think, well, if they attack one personally, it means they have not a single political argument left.

*Margaret, Lady Thatcher*
The Daily Telegraph, *London, 1986*

*115.25* ❧ [T]he media is still dominated by men, many of whom think of women in a very sexist way. They cover them in a sexist way, and they do *not* cover them because of sexism.

*Gloria Allred, lawyer*
Perspectives, *Fall 1996*

*115.26* ❦ [Y]ou're a public figure, which means apparently in America anyone can say anything about you.

Even public figures have feelings and families and reputations.

*Hillary Rodham Clinton*
*Claire G. Osborne,* The Unique Voice of Hillary Rodham Clinton, *1997*

# 116. PRISON

*116.1* ❦ Money never goes to jail.

*Popular wisdom*

*116.2* ❦ [F]orcibly keeping prisoners in detention is what prisons are all about.

*Clarence Thomas*
Hudson v. McMillan, *112 S. Ct.
995 (1992)*

*116.3* ❦ If Lorena Bobbitt was innocent of intentionally dismembering her husband, because she was in the grip of an irresistible impulse, then a large majority of people in prison should probably go free.

*Wendy Kaminer, lawyer and social critic* It's All the Rage, *1995*

# 117. PRIVACY

*117.1* ❦ Public laws favor domestic privacy.

*Legal maxim*

*117.2* ❦ The private life of a citizen ought to be within walls.

*Talleyrand*
*Letter to M. Colomb,
October 31, 1818*

*117.3* ❦ No rights can be dearer to a man of cultivation than exemptions from unseasonable invasions on his time by the coarse-minded and ignorant.

*J. Fenimore Cooper*
The American Democrat, *1838*

*117.4* ❦ A man has a right to pass through this world, if he wills, without having his pictures published, his business enterprises discussed, his successful experiments written up for the benefit of others, or his eccentricities commented upon, whether in handbills, circulars, catalogues, newspapers or periodicals.

*Alton B. Parker, American jurist; Chief*
*Justice, New York Court of Appeals*
Roberson v. Rochater Folding
Box Co. *(1901)*

117.5  ❧  I might have been a gold-fish in a glass bowl for all the privacy I got.

*Saki, pseudonym of H. H. Munro*
The Innocence of Reginald, *1904*

117.6  ❧  The right to be alone—the most comprehensive of rights, and the right most valued by civilized men.

*Louis D. Brandeis*
Olmstead v. United States, *277 U.S.*
*438, 48 S. Ct. 564, 66 ALR 376, 72*
*L.Ed. 944 (1928)*

117.7  ❧  It doesn't matter what you do in the bedroom as long as you don't do it in the street and frighten the horses.

*Mrs. Patrick Campbell, 1865–1940*

117.8  ❧  Civilization is the progress toward a society of privacy. The savage's whole existence is public, ruled by the laws of his tribe. Civilization is the process of setting man free from men.

*Ayn Rand*
The Fountainhead, *1943*

117.9  ❧  The right to be let alone is indeed the beginning of all freedom.

*William O. Douglas*
Public Utilities Comm'n. v. Pollak,
*343 U.S. 451, 467 (1952)*

117.10  ❧  The Fourth Amendment and the personal rights it secures have a long history. At the very core stands the right of a man to retreat into his own home and there be free from unreasonable governmental intrusion.

*Potter Stewart*
New York Times, *March 6, 1961*

117.11  ❧  A state has no business telling a man, sitting alone in his own house, what books he may read or what films he may watch . . . Whatever may be the justifications for other statutes regulating obscenity, we do not think they reach into the privacy of one's own home.

*Thurgood Marshall*
Supreme Court decision, *April 7, 1969*

117.12  ❧  If the right of privacy means anything, it is the right of the individual, married or single, to be free from unwarranted governmental intrusion into matters so fundamentally affecting a person as the decision whether to bear or beget a child.

*William J. Brennan, Jr.*
Eisenstadt v. Baird, *1972*

*117.13* ❦ There is nothing new in the realization that the Constitution sometimes insulates the criminality of a few in order to protect the privacy of us all.

> *Antonin Scalia, majority opinion,*
> *Arizona v. Hicks, March 3, 1987*
> *Daniel B. Baker,* Power Quotes, *1992*

*117.14* ❦ Even if you don't cruise the superhighway, your personal profile will. A portrait of you in I's and O's, the language of computers, will exist in cyberspace.

> *Ellen Alderman and Caroline Kennedy*
> The Right to Privacy, *1995*

*117.15* ❦ There is simply no comprehensive body of law established to deal with all of the privacy concerns arising in the digital age.

> *Ellen Alderman and Caroline Kennedy*
> The Right to Privacy, *1995*

*117.16* ❦ One of the things we cherish most about being Americans is our freedom to move about in relative privacy. If we lose that . . . we will have lost something irreplaceable.

> *Don Haines*
> *Mark Hansen, "No Place to Hide,"*
> ABA Journal, *August 1997*

*117.17* ❦ Civil laws against adultery and fornication have been on the books forever, in every country. That's not the law's business; that's God's business. He can handle it.

> *Thomas G. Kavanagh, American jurist;*
> *Chief Justice,*
> *Supreme Court of Michigan*
> San Francisco Examiner &
> Chronicle, *March 5, 1978*

# *118.* PROPERTY

*118.1* ❦ An assignee is clothed with the rights of his principal.

> *Legal maxim*

*118.2* ❦ He who possesses land possesses also that which is above it.

> *Legal maxim*

*118.3* ❦ He has the better title who was first in point of time.

> *Legal maxim*

*118.4* ❦ In a case of equal right, the position of the person in possession is the better.

> *Legal maxim*

118.5 ❧ Possession is nine points of the law.

*Legal maxim*
*Rosalind Fergusson,* The Facts On File
Dictionary of Proverbs, *1983*

118.6 ❧ Right is said to have commenced in possession.

*Legal maxim*

118.7 ❧ For a man's house is his castle.

*Sir Edward Coke*
The Institutes of the Lawes of
England, *vol. 1, 1628–1641*

118.8 ❧ Law, in a free country, is, or ought to be, the determination of those who have property in land.

*Jonathan Swift*
Thoughts on Various Subjects, *c.1714*

118.9 ❧ Laws are always useful to persons of property, and hurtful to those who have none.

*Jean-Jacques Rousseau*
Du Contrat social, *1761*

118.10 ❧ By the laws of England, every invasion of private property, be it ever so minute, is a trespass. No man can set his foot upon my ground without my licence, but he is liable to an action, though the damage be nothing.

*Charles Pratt, English jurist; Lord
Chancellor, Lord Chief Justice*
Entick v. Carrington *(1765), 19
How. St. Tr. 1066*

118.11 ❧ But the most common and durable source of faction has been the various and unequal distribution of property.

*James Madison*
The Federalist, *1787*

118.12 ❧ Property and law are born and must die together.

*Jeremy Bentham*
Principles of the Civil Code, *c. 1843*

118.13 ❧ The highest law gives a thing to him who can use it.

*Henry David Thoreau*
Journal, *November 9, 1852*

118.14 ❧ Property, it is theft.

*Pierre Joseph Proudhon*
Principle of Right, *1858*

118.15 ❧ . . . generosity is not a virtue when dealing with the property of others.

*Robert M. Douglas, American jurist*
Cashion v. Telegraph Co., *123 N.C.
267, 273 (1898)*

118.16 ❧ The notion that with socialized property we should have women free and a piano for everybody seems to me an empty humbug.

*Oliver Wendell Holmes*
"Ideas and Doubts," Collected Legal
Papers, *1921*

118.17 ❧ The bundle of power and privileges to which we give the name of ownership is not constant through the ages. The

faggots must be put together and re-
bound from time to time.

> *Benjamin N. Cardozo, 1870–1938*
> *"The Paradoxes of Legal Science,"*
> Selected Writings of Benjamin N.
> Cardozo, *edited by Margaret Hall,*
> *1947*

*118.18* ❦ The modern mystics of muscle who
offer you the fraudulent alternative
of "human rights" versus "property
rights," as if one could exist without
the other, are making a last, gro-
tesque attempt to revive the doctrine
of soul versus body. Only a ghost
can exist without material property;
only a slave can work with no right
to the product of his effort.

> *Ayn Rand*
> Atlas Shrugged, *1957*

# 119. PROSECUTION

*119.1* ❦ Who ever knew an honest brute at
law his neighbor prosecute?

> *Jonathan Swift*
> The Logicians Refuted, *c.1735*

*119.2* ❦ [A] plaintiff must shew that he
stands on a fair ground when he
calls on a Court of justice to administer relief to him.

> *Sir Lloyd Kenyon, English jurist;*
> *Lord Chief Justice*
> Booth v. Hodgson *(1795), 6 T.R. 409*

*119.3* ❦ Those who make the attack ought
to be very well prepared to
support it.

> *Sir Giles Rooke, English jurist*
> Almgill v. Pierson *(1797), 2 Bos.*
> *& Pull. 104*

*119.4* ❦ There were no accusers; there could
be no judge.

> *Selma Lagerlöf*
> The Story of Gösta Berling, *1891*

*119.5* ❦ One of the most reprehensible
things a prosecutor can do is to attempt to put into evidence before
the jury his own, and his colleagues',
opinion as to the guilt of the defendants he is prosecuting.

> *Owen J. Roberts*
> United States v. Socony-Vacuum Oil
> Co., *310 U.S. 150, 264*
> *(1940)*

*119.6* ❦ Today, the grand jury is the total captive of the prosecutor who, if he is candid, will concede that he can indict anybody, at any time, for almost anything, before any grand jury.

*William J. Campbell, American jurist;*
*judge, U.S. District Court*
U.S. News & World Report,
*June 19, 1978*

# *120.* PROSTITUTION

*120.1* ❦ Prisons are built with stones of law, brothels with bricks of religion.

*William Blake, 1757–1827*
*W. H. Auden and Louis Kronenberger,*
The Viking Book of Aphorisms, *1962*

*120.2* ❦ . . . nothing could be more grotesquely unjust than a code of morals, reinforced by laws, which relieves men from responsibility for irregular sexual acts, and for the same acts drives women to abortion, infanticide, prostitution and self-destruction.

*Suzanne LaFollette*
*American feminist and writer*
*"Women and Marriage,"*
Concerning Women, *1926*

*120.3* ❦ What it comes down to is this: the grocer, the butcher, the baker, the merchant, the landlord, the druggist, the liquor dealer, the policeman, the doctor, the city father and the politician—these are the people who make money out of prostitution, these are the real reapers of the wages of sin.

*Polly Adler*
A House Is Not a Home, *1953*

*120.4* ❦ At a conference on moral and social hygiene last year [1957] Earl Jowitt criticized the law against prostitution for being "based on a fiction that the man who is accosted is annoyed." He remarked that, at his "ripe old age," if he were accosted he would be "complimented."

*Earl Jowitt*
*criticizing prostitution law in 1957*
*Eugene Gerhart,* Quote It! *1969*

*120.5* ❦ It is a further irony that our legal ethic prosecutes those who are forced (economically or psychologically) to offer themselves for sale as objects, but condones the act of buying persons as objects.

*Kate Millet*
The Prostitution Papers, *1971*

120.6 ❦ It is a silly question to ask a prostitute why she does it. . . . These are
the highest-paid "professional"
women in America.

*Gail Sheehy*
*Hustling, 1971*

120.7 ❦ The prostitutes continue to take all
the arrests, the police to suffer
frustration, the lawyers to mine
gold, the operators to laugh, the
landowners to insist they have no
responsibility, the mayor to issue
press releases. The nature of the
beast is, in a word, greed.

*Gail Sheehy*
*Hustling, 1971*

120.8 ❦ . . . if my business could be made legal . . . and the city and state could
derive the money in taxes and licensing fees that I pay off to crooked
cops and political figures.

*Xaviera Hollander*
*The Happy Hooker, 1972*

120.9 ❦ Punishing the prostitute promotes
the rape of all women. When prostitution is a crime, the message con-
veyed is that women who are sexual
are "bad," and therefore legitimate
weapons of sexual assault.

*Margo St. James*
*Mildred Hamilton, "Margo,"*
*The San Francisco Examiner,*
*April 29, 1979*

120.10 ❦ A call girl is simply someone who
hates poverty more than she
hates sin.

*Sydney Biddle Barrows*
*Mayflower Madam, 1986*

120.11 ❦ Most lawyers are like whores. They
serve the client who puts the highest
fee on the table.

*Florynce Rae Kennedy*
*Lawyer's Wit and Wisdom, edited by*
*Bruce Nash, Allan Zullo and compiled*
*by Kathryn Zullo, 1995*

# 121. PSYCHIATRY

121.1 ❦ Where the head is sick there is
no law.

*Proverb*
*B. J. Whiting and H. W. Whiting,*
*Proverbs, Sentences, and Proverbial*
*Phrases: From English Writings*
*Mainly Before 1500, 1968*

121.2 ❦ Sickness has no law.

*John Lydgate*
*Troy Book, 1420*

121.3 ❦ If weakness may excuse,
What murderer, what traitor,
    parricide,
Incestuous, sacrilegious, but may
    plead it?
All wickedness is weakness.

*John Milton*
Samson Agonistes, *1671*

121.4 ❦ Avarice, ambition, lust, etc. are species of madness.

*Spinoza*
Ethics, *1677*

121.5 ❦ I think the law became an ass the
day it let the psychiatrists get their
hands on the law.

*Lynn D. Compton, American lawyer;*
*chief deputy district attorney,*
*Los Angeles*
Summation at Sirhan B. Sirhan Trial,
*reported in* Los Angeles Times,
*April 14, 1969*

# 122. PUBLIC INTEREST

122.1 ❦ Whatever is injurious to the interests
of the public is void, on the grounds
of public policy.

*Sir Nicholas Conyngham Tindal,*
*English jurist; Chief Justice*
Horner v. Graves (1831), 7 Bing. 743

122.2 ❦ The trouble is that lawyers necessarily acquire the habit of assuming the
law to be right. . . . As a rule, the
pure lawyer seldom concerns himself
about the broad aspects of public
policy which may show a law to be
all wrong, and such a lawyer may be
oblivious to the fact that in helping
to enforce the law he is helping to injure the public. Then, too, lawyers
are almost always conservative.
Through insisting upon the mainte-
nance of legal rules, they become instinctively opposed to change, and
thus are frequently found aiding in
the assertion of legal rights under
laws which have once been reasonable and fair, but which, through the
process of social and business development, have become unjust and unfair without the lawyers seeing it.

*Elihu Root, 1845–1937*
*Philip C. Jessup,* Elihu Root, *1938*

122.3 ❦ The most important thing a lawyer
can do is to become an advocate of
powerless citizens.

*Ralph Nader*
Newsweek, *October 3, 1969*

122.4 ❦ Lawyers as a group are no more
dedicated to justice or public service
than a private public utility is dedicated to giving light.

*David Melinkoff, American educator;*
*professor, University of*
*California, Los Angeles*
San Francisco Examiner &
Chronicle, *June 22, 1973*

122.5 ❦ ... I, as a lawyer, believe that some
significant part of my money, time,
thought, and energy belongs—
I don't give it, it *belongs*—to others,
not just to me.

> *R. Sargent Shriver, Jr.*
> Washington Post, *June 6, 1982*

# 123. PUBLIC OPINION

123.1 ❦ Laws they are not which public approbation hath not made so.

> *Richard Hooker*
> Of the Laws of Ecclesiastical Polity,
> *1594*

123.2 ❦ We are always on the side of those
who speak last.

> *Marie de Rabutin-Chantal, Marquise*
> *de Sévigné, 1671*
> Letters of Madame de Sevigne to
> Her Daughter and
> Her Friends, *vol. 1, 1811*

123.3 ❦ The law no passion can disturb. ...
On the one hand, it is inexorable to
the cries and lamentations of the
prisoner; on the other, it is deaf, deaf
as an adder, to the clamours of the
populace.

> *John Adams, in defense of British*
> *soldiers on trial after the Boston*
> *Massacre, 1770*

123.4 ❦ Public policy is a very unruly horse,
and when once you get astride it you
never know where it will carry you.

> *Sir James Burrough, English jurist*
> Richardson v. Mellish *(1824),*
> *2 Bing. 252*

123.5 ❦ Public opinion is stronger than the
Legislature, and nearly as strong as
the Ten Commandments.

> *Charles Dudley Warner*
> My Summer in a Garden, *1875*

123.6 ❦ Public opinion's always in advance
of the law.

> *John Galsworthy*
> Windows, *1922*

123.7 ❦ In America, public opinion is the
leader.

> *Frances Perkins*
> People at Work, *1934*

*123.8* ❦ Compulsory unification of opinion achieves only the unanimity of the graveyard.

> *Robert H. Jackson*
> Board of Education v. Barnette, *319 U.S. 624, 641 (1943)*

*123.9* ❦ There are not enough jails, not enough policemen, not enough courts to enforce a law not supported by the people.

> *Hubert H. Humphrey*
> *Speech, Williamsburg, Virginia, May 1, 1965*

*123.10* ❦ Somewhere "out there," beyond the walls of the courthouse, run currents and tides of public opinion which lap at the courtroom door.

> *William H. Rehnquist*
> *Speech at the Suffolk University Law School, Boston, Massachusetts, April 17, 1986*

# *124.* PUNISHMENT

*124.1* ❦ Law cannot persuade, where it cannot punish.

> *Proverb*
> Rosalind Fergusson, The Facts On File Dictionary of Proverbs, *1983*

*124.2* ❦ Anyone through whom another man has been falsely punished will be barred from Heaven's Gates.

> *Talmud, Shabbat*

*124.3* ❦ The greatest incitement to crime is the hope of escaping punishment.

> *Cicero*
> Pro Milone, *c.50* B.C.

*124.4* ❦ If you did not punish crimes you would help wickedness.

> *Publilius Syrus, Latin writer*
> Sententiae, *c.43* B.C.

*124.5* ❦ What a slight foundation for virtue it is to be good only from fear of the law!

> *Seneca*
> De Ira, *c.43*

*124.6* ❦ Laws do not persuade just because they threaten.

> *Seneca*
> Epistulae Morales ad Lucilium, *63–65*

**124.7** ❦ The rabbis said about capital cases: "We decide by a majority of one for acquittal, but only by a majority of at least two for conviction."

*Rashi, Jewish legal authority*
*Commentaries on the Pentateuch:*
*Exodus, c.late 11th century*

**124.8** ❦ Stay friend, until I put aside my beard, for that never committed treason.

*Sir Thomas More*
*Remark to executioner, before placing*
*his head on the block, 1535*

**124.9** ❦ Sicinius: He hath resisted law,
And therefore law shall scorn him further trial
Than the severity of the public power.

*Shakespeare*
*Coriolanus, I, 3, 1607–1608*

**124.10** ❦ To you, Lord Governor,
Remains the censure of this hellish villain—
The time, the place, the torture.
O enforce it!

*Shakespeare*
*Othello, Act V*

**124.11** ❦ No pain equals that of an injury inflicted under the pretense of a just punishment.

*Lupercio Leonardo de Argensola,*
*Spanish poet and dramatist,*
*1559–1619 Sonetos*

**124.12** ❦ I went to Charing Cross to see Major General Harrison hanged, drawn, and quartered; which was done there, he looking as cheerful as any man could do in that condition.

*Samuel Pepys*
*Diary, October 13, 1660*

**124.13** ❦ No Indian prince has to his palace
More followers than a thief to th' gallows.

*Samuel Butler*
*Hudibras, 1663–1678*

**124.14** ❦ Men are not hang'd for stealing Horses, but that Horses may not be stolen.

*George Savile, 1st marquess of Halifax,*
*English politician, 1633–1695*
*The Complete Works of George*
*Savile, First Marquess of Halifax,*
*1912*

**124.15** ❦ Wherever a Knave is not punished, an honest Man is laugh'd at.

*George Savile, 1st marquess of Halifax,*
*English politician, 1633–1695*
*The Complete Works of George*
*Saville, First Marquess of Halifax,*
*1912*

**124.16** ❦ Hail hieroglyphic State machine, Contrived to punish fancy in;

*Daniel Defoe*
*Hymn to the Pillory, 1703*

**124.17** ❦ Whenever the offense inspires less horror than the punishment, the rigour of penal law is obliged to give way to the common feelings of mankind.

*Edward Gibbon*
*Decline and Fall of the Roman*
*Empire, 1776*

124.18 ❧ My machine will take off a head in a twinkling, and the victim will feel nothing but a slight sense of refreshing coolness on the neck. We cannot make too much haste, gentlemen, to allow the nation to enjoy this advantage.

> *Joseph Ignace Guillotin,*
> *French physician*
> *To the French Assembly, 1789*

124.19 ❧ Said a man ingenuously to one of his friends: "This morning we condemned three men to death. Two of them definitely deserved it."

> *Sébastien Roch Nicolas Chamfort,*
> *French writer, 1740–1794*
> *W. H. Auden and Louis Kronenberger,*
> *The Viking Book of Aphorisms, 1962*

124.20 ❧ An avidity to punish is always dangerous to liberty.

> *Thomas Paine*
> *"Dissertation on First Principles of*
> *Government" (speech), July 7, 1795*

124.21 ❧ The law doth punish man or woman
That steals the goose from off the
    common
But lets the greater felon loose
That steals the common from
    the goose.

> *Anonymous*
> *On the Enclosure Movement, 18th*
> *century*

124.22 ❧ The Tarpeian rock [the Roman place of execution] is near the Capitol [the place of official distinction].

> *Jony-Spontini*
> *W. Gurney Benham,* Putnam's
> Complete Book of Quotations,
> Proverbs and Household Words, *1927*

124.23 ❧ The tree must lie where it has fallen.

> *Justice North, English jurist*
> In re Bridgewater Navigation Co., Ltd.
> (1890), 60 L.J. Rep. (N.S.) C.D. 422

124.24 ❧ We enact many laws that manufacture criminals, and then a few that punish them.

> *Benjamin R. Tucker, American*
> *journalist and anarchist*
> Instead of a Book, *1893*

124.25 ❧ Gentlemen of the jury, you have a solemn duty to discharge. The life of the prisoner at the bar is in your hands. You can take it—by a word. You can extinguish that life as the candle by your side was extinguished a moment ago. But it is not in your power, it is not in the power of any of us—of any one in the court or out of it,—to restore that life, when once taken, as that light has been restored.

> *John Duke Coleridge, English jurist;*
> *Lord Chief Justice, 1820–1894*
> *Plea in a murder case during which a*
> *candle in the jury box went out, leaving*
> *the court in darkness*

124.26 ❧ A community is infinitely more brutalized by the habitual employment of punishment than . . . by the occasional occurrence of crime.

> *Oscar Wilde, 1854–1900*
> *W. H. Auden and Louis Kronenberger,*
> *The Viking Book of Aphorisms, 1962*

124.27 ❧ Corporal punishment is as humiliating for him who gives it as for him who receives it; it is ineffective besides.

> *Ellen Key, Swedish writer and feminist*
> The Century of the Child, *1909*

124.28 ❧ . . . laws are felt only when the individual comes into conflict with them.

*Suzanne LaFollette, American
feminist and writer
"The Beginnings of Emancipation,"
Concerning Women,
1926*

124.29 ❧ The reformative effect of punishment is a belief that dies hard, chiefly, I think, because it [punishment] is so satisfying to our sadistic impulses.

*Bertrand Russell
Ideas That Have Harmed Mankind,
1946*

124.30 ❧ Punishment must be an honour. It must not only wipe out the stigma of the crime, but must be regarded as a supplementary form of education, compelling a higher devotion to the public good. The severity of the punishment must also be in keeping with the kind of obligation which has been violated, and not with the interests of public security.

*Simone Weil, French philosopher
L'Enracinement, 1949; tr. as
The need for Roots, 1952*

124.31 ❧ Let us revise our views and work from the premise that all laws should be for the welfare of society as a whole and not directed at the punishment of sins.

*John Biggs, Jr., American jurist
"Procedures for Handling the
Mentally-Ill Offender in Some
European Countries,"
Temple Law Quarterly, 1956*

124.32 ❧ "Only lies and evil come from letting people off. . . ."

*Iris Murdoch
A Severed Head, 1961*

124.33 ❧ "Nothing can be right and balanced again until justice is won—the injured party has to have justice. Do you understand that? Nothing can be right, for years, for lifetimes, until that first crime is punished. Or else we'd all be animals."

*Joyce Carol Oates
"Norman and the Killer," Upon the
Sweeping Flood and Other Stories,
1965*

124.34 ❧ This Court inescapably has the duty, as the ultimate arbiter of the meaning of our Constitution, to say whether, when individuals condemned to death stand before our Bar, "moral concepts" require us to hold that the law has progressed to the point where we should declare that the punishment of death, like punishments on the rack, the screw, and the wheel, is no longer morally tolerable in our society.

*William J. Brennan, Jr.
Gregg v. Georgia, 428 U.S. 153, 96
St. Ct. 2909, 49 L.Ed.2d 859 (1976)*

124.35 ❧ If the Menendez brothers are innocent because they were abused, so are many inmates on death row. Death row is filled with people who have had worse childhoods than Erik and Lyle Menendez, in addition to worse lawyers.

*Wendy Kaminer,
lawyer and social critic
It's All the Rage, 1995*

124.36 ❦ The cost of custody should rest with the parents, not with the state.

> *Judy Sheindlin, with Josh Getlin, on*
> *juvenile incarceration*
> Don't Pee on My Leg and Tell Me
> It's Raining, *1996*

# *125.* RAPE

**125.1** ❦ Part of the horror of sexual irregularity so-called is due to the fact that everyone knows himself essentially guilty.

*Aleister Crowley*
The Confessions of Aleister Crowley,
*1929; rev. 1970*

**125.2** ❦ History, sacred and profane, and the common experience of mankind teach that women of the character shown in this case are prone to make false accusations both of rape and of insult upon the slightest provocation or without even provocation, for ulterior purposes.

*James E. Horton, American jurist*
*Memorandum granting a new trial in*
*the Scottsboro case, June 22, 1933*

**125.3** ❦ Woman was and is condemned to a system under which the lawful rapes exceed the unlawful ones a million to one.

*Margaret Sanger, 1883–1966*
Lawyer's Wit and Wisdom, *edited by*
*Bruce Nash, Allan Zullo and compiled*
*by Kathryn Zullo, 1995*

**125.4** ❦ In no state can a man be accused of raping his wife. How can any man steal what already belongs to him?

*Susan Griffin, American poet*
Ramparts, *September 1971*

**125.5** ❦ Rape is a culturally fostered means of suppressing women. Legally we say we deplore it, but mythically we romanticize and perpetuate it, and privately we excuse and overlook it. . . .

*Victoria Billings, American journalist*
*"Sex: We Need Another Revolution,"*
The Womansbook, *1974*

**125.6** ❦ [Rape] is the only crime in which the victim becomes the accused and, in reality, it is she who must prove her good reputation, her mental soundness, and her impeccable propriety.

*Freda Adler, American educator*
Sisters in Crime, *1975*

**125.7** ❦ It is like the old maxim in a rape case: If you can get laughter, you won't get a conviction. The two just don't mix.

*F. Lee Bailey, referring to his reputation*
*for being flamboyant*
Los Angeles Herald Examiner,
*December 7, 1978*

**125.8** ❦ For many feminists, pornography is the theory and rape is the practice.

*Cheris Kramarae and*
*Paula A. Treichler*
A Feminist Dictionary, *1987*

**125.9** ❧ Sexual abuse is like a corpse on a slab, saying nothing. You've got nothing to go on. It's a police officer's nightmare. You just want it to go away.

*Beatrix Campbell, quoting*
*a police source*
Unofficial Secrets, *1988*

**125.10** ❧ Each false accusation makes too many skeptics think that every accusation is a false one—which is a danger that cannot be overstated.

*Linda Fairstein, prosecuting attorney*
*Cathy Young, "Rancorous*
*Liasons—The Morning After,"*
Reason, *February 1994*

# *126.* REASON

**126.1** ❧ What is inconsistent with and contrary to reason is not permitted in law.

*Legal maxim*

**126.2** ❧ A man without reason is a beast in season.

*Proverb*
*John Ray,* English Proverbs, *1678*

**126.3** ❧ Law governs man, reason the law.

*Proverb*
*Rosalind Fergusson,* The Facts On File
Dictionary of Proverbs, *1983*

**126.4** ❧ Reason lies between the spur and the bridle.

*Proverb*
*George Herbert,* Outlandish Proverbs,
*1640*

**126.5** ❧ Reason is the wise man's guide, example the fool's.

*Welsh proverb*

**126.6** ❧ The law of things is a law of universal reason, but most men live as if they had a wisdom of their own.

*Heraclitus*
Cosmic Fragments, *c.500* B.C.

**126.7** ❧ The law is reason free from passion.

*Aristotle*
Politics, *c.322* B.C.

**126.8** ❧ Law is nothing else but right reason, calling us imperiously to our duty, and prohibiting every violation of it.

*Cicero*
Orationes Philippicae, *c.60* B.C.

**126.9** ❧ Reason is the mistress and queen of all things.

*Cicero*
Tusculanae Disputationes,
*45* B.C.

*126.10* ❦ That which natural reason has established amongst all men is called the law of nations.

> *Gaius, Roman jurist,* 130–180
> Institutes

*126.11* ❦ Law is a regulation in accord with reason, issued by a lawful superior for the common good.

> *Thomas Aquinas*
> Summa Theologica, *c.1258–1260*

*126.12* ❦ Every why hath a wherefore.

> *Shakespeare*
> The Comedy of Errors, *II, 2,*
> *1592–1593*

*126.13* ❦ . . . for like reason doth make like law. . . .

> *Sir Edward Coke*
> The Institutes of the Lawes of
> England, *vol. 1, 1628–1641*

*126.14* ❦ How long soever it hath continued, if it be against reason, it is of no force in law.

> *Sir Edward Coke*
> The Institutes of the Lawes of
> England, *vol. 1, 1628–1641*

*126.15* ❦ Reason is the life of the law; nay, the common law itself is nothing else but reason.

> *Sir Edward Coke*
> The Institutes of the Lawes of
> England, *vol. 1, 1628–1641*

*126.16* ❦ Reason is but choosing.

> *John Milton*
> Areopagitica, *1644*

*126.17* ❦ The law of England is, at best, but the reason of Parliament.

> *John Milton*
> Eikonoclastes, *1649*

*126.18* ❦ Men never wish ardently for what they only wish for from reason.

> *La Rochefoucauld*
> Maximes, *1665*

*126.19* ❦ God so commanded, and left that command
> Sole daughter of his voice; the rest we live
> Law to ourselves, our reason is our law.

> *John Milton*
> Paradise Lost, *1667*

*126.20* ❦ 'Tis more than reason that goes to persuasion.

> *Quoted by Thomas Twisden,*
> *English jurist*
> Manby v. Scott *(1672), 1 Levinz. 4;*
> *2 Sm. L.C. (8th Ed.) 462*

*126.21* ❦ In vain thy Reason finer webs shall draw,
> Entangle justice in her net of law,
> And right, too rigid, harden into wrong,
> Still for the strong too weak, the weak too strong.

> *Alexander Pope*
> An Essay on Man, *1732*

126.22 ❦ If you will not hear reason,
She will surely rap your knuckles.

*Benjamin Franklin*
*Poor Richard's Almanack, 1757*

126.23 ❦ Within the brain's most secret cells
A certain Lord Chief Justice dwells
Of sovereign power, whom one and
all,
With common voice, we Reason call.

*Charles Churchill, English poet*
*and satirist*
*The Ghost, 1762–1763*

126.24 ❦ Passion and prejudice govern the
world; only under the name of
reason.

*John Wesley*
*Letter to Joseph Benson,*
*October 5, 1770*

126.25 ❦ Reason and free enquiry are the only
effectual agents against error.

*Thomas Jefferson*
*Notes on the State of Virginia, 1785*

126.26 ❦ I told [John Marshall] it was law
logic—an artificial system of
reasoning, exclusively used in the
courts of justice, but good for
nothing anywhere else.

*John Quincy Adams*
*Clifton Fadiman and Charles van*
*Doran, The American Treasury,*
*1455–1955, 1955*

126.27 ❦ Reason alone can make the laws
obligatory and lasting.

*Honoré Sabriel Riquetti, comte de*
*Mirabeau, 1749–1791*
*W. Gurney Benham,* Putnam's
Complete Book of Quotations,
Proverbs and Household Words,
*1927*

126.28 ❦ Reason is founded on the evidence
of our senses.

*Percy Bysshe Shelley*
*Queen Mab, notes, 1813*

126.29 ❦ Reason is nothing but the analysis
of belief.

*Franz Schubert*
*Diary, March 27, 1824*

126.30 ❦ Reason dissipates the illusions of
life, but does not console us for their
departure.

*Countess of Blessington*
*Desultory Thoughts and*
*Reflections, 1839*

126.31 ❦ Doth not the idiot eat? Doth not
the idiot drink? Doth not the idiot
know his father and mother? . . .
Think you he does this for nothing?
He does it all because he is a man,
and because, however imperfectly,
he exercises his reason.

*William H. Seward*
*Freeman Case, 1846*

126.32 ❦ Reason is only a tool.

*Nietzsche*
*Beyond Good and Evil, 1886*

126.33 ❧ I take it that reasonable human
conduct is part of the ordinary
course of things.

*Nathaniel Lindley, English jurist*
The City of Lincoln *(1889),*
*L.R. 15 P.D. 18*

126.34 ❧ I can stand brute force, but brute
reason is quite unbearable.

*Oscar Wilde*
The Picture of Dorian Gray, *1891*

126.35 ❧ The life of reason is no fair
reproduction of the universe, but the
expression of man alone.

*George Santayana*
The Life of Reason, *1901*

126.36 ❧ A page of history is worth a volume
of logic.

*Oliver Wendell Holmes*
New York Trust Co. v. Eisner, *256
U.S. 345 (1921)*

126.37 ❧ If we would guide by the light of reason, we must let our minds be bold.

*Louis D. Brandeis*
New State Ice Co. v. Liebmann,
*285, U.S. 262 (1932)*

126.38 ❧ . . . two and two will always make
four, despite reports of presidents
and financial advisers who insist on
stretching it into five.

*Louis D. Brandeis, 1856–1941*
*Alpheus Thomas Mason,* Brandeis:
A Free Man's Life, *1946*

126.39 ❧ A rational process is a moral process.

*Ayn Rand*
Atlas Shrugged, *1957*

126.40 ❧ The eternal struggle in the law between constancy and change is
largely a struggle between history
and reason, between past reason and
present needs.

*Felix Frankfurter*
Mr. Justice Holmes and the
Supreme Court, *1961*

126.41 ❧ Ever since Kant divorced reason
from reality, his intellectual descendants have been diligently widening
the breach.

*Ayn Rand*
*"The Cashing-In: The Student
'Rebellion',"* The New Left, *1968*

126.42 ❧ As soon as man began considering
himself the source of the highest
meaning in the world and the
measure of everything, the world
began to lose its human dimension,
and man began to lose control of it.

*Vaclav Havel, Czech
playwright, president*
Disturbing the Peace, *1986, tr. 1990*

# *127.* RELIGION

---

*127.1* ❧ The act of God does no injury to
any person.

*Latin legal phrase*

*127.2* ❧ He that is void of fear, may soon be
just; And no religion binds men to
be traitors.

*Ben Jonson*
*Catiline, 1611*

*127.3* ❧ He that seemeth to be religious, and
bridleth not his tongue, his religion
is vain.

*John Lisle, English jurist*
*Hewet's Case (1658), 5 How.*
*St. Tr. 894*

*127.4* ❧ Fanatic fools, that in those twilight
times,
With wild religion cloaked the worst
of crimes!

*John Langhorne*
*The Country Justice, c.1766*

*127.5* ❧ I for one would never be a party,
unless the law were clear, to saying
to any man who put forward his
views on those most sacred things,
that he should be branded as
apparently criminal because he
differed from the majority of
mankind in his religious views or
convictions on the subject of
religion. If that were so, we should
get into ages and times which, thank

God, we do not live in when people
were put to death for opinions and
beliefs which now almost all of us
believe to be true.

*John Duke Coleridge, English jurist;*
*Lord Chief Justice*
*Reg. v. Bradlaugh and others (1883),*
*15 Cox, C.C. 230*

*127.6* ❧ Indeed, nothing is so likely to lead
us astray as an abject reliance upon
canons of any sort.

*Learned Hand*
*Van Vranken v. Helvering, 313 U.S.,*
*585, 61 S. Ct. 1095, 85 L.Ed. 1541*
*(1940)*

*127.7* ❧ If nowhere else, in the relation
between Church and State, "good
fences make good neighbors."

*Felix Frankfurter*
*McCollum v. Board of Education,*
*333 U.S. 203, 232 (1948)*

*127.8* ❧ The day that this country ceases to
be free for irreligion, it will cease to
be free for religion.

*Robert H. Jackson*
*Zorach v. Clausor, 1952*

*127.9* ❧ In the relationship between man
and religion, the state is firmly
committed to a position of
neutrality.

*Tom C. Clark*
*New York Herald Tribune,*
*June 18, 1963*

127.10 ❧ The hazards of churches supporting government are hardly less in their potential than the hazards of governments supporting churches. . . .

*Warren E. Burger*
*Walz v. Tax Commission, 397 U.S.*
*664, 90 S. Ct. 1409, 25 L.Ed.2d 697*
*(1970)*

127.11 ❧ The court has unambiguously concluded that the individual freedom of conscience protected by the First Amendment embraces the right to select any religious faith or none at all.

*John Paul Stevens*
*Wallace v. Jaffree, No. 83–812 (1985)*

127.12 ❧ As the rights of the majority have been replaced by the rights of the minority, so the spiritual foundations of the nation have been replaced by an entirely secular view of man.

*Pat Robertson*
*America's Dates with Destiny, 1986*

# 128. REVENGE

128.1 ❧ If a man has caused the loss of a gentleman's eye, his eye one shall cause to be lost.

*Hammurabi's Code 1792–1750 B.C.*

128.2 ❧ The law forbids revenge.

*Adapted from Abot de Rabbi Nathan*

128.3 ❧ Revenge is a kind of wild justice, which the more man's nature runs to, the more ought law to weed it out. . . .

*Francis Bacon*
*"Of Revenge," Essayes, 1625*

128.4 ❧ An injured friend is the bitterest of foes.

*Thomas Jefferson*
*French Treaties opinion, April 28, 1793*

128.5 ❧ Cases were decided in the chambers of a six-shooter instead of a supreme court.

*Thomas Babington Macaulay*
*"Burleigh,"*
*Essays, 1832*

128.6 ❧ Wisdom has taught us to be calm and meek,
To take one blow, and turn the other cheek;
It is not written what a man shall do,
If the rude caitiff smite the other too!

*Oliver Wendell Holmes, American physician and author*
*"Non-Resistance," The Works of Oliver Wendell Holmes:*
*The Poetical Works, 1877*

128.7 ❧ The avenger of blood . . . would now be himself punished as a criminal for taking the law into his own hands.

*E. B. Taylor, English anthropologist*
Anthropology, *1881*

128.8 ❧ The instinct for retribution is part of the nature of man.

*Potter Stewart*
Gregg v. Georgia, *428 U.S. 153, 96*
St. Ct. 2909, 49 L.Ed.2d 859 *(1976)*

# 129. REVOLUTION

129.1 ❧ All men recognize the right of revolution.

*Henry David Thoreau*
Civil Disobedience, *1849*

129.2 ❧ Raise less corn and more hell!

*Mary Clyens Lease, 1850–1933,*
*Kansas lawyer*
*Dawn Bradley Berry,* The 50
Most Influential Women in
American Law, *1996*

129.3 ❧ People never move towards revolution; they are pushed towards it by intolerable injustices in the economic and social order under which they live.

*Suzanne La Follette*
*"Institutional Marriage and*
*its Economic Aspects,"*
Concerning Women, *1926*

129.4 ❧ Revolution is the festival of the oppressed.

*Germaine Greer "Revolution,"*
The Female Eunuch, *1970*

129.5 ❧ The most radical revolutionary will become a conservative the day after the revolution.

*Hannah Arendt*
*"Civil Disobedience,"* Crises of
the Republic, *1972*

# *130.* RIGHTS

130.1 ❧ Rights are lost by disuse.

*Latin legal phrase*

130.2 ❧ The laws assist those who are vigilant, not those who sleep over their rights.

*Legal maxim*

130.3 ❧ When a greater right belongs to a man, the lesser right ought to be included.

*Legal maxim*

130.4 ❧ If the abstract rights of man will bear discussion and explanation, those of woman, by a parity of reasoning, will not shrink from the same test: though a different opinion prevails in the country.

*Mary Wollstonecraft*
*A Vindication of the Rights*
*of Women, 1792*

130.5 ❧ Old rights must remain: it would be very unreasonable if it should be otherwise.

*Sir Joseph Yates, English jurist*
*Mayor, &c. of Colchester v. Seaber*
*(1765), 3 Burr. Part IV. (1872)*

130.6 ❧ We hold these truths to be self-evident, that all men are created equal, that they are endowed by their Creator with certain unalienable Rights, that among these are Life, Liberty and the pursuit of Happiness. That to secure these rights, Governments are instituted among Men, deriving their just powers from the consent of the governed. That whenever any Form of Government becomes destructive of those ends, it is the Right of the People to alter or abolish it, and to institute a new Government, laying its foundation on such principles and organizing its power in such form, as to them shall seem most likely to effect their Safety and Happiness.

*Thomas Jefferson*
*Declaration of Independence, 1776*

130.7 ❧ Human beings have *rights*, because they are *moral* beings: the rights of *all* men grow out of their moral nature; and as all men have the same moral nature, they have essentially the same rights.

*Angelina Grimké, American abolitionist*
*Letters to Catherine Beecher, ed. by*
*Isaac Knapp, 1836*

130.8 ❧ I recognize no rights but *human* rights—I know nothing of men's rights and women's rights. . . .

*Angelina Grimké, American abolitionist*
*Letters to Catherine Beecher, ed. by*
*Isaac Knapp, 1836*

130.9 ❧ Men their rights and nothing more; women their rights and nothing less.

*Susan B. Anthony and*
*Elizabeth Cady Stanton*
*Motto of newspaper,*
*The Revolution, 1868*

130.10 ✠ Most rights are qualified.

*Oliver Wendell Holmes*
American Bank and Trust Co. v.
Federal Reserve Bank of Atlanta,
Georgia, *256 U.S. 350, 41 S. Ct. 499,*
*25 ALR 971, 65 L.Ed. 983 (1921)*

130.11 ✠ Such words as "right" are a constant solicitation to fallacy.

*Oliver Wendell Holmes*
Jackman v. Rosenbaum Co., *260 U.S.*
*22, 31 (1922)*

130.12 ✠ They [the makers of the Constitution] conferred, as against the government, the right to be let alone—the most comprehensive of rights and the right most valued by civilized men.

*Louis D. Brandeis, Supreme Court opinion,*
Olmstead v. United States, *1928*
*Daniel B. Baker,* Power Quotes, *1992*

130.13 ✠ . . . peaceable assembly for lawful discussion cannot be made a crime.

De Jonge v. Oregon, *299 U.S. 353 (1937)*

130.14 ✠ Certain rights can never be granted to the government, but must be kept in the hands of the people.

*Eleanor Roosevelt*
New York Times, *May 3, 1947*

130.15 ✠ A right which goes unrecognized by anybody is not worth very much.

*Simone Weil*
The Need for Roots, *1949*

130.16 ✠ In these days, it is doubtful that any child may reasonably be expected to succeed in life if he is denied the opportunity of an education. Such an opportunity, where the State has undertaken to provide it, is a right which must be made available to all on equal terms.

*Earl Warren*
Brown v. Board of Education of
Topeka, *347 U.S. 483, 74 S. Ct. 686,*
*98 L.Ed. 873 (1954)*

130.17 ✠ Prior to any questioning, the person must be warned that he has a right to remain silent, that any statement he does make may be used as evidence against him, and that he has a right to the presence of an attorney, either retained or appointed.

*Earl Warren*
Miranda v. Arizona,
*384 U.S. 436, 86 S. Ct. 1602,*
*16 L.Ed.2d 694 (1966)*

130.18 ✠ People tend to forget their duties but remember their rights.

*Indira Gandhi*
Last Words, *1984*

130.19 ✠ The American people have the Constitutional right to be wrong.

*Warren Rudman*
*Select Senate Committee Hearing on*
*Iran-Contra, July 1987*

130.20 ✠ If there is one message that echoes forth from this conference, let it be that human rights are women's rights, and women's rights are human rights, for once and for all.

*Hillary Rodham Clinton*
Speech, Fourth World Conference on
Women, Beijing, China,
*September 5, 1995*

# *131.* RULE OF LAW

*131.1* ❧ Right is the rule of law, and law is declaratory of right.

*Aphorism*
*Benjamin Whichcote,* Moral and
Religious Aphorisms, *1753*

*131.2* ❧ Therefore he who bids the law rule may be deemed to bid God and Reason alone rule, but he who bids man rule adds an element of the beast; for desire is a wild beast, and passion perverts the minds of rulers, even when they are the best of men.

*Aristotle*
Politics, *c.322* B.C.

*131.3* ❧ Even habitual disobedience in some things is consistent with the rule of law: it is certain that only a minority of motorists observe the statutory speed limit on a clear road, but England is not therefore in a state of anarchy.

*Sir Frederick Pollock, English jurist*
*Mark De Wolfe Howe,*
Holmes-Pollock Letters, *1946*

*131.4* ❧ Great states, able to defend *themselves,* do not entrust matters of life and death to a head count of states that can do neither. The "sovereign equality of all states" is an illusion. A universal "rule of Law" can neither be formulated in a manner acceptable to people with different concepts of law nor enforced under present conditions except by war.

*Dorothy Thompson*
*"The Discrepancy Between Democratic*
*Ideals and Realities,"* Ladies' Home
Journal, *October 1960*

*131.5* ❧ The first step in the direction of a world rule of law is the recognition that peace no longer is an unobtainable ideal but a necessary condition of continued human existence.

*Margaret Mead*
New York Times Magazine,
*November 26, 1961*

*131.6* ❧ What the rule of law means for Englishmen, what due process of law means to Americans, is inseparably bound up with our traditional notions of Magna Carta. Whether all that has been read into the document is historically or legally sound, is not of the first importance; every historian knows that belief itself is a historical fact, and that legend and myth cannot be left out of account in tracing the sequence of cause and effect.

*Helen M. Cam, English historian*
*"Magna Carta—Event*
*or Document?" (lecture),*
*July 7, 1967*

131.7 ❧ The rule of law can be wiped out in one misguided, however well-intentioned generation. And if that should happen, it could take a century of striving and ordeal to restore it, and then only at the cost of the lives of many good men and women.

*William T. Gossett, American*
*lawyer; president, American*
*Bar Association*
*Speech,*
*American Bar Association,*
*August 11, 1969*

131.8 ❧ Too often, practitioners of the law are simply journeymen of legal practice. . . not creators of legal justice and do not, in fact, understand, the philosophical bases of law, its ultimate goals, or its importance. . . in a democratic society. . . . It should be the role of universities to constantly explore the possibilities of improving the rule of

law, of constantly studying the extension of the rule of law, of constantly working for the universalization of the basic principles which lead to an international conformity of basic law. It should be the role of universities to study the extension of law to other areas of human disputes and arguments and violence, so as to substitute basic principles and rational procedures for prejudice and violence.

*Robert John Henle, American educator;*
*president, Georgetown University*
Vital Speeches, *October 15, 1972*

131.9 ❧ [Rule of law] places restraints on individuals and on governments alike. This is a delicate, a fragile balance to maintain. It is fragile because it is sustained only by an ideal that requires each person in society, by an exercise of free will, to accept and abide the restraints of a structure of laws.

*Warren E. Burger*
*Address, Law Day Service, St. John's*
*Cathedral, Jacksonville, Florida,*
*June 15, 1973*

131.10 ❧ Woman throughout the ages has been mistress to the law, as man has been its master. . . . The controversy between rule of law and rule of men was never relevant to women—because, along with juveniles, imbeciles, and other classes of legal nonpersons, they had no access to law except through men.

*Freda Adler, American educator*
Sisters in Crime, *1975*

# *132.* SELF-INCRIMINATION

*132.1* ❧ No one need accuse himself except before God.

*Latin legal phrase*
*W. Gurney Benham,* Putnam's
Complete Book of Quotations,
Proverbs and Household Words, *1927*

*132.2* ❧ A man may not accuse himself of a crime.

*Talmud, Yevamot*

*132.3* ❧ No man is bound to accuse himself.

*John Selden, 1584–1654*
Table-Talk, *1689*

*132.4* ❧ I hope your Worship will not be angry; . . . am I obliged to accuse myself?

*Daniel Defoe*
The Behavior of Servants, *1724*

*132.5* ❧ . . . nor shall any person . . . be compelled in any Criminal Case to be a witness against himself. . . .

*Constitution of the United States, Fifth*
*Amendment, 1791*

*132.6* ❧ The Fifth Amendment is an old friend and a good friend. It is one of the great landmarks in men's struggle to be free of tyranny, to be decent and civilized.

*William O. Douglas*
An Almanac of Liberty, *1954*

*132.7* ❧ Too many, even those who should be better advised, view this privilege as a shelter for wrongdoers. They too readily assume that those who invoke it are either guilty of a crime or commit perjury in claiming the privilege. Such a view does scant honor to the patriots who sponsored the Bill of Rights as a condition to acceptance of the Constitution by the ratifying States.

*Felix Frankfurter*
Ullman v. United States, *350 U.S.*
*422, 100 L.Ed. 511, 76 Sup. Ct.*
*497 (1956)*

*132.8* ❧ The critical point is that the Constitution places the right of silence *beyond the reach of government.*

*William O. Douglas*
Ullman v. United States, *350 U.S.*
*422, 100 L.Ed. 511, 76 Sup. Ct. 497*
*(1956)*

*132.9* ❧ Volunteered statements of any kind are not barred by the Fifth Amendment. . . .

*Earl Warren*
Miranda v. Arizona, *384 U.S. 436,*
*86 S. Ct. 1602, 16 L.Ed.2d 694*
*(1966)*

## 133. SENTENCES

**133.1** ❦ From a foolish judge, a quick
sentence.

*Proverb*
*Rosalind Fergusson,* The Facts On File
Dictionary of Proverbs, *1983*

**133.2** ❦ No! No! Sentence first—Verdict
afterwards.

*Lewis Carroll*
Alice's Adventures in Wonderland,
*1865*

**133.3** ❦ You only have so many options when
you sentence. You can put a defendant
on probation, order him to be put on
work-release and go to a half-way
house, or send him to an institution.
But what it comes right down to is
that there is no alternative that's any
good. I guess you could call it a judge's
dilemma.

*Charles W. Halleck, American jurist;*
*judge, Superior Court of*
*the District of Columbia*
Washington Post,
*October 9, 1971*

**133.4** ❦ I think a judge's education is very
imperfect when it comes to the
sentencing process.

*Edward M. Davis, American law*
*enforcement official;*
*chief of police, Los Angeles*
Interview, Human Events,
*March 22, 1975*

**133.5** ❦ The toughest part of this job is
sentencing. I've lost all kinds of
sleep over sentences. I find it
dreadful.

*Malcolm Muir, American jurist; judge,*
*U.S. District Court*
San Francisco Examiner &
Chronicle, *March 8, 1981*

## 134. SEVERITY

**134.1** ❦ In a thousand pounds of law, there's
not an ounce of love.

*Proverb*
*Rosalind Fergusson,* The Facts On File
Dictionary of Proverbs, *1983*

**134.2** ❦ In making laws, severity; in
administering laws, clemency.

*Chinese proverb*
*William Scarborough,* Chinese
Proverbs, *1875*

*134.3* ✣ There is a point beyond which even justice becomes unjust.

*Sophocles*
Electra, *c.409* B.C.

*134.4* ✣ Rigorous law is often rigorous injustice.

*Terence,* c. l85–159 B.C.
The Self-Tormentor, *163* B.C.

*134.5* ✣ It is hard, but the law is so written.

*Ulpian,* c.2nd–3rd century
*W. Gurney Benham,* Putnam's
Complete Book of Quotations,
Proverbs and Household Words, *1927*

*134.6* ✣ It is better that a judge should lean on the side of compassion than severity.

*Cervantes*
Don Quixote, *1605*

*134.7* ✣ Is not this a lamentable thing, that of the skin of an innocent lamb should be made parchment? That parchment, being scribbled o'er, should undo a man?

*Shakespeare*
2 Henry VI, *IV, 2, 1589–1591*

*134.8* ✣ Lucio:
He arrests him on it;
And follows close the rigour of the statute,
To make him an example.

*Shakespeare*
Measure for Measure,
*I, 4, 1604–1605*

*134.9* ✣ The bloody book of law
You shall yourself read in the bitter letter
After your own sense.

*Shakespeare*
Othello, *I, 3, 1604–1605*

*134.10* ✣ The law is blind and speaks in general terms;
She cannot pity where occasion serves.

*Thomas May, English poet
and playwright*
The Heir, *1620*

*134.11* ✣ At Halifax the law so sharpe doth deale,
That who so more than thirteen pence doth steale,
They have a jyn that wondrous quick and well,
Sends thieves all headless into heaven or hell.

*John Taylor, English journalist
and pamphleteer*
Halifax Law, *1630*

*134.12* ✣ Extremity of law is extremity of wrong.

*John Clarke, English clergyman,*
Paroemiologia Anglo-Latina, *1639*

*134.13* ✣ I oft have heard of Lydford Law,
How in the morn they hang and draw,
And sit in judgment after.

*William Browne, English poet*
Lydford Castle, *1644*

**134.14** ❦ Thwackum was for doing justice,
and leaving mercy to Heaven.

*Henry Fielding*
Tom Jones, *1749*

**134.15** ❦ Ambiguity lurks in generality and
may thus become an instrument
of severity.

*Felix Frankfurter*
McComb v. Jacksonville Paper Co.,
*336 U.S. 187, 197 (1949)*

**134.16** ❦ All laws are an attempt to
domesticate the natural ferocity of
the species. We can't stop murder,
but we can make it tougher to get
away with it. We can't stop a banker
from stealing the widow's money,
but we can make it harder for him
to steal it.

*John W. Gardner*
San Francisco Examiner, *July 3, 1974*

# *135.* SEX

**135.1** ❦ It is true from early habit, one must
make love mechanically as one
swims; I once was very fond of both,
but now as I never swim unless
I tumble into the water, I don't
make love till almost obliged.

*Lord Byron, letter, 10 Sept. 1812*
*Published in* Byron's Letters and
Journals, *vol. 2, ed. by Leslie A.
Marchand, 1973–1981*

**135.2** ❦ Sex. In America an obsession. In
other parts of the world a fact.

*Marlene Dietrich*
Marlene Dietrich's ABC, *1962*

**135.3** ❦ However muted its present appearance may be, sexual dominion ob-
tains nevertheless as perhaps the
most pervasive ideology of our culture and provides its most fundamental concept of power.

*Kate Millet*
Sexual Politics, *1970*

**135.4** ❦ Profanation and violation are part
of the perversity of sex, which never
will conform to liberal theories of
benevolence. Every model of
morally or politically correct sexual
behavior *will be subverted,* by
nature's daemonic law.

*Camille Paglia*
Sexual Personae, *1990*

# *136.* SEXUAL HARASSMENT

*136.1* ❦ When courts learn that sexual harassment is as vicious and pervasive and damaging to women in workplaces everywhere as rape is to women guards in male prisons, and as disruptive to production as rape is to prison security, will women be excluded from the workplace altogether?

*Catharine A. MacKinnon*
*"On Exceptionality: Women as Women in Law,"* Feminism Unmodified, *1987*

*136.2* ❦ We need to turn the question around to look at the harasser, not the target. We need to be sure that we can go out and look anyone who is a victim of harassment in the eye and say, "You do not have to remain silent anymore."

*Anita Hill*
New York Times, *1992*

*136.3* ❦ The only women who don't believe that sexual harassment is a real problem in this country are women who have never been in the workplace.

*Cynthia Heimel*
Get Your Tongue Out of My Mouth,
I'm Kissing You Good-Bye!, *1993*

# *137.* SIN

*137.1* ❦ The law grows of sin, and chastises it.

*Proverb*
*Rosalind Fergusson,* The Facts On File
Dictionary of Proverbs, *1983*

*137.2* ❦ The law groweth of sin, and doth punish it.

*John Florio*
Firste Fruites, *1578*

*137.3* ❦ Law can discover sin, but not remove.

*John Milton*
Paradise Lost, *1667*

*137.4* ❦ As the aim of the law is not to punish sins, but is to prevent certain external results. . . .

*Oliver Wendell Holmes*
Commonwealth v. Kennedy, *170*
*Mass. 18, 20 (1897)*

137.5 ❦ I may hate the sin but never the
sinner.

> *Clarence Darrow, 1857–1938*
> *Irving Stone,* Clarence Darrow for
> the Defense, *1941*

137.6 ❦ Is it wise constantly to advertise the
fact that the wages of sin are often
very high?

> *Lord Hartley Shawcross, English lawyer*
> New York Times, *June 19, 1963*

## 138. SLANDER

138.1 ❦ Done to death by slanderous
tongues,
Was the Hero that here lies.

> *Shakespeare*
> Much Ado About Nothing, *III, 1,
> 1598–1599*

138.2 ❦ Slander,
Whose whisper o'er the world's
diameter,
As level as the cannon to his blank,
Transports his poison'd shot.

> *Shakespeare*
> Hamlet, *IV, 1, 1600–1601*

138.3 ❦ Hurl your calumnies boldly;
Something is sure to stick.

> *Francis Bacon*
> De Augmentis Scientiarum, *1623*

138.4 ❦ I hate the man who builds his name
On ruins of another's fame.

> *John Gay*
> Fables, *1727*

138.5 ❦ Squint-eyed Slander.

> *James Beattie, 1735–1803*
> The Judgment of Paris

138.6 ❦ Slander, the foulest whelp of sin.

> *Robert Pollock, Scottish poet*
> Course of Time, *1827*

## 139. SOCIETY

139.1 ❦ I am of a mind that said, "Better is it
to live where nothing is lawful, than
where all things are lawful."

> *Francis Bacon*
> Of Church Controversies, *1589*

139.2 ❦ Society, that first of blessings, brings
with it evils death only can cure.

> *Sophia Lee*
> The Recess, *1785*

*139.3* ❦ One of the eternal conflicts out of which life is made up is that between the effort of every man to get the most he can for his services, and that of society, disguised under the name of capital, to get his services for the least possible return.

*Oliver Wendell Holmes*
Vegelahn v. Guntner, *167 Mass. 92,*
*1081, 44 N.E. 1077 (1896)*

*139.4* ❦ Society is like the air, necessary to breathe, but insufficient to live on.

*George Santayana*
Little Essays, *1920*

*139.5* ❦ I say that all society is founded on the death of men. Certainly the romance of the past is.

*Oliver Wendell Holmes*
Letter to Doctor Wu,
*September 6, 1925*

*139.6* ❦ Inevitably we look upon society, so kind to you, so harsh to us, as an ill-fitting form that distorts the truth; deforms the mind; fetters the will.

*Virginia Woolf*
Three Guineas, *1938*

*139.7* ❦ Civilization is nothing else but the attempt to reduce force to being the last resort.

*Ortega y Gasset, 1883–1955*
*W. H. Auden and Louis Kronenberger,*
The Viking Book of Aphorisms, *1962*

*139.8* ❦ No good society can be unprincipled; and no viable society can be principle-ridden.

*Alexander M. Bickel*
The Least Dangerous Branch, *1962*

*139.9* ❦ Any society that cannot respect its past by granting those who built it financial security faces moral bankruptcy in the future.

*Geraldine A. Ferraro*
Ferraro: My Story, *1985, with*
*Linda Bird Franke*

*139.10* ❦ It is important to recognize the limited ability of the legal system to prescribe and enforce the quality of social arrangements.

*Hillary Rodham Clinton, 1973*
*Judith Warner,* Hillary Clinton, *1993*

*139.11* ❦ I don't think society is ready for a judicial decision that life begins at conception.

*William Dale Young,* Davis v. Davis
*Ellen Alderman and Caroline Kennedy,*
The Right to Privacy, *1995*

*139.12* ❦ We want a society where people are free to make choices, to make mistakes, to be generous and compassionate. This is what we mean by a moral society; not a society where the state is responsible for everything, and no one is responsible for the state.

*Margaret, Lady Thatcher*
Speech, *1977*

**139.13** ❧ At the end of the day we are right to judge a society by the character of the people it produces. That is why statecraft is, inevitably, soulcraft.

*George Will*
*Introduction,* The Pursuit of
Happiness, and Other
Sobering Thoughts, *1978*

**139.14** ❧ Society as a whole benefits immeasurably from a climate in which all persons, regardless of race or gender, may have the opportunity to earn respect, responsibility, advancement and remuneration based on ability.

*Sandra Day O'Connor*
*Peter Huber,* Sandra Day O'Connor,
*1990*

**139.15** ❧ American civilization cannot survive with twelve-year-olds having babies, fifteen-year-olds shooting one another, seventeen-year-olds dying of AIDS, and eighteen-year-olds graduating with diplomas they cannot read.

*Newt Gingrich*
*Commentary, August 1994*

# *140.* SPEECH

**140.1** ❧ An unprincipled orator subverts the laws.

*Latin phrase*
*W. Gurney Benham,* Putnam's
Complete Book of Quotations,
Proverbs and Household Words, *1927*

**140.2** ❧ . . . every man speaks more virtuously than he either thinks or acts.

*Francis Bacon*
The Advancement of Learning, *1605*

**140.3** ❧ Liberty of speech inviteth and provoketh liberty to be used again, and so bringeth much to a man's knowledge.

*Francis Bacon*
The Advancement of Learning, *1605*

**140.4** ❧ Give me the liberty to know, to utter, and to argue freely according to conscience, above all liberties.

*John Milton*
Areopagitica, *1644*

**140.5** ❧ Sweet words are like honey, a little may refresh, but too much gluts the stomach.

*Anne Bradstreet*
*"Meditations Divine and Mortal,"*
*1664*

**140.6** ❧ I disapprove of what you say, but I will defend to the death your right to say it.

*Attributed to Voltaire,* 1694–1778
Bartlett's Familiar Quotations, *15 ed.,*
*1980*

140.7 ❧ Only the suppressed word is dangerous.

> *Ludwig Boerne, German writer*
> An Kundigurg der Wage, *1818*

140.8 ❧ If all mankind minus one were of one opinion and only one person were of the contrary opinion, mankind would be no more justified in silencing that person than he, if he had the power, would be justified in silencing mankind. . . . If the opinion is right, they are deprived of the opportunity of exchanging error for truth; if wrong, they lose, what is almost as great a benefit, the clearer perception and livelier impression of truth, produced by its collision with error.

> *John Stuart Mill*
> On Liberty, *1859*

140.9 ❧ Blessed is the man who, having nothing to say, abstains from giving us wordy evidence of the fact.

> *George Eliot*
> Impressions of Theophrastus Such, *1879*

140.10 ❧ The most stringent protection of free speech would not protect a man from falsely shouting fire in a theater and causing a panic.

> *Oliver Wendell Holmes*
> Schenck v. United States, *249 U.S. 47, 52, 63 L.Ed. 470, 473, 39 S. Ct. 247 (1919)*

140.11 ❧ The question in every case is whether the words are used in such circumstances and are of such a nature as to create a clear and present danger.

> *Oliver Wendell Holmes*
> Schenck v. United States, *249 U.S. 47, 52, 63 L.Ed. 470, 473, 39 S. Ct. 247 (1919)*

140.12 ❧ Eloquence may set fire to reason.

> *Oliver Wendell Holmes*
> Gitlow v. New York, *268 U.S. 652, 673 (1925)*

140.13 ❧ If there be time to expose through discussion the falsehood and fallacies, to avert the evil by the process of education, the remedy to be applied is more speech, not enforced silence.

> *Louis D. Brandeis*
> Whitney v. California, *274 U.S. 357, 377 (1927)*

140.14 ❧ Utterance in a context of violence can lose its significance as an appeal to reason and become part of an instrument of force. Such utterance was not meant to be sheltered by the Constitution.

> *Felix Frankfurter*
> Milk Wagon Drivers Union of Chicago v. Meadowmoor Dairies, *312 U.S. 287, 293 (1941)*

140.15 ❧ Free speech is not to be regulated like diseased cattle and impure butter. The audience . . . that hissed yesterday may applaud today, even for the same performance.

> *William O. Douglas*
> Kingsley Books, Inc. v. Brown, *354 U.S. 436, 447 (1957)*

140.16 ❦ . . . I had rather take my chance that some traitors will escape detection than spread abroad a spirit of general suspicion and distrust, which accepts rumor and gossip in place of undismayed and unintimidated inquiry. I believe that that community is already in process of dissolution where each man begins to eye his neighbor as a possible enemy, where non-conformity with the accepted creed, political as well as religious, is a mark of disaffection; where denunciation, without specification or backing, takes the place of evidence; where orthodoxy chokes freedom of dissent; where faith in the eventual supremacy of reason has become so timid that we dare not enter our convictions in the open lists, to win or lose.

*Learned Hand*
*Irving Dilliard,* The Spirit of Liberty,
*1960*

140.17 ❦ The only way to make sure people you agree with can speak is to support the rights of people you don't agree with.

*Eleanor Holmes Norton*
New York Post, *March 28, 1970*

140.18 ❦ Free speech carries with it some freedom to listen.

*Warren E. Burger*
Richmond Newspapers, Inc. v.
Virginia, *488 U.S. 555, 100 S. Ct.*
*2814, 65 L.Ed.2d 973 (1980)*

140.19 ❦ By placing discretion in the hands of an official to grant or deny a license, such a statute creates a threat of censorship that by its very existence chills free speech.

*Harry A. Blackmun, majority opinion,*
Roe v. Wade; Doe v. Bolton,
*January 22, 1973*
*Daniel B. Baker,* Power Quotes, *1992*

140.20 ❦ [To restrict political spending] is much like allowing a speaker in a public hall to express his views while denying him the use of an amplifying system.

*William H. Rehnquist, majority*
*opinion, June 18, 1986*
*Daniel B. Baker,* Power Quotes, *1992*

140.21 ❦ The First Amendment essentially presumes some level of social equality among people and hence essentially equal social access to the means of expression. In a context of inequality between the sexes, we cannot presume that that is accurate.

*Catharine A. MacKinnon*
*"Linda's Life and Andrea's Work,"*
Feminism Unmodified, *1987*

# *141.* STATE

141.1   Many laws in a state are a bad sign.

*Italian proverb*
W. *Gurney Benham,* Putnam's
Complete Book of Quotations,
Proverbs and Household Words, *1927*

141.2   For this is the bond of men in cities, that all shall rightly preserve the laws.

*Euripides*
Supplices, *c.420* B.C.

141.3   I see that the State in which the law is above the rulers . . . has salvation.

*Plato, 428–c.348* B.C.
Laws

141.4   The more corrupt the state, the more numerous the laws.

*Tacitus*
Annals, *c.116*

141.5   The principal foundations of all states are good laws and good aims; and there cannot be good laws where there are not good aims.

*Machiavelli*
The Prince, *1532*

141.6   Whatever the state permits, it commands.

*Sixtus V, pope, 1520–1590*

141.7   A state, useful and valuable as the contrivance is, is the inferior contrivance of man; and from his native dignity derives all its acquired importance. . . . Let a state be considered as subordinate to the people: But let everything else be subordinate to the state.

*James Wilson*
Chisholm v. Georgia, *2 U.S. (2 Dall.)*
*419, 455 (1793)*

141.8   By a state I mean, a complete body of free persons united together for their common benefit, to enjoy peaceably what is their own, and to do justice to others.

*James Wilson*
Chisholm v. Georgia, *2 U.S. (2 Dall.)*
*419, 455 (1793)*

141.9   Rights that depend on the sufferance of the State are of uncertain tenure. . . .

*Suzanne LaFollette, American feminist*
*and writer*
*"What Is to Be Done,"*
Concerning Women, *1926*

141.10   Federal intrusions into states' criminal trials frustrate both the states' sovereign power to punish offenders and their good faith attempts to honor constitutional rights.

*Sandra Day O'Connor*
Engle v. Isaac, *456 U.S. 107 (1982)*

141.11 ❦ State legislative and administrative bodies are not field offices of the national bureaucracy.

> *Sandra Day O'Connor*
> Federal Energy Regulatory
> Commission v. Mississippi, *456 U.S.*
> *742 (1982)*

# 142. SUCCESS

142.1 ❦ A man may he reputed an able man this year, and yet be a beggar the next: it is a misfortune that happens to many men, and his former reputation will signify nothing.

> *Sir John Holt, English jurist;*
> *Chief Justice*
> Reg. v. Swendsen *(1702), 14 How.*
> *St. Tr. 596*

142.2 ❦ Always bear in mind that your own resolution to succeed is more important than any other one thing.

> *Abraham Lincoln*
> *Letter to Isham Reavis,*
> *November 5, 1855*

142.3 ❦ But I refused to be defeated by the shadow of a bygone day.

> *Sir Edward Clarke, English lawyer*
> The Story of My Life, *1923*

142.4 ❦ . . . no man is unsuccessful who has plenty to do. So long as one can honestly perform his share of the world's work he enjoys the only success it is possible for anybody to achieve.

> *Joseph H. Choate, 1832–1917*
> *Theron G. Strong,* Joseph H. Choate,
> *1917*

142.5 ❦ Fulfillment may fall short of expectation.

> *Benjamin N. Cardozo*
> Walton Water Co. v. Village of
> Walton, *238 N.Y. 46, 50 (1924)*

142.6 ❦ Reputation and learning are akin to capital assets, like the good will of an old partnership. . . . For many, they are the only tools with which to hew a pathway to success.

> *Benjamin N. Cardozo*
> Welch v. Helvering, *290 U.S. 111,*
> *115–16 (1933)*

142.7 ❦ Achievement brings with it its own anticlimax.

> *Agatha Christie*
> They Came to Baghdad, *1951*

*142.8* ❦ Good and bad come mingled always. The long-time winner is the man who is not unreasonably discouraged by persistent streaks of ill fortune nor at other times made reckless with the thought that he is fortune's darling. He keeps a cool head and trusts in the mathematics of probability, or as often said, the law of averages.

*Roy A. Redfield, American lawyer*
Factors of Growth in a Law Practice,
*1962*

# *143.* SUITS

*143.1* ❦ A piece of paper blown by the wind into a law-court may in the end only be drawn out again by two oxen.

*Chinese proverb*
*S. G. Champion,* Racial Proverbs,
*1938*

*143.2* ❦ Winning a cat you lose a cow.

*Chinese proverb*
*William Scarborough,*
Chinese Proverbs, *1875*

*143.3* ❦ Win your lawsuits and lose your money.

*Chinese proverb*
*William Scarborough,*
Chinese Proverbs, *1875*

*143.4* ❦ One goes to court with one lawsuit and comes home with two.

*Danish proverb*
*H. L Mencken,* A New Dictionary
of Quotations, *1946*

*143.5* ❦ I'll make him water his horse at Highgate [I'll sue him and make him take a journey to London].

*English proverb*
*John Ray,* English Proverbs, *1678*

*143.6* ❦ If you've a good case, try to compromise; if a bad one, take it to court.

*French proverb*
*H. L. Mencken,* A New Dictionary
of Quotations, *1946*

143.7 ❦ May you have a lawsuit in which you know you are in the right.

*Gypsy curse*
*W. H. Auden and Louis Kronenberger,*
The Viking Book of Aphorisms, *1962*

143.8 ❦ A lawsuit is a fruit-tree planted in a lawyer's garden.

*Italian proverb*
*H. L. Mencken,* A New Dictionary
of Quotations, *1946*

143.9 ❦ Lawsuits consume time, and money, and rest, and friends.

*Proverb*
*Rosalind Fergusson,* The Facts On File
Dictionary of Proverbs, *1983*

143.10 ❦ Sue a beggar and get a louse.

*Proverb*
*John Clarke,* Paroemiologia
Anglo-Latina, *1639*

143.11 ❦ A happy death is better than a lawsuit.

*Spanish proverb*
*H. L. Mencken,* A New Dictionary of
Quotations, *1946*

143.12 ❦ I can try a lawsuit as well as other men, but the most important thing is to prevent lawsuits.

*Confucius*
Analects, *c.500* B.C.

143.13 ❦ We should make it our aim that there may be no lawsuits at all.

*Confucius, c. 500* B.C.
*Joseph I. Lieberman, "Confucius's
Lesson to Litigants,"*
New York Times, *July 9, 1984*

143.14 ❦ [Hippodamus] maintained that there are three subjects of lawsuits—insult, injury and homicide.

*Aristotle*
Poetics, *c.340* B.C.

143.15 ❦ Suits at court are like winter nights, long and wearisome.

*Thomas Deloney, English ballad writer
and pamphleteer*
Jack of Newbury, *1597*

143.16 ❦ To go to law is for two persons to kindle a fire, at their own cost, to warm others and singe themselves to cinders.

*Owen Felltham, English writer*
Resolves, *1623*

143.17 ❦ For 'tis a low, newspaper, humdrum, lawsuit Country.

*Lord Byron*
Don Juan, *1819–1824*

143.18 ❦ [*Court fool.*] *The plaintiff.*

*Ambrose Bierce*
The Devil's Dictionary, *1906*

143.19 ❦ Fairness and honesty are finding it increasingly hard to prevail in a

judicial system clogged with
frivolous suits.

> *William B. Spann, Jr., American
> lawyer; president, American Bar
> Association*
> Wall Street Journal,
> *June 20, 1978*

143.20 ❧ If a lawyer is worth his salt, has done
his investigation on the suit, talked
to the experts, and has grounds to

believe his client's claims, he should
proceed fullsteam ahead with the
law suit. This will be a deterrent to
any lawyer with an ounce of brains
to stop filing any frivolous suits.

> *Ivan E. Barris, American lawyer; vice
> president, Michigan Bar Association*
> Los Angeles Times, *August 27, 1978*

# *144.* SUPREME COURT

144.1 ❧ Like all human institutions, the
Supreme Court must earn revere
through the test of truth.

> *Felix Frankfurter*
> "Mr. Justice Holmes and the
> Constitution,"
> 41 Harvard Law Review *(1927)*

144.2 ❧ No matter whether th' constitution
follows th' flag or not, th' supreme
court follows th' illiction returns.

> *Finley Peter Dunne, 1867–1936*
> Edward J. Bander, ed., Mr. Dooley on
> the Choice of Law, *1963*

144.3 ❧ . . . on a question of public policy it
is no disrespect to the Supreme
Court to say that the majority of the
Court were mistaken. There is no
reason why five gentlemen of the
Supreme Court should know better

what public policy demands than
five gentlemen of Congress.

> *Louis D. Brandeis,* 1856–1941
> Alpheus Thomas Mason, *Brandeis: A
> Free Man's Life, 1946*

144.4 ❧ Civil liberties had their origin and
must find their ultimate guaranty in
the faith of the people. If that faith
should be lost, five or nine men in
Washington could not long supply
its want.

> *Robert H. Jackson*
> Douglas v. Jeannette, *319 U.S. 157,
> 182 (1943)*

144.5 ❧ This Court is forever adding new
stories to the temples of constitutional law, and the temples have a
way of collapsing when one story
too many is added.

> *Robert H. Jackson*
> Douglas v. Jeannette, *319 U.S. 157,
> 181 (1943)*

**144.6** ❦ The people can change Congress but only God can change the Supreme Court.

*George W. Norris, 1861–1944*
*Laurence J. Peter, Peter's Quotations,*
*1977*

**144.7** ❦ We want a Supreme Court which will do justice under the Constitution—not over it. In our courts we want a government of laws and not of men.

*Franklin Delano Roosevelt, 1882–1945*
*Laurence J. Peter,*
Peter's Quotations, *1977*

**144.8** ❦ By the very nature of the functions of the Supreme Court, each member of it is subject only to his own sense of the trusteeship of what are perhaps the most revered traditions in our national system.

*Felix Frankfurter*
*"'The Administrative Side' of Chief*
*Justice Hughes," 63* Harvard
Law Review, *1, 2 (1949)*

**144.9** ❦ One is entitled to say without qualification that the correlation between prior judicial experience and fitness for the functions of the Supreme Court is zero.

*Felix Frankfurter*
*"Supreme Court in the Mirror of*
*Justice," 105* University of
Pennsylvania Law Review *(1957)*

**144.10** ❦ The difficulty in modification of the Constitution makes the Supreme Court a very powerful body in shaping the course of our civilization. In dealing with the constitutional guarantees of human dignity, it often has the application of the national con-

science in its keeping. It is a sort of diplomatic priesthood.

*F. D. G. Ribble*
*167* Washington and Lee
Law Review *(1957)*

**144.11** ❦ Whenever you put a man on the Supreme Court he ceases to be your friend.

*Harry S Truman*
New York Times, *1959*

**144.12** ❦ It is nine men, nine very human men, participating in a process that can be impressive or disturbing, grave or funny. And contrary to the general impression, the process is more visible than most of what goes on in government.

*Anthony Lewis*
*"Nine Very Human Men,"* New York
Times Magazine, *January 17, 1965*

**144.13** ❦ I have no objection to nine aging gentlemen appointed for life interpreting the law; but I would deprive them of the last word. . . .

*Robert M. Hutchins, president, Center*
*for the Study of Democratic Institutions*
*Interview,* Los Angeles Times,
*June 17, 1969*

**144.14** ❦ It is not likely ever, with human nature as it is, for nine men to agree always on the most important and controversial issues of life. If it ever comes to such a pass I would say that the Supreme Court will have lost its strength and will no longer be a real force in the affairs of our country.

*Earl Warren*
New York Times, *June 23, 1969*

144.15 ❦ The vision of America held and defined by the Warren Court was the noblest and most honorable of them all—a vision of justice in its ultimate form, the form of freedom. It may not have been perfect. . . . But it dared to turn from darkness to face the sun.

*Archibald MacLeish*
New York Post, *October 14, 1969*

144.16 ❦ . . . there are a lot of mediocre judges and people and lawyers, and they are entitled to a little representation [on the U.S. Supreme Court], aren't they? We can't have all Brandeises, Frankfurters, and Cardozos and stuff like that there.

*Roman L. Hruska, American*
*politician; U.S. senator, Nebraska*
Address, U.S. Senate, *reported in the*
New York Times, *March 17, 1970*

144.17 ❦ I can't get alarmed when [the Supreme Court] overrules a prior decision, especially if it is 5–4. Who is to say that five men 10 years ago were right whereas five men looking the other direction today are wrong.

*Harry A. Blackmun*
*Interview,* Los Angeles
Herald-Examiner, *April 20, 1970*

144.18 ❦ One of the first things I was taught when I went through law school was that we should have predictability in our laws. What has happened is that the Supreme Court has too often de-

stroyed predictability . . . because of its assumption of the legislative authority.

*James L. Buckley*
Washington Post,
*January 10, 1971*

144.19 ❦ The Court is the creature of the litigation the lawyers bring to it.

*Earl Warren*
*Interview,*
Washington Post,
*March 15, 1971*

144.20 ❦ . . . the primary role of the Court is to decide cases. From the decision of cases, of course, some changes develop. But to try to create or substantially change civil or criminal procedure, for example, by judicial decision is the worst possible way to do it. The Supreme Court is simply not equipped to do that job properly.

*Warren E. Burger*
*Address, American Law Institute,*
*Washington, D.C., reported in the*
National Observer,
*May 24, 1971*

144.21 ❦ I go onto the Court with deep personal misgivings whether I'll like it. In fact, I rather suppose I won't. . . . But the Supreme Court has a very special place in the life and attitude of any lawyer of my age. . . . For those of my generation, it is a revered institution, the pinnacle of our profession.

*Lewis F. Powell, Jr.*
*Interview,* Washington Post,
*October 24, 1971*

144.22 ❦ At least, my role in presenting the foreign policy statement will have the merit which John G. Johnson found in staying at the bar instead of accepting President Cleveland's offer of a place on the Supreme Court. "I would rather talk to the damned fools," he said, "than listen to them."

*Dean Acheson, 1893–1971*
*Among Friends: Letters of*
*Dean Acheson, 1980*

144.23 ❦ I feel about the future of the United States whenever the president starts out on his travels the way the marshal of the Supreme Court feels about the law when he opens a session of the court. You will recall that he ends up his liturgy by saying, "God save the United States for the Court is now sitting."

*Dean Acheson,1893–1971*
*Among Friends: Letters of*
*Dean Acheson, 1980*

144.24 ❦ The Supreme Court is becoming a wholly owned subsidiary of the rich and powerful, instead of the impartial and compassionate tribunal it has been.

*Arthur M. Schlesinger, Jr.*
*New York Times,*
*October 24, 1972*

144.25 ❦ A man might be a very great liberal in political life and he might be equally as conservative in judicial process because they are entirely different. You see, in the political process, the legislative bodies have the oversight, within Constitutional limits, of everything in their jurisdiction. . . . But the Court is not a self-starter in that respect. It

can never reach out and grab any issue and bring it into court and decide it, no matter how strongly it may feel about the condition it's confronted with.

*Earl Warren*
*New York Times, December 20, 1972*

144.26 ❦ We [on the Supreme Court] never have the hours and the moments to put our feet on the window sills and reflect a bit.

*Harry A. Blackmun*
*San Francisco Examiner,*
*February 13, 1973*

144.27 ❦ The first opinion the Court ever filed had a dissenting opinion. Dissent is a tradition of this court. . . . When someone is writing for the Court, he is hoping to get eight others to agree with him, so many of the majority opinions are rather stultified.

*William O. Douglas*
*Interview, New York Times,*
*October 29, 1973*

144.28 ❦ The Court's great power is its ability to educate, to provide moral leadership.

*William O. Douglas*
*Interview, Time, November 12, 1973*

144.29 ❦ I think it's so easy, because of the pressures here [on the Court] and the demands on our time, for us [justices] to stay in our ivory tower and not get out. I think we are too confined at times. It doesn't seem to me that we should hit the political circuit, but it's good to hear the voices of America from a different podium than the rostrum before us.

*Harry A. Blackmun*
Interview, New York Times,
*July 14, 1975*

144.30 ❦ I have been told that there is no precedent for admitting a woman to practice in the Supreme Court of the United States. The glory of each generation is to make its own precedents. As there was none for Eve in the Garden of Eden, so there need be none for her daughters on entering the colleges, the church, or the courts.

*Belva Lockwood*
*American lawyer*
*and feminist*
*Mary Virginia Fox,* Lady for
the Defense, *1975*

144.31 ❦ The Court is . . . perhaps one of the last citadels of jealously preserved individualism. For the most part, we function as nine, small independent law firms.

*Lewis F. Powell, Jr.*
Los Angeles Times, *July 9, 1978*

144.32 ❦ I do not believe it is the function of the judiciary to step in and change the law because the times have changed. I do well understand the difference between legislating and judging. As a judge, it is not my function to develop public policy.

*Sandra Day O'Connor*
Washington Post, *September 10, 1981*

144.33 ❦ The vast majority of the filings [before the U.S. Supreme Court] are from lawyers who have never been there. They have no intuitive sense of what's worthy, and no one to tell them. So they go to the big court . . . . There's also an ego factor. A lawyer wants a moment of glory.

*A. E. Howard, American educator;*
*professor, University of Virginia*
Washington Post, *September 24, 1982*

144.34 ❦ According to information available to me, and which I had assumed was generally available, for over two years now SCOTUS [the Supreme Court of the United States] has not consisted of nine men. If you have any contradictory information, I would be grateful if you would forward it as I am sure the POTUS [President of the United States], the SCOTUS and the undersigned (the FWOTSC [first woman on the Supreme Court]) would be most interested in seeing it.

*Sandra Day O'Connor*
Letter to the editor, New York Times,
*September 1983*

144.35 ❦ . . . the proper role of the judiciary is one of interpreting and applying the law, not making it. . . .

*Sandra Day O'Connor, at her*
*confirmation hearing*
New York Times, *February 23, 1984*

*144.36* ❧ The Court's only armor is the cloak of public trust; its sole ammunition, the collective hopes of our society.

*Irving R. Kaufman, American jurist*
*"Keeping Politics Out of the Court,"*
New York Times, *December 9, 1984*

*144.37* ❧ Something about our courtroom scares lawyers to death. Some fellows have fainted.

*William J. Brennan, Jr.*
Lawyer's Wit and Wisdom, *edited by*
*Bruce Nash, Allan Zullo and compiled*
*by Kathryn Zullo, 1995*

*144.38* ❧ They were political animals before they got to the Supreme Court, and they don't change when they get there.

*Christine Kellett*
Lawyer's Wit and Wisdom, *edited by*
*Bruce Nash, Allan Zullo and compiled*
*by Kathryn Zullo, 1995*

# *145.* TAXATION

145.1 ❦ To tax and to please, no more than to love and be wise, is not given to men.

*Edmund Burke, 1729–1797*
*36 Harvard Business Review 1,*
*January–February 1958*

145.2 ❦ . . . the power to tax involves the power to destroy; . . .

*John Marshall*
M'Culloch v. Maryland, *17 U.S.*
*(4 Wheat.) 316, 431 (1819)*

145.3 ❦ Of all debts men are least willing to pay the taxes.

*Ralph Waldo Emerson*
*"History," Essays, 1830–1840*

145.4 ❦ The Income-Tax presses more heavily on the possessors of small incomes than on the possessors of large incomes.

*Millicent Garrett Fawcett*
Political Economy for Beginners,
*1870*

145.5 ❦ The liberty of the citizen to do as he likes so long as he does not interfere with the liberty of others to do the same, which has been a shibboleth for some well-known writers, is interfered with . . . by every state or municipal institution which takes his money for purposes thought desirable, whether he likes it or not.

*Oliver Wendell Holmes*
Lochner v. New York, *198 U.S. 45,*
*49 L.Ed. 937, 25 Sup. Ct. 539 (1905)*

145.6 ❦ . . . even the fixing of a tariff rate must be moral.

*Ida Tarbell, American writer*
The Tariff in Our Times, *1906*

145.7 ❦ Taxes are what we pay for civilized society. . . .

*Oliver Wendell Holmes*
Compania General de Tabacos de
Filipinas v. Collector of Internal
Revenue, *275 U.S. 87, 100 (1927)*

145.8 ❦ The power to tax is not the power to destroy while this Court sits.

*Oliver Wendell Holmes*
Panhandle Oil Co. v. Knox, *277*
*U.S. 233 (1928)*

145.9 ❦ Death and taxes and childbirth! There's never any convenient time for any of them!

*Margaret Mitchell*
Gone with the Wind, *1936*

145.10 ❦ As the Chinese poet, Ah Ling, put it (in the wastebasket):
The more the moolah
You make in your racket,
The quicker you go
In a higher bracket.

*Groucho Marx*
Many Happy Returns, *1942*

145.11 ❦ The physical power to get the money does not seem to me a test of the right to tax. Might does not make right even in taxation.

*Robert H. Jackson*
*International Harvester Company v.*
*Wisconsin Department of Taxation,*
*322 U.S. 435, 450 (1944)*

**145.12** ❧ No one has ever suggested that tax exemption has converted libraries, art galleries, or hospitals into arms of the state . . . There is no genuine nexus between tax exemption and establishment of religion.

*Warren E. Burger*
*Walz v. Tax Commission, 397 U.S.*
*664, 90 S. Ct. 1409, 25 L.Ed.2d 697*
*(1970)*

**145.13** ❧ It has been said that one man's loophole is another man's livelihood. Even if this is true, it certainly is not fair, because the loophole-livelihood of those who are reaping undeserved benefits can be the economic noose of those who are paying more than they should.

*Millicent Fenwick*
*Speaking Up, 1982*

**145.14** ❧ The current tax code is a daily mugging.

*Ronald Reagan*
*Speech in Independence, Missouri,*
*May 28, 1985*

**145.15** ❧ We don't pay taxes. Only the little people pay taxes.

*Leona Helmsley*
New York Times, *July 12, 1989*

**145.16** ❧ No matter how much talk we hear about the problems of the tax system or the Internal Revenue Service, we should not forget that our federal tax administration is the envy of the rest of the world.

*Margaret Milner Richardson, U.S.*
*Commissioner of Internal Revenue, to*
*the Ohio Tax Conference*
*Speech, January 16, 1997, in* Vital
Speeches of the Day, *April 1, 1997*

# *146.* TESTIMONY

**146.1** ❧ A man's death-trap may be between his teeth.

*Jewish folk saying*
*Joseph L. Baron,* A Treasury of
Jewish Quotations, *1956*

**146.2** ❧ Half an answer also tells you something.

*Jewish folk*
*saying Joseph L. Baron,*
A Treasury of Jewish Quotations,
*1956*

146.3 ❦ No answer is a type of answer.

*Jewish folk saying*
*Joseph L. Baron,* A Treasury of
Jewish Quotations, *1956*

146.4 ❦ Thou shalt not bear false witness against thy neighbor.

*Old Testament, Exodus, 20:13*

146.5 ❦ If one man says, "You're a donkey," don't mind; if two say so, be worried; if three say so, get a saddle.

*Midrash, Genesis Rabba*

146.6 ❦ Judge a man only by his own deeds and words; the opinions of others can be false.

*Talmud*

146.7 ❦ An oath [in court] is worthless if it affirms the impossible: for instance, that you saw a camel fly.

*Talmud, Shebrioth*

146.8 ❦ Ingenuity is one thing, and simple testimony another, and plain truth, I take it, needs no flowers of speech.

*Sir James Mansfield, English jurist;*
*Chief Justice*
Wilkes v. Wood *(1763), 19*
How. St. Tr. *1176*

146.9 ❦ Every man is bound to leave a story better than he found it.

*Mary Augusta Ward, English*
*social worker*
Robert Elsmer, *1888*

146.10 ❦ Remember that the eyes of God and of her Majesty's police court are upon you.

*London "beak" [magistrate] to a*
*witness who was about to take the oath*
*Marshall Brown,* Wit and Humor of
Bench and Bar, *1899*

# *147.* THOUGHT

147.1 ❦ The thought of man shall not be tried, for the devil himself knoweth not the thought of man.

*Chief Justice Brian*
Great Britain Yearbooks, *17*
Edward IV, *1444*

147.2 ❦ If there be any among us who would wish to dissolve this Union or to change its republican form, let them

stand as monuments of the safety with which error of opinion may be tolerated where reason is left free to combat it.

*Thomas Jefferson*
*First inaugural address,*
*March 4, 1801*

147.3 ✒ A man is bound to be parochial in his practice. . . . But his thinking should be cosmopolitan and detached. He should be able to criticize what he reveres and loves.

*Oliver Wendell Holmes*
*"John Marshall," Speeches, 1913*

147.4 ✒ If there is any principle of the Constitution that more imperatively calls for attachment than any other it is the principle of free thought—not free thought for those who agree with us but freedom for the thought we hate.

*Oliver Wendell Holmes*
*United States v. Schwimmer, 279*
*U.S. 644, 654, 73 L.Ed. 889, 893, 49*
*S. Ct. 448 (1929)*

147.5 ✒ We can have intellectual individualism and the rich cultural diversities that we owe to exceptional minds only at the price of occasional eccentricity and abnormal attitudes.

*Robert H. Jackson*
*Board of Education v. Barnette, 319*
*U.S. 624, 641–42 (1943)*

147.6 ✒ There is no such crime as a crime of thought; there are only crimes of action.

*Clarence Darrow, 1857–1938*
*Arthur Weinberg, ed.,* Attorney
for the Damned, *1957*

147.7 ✒ Much of what Mr. [Vice-President Henry A.] Wallace calls his global thinking is, no matter how you slice it, still globaloney.

*Clare Boothe Luce*
*Speech, 1943*

147.8 ✒ Freedom of speech and freedom of action are meaningless without freedom to think. And there is no freedom of thought without doubt.

*Bergen Evans*
The Natural History of Nonsense,
*1946*

147.9 ✒ There are no dangerous thoughts; thinking itself is dangerous.

*Hannah Arendt*
The Life of the Mind, *vol. 1, 1978*

# 148. TORTS

148.1 ✒ No man should take advantage of his own wrong.

*Legal maxim*

148.2 ✒ Strife produces strife, and injury produces injury.

*Legal maxim*

*148.3* ❦ It makes no difference whether a good man has defrauded a bad man or a bad man defrauded a good man, or whether a good or bad man has committed adultery: the law can look only to the amount of damage done.

> *Aristotle*
> Nicomachean Ethics, *c.340* B.C.

*148.4* ❦ But it is the first function of the law to see that no one shall injure another unless provoked by some wrong.

> *Cicero*
> De Officiis, *45–44* B.C.

*148.5* ❦ The construction of the law does no injury.

> *Sir Edward Coke, 1552–1634*
> *W. Gurney Benham,* Putnam's
> Complete Book of Quotations,
> Proverbs and Household Words, *1927*

*148.6* ❦ The law is an equal dispenser of justice, and leaves none without a remedy, for his right, without his own laches.

> *Justice Vaughn*
> Tustian v. Roper *(1670), Jones's*
> *(Sir Thos.) Rep. 32*

*148.7* ❦ It is a vain thing to imagine a right without a remedy; for want of right and want of remedy are reciprocal.

> *Sir John Holt, English jurist;*
> *Chief Justice*
> Ashby v. White *(1703),*
> *2 Raym. 953*

*148.8* ❦ God forbid that the rights of the innocent should be lost and destroyed by the offence of individuals.

> *Sir John Eardley Wilmot, English*
> *jurist; Chief Justice*
> Mayor etc. of Colchester v. Seaber
> *(1765), 3 Burr. Part IV. (1871)*

*148.9* ❦ Better that an individual should suffer an injury than that the public should suffer an inconvenience.

> *Justice Ashhurst, English jurist*
> Russell v. The Mayor of Devon
> *(1788), 1 T.R. 673*

*148.10* ❦ What a man does in his closet ought not to affect the rights of third persons.

> *Sir Lloyd Kenyon, English jurist;*
> *Lord Chief Justice*
> Outram v. Morewood *(1793),*
> *5 T.R. 123*

*148.11* ❦ The public can have no rights springing from injustice to others.

> *Sir John Romilly, English jurist*
> Walker v. Ware, Hadham, etc. Rail.
> Co. *(1866), 12 Jur. (n.s.) 18*

*148.12* ❦ That great principle of the common law which declares that it is your duty so to use and exercise your own rights as not to cause injury to other people.

> *Sir Charles James Watkin Williams,*
> *English jurist*
> Gray v. North-Eastern Rail. Co.
> *(1883), 48 L.T.R. (n.s.) 905*

**148.13** ❦ A nuisance may be merely a right
thing in the wrong place, like a pig
in the parlor instead of the barnyard.

*George Sutherland, American jurist*
Euclid v. Ambler Co., *272 U.S. 365,*
*388 (1926)*

# *149.* TRIALS

**149.1** ❦ A benefit may be conferred, but not
a disability imposed, on a man in his
absence.

*Talmud, Eruvin*

**149.2** ❦ No man can be declared guilty in his
absence [from the courtroom].

*Talmud, Ketubot*

**149.3** ❦ A man confesses guilt by avoiding
trial.

*Publilius Syrus, Latin writer*
Sententiae, *c. 43* B.C.

**149.4** ❦ It is abominable to convict a man behind his back.

*Sir John Holt, English jurist;*
*Chief Justice*
The Queen v. Dyer *(1703),*
*6 Mod. 41*

**149.5** ❦ All trial is the investigation of
something doubtful.

*Samuel Johnson, 1709–1784*
*Eugene Brussell,* Dictionary of
Quotable Definitions, *1970*

**149.6** ❦ The charge is prepar'd, the lawyers
are met,

The judges all ranged,—a terrible
show!

*John Gay*
Beggar's Opera, *1728*

**149.7** ❦ [*Trial:*] A formal inquiry designed to
prove and put upon record the
blameless characters of judges,
advocates and jurors.

*Ambrose Bierce*
The Devil's Dictionary, *1906*

**149.8** ❦ A trial is still ordeal by battle. For
the broadsword there is the weight
of evidence; for the battle-axe the
force of logic: for the sharp spear,
the blazing gleam of truth; for the
rapier, the quick and flashing knife
of wit.

*Lloyd Paul Stryker, American lawyer*
*Quoted in reports of his death,*
*June 22, 1955*

**149.9** ❦ In criminal trials a state can no more
discriminate on account of poverty
than on account of religion, race or
color.

*Hugo Black*
Griffin v. Illinois, *351 U.S. 12, 19,*
*100 L.Ed. 891, 899, 76 S. Ct. 585,*
*55 ALR2d 1055 (1956)*

149.10 ⚘ In our own lifetime we have seen how essential fair trials are to civilization. The establishment of the modern dictatorships was not the result of a failure of democracy: it was due to a failure of law. There is no "trying" choice between fair trials and free speech, because free speech itself will die if there are no fair trials. For that matter it is almost always the first victim.

*Arthur L. Goodhart, American educator*
*"Fair Trial and Contempt of Court in*
*England," 4 New York Law*
*Journal 1 (June 25, 1964)*

149.11 ⚘ Guilt or innocence become irrelevant in the criminal trial as we flounder in a morass of artificial rules, poorly conceived and often impossible of application. Like the hapless centipede on the flypaper, our efforts to extricate ourselves from this self-imposed dilemma will, if we keep it up, soon have all of us immobilized.

*Warren E. Burger*
*Speech, reported in the*
Washington Post, *May 26, 1969*

149.12 ⚘ I would rather see the law moving toward the day when we could scientifically determine innocence or guilt, instead of having to play the theater that is the trial to see if innocence or guilt can be proved by the cunning of prosecution or defense.

*F. Lee Bailey*
New York Times Magazine,
*September 20, 1970*

149.13 ⚘ Those who think the information brought out at a criminal trial is the truth, the whole truth and nothing but the truth are fools. Prosecuting or defending a case is nothing more than getting to those people who will talk for your side, who will say what you want said. . . . I use the law to frustrate the law. But I didn't set up the ground rules.

*F. Lee Bailey*
New York Times Magazine,
*September 20, 1970*

149.14 ⚘ An incompetent attorney can delay a trial for years or months. A competent attorney can delay one even longer.

*Evelle J. Younger, American lawyer;*
*attorney general, California*
Los Angeles Times, *March 3, 1971*

149.15 ⚘ The criminal trial today is less a test of guilt or innocence than a competition in which the knowledge of the rules, gamesmanship, and, above all, self-control is likely to decide the outcome; a kind of showjumping contest in which the rider for the prosecution must clear every obstacle to succeed.

*Robert Mark, English law enforcement*
*official; commissioner,*
*London Metropolitan Police*
Washington Post, *November 23, 1971*

149.16 ⚘ I'll tell you what my daddy told me after my first trial. I asked him, "How did I do?" He paused and said, "You've got to guard against speaking more clearly than you think."

*Howard H. Baker, Jr.*
Interview, Washington Post,
*June 24, 1973*

149.17 ❧ The institution of trial by jury is almost 1000 years old. But it may not last another 50 unless we can show the public that it is an efficient tool for the administration of justice.

*Irving Kaufman, American jurist*
Reader's Digest, *September 1973*

149.18 ❧ [Preparation] is the be-all of good trial work. Everything else—felicity of expression, improvisational brilliance—is a satellite around the sun. Thorough preparation is that sun.

*Louis Nizer*
Newsweek, *December 11, 1973*

149.19 ❧ Public participation—as in the jury trial—is the cornerstone in the administration of justice and vital to our system of law.

*June L. Tapp, American psychologist*
*Gordon Bermant, "The Notion of*
*Conspiracy Is Not Tasty to Americans,"*
Psychology Today, *May 1975*

149.20 ❧ Law is not justice and a trial is not a scientific inquiry into truth. A trial is the resolution of a dispute.

*Edison Haines*
*Laurence J. Peter,* Peter's Quotations,
*1977*

149.21 ❧ To work effectively, it is important that society's criminal process "satisfy the appearance of justice," . . . and the appearance of justice can best be provided by allowing people to observe it.

*Warren E. Burger*
Richmond Newspapers, Inc. v.
Virginia, *488 U.S. 555, 100 S. Ct.*
*2814, 65 L.Ed.2d 973 (1980)*

149.22 ❧ It is not the bad lawyers who are screwing up the justice system in this country—it's the good lawyers. If you have two competent lawyers on opposite sides, a trial that should take three days could easily last six months.

*Art Buchwald*
*Kenneth Redden,* Modern
Legal Glossary, *1983*

149.23 ❧ If you measured our progress by any normal pretrial schedule, we were proceeding at the goddamned speed of light.

*Marcia Clark*
Without a Doubt, *with Teresa*
*Carpenter, 1997*

# 150. TRUTH

150.1 ❧ The thing is true, according to the law of Medes and Persians, which altereth not.

Old Testament, Daniel *6:12*

150.2 ❧ What is truth? said jesting Pilate; and would not stay for an answer.

*Francis Bacon, 1561–1626*
*"Of Truth,"* Essayes

150.3 ❦ Truth is the same in all persuasions.

*George Jeffreys*
*Titus Oates' Case (1685), 10 How.*
*St. Tr. 1262*

150.4 ❦ It is error alone which needs the support of government. Truth can stand by itself.

*Thomas Jefferson*
*Notes on the State of Virginia, 1785*

150.5 ❦ The greater the truth, the greater the libel.

*William Murray, 1st earl of Mansfield,*
*English jurist; Chief Justice*
*Presiding in 1784, over the king's*
*bench, probably quoting a legal maxim*

150.6 ❦ And, finally, that truth is great and will prevail if left to herself; that she is the proper and sufficient antagonist to error, and has nothing to fear from the conflict unless by human interposition disarmed of her natural weapons, free argument and debate; errors ceasing to be dangerous when it is permitted freely to contradict them.

*Thomas Jefferson*
*Virginia Act for Religious Freedom,*
*1786*

150.7 ❦ What a weak barrier is truth when it stands in the way of an hypothesis!

*Mary Wollstonecraft*
*A Vindication of the Rights*
*of Women, 1792*

150.8 ❦ Presumption means nothing more than, as stated by *Lord Mansfield*, the weighing of probabilities, and deciding, by the powers of common sense, on which side the truth is.

*Sir William Draper Best, Lord*
*Wynford, British jurist; Chief Justice*
*King v. Burdett (1820),*
*1 St. Tr. (n.s.) 114*

150.9 ❦ It was a wise saying, that the farthest way about was often the nearest way home.

*John Mitford, Lord Redesdale,*
*English jurist*
*Corporation of Ludlow v.*
*Greenhouse (1827), 1 Bligh,*
*New Rep. 49*

150.10 ❦ Truth, like all other good things, may be loved unwisely—may be pursued too keenly—may cost too much.

*Sir James Lewis Knight-Bruce,*
*English jurist*
*Pearse v. Pearse (1846), 1 De Gex &*
*Sm. 28, 29*

150.11 ❦ The lawyer's truth is not Truth, but consistency or a consistent.

*Henry David Thoreau*
*Civil Disobedience, 1849*

150.12 ❦ Truth is always in harmony with herself, and is not concerned chiefly to reveal the justice that may consist with wrong doings.

*Henry David Thoreau*
*Civil Disobedience, 1849*

150.13 ❦ Let us accept truth, even when it sur-
prises us and alters our views.

*George Sand, 1863*
*Raphael Ledos de Beafort, ed.,*
Letters of George Sand, *1886*

150.14 ❦ Truth and falsehood, it has been well
said, are not always opposed to each
other like black and white, but
oftentimes, and by design, are made
to resemble each other so as to be
hardly distinguishable; just as the
counterfeit thing is counterfeit
because it resembles the genuine
thing.

*Sir Anthony Cleasby, English jurist*
Johnson v. Emerson *(1871), L.R. 6*
*Ex. Ca. 357*

150.15 ❦ But O the truth, the truth!
The many eyes
That look on it! the diverse things
they see.

*George Meredith*
*"The Ballad of Fair Ladies in Revolt,"*
*c.1887*

150.16 ❦ Truth is the only safe ground to
stand upon.

*Elizabeth Cady Stanton*
The Woman's Bible, *1895*

150.17 ❦ I used to say, when I was young, that
truth was the majority vote of that
nation that could lick all others.

*Oliver Wendell Holmes*
*"Natural Law,"* Collected
Legal Papers, *1920*

150.18 ❦ No poet ever interpreted nature as
freely as a lawyer interprets the truth.

*Jean Giraudoux, 1882–1944*
*Laurence J. Peter,* Peter's Quotations,
*1977*

150.19 ❦ For the trouble with lying and
deceiving is that their efficiency
depends entirely upon a clear notion
of the truth that the liar and
deceiver wishes to hide. In this
sense, truth, even if it does not
prevail in public, possesses an
ineradicable primacy over all
falsehoods.

*Hannah Arendt*
*"Lying in Politics,"* Crises of the
Republic, *1972*

150.20 ❦ All sides in a trial want to hide at
least some of the truth. The defendant wants to hide the truth because
he's generally guilty. The defense attorney's job is to make sure the jury
does not arrive at that truth. The
prosecution is perfectly happy to
have the truth of guilt come out,
but it, too, has a truth to hide: it
wants to make sure the process by
which the evidence was obtained is
not truthfully presented because, as
often as not, that process will raise
questions.

*Alan M. Dershowitz*
*Interview,* U.S. News & World
Report, *August 9, 1982*

150.21 ❦ There is something wonderful in
seeing a wrong-headed majority
assailed by truth.

*John Kenneth Galbraith,*
*U.S. economist*
Guardian, *London, July 28, 1989*

150.22 ❦ The speedy trial statute is a mathematical calculation that renders the quest for truth irrelevant.

*Judge Harold J. Rothwax*
Guilty: The Collapse of
Criminal Justice, *1996*

150.23 ❦ They don't want the truth; they want to hide evidence.

*Marcia Clark*
Without a Doubt, *with Teresa
Carpenter, 1997*

# 151. TYRANNY

151.1 ❦ The more by law, the less by right.

*Danish proverb*
H. L. Mencken, A New Dictionary of
Quotations, *1946*

151.2 ❦ [A king] is above his laws.

*Proverb*
"Jack Cade's Proclamation," *in James
Gairdner,* Three Fifteenth-Century
Chronicles *(1460), Camden Society
Publications: London, 1838*

151.3 ❦ The purpose of law is to prevent the strong always having their way.

*Ovid,* 43 B.C.–A.D. 17
Fasti, *c.8*

151.4 ❦ Wherever Law ends, Tyranny begins.

*John Locke*
Second Treatise of Government, *1690*

151.5 ❦ The voice of nations and the course of things
Allow that laws superior are to kings.

*Daniel Defoe*
The True-Born Englishman, *1701*

151.6 ❦ There is no crueler tyranny than that which is perpetuated under the shield of law and in the name of justice.

*de Montesquieu,* 1689–1755
Laurence J. Peter, *Peter's Quotations,
1977*

151.7 ❦ God forbid, my lords, that there should be a power in this country of measuring the civil rights of the subject by his moral character, or by any other rule but the fixed laws of the land! . . . Unlimited power is apt to corrupt the minds of those who possess it; and this I know, my lords, that where law ends, tyranny begins!

*William Pitt*
"The English Constitution," *speech
delivered in the House of Lords in reply
to Lord Mansfield in the
Case of Wilkes, January 9, 1770*

151.8 ❦ One law for the lion and ox is oppression.

*William Blake*
The Marriage of Heaven and Hell,
*1790*

*151.9* ❦ O Paddy dear, an' did ye hear the
      news that's goin' round?
    The shamrock is by law forbid to
      grow on Irish ground!
    No more St. Patrick's Day we'll
      keep, his color can't be seen,
    For there's a cruel law agin the
      wearin' o' the Green!

> *Anonymous*
> *"The Wearing O' the Green," c.1795*

*151.10* ❦ The Law is the true embodiment
    Of everything that's excellent.
    It has no kind of fault or flaw,
    And I, my lords, embody the Law.

> *Sir W. S. Gilbert*
> Iolanthe, *1882*

*151.11* ❦ A crown and justice? Night and day
    Shall first be yoked together.

> *Algernon Charles Swinburne*
> Marino Faliero, *1885*

*151.12* ❦ Legality and oppression are not
    unknown to run hand in hand.

> *Sir Henry Hawkins, Baron Brampton,*
> *English jurist*
> Roberts v. Jones; Willey v. Great
> Northern Railway Co. *(1891), L.R. 2*
> *Q.B. (1891)*

*151.13* ❦ A good deal of tyranny goes by the
    name of protection.

> *Crystal Eastman*
> Equal Rights, *1924*

*151.14* ❦ This testimony of centuries, in
    governments of varying kinds over
    populations of different races and
    beliefs, stood as proof that physical
    and mental torture and coercion
    had brought about the tragically
    unjust sacrifices of some who were
    the noblest and most useful of their
    generations.

> *Hugo Black*
> Chambers v. Florida, *309 U.S. 227,*
> *84 L.Ed. 716,*
> *60 Sup. Ct. 472 (1940)*

*151.15* ❦ . . . it is from petty tyrannies that
    large ones take root and grow. This
    fact can be no more plain than
    when they are imposed on the most
    basic rights of all. Seedlings planted
    in that soil grow great and, growing,
    break down the foundations of
    liberty. . . .

> *Wiley B. Rutledge*
> Thomas v. Collins, *323 U.S. 516,*
> *89 L.Ed. 430,*
> *65 Sup. Ct. 315 (1944)*

*151.16* ❦ Tyranny and anarchy are alike in-
    compatible with freedom, security,
    and the enjoyment of opportunity.

> *Jeane Kirkpatrick*
> *Speech, Third Committee of United*
> *Nations General Assembly,*
> *November 24, 1981*

# *152.* USURY

*152.1*  Usury is murder.

*Hebrew proverb*

*152.2*  To borrow upon Usury bringeth on Beggary.

*Proverb*
Thomas Fuller, Gnomologia, *1732*

*152.3*  The usurer is as deaf as a doornail.

*Thomas Wilson*
A Discourse upon Usury, *1572*

*152.4*  These eyght thynges are rare times seene . . . an old usurer without money. . . .

*John Florio*
Firste Fruites, *1578*

*152.5*  A legal thief, a bloodless murderer, A fiend incarnate, a false usurer.

*Joseph Hall, English clergyman;*
*bishop of Norwich*
Virgidemarium, *IV, 1598*

*152.6*  Usurers live by the fall of young heirs, as swine by the dropping of acorns.

*George Wilkins*
The Miseries of Inforst Marriage,
*1607*

*152.7*  To speak of a usurer at the table mars the wine.

*George Herbert*
Jacula Prudentum, *1640*

*152.8*  There are three forms of usury: interest on money, rent of land and houses, and profit in exchange. Whoever is in receipt of any of these is a usurer.

*Benjamin R. Tucker*
Instead of a Book, *1893*

*152.9*  Man was lost if he went to a usurer, for the interest ran faster than a tiger upon him. . . .

*Pearl S. Buck*
*"The Frill,"* First Wife and
Other Stories, *1933*

# *153.* VICTIMS

**153.1** ❦ There's no weapon that slays
Its victim so surely (if well aimed) as
praise.

*Edward Robert Bulwer-Lytton,*
*1st earl of Lytton*
Lucile, *1860*

**153.2** ❦ The first thing to be done by a biographer in estimating character is to examine the stubs of the victim's cheque books.

*Silas Weir Mitchell,* 1829–1891
*Harvey William Cushing,* Life of
Sir William Osler, *1925*

**153.3** ❦ The rain it raineth on the just
And also on the unjust fella:

But chiefly on the just, because
The unjust steals the just's umbrella.

*Charles Bowen*
*Thad Stem, Jr. and*
*Alan Butler,* Sam Ervin's
Best Short Stories, *1973*

**153.4** ❦ Do you think there could be
something like victims without
crimes?

*Rosellen Brown, American writer*
*"A Letter to Ismael in the*
*Grave,"* Street Games, *1974*

**153.5** ❦ People find victimhood appealing
because they believe it absolves them
of their own misdeeds; it imbues
them with a sense of righteousness.

*Wendy Kaminer, lawyer and social critic*
It's All the Rage, *1995*

# *154.* WAR

154.1 ❧ Where drums beat, laws are silent.

> *Proverb*
> *Rosalind Fergusson,* The Facts On File
> Dictionary of Proverbs, *1983*

154.2 ❧ But we fight for our lives and our laws.

> *Old Testament, 1 Maccabees 3:21*

154.3 ❧ Go, tell the Spartans, thou who
>        passest by,
> That here obedient to their laws
>        we lie.

> *Simonides of Ceos, 556–c.468* B.C.
> *J. M. Cohen and M. J. Cohen,*
> The Penguin Dictionary
> of Quotations, *1960*

154.4 ❧ The law speaks too softly to be heard amid the din of arms.

> *Caius Marius,* c.157–86 B.C
> "Caius Marius" Plutarch, Lives

154.5 ❧ Hotspur: The arms are fair,
> When the intent of bearing them is
> just.

> *Shakespeare*
> I Henry IV, V, 2, *1597–1598*

154.6 ❧ Religious cannons, civil laws are
>        cruel;
> Then what should war be?

> *Shakespeare*
> Timon of Athens, *1607–1608*

154.7 ❧ Force and fraud are in war the two cardinal virtues.

> *Thomas Hobbes*
> Leviathan, *1651*

154.8 ❧ Who overcomes by force hath overcome but half his foe.

> *John Milton*
> Paradise Lost, *1667*

154.9 ❧ Force first made conquest, and that conquest law.

> *Alexander Pope*
> An Essay on Man, *1733*

154.10 ❧ One to destroy, is murder by the law,
> And gibbets keep the lifted hand
>        in awe;
> To murder thousands takes a
>        specious name,
> War's glorious art, and gives
>        immortal fame.

> *Edward Young, 1683–1765*
> Love of Fame

154.11 ❧ Ez fer war, I call it murder—
> Ther you hev it plain and flat;
> I don't want to go no further
> Than my testament fer that.

> *James Russell Lowell*
> The Biglow Papers, *1848*

154.12 ❧ Follow law, and forms of law, as far as convenient.

*Abraham Lincoln*
*Instructions to Ulysses S. Grant,*
*October 21, 1862*

154.13 ❧ We are not interested in the possibilities of defeat.

*Queen Victoria*
*Letter to Arthur J. Balfour,*
*December 1899*

154.14 ❧ A bayonet in the hands of one man is no better than in the hand of another. It is the bayonet that is evil and all of its fruits are bad.

*Clarence Darrow*
Resist Not Evil, *1903*

154.15 ❧ To call war the soil of courage and virtue is like calling debauchery the soil of love.

*George Santayana*
The Life of Reason: Reason
in Society, *1905–1906*

154.16 ❧ And lo, there dawns another, swift and stern,
When on the wheels of wrath, by Justice' token,
Breaker of God's own Peace, you shall in turn
Yourself be broken.

*Sir Owen Seaman*
*English humorist and author*
*"To the German Kaiser,"* Punch,
*August 19, 1914*

154.17 ❧ [E]stablish new values, to create an overpowering sense of the sacred-

ness of life, so that war would be unthinkable.

*Crystal Eastman, between 1914*
*and 1917*
*Dawn Bradley Berry,*
The 50 Most Influential Women in
American Law, *1996*

154.18 ❧ The appalling thing about war is that it kills all love of truth.

*Georg Brandes*
*Letter to Georges Clemenceau,*
*March 1915*

154.19 ❧ As a woman I can't go to war, and I refuse to send anyone else.

*Jeannette Rankin, 1941*
*Hannah Josephson,* Jeannette Rankin,
*1974*

154.20 ❧ I can not believe that war is the best solution. No one won the last war, and no one will win the next.

*Eleanor Roosevelt, letter to*
*Harry S Truman, 1948*
*Joseph P. Lash,* Eleanor: The Years
Alone, *1972*

154.21 ❧ In the long course of history, having people who understand your thought is much greater security than another submarine.

*J. William Fulbright*
The New Yorker, *May 10, 1958*

154.22 ❧ You can no more win a war than you can win an earthquake.

*Jeannette Rankin, c. 1941*
*Hannah Josephson,* Jeannette Rankin,
*1974*

*154.23* ❧ If men recognize no law superior to their desires, then they must fight when their desires collide.

> *R. H. Tawney*
> Laurence J. Peter, Peter's Quotations, *1977*

*154.24* ❧ You cannot shake hands with a clenched fist.

> *Indira Gandhi, 1917–1984*

*154.25* ❧ The calamity of war, wherever, whenever and upon whomever it descends, is a tragedy for the whole of humanity.

> *Raisa M. Gorbachev*
> I Hope, *1991*

*154.26* ❧ War has crossed out the day and replaced it with horror, and now horrors are unfolding instead of days.

> *Zlata Filipovic*
> Zlata's Diary, *1994*

*154.27* ❧ We have war when at least one of the parties to a conflict wants something more than it wants peace.

> *Jeane J. Kirkpatrick*
> Reader's Digest, *1994*

*154.28* ❧ Force, and the credible possibility of its use, are essential to defend our vital interests and to keep America safe. But force alone can be a blunt instrument, and there are many problems it cannot solve.

> *Madeleine Albright*
> Speech, February 7, *1997*; Vital Speeches of the Day, *April 15, 1997*

# *155.* WITNESSES

*155.1* ❧ Woe to the dough that the baker testifies against.

> *Babylonian Talmud, Pesahim*

*155.2* ❧ A witness may not act as a judge.

> *Talmud, Bava Qamma*

*155.3* ❧ These are ineligible to serve as judges or witnesses: a gambler, a usurer, and a dealer in forbidden produce.

> *Talmud, Sanhedrin*

*155.4* ❧ One eye-witness is worth more than ten who tell what they have heard.

> *Plautus, c.254–184 B.C.*
> Truculentus

*155.5* ❧ The innocent man on trial fears fortune, but not a witness.

> *Publilius Syrus, Latin writer*
> Sententiae, *c.43* B.C.

155.6 ❦ Witnesses, not hired in any honest fashion, sell their perjuries.

*Ovid, 43 B.C.–?A.D. 18*
*Amores*

155.7 ❦ Witnesses may lie, either be mistaken themselves, or wickedly intend to deceive others . . . but . . . circumstances cannot lie.

*Richard Mounteney,*
*Irish jurist*
*Annesley v. Lord Anglesea (1743),*
*17 How. St. Tr. 1430*

155.8 ❦ . . . the lawyer's vacation is the space between the question put to a witness and his answer!

*Rufus Choate, 1799–1859*
*Samuel Gilman Brown, The Works*
*of Rufus Choate, 1862*

155.9 ❦ We better know there is a fire whence we see much smoke rising than we could know it by one or two witnesses swearing to it. The witnesses may commit perjury, but the smoke cannot.

*Abraham Lincoln*
*Unsent letter to J. R. Underwood and*
*Henry Grider, October 26, 1864*

155.10 ❦ Wherever a man commits a crime, God finds a witness. . . . Every secret crime has its reporter.

*Ralph Waldo Emerson*
*"Natural Religion," Essays, c.1875*

155.11 ❦ And summed it so well that it came to far more
Than the witness ever had said!

*Lewis Carroll*
*The Hunting of the Snark, 1876*

# 156. WOMEN

156.1 ❦ Men make laws, women make manners.

*Guibert, French writer, 18th century*
*W. Gurney Benham, Putnam's*
*Complete Book of Quotations,*
*Proverbs and Household Words, 1927*

156.2 ❦ If particular care is not paid attention to the ladies, we are determined to foment a rebellion, and will not hold ourselves bound by any laws in which we have no voice, no representation.

*Abigail Adams*
*Letter to John Adams, March 31, 1776*

156.3 ❦ I cannot say that I think that you are very generous to the ladies; for, whilst you are proclaiming peace and goodwill to men, emancipating all nations, you insist on retaining an absolute power over wives.

*Abigail Adams*
*Letter to John Adams, May 7, 1776*

**156.4** ❦ . . . there is no country in the world where there is so much boasting of the "chivalrous" treatment she enjoys. . . . In short, indulgence is given her as a substitute for justice.

*Harriet Martineau, American writer*
*"Women," Society in America, 1837*

**156.5** ❦ . . . all laws which prevent women from occupying such a station in society as her conscience shall dictate, or which place her in a position inferior to that of man, are contrary to the great precept of nature, and therefore of no force or authority.

*Elizabeth Cady Stanton*
History of Woman Suffrage, *1881*

**156.6** ❦ . . . such laws as conflict, in any way, with the true and substantial happiness of women, are contrary to the great precept of nature and of no validity, for this is "superior in obligation to any other."

*Elizabeth Cady Stanton*
History of Woman Suffrage, *1881*

**156.7** ❦ Thus far women have been the mere echoes of men. Our laws and constitutions, our creeds and codes, and the customs of social life are all of masculine origin. The true woman is as yet a dream of the future.

*Elizabeth Cady Stanton*
*Speech, International Council of*
*Women, 1888*

**156.8** ❦ Nature gave women too much power; the law gives them too little.

*Will Henry, American political adviser*
*and columnist,* 1890–1970
Reader's Digest, *August 1971*

**156.9** ❦ True, the movement for women's rights has broken many old fetters, but it has also forged new ones.

*Emma Goldman*
*"The Tragedy of Women's*
*Emancipation," Anarchism and Other*
Essays, *1911*

**156.10** ❦ The basic freedom of the world is woman's freedom.

*Margaret Sanger*
Woman and the New Race, *1920*

**156.11** ❦ It's hard for a mere man to believe that women don't have equal rights.

*Dwight D. Eisenhower*
*Speech, August 7, 1957*

**156.12** ❦ To conclude that women are unfitted to the task of our historic society seems to me the equivalent of closing male eyes to female facts.

*Lyndon Baines Johnson*
*On swearing-in of women appointees,*
*April 13, 1964*

**156.13** ❦ We're half the people, we should be half the congress.

*Jeannette Rankin, 1966*
*Hannah Josephson,* Jeannette Rankin,
*1974*

156.14 ✾ Of my two "handicaps," being female put many more obstacles in my path than being black.

*Shirley Chisholm*
Unbought and Unbossed, *1970*

156.15 ✾ On the road to equality there is no better place for blacks to detour around American values than in forgoing its example in the treatment of its women and the organization of its family life.

*Eleanor Holmes Norton*
*"For Sadie and Maude," Robin*
*Morgan, ed.,* Sisterhood Is Powerful,
*1970*

156.16 ✾ It is horrible to listen to men in black togas having discussions about your morals, your cystitis, your feelings, your womb, the way you straddled your legs.

*Gigliola Pierobon, Italian feminist*
*"Gazette News: Abortion in Italy,"*
Ms., *October 1973*

156.17 ✾ The controversy between rule of law and rule of men was never relevant to women—because, along with juveniles, imbeciles and other classes of legal nonpersons, they had no access to law except through men.

*Freda Adler*
Sisters in Crime, *1975*

156.18 ✾ Men are generally more law-abiding than women . . . Women have a feeling that since they didn't make the rules, the rules have nothing to do with them.

*Diane Johnson*
Lying Low, *1978*

156.19 ✾ . . . classifications based on sex, like classification based on race, alienage, or national origin, are inherently suspect, and must therefore be subjected to strict judicial scrutiny.

Frontiero v. Richardson, *411 U.S.*
*677 (1973)*

156.20 ✾ The Constitution requires that Congress treat similarly situated persons similarly, not that it engage in gestures of superficial equality.

*William H. Rehnquist*
Rostker v. Goldberg, *June 25, 1981*

156.21 ✾ The law sees and treats women the way men see and treat women.

*Catharine MacKinnon*
*"Viewpoint: Feminism, Marxism,*
*Method, and the State: Towards*
*Feminist Jurisprudence,"* Signs, *1983*

156.22 ✾ If women are to restrict our demands for change to spheres we can trust, spheres we already control, there will not be any.

*Catharine A. MacKinnon*
*Afterword,* Feminism Unmodified,
*1987*

156.23 ✾ Whatever class and race divergences exist, top cats are tom cats.

*Elizabeth Janeway*
Improper Behavior, *1987*

156.24 ✾ When asked what it felt like to have gotten her job because she was a woman, Barbara Babcock developed a stock reply: "It feels a lot better than not getting it because I am a woman."

*Deborah L. Rhode*
Justice and Gender, *1989*

156.25 ❦ When Clara Shortridge Foltz, the first woman lawyer on the Pacific coast, was leaving court one day around 1885, her losing opponent snapped that a woman should be home taking care of her children. Foltz flashed back: "A woman would be better off almost anywhere than home raising men like you."

*Sandra Day O'Connor*
*Forword (First Women: Contribution*
*of American Women to the Law), 28*
Valparaiso Law Review *xiii (1994)*

156.26 ❦ Who can claim to represent the interests of women when women themselves disagree about what those interests are . . .

*Deborah L. Rhode*
*"Feminism and the State," 107*
Harvard Law Review *1181 (1994)*

156.27 ❦ Questions surrounding social development, especially of women, are at the center of our political and economic challenges.

*Hillary Rodham Clinton*
*"Investing in Sisterhood: An Agenda*
*for the World's Women,"*
Washington Post, *1995*

156.28 ❦ I do think that being the second woman is wonderful, because it is a sign that being a woman in a place of importance is no longer extraordinary.

*Ruth Bader Ginsberg, remarking to the*
*ABA Journal on her appointment as a*
*Supreme Court Justice*
*Dawn Bradley Berry,* The 50 Most
Influential Women in American Law,
*1996*

156.29 ❦ Being called a bitch by some old-time gender bigot doesn't bother me. In context, it's a compliment. It means I've stood up to him, I haven't let him have his way, and now he's throwing his little tantrum. *But from women?*

*Marcia Clark*
Without a Doubt, *with Teresa*
*Carpenter, 1997*

156.30 ❦ A lot of skills women have are undervalued and rainmaking is overvalued. The woman lawyer in an average professional setting in an average city still needs a lot of support.

*Estelle H. Rogers*
*"Back to the Future,"* Perspectives,
*Fall 1997*

# *157.* WORDS

157.1 ❦ The thought hath good lips and the quill a good tongue.

*Italian proverb*
*W. Gurney Benham,* Putnam's Complete Book of Quotations, Proverbs
and Household Words, *1927*

*157.2* ❧ Then words came like a fall of winter snow.

> *Homer*
> Iliad, *c.8th century* B.C.

*157.3* ❧ Usage, in which lies the decision, the law, and the norm of speech.

> *Horace*
> Ars Poetica, *13* B.C.

*157.4* ❧ By men's words we know them.

> *Marie de France,* 12th century
> Medieval Fables of Marie de France,
> *Jeannette Beer, tr., 1981*

*157.5* ❧ All laws are promulgated for this end: that every man may know his duty; and therefore the plainest and most obvious sense of the words is that which must be put on them.

> *Sir Thomas More*
> Utopia, *1516*

*157.6* ❧ The heaviest thing that is, is one Et cetera.

> *John Florio*
> Firste Fruites, *1578*

*157.7* ❧ There must be no departure from the words of the law.

> *Sir Edward Coke, 1552–1634*
> *W. Gurney Benham,* Putnam's
> Complete Book of Quotations,
> Proverbs and Household Words, *1927*

*157.8* ❧ We can judge of the intent of the parties only by their words.

> *Sir John Powell, English jurist*
> Idle v. Cooke *(1704), 2 Raym. 1149*

*157.9* ❧ Words pass from men lightly.

> *Sir John Eardley Wilmot, English jurist;*
> *chief justice*
> Pillans v. Van Mierop *(1764), 3 Burr.*
> *Part IV. 1671*

*157.10* ❧ Most of the disputes in the world arise from words.

> *William Murray, 1st earl of Mansfield,*
> *English jurist; Chief Justice*
> Morgan v. Jones *(1773), Lofft. 177*

*157.11* ❧ Language, like all art, becomes pale with years; words and figures of speech lose their contagious and suggestive power.

> *George Santayana*
> The Life of Reason, *1905–1906*

*157.12* ❧ The search is for the just word, the happy phrase, that will give expression to the thought, but somehow the thought itself is transfigured by the phrase when found.

> *Benjamin N. Cardozo*
> The Growth of the Law, *1924*

*157.13* ❧ We seek to find peace of mind in the word, the formula, the ritual. The hope is an illusion.

> *Benjamin N. Cardozo*
> The Growth of the Law, *1924*

**157.14** ❦ In the case at bar, also, the logic of words should yield to the logic of realities.

*Louis D. Brandeis*
Di Santo v. Pennsylvania, *273 U.S.*
*34, 47 S. Ct. 267, 71 L.Ed. 524*
*(1927)*

**157.15** ❦ Words after all are symbols, and the significance of the symbols varies with the knowledge and experience of the mind receiving them.

*Benjamin N. Cardozo*
Cooper v. Dasher, *290 U.S. 106, 54*
*S. Ct. 6, 78 L.Ed. 203 (1933)*

**157.16** ❦ We live by symbols, and what shall be symbolized by any image of the sight depends upon the mind of him who sees it.

*Oliver Wendell Holmes*
*"John Marshall," Speeches, 1934*

**157.17** ❦ . . . words acquire scope and function from the history of events which they summarize.

*Felix Frankfurter*
Phelps Dodge Corporation v.
National Labor Relations Board, *313*
*U.S. 177, 61 S. Ct. 845, 133 ALR*
*1217, 85 L.Ed. 1271 (1941)*

**157.18** ❦ Words are not pebbles in alien juxtaposition.

*Learned Hand*
NLRB v. Federbush Co., Inc., *1941*

**157.19** ❦ Words, especially those of a constitution, are not to be read with such stultifying narrowness.

*Harlan F. Stone*
United States v. Classic, *313 U.S.*
*299, 85 L.Ed. 1368, 61 Sup. Ct. 1031*
*(1941)*

**157.20** ❦ There is no surer way to misread any document than to read it literally.

*Learned Hand*
Guiseppi v. Walling, *324 U.S. 244,*
*65 S. Ct. 605, 89 L.Ed. 921 (1944)*

**157.21** ❦ Words are chameleons, which reflect the color of their environment.

*Learned Hand*
Cabell v. Markham, *1945*

**157.22** ❦ In law also the emphasis makes the song.

*Felix Frankfurter*
Bethlehem Co. v. State Board, *330*
*U.S. 767, 780 (1947)*

**157.23** ❦ Law has always been unintelligible, and I might say that perhaps it ought to be. And I will tell you why, because I don't want to deal in paradoxes. It ought to be unintelligible because it ought to be in words— and words are utterly inadequate to deal with the fantastically multiform occasions which come up in human life. . . .

*Learned Hand*
*"Thou Shalt Not Ration Justice,"*
Brief Case, *November 4, 1951*

157.24 ❦ Man does not live by words alone, despite the fact that sometimes he has to eat them.

*Adlai Stevenson*
*Speech, September 5, 1952*

157.25 ❦ One must be chary of words because they turn into cages.

*Viola Spolin*
*In article by Barry Hyams,*
*Los Angeles Times, May 26, 1974*

157.26 ❦ Most conduct is expressive as well as active; words are as often tantamount to acts as they are vehicles for removed cerebration.

*Catharine A. MacKinnon*
*"The Sexual Politics of the First Amendment," Feminism Unmodified,*
*1987*

157.27 ❦ This has been at the heart of every women's initiative for civil equality from suffrage to the Equal Rights Amendment: the simple notion that law—only words, words that set conditions as well as express them, words that are their own kind of art, words in power, words in authority, words in life—respond to women as well as men.

*Catharine A. MacKinnon*
*Afterword, Feminism Unmodified,*
*1987*

157.28 ❦ It took man thousands of years to put words down on paper, and his lawyers still wish he wouldn't.

*Mignon McLaughlin*
*Lawyer's Wit and Wisdom, edited by*
*Bruce Nash, Allan Zullo and compiled*
*by Kathryn Zullo, 1995*

# SELECTIVE BIBLIOGRAPHY

Abramson, Leslie, and Richard Flaste. *The Defense Is Ready.* New York: Simon Schuster, 1997.

Adams, Abigail. *Letters to Mrs. Adams.* Boston: Charles and James Brown, 1840.

Adams, Franklin Pierce. *F.P.A.'s Book of Quotations.* New York: Funk and Wagnalls, 1952.

Addams, Jane. Introduction to *Democracy and Social Ethics.* New York: Macmillan, 1908.

Adler, Freda. *Sisters in Crime.* New York: McGraw-Hill, 1975.

Alderman, Ellen, and Caroline Kennedy. *The Right to Privacy.* New York: Knopf, 1995.

Allen, Florence Ellinwood. *This Constitution of Ours.* New York: Putnam, 1940.

Allen, Woody, *Without Feathers.* New York: Random House, 1975.

Andrews, William, ed. *The Lawyer in History, Literature, and Humour.* London: Wm. Andrews and Co., 1896.

Arendt, Hannah "Civil Disobedience." In *Crisis of the Republic.* New York: Harcourt Brace Jovanovich, 1972.

———. *Eichmann in Jerusalem.* New York: Viking Press, 1963.

———. *The Life of the Mind.* Vol. 1. New York: Harcourt Brace Jovanovich, 1987.

Auden, W. H., ed., and Louis Kronenberger. *The Viking Book of Aphorisms: A Personal Selection.* New York: Viking Press, 1962, 1966.

Baker, Daniel B. *Power Quotes.* Detroit: Visible Ink, 1992.

Bankier, Joanna, and Deirdre Lashgari, eds. *Women Poets of the World.* New York: Macmillan; London: Collier Macmillan, 1983.

Baron, Joseph L., ed. *A Treasury of Jewish Quotations.* South Brunswick, N.J.: A.S. Barnes and Co., 1956, 1965.

Barrows, Signey Biddle. *Mayflower Madam.* New York: Arbor House, 1986.

Bartlett, John. *Familiar Quotations: A Collection of Passages, Phrases and Proverbs Traced to Their Sources in Ancient and Modern Literature.* Boston: Little, Brown and Company, 1948.

Beeton, Isabella. *The Book of Household Management.* London: S.O. Beeton, 1861.

Behn, Aphra. *The Rover.* Lincoln: University of Nebraska Press, 1967.

Benedict, Agnes E. *Progress to Freedom.* New York: G.P. Putnam's Sons, 1942.

Benham, W. Gurney. *Putnam's Complete Book of Quotations, Proverbs and Household Words.* New York: G.P. Putnam's Sons, 1927.

Berry, Dawn Bradley. *The 50 Most Influential Women in American Law.* Los Angeles: Lowell House, 1996.

Bickel, Alexander M. *The Least Dangerous Branch.* Indianapolis: Bobbs-Merril, 1962.

Bloom, Allan. *The Closing of the American Mind.* New York: Simon & Schuster, 1987.

Bork, Robert. *The Tempting of America.* New York: Free Press, 1990.

Bowen, Catherine. *Yankee from Olympus.* Boston: Little, Brown and Co., 1944.

Braude, Jacob M. *Lifetime Speaker's Encyclopedia.* Vol. 2. Englewood Cliffs, N.J.: Prentice Hall, 1962.

Broom, Herbert. *A Selection of Legal Maxims.* Philadelphia: T. & J.W. Johnson & Co., 1868.

Brown, Marshall. *Wit & Humor of Bench and Bar.* Chicago: T.M. Flood & Co., 1899.

Brussell, Eugene E., ed. *Dictionary of Quotable Definitions.* Englewood Cliffs, N.J.: Prentice Hall, 1970.

Buck, Pearl S. *What America Means to Me.* New York: Day, 1943.

Bunch, Charlotte. "Speaking Out, Reaching Out." In *Passionate Politics.* New York: St. Martin's Press, 1987.

Cardozo, Benjamin. *The Growth of the Law.* 1924. Reprint, Westport: Greenwood Press, 1973.

Carson, Rachel. *Silent Spring.* Boston: Houghton Mifflin Riverside Press, 1962.

Carter, Rosalyn. *First Lady of the Plains.* Boston: Houghton Mifflin, 1984.

Carter, Stephen. *Reflections of an Affirmative Action Baby.* New York: Basic Books, 1991.

Cather, Willa. *The Song of the Lark.* Boston: Houghton Mifflin, 1915.

Chase-Ribound, Barbara. *Echo of Lions.* New York: Morrow, 1989.

Childress, Alice. *A Hero Ain't Nothin' But a Sandwich.* Santa Barbara: Corner Stone Books, 1973.

Chisholm, Shirley. *Unbought and Unbossed.* New York: Avon Books, 1971.

Christie, Agatha. *The Mysterious Affair at Styles.* Boston: G.K. Hall, 1976.

———. *The Pale Horse.* New York: Dodd, Mead, 1961.

———. *They Came to Baghdad.* New York: Dodd, Mead, 1951.

Clark, Marcia, with Teresa Carpenter. *Without a Doubt.* New York: Viking, 1997.

Clinton, Hillary Rodham. *It Takes a Village and Other Lessons Children Teach Us.* New York: Simon & Schuster, 1996.

Cochran, Johnnie L., with Tim Rutten. *Journey to Justice.* New York: Ballentine Books, 1996.

Cohen, J. M., and M. J. Cohen. *The Penguin Dictionary of Quotations.* New York: Allen Lane/Viking Press, 1960, 1977.

Collison, Robert, and Mary Collison. *The Dictionary of Foreign Quotations.* New York: Facts On File, 1980.

Commager, Henry Steel. *Freedom, Loyalty, Dissent.* New York: Oxford University Press, 1954.

Cook, Paul C. *A Treasury of Legal Quotations Selected by Paul C. Cook.* New York: Vantage Press, 1961

Cooper, James Fenimore. *The Redskins.* New York: Putnam, 1846.

Cross, Amanda. *Poetic Justice.* New York: Knopf, 1970.

Crowley, Aleister. *The Confessions of Aleister Crowley.* New York: Hill and Wang, 1969.

Cushman, Robert F. *Leading Constitutional Decisions.* Englewood Cliffs, N.J.: Prentice-Hall, 1977.

Darden, Christopher, with Jess Walter. *In Contempt.* New York: Regan Books, 1996.

de Beaufort, Raphael Ledos. *Letters of George Sand.* Boston: Houghton Mifflin, 1886.

de Rabutin-Chantal, Marie. *Letters of Madame de Sévigné to Her Daughter and Friends.* Vol. 1. New York: E. P. Dutton, 1937.

Dietrich, Marlene. *Marlene Dietrich's ABC.* Garden City, N.Y.: Doubleday, 1962.

Dorr, Julia C. R. "A New Beatitude." In *Poems.* New York: Scribner's Sons, 1892.

Edelhart, Mike, and James Tinen. *America the Quotable.* New York: Facts On File, 1983.

Edelman, Marian Wright. *Families in Peril.* Cambridge: Harvard University Press, 1987.

Eliot, George. *Impressions of Theophrastus, Such.* Iowa City: University of Iowa Press, 1994.

———. *The Spanish Gypsy.* New York: A. L. Burt, 1868.

Ellerbee, Linda. *Move On.* New York: G. P. Putnam's Sons, 1991.

Evans, Bergen. *Dictionary of Quotations.* New York: Delacorte Press, 1969.

Fadiman, Clifton, and Charles Van Doren. *The American Treasury, 1455–1955.* New York: Harper and Brothers, 1955.

Fawcett, Millicent Garrett. *Political Economy for Beginners.* London: Macmillan, 1874.

Fenwick, Millicent. *Speaking Up.* New York: Harper & Row, 1982.

Fergusson, Rosalind. *The Facts On File Dictionary of Proverbs.* New York: Facts On File, 1983.

Filipovic, Zlata. *Zlata's Diary.* New York: Viking, 1994.

Franke, Linda Bird. *Ferraro: My Story.* New York: Bantam Books, 1985.

Fulbright, William. *Old Myths and New Realities.* New York: Random House, 1964.

Gerhart, Eugene. *Quote It? Memorable Legal Quotations.* New York: Clark Boardman Co.; Albany: Sage Hill Publishers, 1969.

Gilmer, Elizabeth Meriweather. *Dorothy Dix, Her Book.* New York: Funk & Wagnalls, 1926.

Glasgow, Ellen. *The Voice of the People.* New York: Doubleday, 1900.

Goldman, Emma. *Anarchism.* New York: Dover, 1969.

———. "The Individual, Society and State." In *Red Emma Speaks.* Alix Kates Shulman, ed. Random House, 1972.

Gorbachev, Raisa M. *I Hope.* New York: HarperCollins, 1991.

Gordon, Lois, and Alan Gordon. *American Chronicle.* New York: Atheneum Publishers, 1987.

Grafton, Sue. *"H" is for Homicide.* New York: Henry Holt, 1991.

Green, Lee. *Sportswit.* New York: Harper & Row, 1984.

Greer, Germaine. *The Female Eunuch.* New York: McGraw Hill, 1971.

Hamilton, Edith. *Witness to the Truth.* New York: W. W. Norton, 1948

Harnsberger, Caroline Thomas. *Treasury of Presidential Quotations.* Chicago: Follet Publishing Co., 1964.

Havel, Vaclav. *Disturbing the Peace.* New York, Knopf; distributed by Random House, 1990.

Heimel, Cynthia. *Get Your Tongue Out of My Mouth, I'm Kissing You Good-Bye!* New York: Atlantic Monthly Press, 1993.

Huber, Peter. *Sandra Day O'Conner.* Cooper Station: Chelsea House, 1990.

Jackson, Robert H. *The Supreme Court in the American System of Government.* Cambridge: Harvard University Press, 1955.

James, P. D. *A Taste of Death.* New York: Knopf, 1986.

Janeway, Elizabeth. *Improper Behavior.* New York: Morrow, 1987.

Johnson, Diane. *Lying Low.* New York: Knopf, 1978.

Jones, Mother. *The Autobiography of Mother Jones.* Edited by Mary Field Parton. Chicago: C.H. Kerr & Co., 1972.

Josephson, Hannah. *Jeannette Rankin.* Indianapolis: Bobbs-Merril, 1974.

Kraminer, Wendy. *It's All the Rage.* Reading, Mass.: Addison Wesley, 1995.

Katz, Marjorie, and Jean Arbeiter. *Pegs to Hang Ideas On.* New York: M. Evans and Co., 1973

Keller, Helen. *Optimism.* New York: T.Y. Crowell and Company, 1903.

Kenin, Richard, and Justin Wintle, eds. *The Dictionary of Biographical Quotations.* New York: Alfred A. Knopf, 1968.

King, Martin Luther, Jr. *Where Do We Go from Here: Chaos or Community?* Boston: Beacon Press, 1967.

Kramarae, Cheris, and Paula A. Treichler. *A Feminist Dictionary.* London and Boston: Pandora Press, 1985.

LaFollette, Suzanne. *Concerning Women.* New York: A. & C. Boni, 1926.

Lanker, Brian. *I Dream a World.* New York: Stewart, Tabori & Chang, distributed in U.S. by Workman, 1989.

Lash, Joseph P. *Eleanor: The Years Alone.* New York: Norton, 1972.

Lawrenceson, Helen. *Whistling Girl.* New York: Doubleday, 1978.

*Lawyers Wit and Wisdom.* Edited by Bruce Nash and Allan Zullo from materials compiled by Katerine Zullo. Philadelphia: Running Press, 1995.

Lee, Harper. *To Kill a Mockingbird.* Philadelphia: Lippincott, 1960.

Lee, Sophia. *The Recess.* New York: Arno Press, 1972.

Lewis, Sinclair. *It Can't Happen Here.* New York: P.F. Collier and Son, 1935.

Lifton, Robert J., ed. *The Women in America.* Boston: Houghton Mifflin, 1984.

MacDonald, William, ed. *Select Documents Illustrative of the History of the United States, 1776–1861.* New York and London: Macmillan Co., 1911.

MacKinnon, Catherine A. *Feminism Unmodified.* Cambridge: Harvard University Press, 1987.

Mansfield, Katherine. *The Journal of Kate Mansfield.* New York: Knopf, 1927.

Marchand, Leslie A. *Letters and Journals.* Vol. 2. Cambridge: Belnap Press of Harvard University, 1982.

Martin, Ralph G. *A Hero for Our Time.* New York: Macmillan, 1983.

Marx, Groucho. *Many Happy Returns.* New York: Simon & Schuster, 1942.

McCaffery, Edward J. *Taxing Women.* Chicago: University of Chicago Press, 1997.

McCarthy, Mary. "My Confession." In *On the Contrary.* New York: Farrar, Straus and Cudahy, 1961.

McNamara, M. Francis. *Ragbag of Legal Quotations Compiled by Francis McNamara.* New York: Matthew Bender and Co., 1960.

———. *2000 Famous Legal Quotations.* Rochester, N.Y.: Aqueduct Books, 1967.

Mencken, H. L. *A Mencken Chrestomathy.* New York: Knopf, 1949.

Mencken, H. L., ed. *A New Dictionary of Quotations on Historical Principles from Ancient and Modern Sources.* New York: Knopf, 1946.

———. *Prejudices.* New York: Knopf, 1926.

Millay, Edna St. Vincent. "Dirge Without Music." In *The Buck in the Snow.* New York and London: Harper Brothers, 1928.

Millet, Kate. *Sexual Politics.* New York: Ballantine, 1970.

Moncreiff, F. C. *Wit and Wisdom of the Bench and Bar.* London, Paris, and New York: Cassel, Peter, Golpin and Co., 1882.

Montessori, Maria. *The Secret of Childhood.* c. 1936. Reprint, London: Sangam Books, 1983.

Morgan, Robin, ed. *Sisterhood Is Powerful.* New York: Random House, 1970.

Moyers, Bill. *A World of Ideas.* New York: Doubleday, 1989.

Norton-Kyshe, James William *The Dictionary of Legal Quotations.* London: Sweet and Maxwell, 1904.

Osborne, Claire G. *The Unique Voice of Hillary Rodham Clinton.* New York: Avon Books, 1997.

*The Oxford Dictionary of Quotations.* 3d ed. New York: Oxford Univeristy Press, 1979.

Paglia, Carmille. *Sexual Personae.* New York: Vintage Books, 1990.

Paretsky, Sara. *Blood Shot.* New York: Delcourt Press, 1988.

Parker, Dorothy. "Unfortunate Coincidence." In *Enough Rope.* New York: H. Liveright, 1926.

Partnow, Elaine, ed. *The Quotable Woman.* New York: Facts On File, 1992.

————. *The Quotable Woman Eve to 1799.* New York: Facts On File, 1985.

————. *The Quotable Woman 1800–1981.* New York: Facts On File, 1982.

Perkins, Frances. *People at Work.* New York: The John Day Co., c.1934.

Peter, Laurence J. *Peter's Quotations: Ideas for Our Times.* New York: William Morrow Co., 1977.

Rand, Ayn. *Atlas Shrugged.* New York: Random House, 1957.

Rathbone, Eleanor. *The Disinherited Family.* London: E. Arnold & Co., 1924.

Reader's Digest Press editors. *Reader's Digest Treasury of Modern Quotations.* New York: Thomas Y. Crowell Co., 1975.

Reagan, Nancy. *Nancy.* New York: Morrow, 1980.

Rhode, Deborah L. *Speaking of Sex.* Cambridge: Harvard University Press, 1997.

Robertson, Pat. *America's Dates with Destiny.* Nashville: Nelson, 1986.

Ross, Susan. *The Rights of Women.* New York: Avon, 1973.

Rosten, Leo. *Leo Rosten's Treasury of Jewish Quotations.* New York: McGraw-Hill, 1972.

Rothwax, Judge Harold J. *Guilty: The Collapse of Criminal Justice.* New York: Random House, 1996.

Sanger, Margaret. *Women and the New Race.* New York: Brentano's, 1920.

Santayana, George. *Little Essays.* 1920. Reprint, Freeport, N.Y.: Books for College Libraries, 1967.

————. *The Life of Reason: Reason in Society.* New York: Scribner, 1954.

Seldes, George, ed. *The Great Quotations.* Secaucus, N.J.: Citadel Press, 1960, 1966, 1983.

Shelly, Mary Wollstonecraft. *Frankenstein.* New York: Harper Paperbacks, 1996.

Shendlin, Judy, with Josh Getlin. *Don't Pee on My Leg and Tell Me It's Raining.* New York: HarperCollins Publishing, 1996.

Simpson, James B. *Contemporary Quotations: A Treasury of Notable Quotes Since 1930.* New York: Thomas Y. Crowell, 1964.

Sontag, Susan. *AIDS and Its Metaphors.* New York: Farrar, Straus and Giroux, 1989.

de Spinoza, Baruch Benedictus. *Tractatus Politicus.* New York: Oxford University Press, 1958.

Stanton, Elizabeth Cady. *The Woman's Bible.* New York: European Publishing Co., 1895.

Stanton, Elizabeth Cady, Susan B. Anthony, and Matilda J. Gage, eds. *History of Woman Suffrage.* Vol 1. 1881. Reprint, Salem, N.H.: Ayer Company, Publisher, 1985.

Steinem, Gloria. *Outrageous Acts and Everyday Rebellions.* New York: Holt, Rinehart, and Winston, 1983.

Stem, Thad, Jr., and Alan Butler. *Senator Sam Ervin's Best Stories.* Dunham, N.C. Moore Publishing Co., 1973.

Stevenson, Burton. *Home Book of Proverbs, Maxims & Familiar Phrases.* New York: Macmillan Co., 1948.

Stineman, Esther. *American Political Women.* Englewood, N.J.: Libraries Unlimited, 1980.

Stowe, Harriet Beecher. *Uncle Tom's Cabin.* New York: Chelsea House, 1996.

Twain, Mark. *Following the Equator.* New York: Harper, 1906.

Veeck, Bill. *The Hustler's Handbook.* New York: Putnam, 1965.

Viereck, Peter. *The Unadjusted Man.* Boston: Beacon, 1956.

Walker, Alice. *In Search of Our Mother's Gardens.* San Diego: Harcourt Brace Jovanovich, 1983.

Walsh, William S. *International Encyclopedia of Prose and Political Quotations.* New York: Holt, Rinehart and Winston, 1951.

Warner, Judith. *Hillary Rodham Clinton.* New York: Penguin, 1993.

Weil, Simon. *The Need for Roots.* New York: Putnam, 1952.

Whiting, Bartlett Jere, and Helen Wescott Whiting. *Proverbs, Sentences, and Proverbial Phrases: From English Writings Mainly Before 1500.* Cambridge, Mass.: Belknap Press, Harvard University Press, 1968.

Will, George. *The Pursuit of Happiness and Other Sobering Thoughts.* Introduction. New York: Harper & Row, 1978.

Wollstonecraft, Mary. *Political Writings.* Edited by Janet Todd. Toronto: University of Toronto Press, 1993.

———. *A Vindication of the Rights of Women.* New York: Penguin, 1984.

*Woolf, Virginia. Montaigne.* The Common Reader, 1st ser. Toronto: Harcourt, Brace, 1925.

———. *Three Guineas.* New York: Harcourt Brace, 1938.

# ᴊUBJECT INDEX

# AUTHOR INDEX